ORACLE®

Oracle Press™

Database Cloud Storage: The Essential Guide to Oracle Automatic Storage Management

Nitin Vengurlekar

Prasad Bagal

Mc
Graw
Hill
Education

New York   Chicago   San Francisco   Athens
London   Madrid   Mexico City   Milan
New Delhi   Singapore   Sydney   Toronto

Library of Congress Cataloging-in-Publication Data

Vengurlekar, Nitin.
    Database cloud storage : the essential guide to Oracle automatic storage management /
Nitin Vengurlekar, Prasad Bagal.—First edition.
        pages cm
    ISBN 978-0-07-179015-4 (pbk.)
    1. Cloud computing.   2. Database management.   3. Oracle (Computer file)   I. Bagal, Prasad.
    II. Title.   III. Title: Essential guide to Oracle automatic storage management.
        QA76.585.V46 2013
        004.67'82—dc23   2013021940

McGraw-Hill Education books are available at special quantity discounts to use as premiums and sales promotions, or for use in corporate training programs. To contact a representative, please visit the Contact Us pages at www.mhprofessional.com.

Database Cloud Storage: The Essential Guide to Oracle Automatic Storage Management

1 2 3 4 5 6 7 8 9 0   DOC DOC   1 0 9 8 7 6 5 4 3

ISBN   978-0-07-179015-4
MHID   0-07-179015-2

Sponsoring Editor Paul Carlstroem	**Technical Editor** Anil Nair	**Production Supervisor** Jean Bodeaux
Editorial Supervisor Patty Mon	**Copy Editor** Bart Reed	**Composition** Cenveo Publisher Services
Project Manager Sandhya Gola, Cenveo® Publisher Services	**Proofreader** Paul Tyler	**Illustration** Cenveo Publisher Services
Acquisitions Coordinator Amanda Russell	**Indexer** Jack Lewis	**Art Director, Cover** Jeff Weeks

This book is dedicated to Nisha, Ishan, Priya, my Mom, Marlie, and the Bhide family. But most importantly this is for my Dad, for all the guidance and support he gave me.
—Nitin Vengurlekar

I dedicate this book to my sons, Kavin and Vihan, and my wife, Anu.
—Prasad Bagal

About the Authors

Nitin Vengurlekar is the co-founder and CTO of Viscosity North America, a leader in virtualization, Oracle Engineered Systems, Private Database Cloud, and RAC implementations.

With more than 25 years of IT experience, including OS390 systems programming, storage administration, system and database administration, Nitin is a seasoned systems architect who has successfully assisted numerous customers in deploying highly available Oracle systems.

Prior to joining Viscosity, Nitin worked for Oracle for more than 17 years, mostly in the Real Application Clusters (RAC) engineering group, with a primary emphasis on ASM and storage, and was a Database Cloud Architect/Evangelist in the Oracle's Cloud Strategy Group.

Nitin is a well-known Oracle technologist and speaker in the areas of Oracle Storage, high availability, Oracle RAC, and Private Database Cloud. He is the co-author of *Oracle Automatic Storage Management* and *Oracle Data Guard 11g Handbook* (both from Oracle Press) and has written many papers on storage, database internals, and database tuning as well as having served as a contributor to Oracle documentation and Oracle education material.

Prasad Bagal started working on ASM from its earliest days. He is currently the Senior Director of Development at Oracle Corporation and is responsible for developing ASM-based storage solutions.

About the Technical Editor

Anil Nair has been involved with Oracle database technologies since the mid-1990s, starting with Oracle 7, and is currently working on Engineered Systems in the Oracle Server Technologies group. During his career, Anil has helped maintain, tune, and troubleshoot the most business-critical systems, including the largest Oracle Parallel customer implementation, with 52 nodes, as a Global Technical Lead for Oracle Clusterware and Real Application Clusters (RAC).

Contents at a Glance

1 Automatic Storage Management in a Cloud World 1
2 ASM and Grid Infrastructure Stack 11
3 ASM Instances. 29
4 ASM Disks and Disk Groups 49
5 Managing Databases in ASM 105
6 ASMLIB Concepts and Overview 159
7 ASM Files, Aliases, and Security 179
8 ASM Space Allocation and Rebalance. 195
9 ASM Operations 215
10 ACFS Design and Deployment 239
11 ACFS Data Services. 271
12 ASM Optimizations in Oracle Engineered Solutions .309
13 ASM Tools and Utilities 325
14 Oracle 12c ASM: A New Frontier 353
A Best Practices for Database Consolidation in Private Clouds 365
   Index 377

Contents

Acknowledgments xv
Introduction xvii

1 Automatic Storage Management in a Cloud World 1
    The Early Years 2
    First Release of ASM and Beyond 4
    The Cloud Changes Everything 6
        What Is the Cloud? 6
        Relational Databases in the Cloud 6
    ASM in the Cloud 8
        Common Storage Management 9
        Enterprise Cloud Robustness 9
        Enterprise Cloud Policy Management 10
        Cross-Cluster Sharing 10
    Summary 10

2 ASM and Grid Infrastructure Stack 11
    Clusterware Primer 12
        OCR Overview 12
        Voting File Overview 13
    Grid Infrastructure Stack Overview 13
        Grid Infrastructure for Standalone Server 15
        Grid Infrastructure for Cluster 15
        Voting Files and Oracle Cluster Repository Files in ASM 18
        Voting Files in ASM 18
        Voting File Discovery 20
        Voting File Recovery 20
        Oracle Cluster Registry (OCR) 21
        OCR Recovery 22

The Quorum Failure Group 23
Clusterware Startup Sequence—
    Bootstrap If OCR Is Located in ASM 24
Disk Groups and Clusterware Integration 26
Summary 28

3   ASM Instances **29**
Managing ASM Instance 31
    Starting Up an ASM Instance 31
    Stopping the ASM Instance 32
    Authentication for Accessing ASM Instances 33
    ASM and ASM SPFILE 38
    Managing the ASM SPFILE 40
    ASM Background Processes 42
    ASM SGA and Parameter Sizing 43
ASM Health Check Monitor 46
Summary 48

4   ASM Disks and Disk Groups **49**
ASM Storage Provisioning 50
    ASM Storage Device Configuration 51
    ASM Disk Device Discovery 52
Third-Party Volume Managers and ASM 57
Preparing ASM Disks on NFS 57
    Direct NFS 59
Preparing ASM Disks on OS Platforms 59
    Linux 59
    Solaris 61
    AIX 61
ASM and Multipathing 64
    Linux Device Mapper 65
Disk Group 71
    Disk Group Management 72
    ASM Redundancy and Failure Groups 78
    ASM and Intelligent Data Placement 80
    ASM and Extended Clusters 84
    Recovering from Transient and Permanent Disk Failures 88
    ASM and I/O Error Failure Management 92
    Space Management Views for ASM Redundancy 96
    Disk Groups and Attributes 97
Attributes Overview 97
Summary 102

5 Managing Databases in ASM **105**
   Interaction Between ASM and Database 106
   Cloning ASM and Database Homes 107
   Create Database in Command-Line Mode 111
   Database Interaction with ASM 117
   Disk Groups and Databases 122
   Transportable Tablespaces and ASM 124
      Performing the Preliminary Steps to Set Up the TTSs 124
   Alert Log Monitoring 129
   Monitoring the ASM Disk Group 133
   Issues DBAs Encounter with ASM 136
      Spfile with an Incorrect Initialization Parameter 137
      Archiver Is Stuck 137
      Moving the Control Files to ASM 139
   Use Cases for DBAs 141
      Impact of DB_UNIQUE_NAME
         for the ASM Directory Structure 141
      Backing Up the Database to the FRA Disk Group 142
      Specifying Default Locations
         for Data Files and Redo Logs 143
      Copying Files from One ASM Instance to Another 145
      How to Migrate from File System
         to ASM with Minimal Downtime 149
      How to Move a Tablespace from
         One Disk Group to Another 153
      Create Multiplexed Redo Logs 155
   Summary 156

6 ASMLIB Concepts and Overview **159**
   Benefits of ASMLIB 160
      Device Discovery 160
      I/O Processing 161
   ASMLIB Implementation 162
      ASMLIB Installation 162
      Setting Up and Configuring ASMLIB 165
      Managing Disks in ASMLIB 166
      Troubleshooting ASMLIB 173
   Summary 177

7 ASM Files, Aliases, and Security **179**
   ASM Filenames 180
   ASM Directories 183

ASM Aliases 184
    Templates 185
    V$ASM_TEMPLATE 187
ASM File Access Control 187
    ASM ACL Overview 188
    ASM ACL Setup Example 189
Summary 194

8   ASM Space Allocation and Rebalance **195**
ASM Space Allocation 196
    ASM Allocation Units 196
    ASM Extents 197
    ASM Striping 198
    Setting Larger AU Sizes for VLDBs 199
ASM Rebalance 200
    Rebalance Operation 200
    Fast Rebalance 207
    Effects of Imbalanced Disks 208
    ASM and Storage Array Migration 210
    ASM and OS Migration 211
    Important Points on ASM Rebalance 212
Summary 213

9   ASM Operations **215**
ASM Instance Discovery 216
RDBMS Operations on ASM Files 216
    File Create 217
    File Open 218
    File I/O 218
    File Close 219
    File Delete 219
ASM File Allocation 219
    External Redundancy Disk Groups 219
    Variable-Sized Extents 220
    ASM Striping 221
ASM Redundancy 224
    Failure Groups 225
    Disk Partners 225
    Allocation with ASM Redundancy 226
    I/O to ASM Mirrored Files 226
Rebalance 230
Resync 232
Relocation 233
ASM Instance Recovery and Crash Recovery 234

Disk Discovery 235
Mount Disk Group 236
   Create Disk Group 237
   Add Disk 237
   Online Disk 237
   Select from V$ASM_DISK and V$ASM_DISKGROUP 237
Summary 238

10 ACFS Design and Deployment 239
ASM Cluster File System Overview 240
ACFS File System Design 243
   ACFS File I/O 243
   ACFS Space Allocation 244
   Distributed Lock Manager (DLM) 245
   Metadata Buffer Cache 246
   Recovery 246
ADVM Design 248
ACFS Configuration and Deployment 249
   Configuring the Environment for ACFS 250
   ACFS Deployment 251
   CRS Managed ACFS File Systems 251
Managing ACFS and ADVM 257
   ACFS File System Resize 257
   Unmounting File Systems 258
   Deleting File Systems 259
   ADVM Management 260
   ACFS Management 261
Summary 269

11 ACFS Data Services 271
ACFS Snapshots 272
   ACFS Read-Only Snapshots 272
   ACFS Read-Write Snapshots 273
   ACFS Snapshot by Example 273
ACFS Tagging 275
ACFS Replication Overview 276
Primary File System 276
   Current Restrictions (11.2.0.3) 277
   Standby File System 277
   Planning for ACFS Replication 277
   Tagging Considerations 278
   Setting Up Replication 279
   Replication Configuration and Initiation 285
   Pause and Resume Replication 288

Sizing ACFS File Systems 290
ACFS Compare Command 291
Termination of Replication 292
ACFS Security and Encryption 293
Databases and Security 293
ACFS Security 294
Databases and Encryption 299
ACFS and File Encryption 299
ACFS Encryption Key Management 300
ACFS Encryption Configuration and Use 302
ACFS Snapshots, Security, and Encryption 303
ACFS Security and Encryption Implementation 303
Summary 308

12 ASM Optimizations in Oracle Engineered Solutions **309**
Overview of Exadata 310
Exadata Components 310
11gR2 Database Optimizations for Exadata 313
ASM Optimizations for Exadata 314
ODA Overview 318
ODA Components 318
ASM Optimizations for ODA 320
ODA and NFS 323
Summary 323

13 ASM Tools and Utilities **325**
ASMCA 326
ASMCMD 330
Renamedg 332
ASM Storage Reclamation Utility (ASRU) 338
Overview of ASRU Operation 338
When to Use ASRU to Reclaim Storage 339
Using ASRU to Reclaim Storage on 3Par: Use Cases 340
KFOD 344
AMDU 346
Summary 352

14 Oracle 12c ASM: A New Frontier **353**
Password Files in ASM 354
Disk Management and Rebalance New Features 355
Fast Disk Resync and Checkpoints 355
Fast Disk Replacement 356
Failure Group Repair Timer 357
Rebalance Time Estimations 357
File Priority Rebalance 358

Flex ASM 358
    Flex ASM Clustering 359
    Flex ASM Listeners 360
    Flex ASM Network 360
    Remote ASM Access 361
ASM Optimizations on Engineered Systems 361
Error Checking and Scrubbing 362
Other Miscellaneous Flex ASM Features 363
Summary 363

A   **Best Practices for Database Consolidation in Private Clouds** **365**
Private Database Cloud Consolidation: The Business Drivers 366
Initial Server Pool Sizing 367
    CPU 368
    Partitioning vs. Overprovisioning 369
    Memory 370
    Storage 370
    Complementary Workloads 371
Isolation 371
    Database Consolidation 372
    Schema Consolidation 372
Summary 376

Index **377**

Acknowledgments

I would like to thank the following people for helping with the content in this book: John McHugh, Markus Michaelwicz, Sohan Demel, Michael Timpanaro-Perrotta, Angelo Pruscino, Rich Long, the ASM development team, Srinivas Eeda, P. Venkatraman, Anil Nair, Raj Kammend, Martin K. Petersen, and Sundar Matpadi, Rich Long, Bill Bridge, Ara Shakian, and Murali Vallath.

I especially want to thank the following people for their significant contributions, from helping with the review process, all the way to the completion of the book: Jim Williams, the Great Charles Kim, David Friedman, Fred Glover, Barb Glover, Diane Lebel, Samarjeet Tomar, and Bane Radulovic.

Finally, I would like thank all the Oracle Product Managers and Support folks who have assisted in me in the 17 years I was at Oracle. It was a privilege to work with all of you and I hope to continue our relationship.

Introduction

A t the core of most people's idea of cloud computing is a set of concepts speaking to information technology agility, scalability, and cost minimization.

This book focuses on the capabilities of ASM as well as the core components and layers of ASM. It also details the best practices for implementation in a Private Database Cloud.

Chapter 1: Automatic Storage Management in a Cloud World

This chapter's focus is how "cloud computing" influences the management of storage in an Oracle Database world. An important aspect of storage management for Oracle Database is the database feature known as Automatic Storage Management. This chapter addresses many of the recent changes that have been influenced by cloud computing, and how cloud computing will impact ASM into the future.

Chapter 2: ASM and Grid Infrastructure Stack

In 11gR2, ASM has become tightly integrated with the Oracle Clusterware stack. The Grid Infrastructure stack is the foundation of Oracle's Private Database Cloud, and provides the essential cloud pool capabilities, such as growing server and storage capacity as needed. This chapter discusses how the ASM fits into the Oracle Clusterware stack.

Chapter 3: ASM Instances

This chapter describes the basic component of the ASM architecture, the ASM instance. It covers configuring and managing the ASM instance as well as describes how the ASM instance manages the metadata describing the layout of the ASM files to clients.

Chapter 4: ASM Disks and Disk Groups

In this chapter, we cover in detail the core components of ASM, the ASM disk group, and its disks. This chapter discusses how to configure, prepare, and manage the disks that will be part of an ASM disk group.

Chapter 5: Managing Databases in ASM

In this chapter, you'll learn how to manage the databases that are stored in ASM, which includes very typical DBA tasks such as creating a database in ASM, backup/recovery, cloning, managing transportable tablespaces, and monitoring databases.

Chapter 6: ASMLIB Concepts and Overview

This chapter describes how to install, configure, set up, and troubleshoot ASMLIB. You'll learn why ASMLIB is a key part of any ASM and RAC environment.

Chapter 7: ASM Files, Aliases, and Security

In this chapter, you'll understand how files are created and handled in ASM as well as how aliases are managed. In addition, you'll learn about 11gR2 ASM file security features.

Chapter 8: ASM Space Allocation and Rebalance

In this chapter, you'll learn about the essentials of ASM space management. This chapter discusses how ASM allocates space in the disk group and how clients such as the relational database management system (RDBMS) and the ASM Cluster File System (ACFS) use the allocated space.

Chapter 9: ASM Operations

This chapter describes the flow of the critical operations for ASM disk groups and files. It also describes the key interactions between the ASM and relational database management system (RDBMS) instances.

Chapter 10: ACFS Design and Deployment

In this chapter, you'll learn about the essentials of ASM Cluster File System (ACFS), including configuring and managing ACFS.

Chapter 11: ACFS Data Services

One of the key aspects of the ACFS is the support for advanced data services, such as point-in-time snapshots, replication, file tagging, and file system security and encryption features. This chapter covers the inner workings and implementation of these ACFS data services.

Chapter 12: ASM Optimizations in Oracle Engineered Systems

Oracle Exadata Database Machine, Oracle Database Appliance, and Oracle SPARC SuperCluster are solutions designed to be optimal platforms for Oracle Database, and thus an ideal platform for Private Database Cloud computing. This chapter focuses on the ASM optimizations developed specifically for Oracle Exadata and Oracle Database Appliance.

Chapter 13: ASM Tools and Utilities

Many tools can be used to manage ASM and its components. In this chapter, you'll learn how to use these tools and utilities. This chapter provides a step-by-step guide to use these tools.

Chapter 14: ASM 12c: The New Frontier

This chapter previews some of the key features of ASM and cloud storage in Oracle 12c.

Appendix: Best Practices for Database Consolidation in Private Clouds

The book's appendix brings all the concepts together and touches on best practices for consolidating databases.

Intended Audience

This book is suitable for the following readers:

■ Developers who need to write SQL and PL/SQL

■ Database administrators who need in-depth knowledge of SQL

- Business users who need to write SQL queries to get information from their organization's database

- Technical managers or consultants who need an introduction to SQL and PL/SQL

No prior knowledge of the Oracle Database, SQL, or PL/SQL is assumed. Everything you need to know to become a master is contained in this book.

Retrieving the Examples

All the SQL scripts, programs, and other files used in this book can be downloaded from the Viscosity North America website at www.viscosityna.com/asmbook/. The files are contained in a ZIP file and will unzip into series of ksh and sql scripts.

I hope you enjoy this book!

CHAPTER
1

Automatic Storage
Management in
a Cloud World

C loud computing means many things to different people. At the core of most people's concept of cloud computing is a set of concepts speaking to information technology agility, scalability, and cost minimization. Early proponents of cloud computing visualized IT becoming a utility very much like electricity. To some extent, in the mobile platform space, that vision has become reality. The cost of mobile applications has never been lower, and the data feeding these applications is almost universally accessible.

This chapter's focus is how cloud computing influences the management of storage in an Oracle Database world. An important aspect of storage management for Oracle Database is the database feature known as Automatic Storage Management (ASM). ASM is an integrated volume manager and file system for Oracle's database. It takes the place of host-based volume managers and file systems, which have long been the practice when deploying Oracle. Bundled with ASM is ASM Cluster File System (ACFS), which is a POSIX-compliant file system that relies on the volume management provided by ASM as volume space for a file system supporting files outside the database.

The subsequent chapters of this book focus on the currently available capabilities of ASM and related technologies. This chapter addresses many of the recent changes that have been influenced by cloud computing, and how cloud computing will impact ASM in the future.

The Early Years

ASM was developed in the pre–Oracle 9*i* days. This was before the release of Real Application Clusters (RAC) databases providing commodity-class clustered databases. However, the product that became RAC was previously called Oracle Parallel Server, or simply OPS. Although it was expected that ASM would serve a wide selection of needs, from small databases upward, Oracle development believed that ASM would likely be important to OPS and the clustering of database instances. Originally, ASM was called Oracle Storage Manager (OSM), reflecting that relationship with OPS. In those early days, storage management for customers deploying large Oracle databases was rather challenging. As a customer, if you wanted to deploy OPS, you were stuck with only two choices: NFS-based storage and raw-attached storage. This limited choice was because Oracle's clustered database architecture is a shared-everything architecture requiring all storage devices to be accessible by all database servers running in a cluster. Furthermore, host-based global file systems that could accommodate Oracle's shared-everything architecture were not readily available. Consequently, the storage management choices for the customer were either to use the storage provided by network filers or to eliminate the file system altogether and deploy raw volumes for the Oracle database instances to access directly without any intermediary file system. Most customers choose the latter because it was perceived that file servers could not deliver the required I/O performance for large-scale databases.

Although deploying raw storage for the Oracle database can deliver excellent storage performance, it comes with a high management overhead because of the ongoing storage management needed to maintain the data layout as database workloads change. Furthermore, database and systems administrators usually had to work closely together to match the I/O demand requirements of database objects with the I/O capabilities of storage devices.

Elsewhere in the storage industry, vendors began developing enterprise-class cluster-aware storage management products. The most successful of vendors was Veritas with their cluster-aware file system and logical volume manager. Platform vendors, most notably IBM and HP, also introduced products in this space, either through partnering with Veritas or developing cluster-aware storage products independently. Because these products were important to customers, Oracle partnered with these vendors to ensure that they had viable solutions supporting the needs for Oracle Parallel Server, which later became RAC.

To help simplify storage management, Oracle started an initiative called SAME, for "Stripe and Mirror Everything." The idea behind this initiative was simple, yet powerful. It proposed that customers organize database file systems in a way that follows two principles:

- Stripe all files across all disks

- Mirror file systems across disks for high availability

Previously, customers invested considerable time optimizing many separate file systems to match the requirements for each database object. The SAME concept greatly simplified things by reducing the number of file systems and, consequently, the ongoing tuning of storage resources for the Oracle database. At the core of ASM is the SAME concept. ASM stripes all files across all disks and optionally mirrors the files.

With its introduction, ASM offered features that set it apart from conventional file system alternatives. Storage management for an Oracle database environment typically involves operating system–based volume managers and file systems. File systems and volume managers are most often managed by system administrators, who would set up the file system for the database administrator. This means that system administers have frequent and recurring interactions with database administrators. ASM, however, provided a database administrator–centric file system from which database files are managed. The entity of space management in ASM is called a *disk group,* which can be thought of as a file system. The disk group is usually the charter of the database administrator, rather than the system administrator. The effect of this is that it changed the way in which logical space is managed. This change meant that system administrators continue to provide physical volumes that populate a disk group, but DBAs become responsible for managing the disk groups, which is the file system that the database depends on. Furthermore, because ASM inherently implements the Stripe and Mirror Everything concept within the disk group, it eliminates the kind of management overhead previously required from system administrators.

Unlike conventional file systems, ASM is integrated with the Oracle database. This integration provides optimization not possible with a conventional file system. Like the database, ASM utilizes an instance that is simply a collection of processes sharing a region of memory. The ASM instance is responsible for file metadata that maps the locations of file blocks to physical storage locations. However, when the database performs an I/O operation, that operation does not pass through an ASM instance. The database executes I/O directly to the storage device. With a conventional file system, when the database performs an I/O operation, that operation is processed by a layer in the file system. Another way of stating this is that unlike a conventional file system, ASM is not in the I/O path between the database and storage.

Perhaps the most significant aspect of ASM is that it works well with RAC, or Real Application Clusters. As of Oracle Release 11.2, each node of a cluster has an ASM instance. All the database instances depend on the ASM instance operating on that node. The communication between the databases and the ASM instance on the node is efficient. And all the ASM instances within a cluster coordinate their activities and provide the management of the shared disk group space for the associated databases utilizing that cluster. Because of the simplicity of management and efficiency in clusters, usage of ASM for RAC is quite high and believed to be over 85 percent of deployments.

First Release of ASM and Beyond

Automatic Storage Management was introduced with Oracle 10*g*. From a development perspective, the release came at the Oracle Open World conference in September of 2003. During that event, Larry Ellison spoke of grid computing and how Real Application Clusters delivers the reliability and performance of a mainframe at a fraction of the cost. Charles Rozwat, Executive VP of Development at the time, delivered a keynote speech with a demonstration of ASM. ASM fundamentally changed the way in which storage for the Oracle database is managed, and this fact kept all of us very active with customers and storage partners presenting ASM's value to them.

Another product-related activity in the early days is best described as the development of an ASM ecosystem. The development team met with storage vendors presenting the value proposition of ASM to Oracle's customers. Another partner activity in the early days was performance measurements and compatibility testing with the partner's storage arrays. It was in the mutual interest of Oracle and the storage array vendors to ensure that ASM performed well with their equipment. From these measurements, whitepapers were written that documented best-practice procedures for using ASM with their storage hardware. One of these efforts led to the validation of thin provisioning in an ASM environment. Oracle worked with thin provisioning pioneer 3Par to illustrate compatibility between thin provisioning storage and ASM.

ASM provides an integrated volume manager and file system for the Oracle database. While the Oracle database is possibly one of the most important storage deployments for enterprise customers, it is not the only consumer of storage. Obviously, every customer has applications and nonrelational data requiring storage. This means that ASM users had to fragment their storage management between Oracle databases and everything else. Consequently, the ASM development team came up with the idea that it would be really useful to enable ASM as a platform for general-purpose storage management for all of the customer's data needs. This concept became the basis for the next major ASM development focus. Oracle hired an entire development team that had worked on file systems in the VMS operating system and they became the group to deliver ASM's next major stage of evolution.

To expand the data managed outside of the database environment meant that a POSIX-compliant file system had to be able to utilize storage residing in an ASM disk group. The architecture for providing this capability came in two parts. The first is the capability of exposing an ASM file as a logical volume on which a file system resides. The second part is a cluster file system utilizing that exposed logical volume. Exposing ASM files as file system volumes makes sense in that ASM files are normally quite large because they are intended for a database. The component providing this capability is called ASM Device Volume Manager (ADVM). It is a loadable operating system module that talks to an ASM instance for the purpose of acquiring volume extent layout metadata. ADVM, in turn, presents the storage space represented in the extent map metadata as a logical device in the operating system. Finally, ADVM is "cluster aware," meaning it can present its logical volumes coherently across a cluster.

The second part of extending ASM storage management was the development of a cluster file system utilizing the storage space presented by ADVM. That component is called ASM Cluster File System (ACFS). It is a POSIX-compliant cluster file system implementing a wide range of features described in Chapter 10. The combination of ADVM and ACFS enables a platform for storage management that extends beyond the database and is available on all Oracle platforms, except HPUX. (HPUX is not available at this time because of the lack of available HPUX internal information required for the development of drivers for that environment.)

ADVM and ACFS became available with the 11.2 release of Oracle. This was a major release for ASM, which included the ability to support Oracle's Clusterware files in an ASM disk group. Oracle's Clusterware requires two critical storage components called the "voting disks" and the Oracle Clusterware Repository (OCR). Previously, these two entities had to be stored on dedicated storage devices. With the release of 11.2, the Clusterware files can be kept in an ASM disk group, thus eliminating a major management challenge. This feature is a bit of magic because ASM depends on Oracle Clusterware, yet the Clusterware files can now reside in ASM. It's a chicken-and-egg problem that development cleverly solved.

ASM is intimately related to Oracle Clusterware and Real Application Clusters. Although ASM provides many advantages to single-instance databases, the clustered version of the Oracle database (that is, RAC) is where ASM sees most of its use. For these reasons, ASM is now bundled with ACFS/ADVM and Oracle Clusterware into a package called Grid Infrastructure. Although ASM and ACFS can be installed in a non-RAC environment, the Grid Infrastructure bundling greatly simplifies the installation for customers running RAC.

The Cloud Changes Everything

The "cloud" or the enablement of cloud has had a transformative impact not only on the IT industry but in our daily lives as well. This section covers cloud computing as it impacts Private Database Clouds and specifically ASM.

What Is the Cloud?

This chapter started by alluding to a definition for cloud computing. Although many companies re-label their products and features as "cloud enabled" (something we call "cloudification"), the cloud moniker does imply something real with respect to product features and what customers want. At the core of the definition is a customer desire for improved scalability, greater agility, and cost reduction with respect to otherwise conventional products. Cloud enabling generally implies transforming consumer and business applications into a nebulous infrastructure where the applications are managed elsewhere and access is presented via a network, which is generally the Internet. Cloud applications and their related infrastructure are most often thought to be managed by a third party, with the perception that infinite resources are available to meet your changing demands and you only pay for what you use. The electric utility is often used as the perfect metaphor.

Certainly, from a societal impact, the more significant impact of cloud computing is for end consumers. However, the question here is what does cloud computing mean for the Oracle database in general, and the ASM feature in particular? This question is examined by looking at cloud computing trends, what the requirements are for enterprise relational databases, and how the storage-related aspects of the latter question influences product evolution in the future.

Relational Databases in the Cloud

For the purposes of examining the impact of cloud computing on Oracle storage management, we must consider the environments and needs of Oracle's customers. Oracle's largest customers deploy business-critical applications around Oracle's database. It is often the case that if these databases fail, the impact to the underlying application can profoundly affect the business. Oracle customers typically have teams of people managing the operation of their enterprise applications and the underlying infrastructure. It is the case that there can be a cost-savings opportunity for some customers by outsourcing particular applications to third-party companies. Examples of this are seen in the Salesforce.com market as well as Oracle's own hosting business. However, the focus in this discussion is with respect to database and related storage management customer requirements. The more critical application environments deploy a redundant infrastructure that ensures continuity of operation because business continuity depends on the uptime of these environments. Such companies simply cannot depend on a third party to supply the necessary resources.

When discussing the deployment models, the descriptions most often used are *public cloud computing* and *private cloud computing*. Public cloud computing can be thought of as the outsourcing of whole applications to third-party providers delivering access to applications over a public Internet. Obviously, customers could access infrastructure elements of applications, such as databases, over the Internet as well. However, the purpose here is to focus on cloud computing's impact on the inverse of public cloud computing, which is private cloud computing. Private cloud computing is the means of delivering some of the value of cloud computing, but through corporate-managed networks and computing infrastructures. The tradeoff of private clouds is that customers retain control over security and deployment of vital elements, although at a higher cost to the enterprise than could be afforded through a public cloud. For the purposes of the following discussion, private clouds in the enterprise are simply referred to as *enterprise cloud computing*.

What does it mean to manage an Oracle database in an enterprise cloud? The change to an enterprise cloud model is primarily how the databases and underlying infrastructure are managed. In a conventional model, separate applications and databases are deployed in a vertical fashion. This means new applications and supporting infrastructure are committed to their own hardware stack. In an enterprise cloud model, new applications and databases are not deployed on dedicated platforms and software infrastructure, but may share platforms with other applications. One model that supports such sharing is *multitenancy,* which means the sharing of a software component by multiple consumers through logical separation of the consumers by the software component. With respect to a database, an example of multitenancy is the sharing of a single database instance by multiple applications where each application contains its own schema and the database provides the means of enforcing access separation between the applications sharing the database instance.

Another architectural tool used to create enterprise clouds is virtualization. An example of virtualization used in the service of enterprise clouds is server virtualization, where companies deploy several applications and associated infrastructure on a single platform, but each application environment operates on its own virtual server image. There is public debate as to the merits of these approaches for creating an enterprise cloud environment, but from an Oracle perspective, a lot of development attention surrounds product features supporting these trends.

From a conceptual level, there are at least four obvious product development areas, with respect to Oracle's database, that will evolve to support customers creating enterprise clouds:

■ **Large-scale clustering**   An enterprise cloud is a collection of IT resources that is malleable and can expand or contract to changing application demands. From an Oracle database perspective, this flexibility is provided with database clustering. Enterprise clouds dictate that the enterprise will have a growing need for larger clusters of servers and storage that are easily managed.

■ **Large-scale platform sharing**   As much as there is a need to scale database services for demanding applications operating within a cluster, there is also a requirement to effectively share database instances for less demanding applications on a single server. Examples of technologies providing such sharing include database multitenancy and server virtualization.

■ **Efficient cluster reconfiguration**   An enterprise cloud with respect to clustering is not one large single cluster, but many separately managed clusters. An enterprise cloud requires these collections of clusters to be easily reconfigured to adapt to changing needs. There are also unplanned reconfigurations, which are the results of component failures. Consequently, cluster reconfigurations must be as seamless and transparent to the applications as possible.

■ **Enterprise cloud management model**   Cloud computing in the enterprise is as much about a change regarding management mindset as a technology change. The enterprise cloud management model dictates thinking of IT as delivering a set of services rather than components. It does not matter to the end consumer where their business applications run, as long as the expected services are delivered as agreed upon by their service-level agreements (SLAs). This means that the staff managing the enterprise cloud must have tools for ensuring the SLAs are delivered and that services are appropriately charged for.

The preceding key requirements regarding cloud computing in the enterprise will drive product development for the next several years. Next, we'll look at how these requirements will likely affect ASM evolution.

ASM in the Cloud

ASM was originally intended to solve one problem: reduce the management challenge associated with storage used for the Oracle database. However, the original approach implemented with ASM meant that it could not be used for managing storage and data outside of the database. The second major development phase for ASM brought ACFS that extended ASM's storage management model to data outside of the database. Clouds computing in the enterprise will likely further the idea of ASM being the underpinning for storage management for all elements remotely associated with the Oracle database. Cloud computing means applications and supporting infrastructure must be malleable within and across servers and clusters. Storage management that is tied to an isolated platform impedes this malleability.

Common Storage Management

Storage management must be global with respect to the enterprise cloud. From an architectural perspective, global storage management can be achieved either at the storage level or at the host level. At the extremes, global storage management at the storage level implies storage is totally managed and made available to applications and infrastructure through storage array products, such as those available from EMC and Network Appliance. Global storage management at the host means that less is expected from the physical storage and that storage management is principally provided by host management components providing a global management structure with respect to the enterprise cloud. ASM/ACFS is an example of host-based global storage management, and over time it will extend to provide a greater reach of management, not only with respect to application data, but across cluster boundaries. The idea is that ASM/ACFS will be the common storage and data management platform for the enterprise cloud.

Enterprise Cloud Robustness

For ASM to be an effective platform for storage and data management in an enterprise cloud, it must adapt to the four product development areas described in the previous section. It should be expected that ASM evolution will include growing support for larger clusters. An example of this is that as the cluster size increases, ASM will not become an impediment to that growth, which could result from lock contention and reconfiguration overhead. All host-based global storage management components require some form of serialization for access to shared resources. This commonly involves a global lock manager. As the cluster size increases, contention for locks increases. If not implemented effectively, this contention can impede the largest effective size of a cluster.

A related ASM evolution is associated with the cost of cluster reconfiguration. Whenever a cluster is reconfigured—either planned or unplanned—overhead is associated with reconfiguring management elements and updating the metadata associated with all the active members of the cluster. Larger clusters, particularly in the enterprise cloud, imply a far greater frequency of cluster reconfiguration events. It should be expected that ASM will not only evolve to minimize this overhead, but also to limit the impact to services that might otherwise be affected by a reconfiguration event.

Enterprise Cloud Policy Management

The cloud computing environment is far more dynamic than a non-cloud environment. Clusters' membership will change frequently, and the storage management infrastructure must quickly adapt to these frequent changes. Additionally, storage management will require provisioning and must deliver a wide range in service levels with respect to performance and reliability. Matching the available storage capabilities against a consistently changing set of demands could lead to an unmanageable environment.

Cross-Cluster Sharing

A typical enterprise cloud will likely contain many separate cluster environments. Separate cluster environments provide fault and performance isolation between workloads that are highly independent and require varying service levels. Yet, even with this separation, there will be a need to share access to data between the clusters. An example of this is the needed separation between the production environment and the test and development environment of the same application. Although the test and development environment is isolated from the production environment, testing may require controlled access to the production environment. This places a requirement on ASM to enable cross-cluster access of data. This is not easily available in Oracle 11.2, but will be a requirement in the future.

Summary

Cloud computing has been driven by the need to reduce costs, improve utilization, and produce better efficiency. At the center of this cloud movement has been the Private Database Cloud. With its support for all file and content types, Oracle ASM similarly has become a core component of the Oracle Private Database cloud movement.

CHAPTER
2

ASM and Grid
Infrastructure Stack

I n releases prior to 11gR2, Automatic Storage Management (ASM) was tightly integrated with the Clusterware stack. In 11gR2, ASM is not only tightly integrated with the Clusterware stack, it's actually part of the Clusterware stack. The Grid Infrastructure stack is the foundation of Oracle's Private Database Cloud, and it provides the essential Cloud Pool capabilities, such as growing server and storage capacity as needed. This chapter discusses how ASM fits into the Oracle Clusterware stack.

Clusterware Primer

Oracle Clusterware is the cross-platform cluster software required to run the Real Application Clusters (RAC) option for Oracle Database and provides the basic clustering services at the operating system level that enable Oracle software to run in clustered mode. The two main components of Oracle Clusterware are Cluster Ready Services and Cluster Synchronization Services:

- **Cluster Ready Services (CRS)**   Provides high-availability operations in a cluster. The CRS daemon (CRSd) manages cluster resources based on the persistent configuration information stored in Oracle Cluster Registry (OCR). These cluster resources include the Oracle Database instance, listener, VIPs, SCAN VIPs, and ASM. CRSd provides start, stop, monitor, and failover operations for all the cluster resources, and it generates events when the status of a resource changes.

- **Cluster Synchronization Services (CSS)**   Manages the cluster configuration by controlling which nodes are members of the cluster and by notifying members when a member (node) joins or leaves the cluster. The following functions are provided by the Oracle Cluster Synchronization Services daemon (OCSSd):

    - **Group Services**   A distributed group membership system that allows for the synchronization of services between nodes

    - **Lock Services**   Provide the basic cluster-wide serialization locking functions

    - **Node Services**   Use OCR to store state data and update the information during reconfiguration

OCR Overview

The Oracle Cluster Registry is the central repository for all the resources registered with Oracle Clusterware. It contains the profile, state, and ownership details of the resources. This includes both Oracle resources and user-defined application resources. Oracle resources include the node apps (VIP, ONS, GSD, and Listener) and database resources, such as database instances, and database services. Oracle resources are added to the OCR by tools such as DBCA, NETCA, and srvctl.

Voting File Overview

Oracle Clusterware maintains membership of the nodes in the cluster using a special file called *voting disk* (mistakenly also referred to as *quorum disk*). Sometimes, the voting disk is also referred to as the vote file, so you'll see this referenced both ways, and both are correct. This file contains the heartbeat records from all the nodes in the cluster. If a node loses access to the voting file or is not able to complete the heartbeat I/O within the threshold time, then that node is evicted out of the cluster. Oracle Clusterware also maintains heartbeat with the other member nodes of the cluster via the shared private interconnect network. A split-brain syndrome occurs when there is a failure in the private interconnect whereby multiple sub-clusters are formed within the clustered nodes and the nodes in different sub-clusters are not able to communicate with each other via the interconnect network but they still have access to the voting files. The voting file enables Clusterware to resolve network split brain among the cluster nodes. In such a situation, the largest active sub-cluster survives. Oracle Clusterware requires an odd number of voting files (1, 3, 5, …) to be created. This is done to ensure that at any point in time, an active member of the cluster has access to the majority number (n / 2 + 1) of voting files.

Here's a list of some interesting 11gR2 changes for voting files:

- The voting files' critical data is stored in the voting file and not in the OCR anymore. From a voting file perspective, the OCR is not touched at all. The critical data each node must agree on to form a cluster is, for example, miscount and the list of voting files configured.

- In Oracle Clusterware 11g Release 2 (11.2), it is no longer necessary to back up the voting files. The voting file data is automatically backed up in OCR as part of any configuration change and is automatically restored as needed. If all voting files are corrupted, users can restore them as described in the *Oracle Clusterware Administration and Deployment Guide*.

Grid Infrastructure Stack Overview

The Grid Infrastructure stack includes Oracle Clusterware components, ASM, and ASM Cluster File System (ACFS). Throughout this chapter, as well as the book, we will refer to Grid Infrastructure as the GI stack.

The Oracle GI stack consists of two sub-stacks: one managed by the Cluster Ready Services daemon (CRSd) and the other by the Oracle High Availability Services daemon (OHASd). How these sub-stacks come into play depends on how the GI stack is installed. The GI stack is installed in two ways:

- Grid Infrastructure for Standalone Server

- Grid Infrastructure for Cluster

ASM is available in both these software stack installations. When Oracle Universal Installer (OUI) is invoked to install Grid Infrastructure, the main screen will show four options (see Figure 2-1). In this section, the options we want to focus on are Grid Infrastructure for Standalone Server and Grid Infrastructure for Cluster.

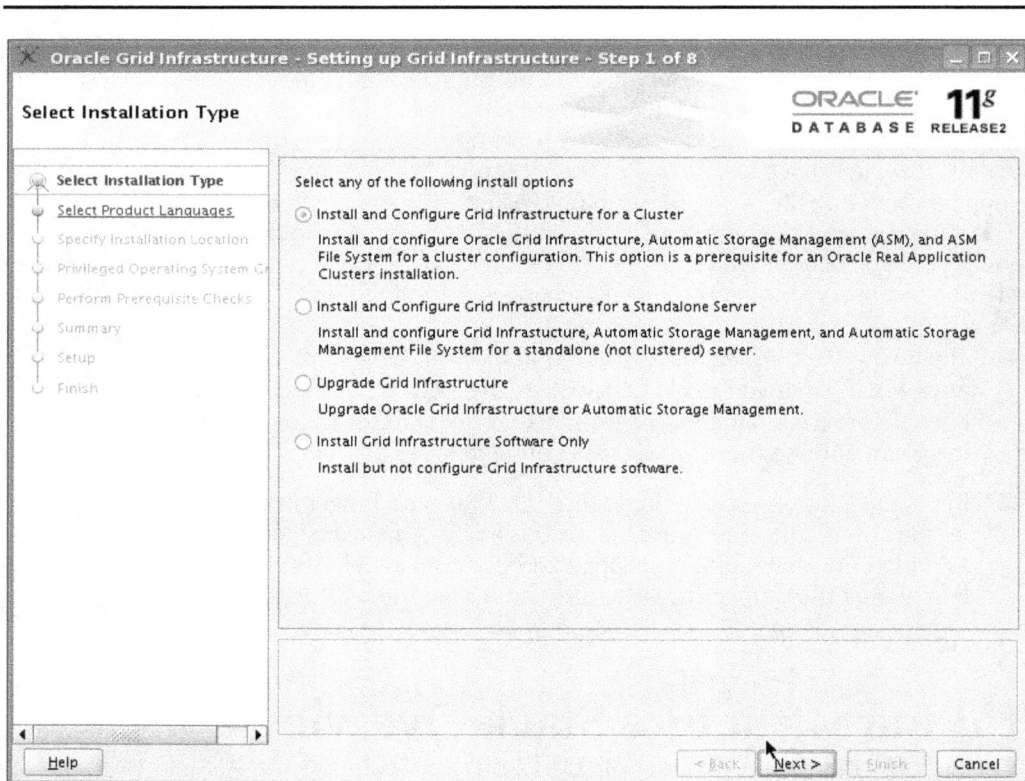

FIGURE 2-1.   *Oracle Universal Installer for Grid Infrastructure install*

Grid Infrastructure for Standalone Server

Grid Infrastructure for Standalone Server is essentially the single-instance (non-clustered) configuration, as in previous releases. It is important to note that in 11gR2, because ASM is part of the GI stack, Clusterware must be installed first before the database software is installed; this holds true even for single-instance deployments. Keep in mind that ASM will not need to be in a separate ORACLE_HOME; it is installed and housed in the GI ORACLE_HOME.

Grid Infrastructure for Standalone Server does not configure the full Clusterware stack; just the minimal components are set up and enabled—that is, private interconnect, CRS, and OCR/voting files are not enabled or required. The OHASd startup and daemon replaces all the existing pre-11.2 init scripts. The entry point for OHASd is /etc/inittab, which executes the /etc/init.d/ohasd and /etc/init.d/init.ohasd control scripts, including the start and stop actions. This OHASD script is the framework control script, which will spawn the $GI_HOME/bin/ohasd.bin executable. The OHASd is the main daemon that provides High Availability Services (HAS) and starts the remaining stack, including ASM, listener, and the database in a single-instance environment.

A new feature that's automatically enabled as part of Grid Infrastructure for Standalone Server installation is Oracle Restart, which provides high-availability restart functionality for failed instances (database and ASM), services, listeners, and dismounted disk groups. It also ensures these protected components start up and shut down according to the dependency order required. This functionality essentially replaces the legacy *dbstart/dbstop* script used in the pre-11gR2 single-instance configurations. Oracle Restart also executes health checks that periodically monitor the health of these components. If a check operation fails for a component, the component is forcibly shut down and restarted. Note that Oracle Restart is only enabled in GI for Standalone Server (non-clustered) environments. For clustered configurations, health checks and the monitoring capability are provided by Oracle Clusterware CRS agents.

When a server that has Grid Infrastructure for Standalone Server enabled is booted up, the HAS process will initialize and start up by first starting up ASM. ASM has a hard-start (pull-up) dependency with CSS, so CSS is started up. Note that there is a hard-stop dependency between ASM and CSS, so on stack shutdown ASM will stop and then CSS will stop.

Grid Infrastructure for Cluster

Grid Infrastructure for Cluster is the traditional installation of Clusterware. It includes multinode RAC support, private interconnect, Clusterware files, and now also installs ASM and ACFS drivers. With Oracle Clusterware 11gR2, ASM is not simply the storage manager for database files, but also houses the Clusterware files (OCR and voting files) and the ASM spfile.

When you select the Grid Infrastructure for Cluster option in OUI, as shown previously in Figure 2-1, you will be prompted next on file storage options for the Clusterware files (Oracle Clusterware Registry and Clusterware voting file). This is shown in Figure 2-2.

Users are prompted to place Clusterware files on either a shared file system or ASM. Note that raw disks are not supported any longer for new installations. Oracle will support the legacy method of storing Clusterware files (raw and so on) in upgrade scenarios only.

When ASM is selected as the storage location for Clusterware files, the Create ASM Disk Group screen is shown next (see Figure 2-3). You can choose external or ASM redundancy for the storage of Clusterware files. However, keep in mind that the type of redundancy affects the redundancy (or number of copies) of the voting files.

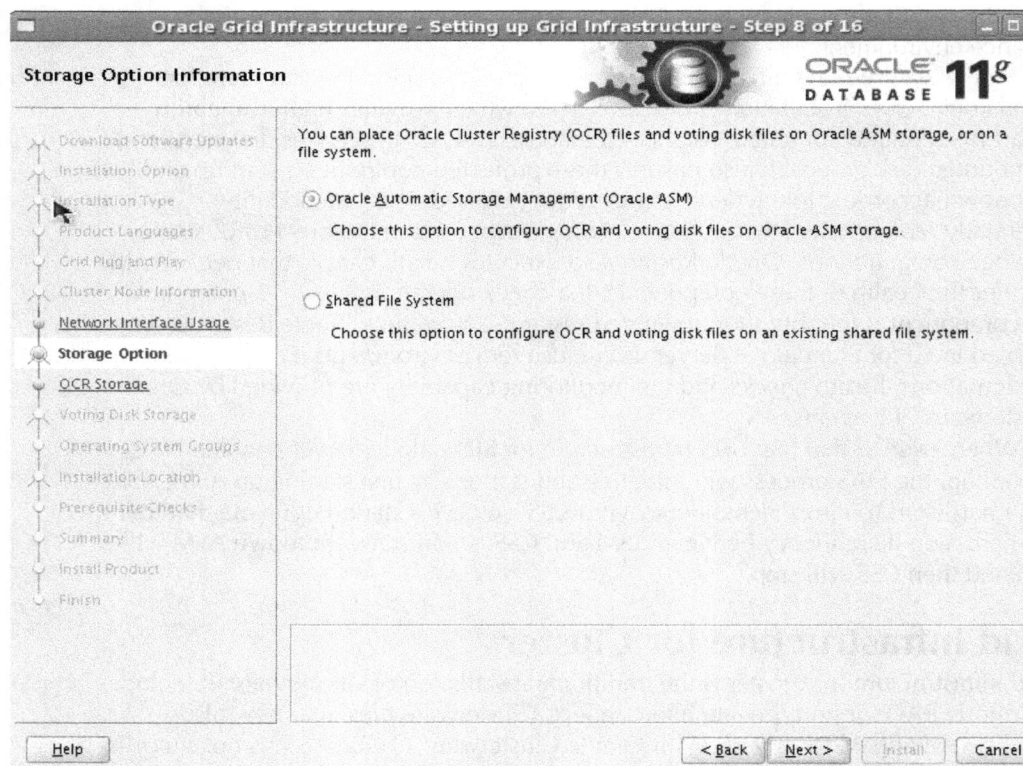

FIGURE 2-2. *Oracle Universal Installer Storage Option screen*

FIGURE 2-3.   *Create ASM Disk Group screen*

For example, for normal redundancy, there needs to be a minimum of three failure groups, and for high redundancy a minimum of five failure groups. This requirement stems from the fact that an odd number of voting files must exist to enable a vote quorum. Additionally this enables to tolerate one or two disk failures and still provide quorums.

This first disk group that is created during the installation can also be used to store database files. In previous versions of ASM, this disk group was referred to as the DATA disk group. Although it is recommended that you create a single disk group for storing the Clusterware files and database files, for users who are employing a third-party vendor snapshot technology against the ASM disk group, users may want to have a separate disk group for the Clusterware files. Users may also deploy a separate disk group for the Clusterware to leverage normal or high redundancy for the Clusterware files. In both of the cases, users should create a small CRSDATA disk group with 1MB AU and enough failure groups to support the redundancy required. Next, the installation users can then use ASMCA to create the DATA disk group.

Voting Files and Oracle Cluster Repository Files in ASM

In versions prior to 11gR2, users needed to configure and set up raw devices for housing the Clusterware files (OCR and voting files). This step creates additional management overhead and is error prone. Incorrect OCR/voting files setup creates havoc for the Clusterware installation and directly affects run-time environments. To mitigate these install preparation issues, 11gR2 allows the storing of the Clusterware files in ASM; this also eliminates the need for a third-party cluster file system and eliminates the complexity of managing disk partitions for the OCR and voting files. The COMPATIBLE.ASM disk group compatibility attribute must be set to 11.2 or greater to store the OCR or voting file data in a disk group. This attribute is automatically set for new installations with the OUI. Note that COMPATIBLE.RDBMS does not need to be advanced to enable this feature. The COMPATIBLE.* attributes topic is covered in Chapter 3.

Voting Files in ASM

If you choose to store voting files in ASM, then all voting files must reside in ASM in a single disk group (in other words, Oracle does not support mixed configurations of storing some voting files in ASM and some on NAS devices).

Unlike most ASM files, the voting files are wholly consumed in multiple contiguous AUs. Additionally, the voting file is not stored as a standard ASM file (that is, it cannot be listed in the asmcmd ls command). However, the disk that contains the voting file is reflected in the V$ASM_DISK view:

```
SQL> select a.name, b.name DG_NAME, voting_file
        from v$asm_disk a, v$asm_diskgroup b
        where a.group_number=b.group_number and voting_file='Y'

NAME                             DG_NAME                         V
-------------------------------  ------------------------------  -
CRSDATA_0000                     CRSDATA                         Y
```

The number of voting files you want to create in a particular Oracle ASM disk group depends on the redundancy of the disk group:

- **External redundancy**   A disk group with external redundancy can store only one voting file. Currently, no supported way exists to have multiple voting files stored on an external redundancy disk group.

- **Normal redundancy** A disk group with normal redundancy can store up to three voting files.

- **High redundancy** A disk group with high redundancy can store up to five voting files.

In this example, we created an ASM disk group with normal redundancy for the disk group containing voting files. The following can be seen:

```
SQL> CREATE DISKGROUP CRSDATA NORMAL REDUNDANCY
FAILGROUP fg1 DISK '/dev/sdm1',
FAILGROUP fg2 DISK '/dev/sdn1',
FAILGROUP fg3 DISK '/dev/sdo1'
  ATTRIBUTE 'compatible.asm' = '11.2.0.0';

# /bin/crsctl query css votedisk
  1.   2 21430e6edf9b4f79bf9acced0b4d7de1 (/dev/sdm1)  [DATA]
  2.   2 41ab2b6fa2ca4f48bf021e5dce37e3fc (/dev/sdn1)  [DATA]
  3.   2 22b755bca80d4fddbf39a9369e99210e (/dev/sdo1)  [DATA]
  Located 3 voting disk(s).
```

ASM puts each voting file in its own failure group within the disk group. A *failure group* is defined as the collection of disks that have a shared hardware component for which you want to prevent its loss from causing a loss of data.

For example, four drives that are in a single removable tray of a large JBOD (just a bunch of disks) array are in the same failure group because the tray could be removed, making all four drives fail at the same time. Conversely, drives in the same cabinet can be in multiple failure groups if the cabinet has redundant power and cooling so that it is not necessary to protect against the failure of the entire cabinet. If voting files are stored on ASM with normal or high redundancy, and the storage hardware in one failure group suffers a failure, then if another disk is available in a disk group in an unaffected failure group, ASM allocates new voting files in other candidate disks.

Voting files are managed differently from other files that are stored in ASM. When voting files are placed on disks in an ASM disk group, Oracle Clusterware records exactly on which disks in that disk group they are located. Note that CSS has access to voting files even if ASM becomes unavailable.

Voting files can be migrated from raw/block devices into ASM. This is a typical scenario for upgrade scenarios. For example, when a user upgrades from 10g to 11gR2, they are allowed to continue storing their OCR/voting files on raw, but at a later convenient time they can migrate these Clusterware files into ASM. It is important to point out that users cannot migrate to Oracle Clusterware 12c from 10g without first moving the voting files into ASM (or shared file system), since raw disks are no longer supported even for upgraded environments in 12c.

The following illustrates this:

```
$ crsctl replace css votedisk +CRSDATA2
```

Voting File Discovery

The method by CSS that identifies and locates voting files has changed in 11.2. Before 11*g*R2, the voting files were located via lookup in OCR; in 11*g*R2, voting files are located via a Grid Plug and Play (GPnP) query. GPnP, a new component in the 11*g*R2 Clusterware stack, allows other GI stack components to query or modify cluster-generic (non-node-specific) attributes. For example, the cluster name and network profiles are stored in the GPnP profile. The GPnP configuration, which consists of the GPnP profile and wallet, is created during the GI stack installation. The GPnP profile is an XML file that contains bootstrap information necessary to form a cluster. This profile is identical on every peer node in the cluster. The profile is managed by gpnpd and exists on every node (in gpnpd caches). The profile should never be edited because it has a profile signature that maintains its integrity.

When the CSS component of the Clusterware stack starts up, it queries the GPnP profile to obtain the disk discovery string. Using this disk string, CSS performs a discovery to locate its voting files.

The following is an example of a CSS GPnP profile entry. To query the GPnP profile, the user should use the supplied (in CRS ORACLE_HOME) gpnptool utility:

```
#gpnptool get

<orcl:CSS-Profile id="css" DiscoveryString="+asm"
LeaseDuration="400"/><orcl:ASM-Profile id="asm" DiscoveryString="/
dev/mapper/*" SPFile="+CRSDATA/nishan-cluster/asmparameterfile/
registry.253.758886543"/>
<orcl:CSS-Profile id="css"
DiscoveryString="+asm"
LeaseDuration="400"/>
<orcl:ASM-Profile id="asm" DiscoveryString="" SPFile=""/>
```

The CSS voting file discovery string anchors into the ASM profile entry; that is, it derives its DiscoveryString from the ASM profile entry. The ASM profile lists the value in the ASM discovery string as '/dev/mapper/*'. Additionally, ASM uses this GPnP profile entry to locate its spfile.

Voting File Recovery

Here's a question that is often heard: If ASM houses the Clusterware files, then what happens if the ASM instance is stopped? This is an important point about the relationship between CSS and ASM. CSS and ASM do not communicate directly. CSS discovers its voting files independently and outside of ASM. This is evident at cluster startup when CSS initializes before ASM is available. Thus, if ASM is stopped, CSS continues to access the voting files, uninterrupted. Additionally, the voting file is backed up into the OCR at every configuration change and can be restored with the crsctl command.

If all voting files are corrupted, you can restore them as described next.

Furthermore, if the cluster is down and cannot restart due to lost voting files, you must start CSS in exclusive mode to replace the voting files by entering the following command:

```
# crsctl start crs -excl (on one node only)
crsctl delete css votedisk voting_disk_guid
# crsctl add css votedisk path_to_voting_disk
```

Oracle Cluster Registry (OCR)

Oracle Clusterware 11*g*R2 provides the ability to store the OCR in ASM. Up to five OCR files can be stored in ASM, although each has to be stored in a separate disk group.

The OCR is created, along with the voting disk, when root.sh of the OUI installation is executed. The OCR is stored in an ASM disk group as a standard ASM file with the file type OCRFILE. The OCR file is stored like other ASM files and striped across all the disks in the disk group. It also inherits the redundancy of the disk group. To determine which ASM disk group the OCR is stored in, view the default configuration location at /etc/oracle/ocr.loc:

```
# cat /etc/oracle/ocr.loc
ocrconfig_loc=+DATA
local_only=FALSE

Or
ASMCMD > find --type OCRFILE / *
+CRSDATA/NISHAN-clust/OCRFILE/REGISTRY.255.758886547
```

The disk group that houses the OCR file is automounted by the ASM instance during startup.

All 11*g*R2 OCR commands now support the ASM disk group. From a user perspective, OCR management and maintenance works the same as in previous versions, with the exception of OCR recovery, which is covered later in this section. As in previous versions, the OCR is backed up automatically every four hours. However, the new backup location is <GRID_HOME>/cdata/<scan name>.

A single OCR file is stored when an external redundancy disk group is used. It is recommended that for external redundancy disk groups an additional OCR file be created in another disk group for added redundancy. This can be done as follows:

```
# ocrconfig -add +DATA
```

In an ASM redundancy disk group, the ASM partnership and status table (PST) is replicated on multiple disks. In the same way, there are redundant extents of OCR file stored in an ASM redundancy disk group. Consequently, OCR can tolerate the loss of the same number of disks as are in the underlying disk group, and it can be relocated/rebalanced in response to disk failures. The ASM PST is covered in Chapter 9.

OCR Recovery

When a process (OCR client) that wants to read the OCR incurs a corrupt block, the OCR client I/O will transparently reissue the read to the mirrored extents for a normal- or high-redundancy disk group. In the background the OCR master (nominated by CRS) provides a hint to the ASM layer identifying the corrupt disk. ASM will subsequently start "check disk group" or "check disk," which takes the corrupt disk offline. This corrupt block recovery is only possible when the OCR is configured in a normal- or high-redundancy disk group.

In a normal- or high-redundancy disk group, users can recover from the corruption by taking either of the following steps:

■ Use the ALTER DISK GROUP CHECK statement if the disk group is already mounted.

■ Remount the disk group with the FORCE option, which also takes the disk offline when it detects the disk header corruption. If you are using an external redundancy disk group, users must restore the OCR from backup to recover from a corruption. Starting in Oracle Clusterware 11.2.0.3, the OCR backup can be stored in a disk group as well.

The workaround is to configure an additional OCR location on a different storage location using the ocrconfig -add command. OCR clients can tolerate a corrupt block returned by ASM, as long as the same block from the other OCR locations (mirrors) is not corrupt. The following guidelines can be used to set up a redundant OCR copy:

■ Ensure that the ASM instance is up and running with the required disk group mounted and/or check ASM alert.log for the status for the ASM instance.

■ Verify that the OCR files were properly created in the disk group, using asmcmd ls. Because the Clusterware stack keeps accessing OCR files, most of the time the error will show up as a CRSD error in the crsd.log. Any errors related to an ocr* command will generate a trace file in the Grid_home/ log/<hostname>/client directory; look for kgfo, kgfp, or kgfn at the top of the error stack.

Use Case Example

A customer has an existing three-node cluster with an 11gR1 stack (CRS 11.1.0.7; ASM 11.1.0.7; DB 11.1.0.7). They want to migrate to a new cluster with new server hardware but the same storage. They don't want to install 11.1.0.7 on the new servers; they just want to install 11.2.0.3. In other words, instead of doing an upgrade, they want to create a new "empty" cluster and then "import" the ASM disks into the 11.2 ASM instance. Is this possible?

Yes. To make this solution work, you will install the GI stack and create a new cluster on the new servers, stop the old cluster, and then rezone the SAN paths to the new servers. During the GI stack install, when you're prompted in the OUI to configure the ASM disk group for a storage location for the OCR and voting files, use the drop-down box to use an existing disk group. The other option is to create a new disk group for the Clusterware files and then, after the GI installation, discover and mount the old 11.1.0.7 disk group. You will need to do some post-install work to register the databases and services with the new cluster.

The Quorum Failure Group

In certain circumstances, customers might want to build a stretch cluster. A *stretch cluster* provides protection from site failure by allowing a RAC configuration to be set up across distances greater than what's typical "in the data center." In these RAC configurations, a third voting file must be created at a third location for cluster arbitration. In pre-11gR2 configurations, users set up this third voting file on a NAS from a third location. In 11gR2, the third voting file can now be stored in an ASM quorum failure group.

The "Quorum Failgroup" clause was introduced for setups with Extended RAC and/or for setups with disk groups that have only two disks (respectively, only two failure groups) but want to use normal redundancy.

A quorum failure group is a special type of failure group where the disks do not contain user data and are not considered when determining redundancy requirements. Unfortunately, during GI stack installation, the OUI does not offer the capability to create a quorum failure group. However, this can be set up after the installation. In the following example, we create a disk group with a failure group and optionally a quorum failure group if a third array is available:

```
SQL> CREATE DISKGROUP DATA_PROD NORMAL REDUNDANCY
FAILGROUP fg1 DISK '<a disk in SAN1>'
FAILGROUP fg2 DISK '<a disk in SAN2>'
QUORUM FAILGROUP fg3 DISK '<another disk or file on a third location>'
ATTRIBUTE 'compatible.asm' = '11.2.0.0';
```

If the disk group creation was done using ASMCA, then after we add a quorum disk to the disk group, Oracle Clusterware will automatically change the CSS vote disk location to the following:

```
$ crsctl query css votedisk
## STATE File Universal Id File Name Disk group
-- ----- ---------------- --------- ---------
1. ONLINE 3e1836343f534f51bf2a19dff275da59 (/dev/sdg10) [DATA]
2. ONLINE 138cbee15b394f3ebf57dbfee7cec633 (/dev/sdf11) [DATA]
3. ONLINE 462722bd24c94f70bf4d90539c42ad4c (/voting_disk/vote_node1)
[DATA]
Located 3 voting file(s).
```

Clusterware Startup Sequence—
Bootstrap If OCR Is Located in ASM

Oracle Clusterware 11*g* Release 2 introduces an integral component called the *cluster agents*. These agents are highly available, multithreaded daemons that implement entry points for multiple resource types.

ASM has to be up with the disk group mounted before any OCR operations can be performed. OHASd maintains the resource dependency and will bring up ASM with the required disk group mounted before it starts the CRSd. Once ASM is up with the disk group mounted, the usual ocr* commands (ocrcheck, ocrconfig, and so on) can be used. Figure 2-4 displays the client connections into ASM once the entire stack, including the database, is active.

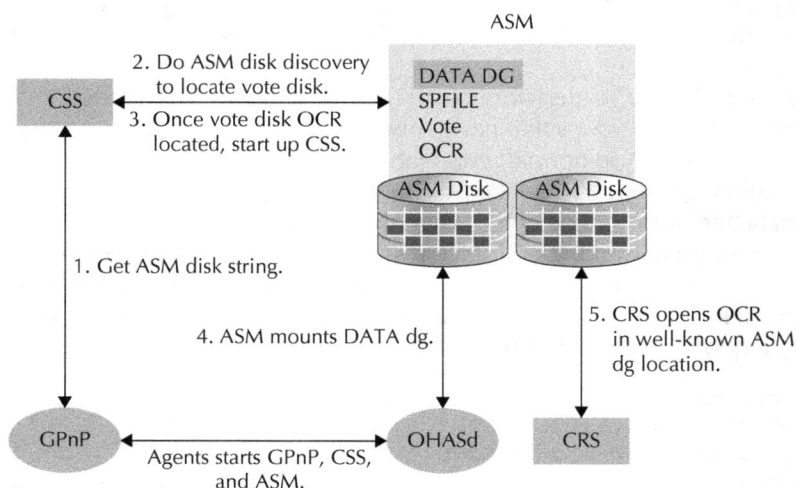

FIGURE 2-4. *Clusterware startup sequence*

NOTE
This lists the processes connected to ASM using the OS ps command. Note that most of these are bequeath connections.

```
[grid@rst-2850-05 trace]$ ps -ef| grep beq
grid      7998     1   0 Sep11 ?        00:00:01 oracle+ASM1_o000_yoda1
(DESCRIPTION=(LOCAL=YES)(ADDRESS=(PROTOCOL=beq)))  ◂database UFG connections into ASM
slaves
grid      8414     1   0 Sep07 ?        00:00:05 oracle+ASM1_ocr
(DESCRIPTION=(LOCAL=YES)(ADDRESS=(PROTOCOL=beq)))  ◂OCR client connection
grid      8416     1   0 Sep07 ?        00:00:05 oracle+ASM1_ocr ◂OCR client connection
(DESCRIPTION=(LOCAL=YES)(ADDRESS=(PROTOCOL=beq)))
grid     10284 10281  0 Aug24 ?        00:00:01 oracle+ASM1 (DESCRIPTION=(LOCAL=YES)
(ADDRESS=(PROTOCOL=beq)))
grid     11147     1   0 Aug11 ?        00:00:00 oracle+ASM1 (DESCRIPTION=(LOCAL=YES)
(ADDRESS=(PROTOCOL=beq)))
grid     11185     1   0 Aug11 ?        00:00:07 oracle+ASM1_asmb_+asm1
(DESCRIPTION=(LOCAL=YES)(ADDRESS=(PROTOCOL=beq)))  ◂ASM local ASMB connection
grid     11581     1   0 Aug11 ?        00:00:11 oracle+ASM1 (DESCRIPTION=(LOCAL=YES)
(ADDRESS=(PROTOCOL=beq)))
grid     17906     1   0 Aug29 ?        00:00:03 oracle+ASM1_asmb_yoda1
(DESCRIPTION=(LOCAL=YES)(ADDRESS=(PROTOCOL=beq)))  ◂database ASMB connection
```

The following output displays a similar listing but from an ASM client perspective:

```
[grid@rst-2850-05 trace]$ asmcmd lsct
DB_Name   Status      Software_Version  Compatible_version  Instance_Name  Disk_Group
+ASM      CONNECTED   11.2.0.3.0        11.2.0.3.0          +ASM1          CRSDATA
+ASM      CONNECTED   11.2.0.3.0        11.2.0.3.0          +ASM1          DATA
asmvol    CONNECTED   11.2.0.3.0        11.2.0.3.0          +ASM1          CRSDATA
asmvol    CONNECTED   11.2.0.3.0        11.2.0.3.0          +ASM1          DATA
yoda      CONNECTED   11.2.0.3.0        11.2.0.0.0          yoda1          DATA_ISHAN01
```

There will be an ASM client listed for the connection OCR:

```
[grid@rst-2850-05 trace]$ asmcmd lsof
DB_Name   Instance_Name  Path
+ASM      +ASM1          +crsdata.255.4294967295
+ASM      +ASM1          +data.255.4294967295
asmvol    +ASM1          +crsdata/DB1.256.760034911
asmvol    +ASM1          +data/SECURE_VOL.256.761163289
yoda      yoda1          +data_ishan01/yoda/controlfile/current.261.760461701
yoda      yoda1          +data_ishan01/yoda/datafile/sysaux.258.760461595
yoda      yoda1          +data_ishan01/yoda/datafile/system.257.760461595
yoda      yoda1          +data_ishan01/yoda/datafile/undotbs1.259.760461595
yoda      yoda1          +data_ishan01/yoda/datafile/undotbs2.265.760461737
yoda      yoda1          +data_ishan01/yoda/datafile/users.260.760461595
yoda      yoda1          +data_ishan01/yoda/onlinelog/group_1.262.760461705
yoda      yoda1          +data_ishan01/yoda/onlinelog/group_2.263.760461705
yoda      yoda1          +data_ishan01/yoda/onlinelog/group_3.266.760461785
yoda      yoda1          +data_ishan01/yoda/onlinelog/group_4.267.760461785
yoda      yoda1          +data_ishan01/yoda/tempfile/temp.264.760461707
```

Here, +data.255 is the OCR file number, which is used to identify the OCR file within ASM.

The voting files, OCR, and spfile are processed differently at bootstrap:

- **Voting file** The GPnP profile contains the disk group name where the voting files are kept. The profile also contains the discovery string that covers the disk group in question. When CSS starts up, it scans each disk group for the matching string and keeps track of the ones containing a voting disk. CSS then directly reads the voting file.

- **ASM spfile** The ASM spfile location is recorded in the disk header(s), which has the spfile data. It is always just one AU. The logic is similar to CSS and is used by the ASM server to find the parameter file and complete the bootstrap.

- **OCR file** OCR is stored as a regular ASM file. Once the ASM instance comes up, it mounts the disk group needed by the CRSd.

Disk Groups and Clusterware Integration

Before discussing the relationship of ASM and Oracle Clusterware, it's best to provide background on CRS modeling, which describes the relationship between a resource, the resource profile, and the resource relationship. A resource, as described previously, is any entity that is being managed by CRS—for example, physical (network cards, disks, and so on) or logical (VIPs, listeners, databases, disk groups, and so on). The resource relationship defines the dependency between resources (for example, state dependencies or proximities) and is considered to be a fundamental building block for expressing how an application's components interact with each other. Two or more resources are said to have a relationships when one (or both) resource(s) either depends on or affects the other. For example, CRS modeling mandated that the DB instance resource depend on the ASM instance and the required disk groups.

As discussed earlier, because Oracle Clusterware version 11gR2 allows the Clusterware files to be stored in ASM, the ASM resources are also managed by CRS. The key resource managed by CRS is the ASM disk group resource.

Oracle Clusterware 11g Release 2 introduces a new agent concept that makes cluster resource management very efficient and scalable. These agents are multithreaded daemons that implement entry points for multiple resource types and spawn new processes for different users. The agents are highly available and, besides oraagent, orarootagent, and cssdagent/cssdmonitor, there can be an application agent and a script agent. The two main agents are oraagent and orarootagent. As the names suggest, oraagent and orarootagent manage resources owned by Oracle and root, respectively. If the CRS user is different from the ORACLE user, then CRSd would utilize two oraagents and one ararootagent. The main agents perform different tasks with respect to ASM. For example, oraagent performs the start/stop/check/clean actions for ora.asm, database, and disk group resources, whereas ararootagent performs start/stop/check/clean actions for the ora.diskmon and ora.drivers.acfs resources.

The following output shows typical ASM-related CRS resources:

```
$ crsctl status resource -t
--------------------------------------------------------------------------
NAME           TARGET  STATE         SERVER          STATE_DETAILS
--------------------------------------------------------------------------
Local Resources
--------------------------------------------------------------------------
ora.DATADG.dg
               ONLINE  ONLINE        racbde1
               ONLINE  ONLINE        racbde2
ora.asm
               ONLINE  ONLINE        racbde1         Started
               ONLINE  ONLINE        racbde2         Started
ora.registry.acfs
               ONLINE  ONLINE        racbde1
               ONLINE  ONLINE        racbde2
```

When the disk group is created, the disk group resource is automatically created with the name, ora.<DGNAME>.dg, and the status is set to ONLINE. The status OFFLINE will be set if the disk group is dismounted, because this is a CRS-managed resource now. When the disk group is dropped, the disk group resource is removed as well. A dependency between the database and the disk group is automatically created when the database tries to access the ASM files. More specifically, a "hard" dependency type is created for the following files types: datafiles, controlfiles, online logs, and SPFile. These are the files that are absolutely needed to start up the database; for all other files, the dependency is set to weak. This becomes important when there are more than two disk groups: one for archive, another for flash or temp, and so on. However, when the database no longer uses the ASM files or the ASM files are removed, the database dependency is not removed automatically. This must be done using the srvctl command-line tool.

The following database CRS profile illustrates the dependency relationships between the database and ASM:

```
$ crsctl status res ora.yoda.db -f
NAME=ora.yoda.db
TYPE=ora.database.type
STATE=OFFLINE
TARGET=ONLINE
ACL=owner:oracle:--x,pgrp:dba:--x,other::r--,group:oinstall:r-x,user:oracle:rwx
ACTION_FAILURE_TEMPLATE=
ACTION_SCRIPT=
ACTIVE_PLACEMENT=1
AGENT_FILENAME=%CRS_HOME%/bin/oraagent%CRS_EXE_SUFFIX%
```

```
AUTO_START=restore
DB_UNIQUE_NAME=yoda
DESCRIPTION=Oracle Database resource
ENABLED=1
SPFILE=+DATA/yoda/spfileyoda.ora
START_DEPENDENCIES=hard(ora.DATA.dg,ora.FRA.dg) weak(type:ora.listener.
type,uniform:ora.ons,uniform:ora.eons) pullup(ora.DATA.dg,ora.FRA.dg)
START_TIMEOUT=600
STATE_CHANGE_TEMPLATE=
STATE_CHANGE_VERS=0
STATE_DETAILS=
STOP_DEPENDENCIES=hard(intermediate:ora.asm,shutdown:ora.DATA.dg,shutdown:ora.FRA.dg)
STOP_TIMEOUT=600
```

Summary

The tighter integration between ASM and Oracle Clusterware provides the capability for quickly deploying new applications as well as managing changing workloads and capacity requirements. This faster agility and elasticity are key drivers for the Private Database Cloud. In addition, the ASM/Clusterware integration with the database is the platform at the core factor of Oracle's Engineered Systems.

CHAPTER

3

ASM Instances

S tarting in Oracle Database 10*g*, the two types of Oracle instances are relational database management system (RDBMS) and Automatic Storage Management (ASM). An ASM instance is similar to any Oracle database instance in that it has a Shared Global Area (SGA) and most of the standard background processes associated with an Oracle database instance. ASM instances do not mount databases, but instead mount disk groups. This chapter focuses on the ASM instance architecture.

ASM instances manage the metadata describing the layout of the ASM files to clients. Databases are one of these clients. ASM metadata is the information that ASM uses to control a disk group. ASM metadata resides within the disk group itself and includes the following information:

- Disks that belong to a disk group

- The amount of space available in a disk group

- The allocation status of blocks on ASM disks

- Filenames of the files in a disk group

- The location of disk group data file extents

- A redo log that records information about atomically changing metadata blocks

- ADVM volume information

The ASM instance provides an extent map to the RDBMS instance and other clients when a file is opened or created, and subsequently the RDBMS instances read and write directly to the disks based on the extent map. The ASM instance is not in the input/output (I/O) path. Database instances access the contents of ASM files directly, communicating with an ASM instance only to get information about the layout of these files. This occurs during certain operations that require ASM intervention, such as a file creation or file extension by a database foreground process. In this case, the database foreground communicates directly with the ASM instance to coordinate the operation (this is covered in Chapter 2). Each database instance maintains a pool of connections to its ASM instance to avoid the overhead of reconnecting for every file operation. Additionally, the RDBMS instances never directly update ASM metadata. ASM metadata is managed and written only by the ASM instance.

Managing ASM Instance

ASM is the volume manager for all databases that employ ASM on a given node. Therefore, only one ASM instance is required per node, regardless of the number of database instances on the node. ASM instances can support various versions of RDBMS instances. Note that because ASM is now part of the Grid Infrastructure stack, thus, ASM as well as the Clusterware must be the highest version in the stack.

Clustering ASM instances is the key to creating a consolidated storage pool. Note that a Real Application Clusters (RAC) license is not required to cluster the ASM instance. In a clustered environment there is one ASM instance per clustered node, and the ASM instances communicate with each other on a peer-to-peer basis. This peer-to-peer communication leverages the RAC Cache Fusion infrastructure (similarly to the RDBMS instance), such as global enqueue services (GES), global cache services (GCS), and global resource directory (GRD). ASM instances message other ASM instances to acknowledge or convey changes to the disk group (for example, disk state changes, disk group membership changes, and ASM cluster membership). ASM's distributed lock manager (DLM) traffic typically is minimal and should not impact the RDBMS interconnect throughput.

Starting Up an ASM Instance

In releases prior to 11gR2, you can start the ASM instance using SQL*Plus, Oracle Enterprise Manager (EM), or the srvctl command (if you are using Oracle Clusterware). However, in 11gR2 the ASM instance is started as part of the Grid Infrastructure stack by the High Availability Services (HAS) process in Grid Infrastructure for Standalone Server or by Grid Infrastructure for Cluster.

The ASM instance is started with the INSTANCE_TYPE=ASM parameter set in the init.ora file. Similarly, the RDBMS instance is identified by INSTANCE_TYPE=RDBMS (which is the default). The following query, when run on the ASM instance, reflects that it is an ASM instance:

```
ASM_SQL> SELECT INSTANCE_NAME FROM V$INSTANCE; INSTANCE_NAME
----------------
+ASM
```

The ASM instance is generally named +ASM, and in RAC configurations, the ASM system identifier (SID) is named the +ASMx instance, where x represents the instance number. The ORACLE_SID environment variable can be set as follows:

```
export ORACLE_SID=+ASM1
```

When the INSTANCE_TYPE=ASM parameter is set, it signals the Oracle initialization routine to start an ASM instance and not an RDBMS instance.

When the 11gR2 Grid Infrastructure software stack is installed with ASM as the storage manager, the Oracle Universal Installer (OUI) will link asm_on in libknlopt.a, and conversely asm_off if ASM is not being used. This linkage entry controls the default value for INSTANCE_TYPE. Enabling asm_on is necessary to store the ASM SPFILE in a disk group, because the instance needs to know that it is an ASM instance before it accesses the parameter file.

The following shows what is linked in libknlopt.a, with kfon.o indicating that ASM is enabled in this Oracle executable:

```
[grid]$ ar -t $ORACLE_HOME/rdbms/lib/libknlopt.a
kkxwtp.o
ksnktd.o
kxmwsd.o
kciwcx.o
ksnkkpo.o
dmndm.o
sllfls.o
xsnoolap.o
kprnts.o
kzlnlbac.o
kzvndv.o
kecnr.o
kdzof.o
joxoff.o
kfon.o
kcsm.o
```

Stopping the ASM Instance

The ASM shutdown process is initiated when you run the SHUTDOWN command in SQL*Plus or the srvctl stop asm command. It is strongly recommended that you shut down all database instances that use the ASM instance and dismount all file systems mounted on ASM Dynamic Volume Manager (Oracle ADVM) volumes before attempting to shut down the ASM instance.

If the Oracle Cluster Registry (OCR) or voting files are stored in a disk group, you can only dismount the disk group by shutting down the ASM instance as part of shutting down the Clusterware on a node. To shut down the Clusterware, run crsctl stop crs.

The following list describes the SHUTDOWN modes and the behavior of the ASM instance in each mode:

- **NORMAL clause** ASM waits for any in-progress SQL to complete before performing an orderly dismount of all the disk groups and shutting down the ASM instance. Before the instance is shut down, ASM waits for all the currently connected users to disconnect from the instance. If any database instances are connected to the ASM instance, the SHUTDOWN command returns an error and leaves the ASM instance running. NORMAL is the default shutdown mode.

■ **IMMEDIATE or TRANSACTIONAL clause**   ASM waits for any in-progress SQL to complete before performing an orderly dismount of all the disk groups and shutting down the ASM instance. ASM does not wait for users currently connected to the instance to disconnect. If any database instances are connected to the ASM instance, the SHUTDOWN command returns an error and leaves the ASM instance running. Because the ASM instance does not contain any transactions, the TRANSACTIONAL mode behaves the same as IMMEDIATE mode.

■ **ABORT clause**   The ASM instance immediately shuts down without the orderly dismount of disk groups. This causes recovery to occur upon the next ASM startup.

If any database instance is connected to the ASM instance, the database instance aborts.

If any ACFS file systems are currently mounted on Oracle ADVM volumes, those file systems should first be dismounted. Otherwise, applications encounter I/O errors, and ACFS user data and metadata might not be written to storage before the ASM storage is fenced.

Authentication for Accessing ASM Instances

An ASM instance does not have a data dictionary, so the only way to connect to an ASM instance is by using one of three system privileges: SYSASM, SYSDBA, or SYSOPER. There are three modes of connecting to ASM instances:

■ Local connection using operating system authentication

■ Local connection using password authentication

■ Remote connection by way of Oracle Net Services using password authentication

The ASM and database instances must have read/write operating system access rights to disk groups. For example, the ASM instance and the database instance must have identical read and write permissions for the disks that comprise the related ASM disk group. For Linux and UNIX systems, this is typically provided through shared Linux and UNIX group membership (OSASM group). On Windows systems, the ASM service must be run as Administrator.

About Privileges for ASM

During ASM installation, you can use one operating system group for all users or divide system privileges so that database administrators, storage administrators, and database operators each have distinct operating system privilege groups.

Whether you create separate operating system privilege groups or use one group to provide operating system authentication for all system privileges, you should use SYSASM to administer an ASM instance. The SYSDBA privilege cannot be used to administer an ASM instance. If you use the SYSDBA privilege to run administrative commands on an ASM instance, the operation results in an error. The SYSDBA privilege is intended to be used by the database to access disk groups.

It is recommended that you use a less privileged user, such as ASMSNMP with SYSDBA privileges, that is created during installation for monitoring the ASM instance.

Connecting to an ASM instance as SYSASM grants you full access to all the available ASM disk groups and management functions.

Using One Operating System Group for ASM Users

If you do not want to divide the privileges for system access into separate operating system groups, you can designate one operating system group as the group whose members are granted access as OSDBA, OSOPER, and OSASM for ASM privileges. The default operating system group name for all of these is usually dba, and that group is typically chosen for the default configuration.

Table 3-1 shows an example of a Linux deployment without separated privileges for ASM users.

Using Separate Operating System Groups for ASM Users

You can designate separate operating system groups as the operating system authentication groups for privileges on ASM. The following list describes the

Role / Software Owner	User	Group / Privilege
ASM administrator / Oracle Grid Infrastructure home	oracle	dba / SYSASM, SYSDBA, SYSOPER
Database administrator 1 / Database home 1	oracle	dba / SYSASM, SYSDBA, SYSOPER
Database administrator 2 / Database home 2	oracle	dba / SYSASM, SYSDBA, SYSOPER
Operating system disk device owner	oracle	dba

TABLE 3-1. *One Operating System Group and One Set of Privileges for All ASM Users*

separate operating system authentication groups for ASM and the privileges that their members are granted:

- **OSASM group**   This group is granted the SYSASM privilege, which provides full administrative privileges for the ASM instance. For example, the group could be asmadmin.

- **OSDBA for ASM group**   This group is granted the SYSDBA privilege on the ASM instance, which grants access to data stored on ASM. This group has a subset of the privileges of the OSASM group.

  When you implement separate administrator privileges, choose an OSDBA group for the ASM instance that is different from the group you select for the database instance, such as dba. For example, the group could be asmdba.

- **OSOPER for ASM group**   This group is granted the SYSOPER privilege on the ASM instance, which provides operations such as startup, shutdown, mount, dismount, and check disk group. This group has a subset of the privileges of the OSASM group. For example, the group could be asmoper.

When you implement separate ASM and database administrator duties, this configuration requires different group and different software owners. Implicitly this implementation requires that the OSASM and OSDBA are different groups. For this configuration, you must create an OSDBA for ASM group, and a database instance must be a member of that group to access the ASM instance.

In an installation that has been configured as Oracle Grid Infrastructure, the ASM user (such as grid) does not have to be a member of the Oracle Database OSDBA group (such as dba1 or dba2) because the Oracle Clusterware database agent runs as the database owner and can use SYSDBA to connect to the database.

However, in an Oracle Restart configuration, the ASM user (grid) must be a member of the OSDBA group (dba1, dba2, and so on) of every database. This requirement is necessary because Oracle Restart software runs as the ASM user (grid), and this user must be able to start and stop the databases using the CONNECT / AS SYSDBA authentication.

Additionally, the owner of the operating system disk devices should be the same as the owner of the ASM software.

Table 3-2 shows an example of a Linux deployment using separate operating system privilege groups for ASM users.

The SYSASM Privilege for Administering ASM

SYSASM is a system privilege that enables the separation of the SYSDBA database administration privilege from the ASM storage administration privilege. Access to the SYSASM privilege is granted by membership in an operating system group that

Role / Software Owner	User	Group / Privilege
ASM administrator / Oracle Grid Infrastructure home	grid	asmadmin (OSASM) / SYSASM asmdba (OSDBA for ASM) / SYSDBA asmoper (OSOPER for ASM) / SYSOPER dba1, dba2, ... (OSDBA for the databases when in an Oracle Restart configuration)
Database administrator 1 / Database home 1	oracle1	asmdba (OSDBA for ASM) / SYSDBA oper1 (OSOPER for database 1) / SYSOPER dba1 (OSDBA for database 1) / SYSDBA
Database administrator 2 / Database home 2	oracle2	asmdba (OSDBA for ASM) / SYSDBA oper2 (OSOPER for database 2) / SYSOPER dba2 (OSDBA for database 2) / SYSDBA
Operating system disk device owner	grid	asmadmin (OSASM)

TABLE 3-2. *Separated Operating System Groups and Privileges for ASM Users*

is designated as the OSASM group. This is similar to the SYSDBA and SYSOPER privileges, which are system privileges granted through membership in the groups designated as the OSDBA and OSOPER operating system groups. You can designate one group for all these system privileges, or you can designate separate groups for each operating system privilege.

You can also grant the SYSASM privilege with password file authentication, as discussed in "Password File Authentication for ASM," later in this chapter.

To connect locally as SYSASM using password authentication with SQL*Plus, use the following statement:

```
sqlplus "SYS AS SYSASM"
...
```

Enter password:

To connect remotely as SYSASM using password authentication with SQL*Plus, use the following statement:

```
sqlplus sys@\"myhost.mydomain.com:1521/+ASM\" AS SYSASM
...
```

Enter password:

In the previous example, +ASM is the service name of the ASM instance.

To connect locally as SYSASM to an ASM instance using operating system authentication with SQL*Plus, use the following statement:

```
sqlplus / AS SYSASM
```

The SYSDBA Privilege for Managing ASM Components

You can connect as SYSDBA to use SQL*Plus or ASMCMD commands to manage ASM components associated with the database. When running SQL, or ASMCMD operations, with the SYSDBA privilege, connect to the database instance rather than the ASM instance.

Connecting as SYSDBA to the database instance has a limited set of ASM privileges. For example, you cannot create a disk group when connected with the SYSDBA privilege.

When you are connected as SYSDBA to the database instance, the ASM operations are limited to the following:

- Create and delete files, aliases, directories, and templates

- Examine various ASM instance views

- Operate on files that were created by this user or only access files to which another user had explicitly granted access

- Granting ASM File Access Control to other users

Creating Users with the SYSASM Privilege

When you are logged in to an ASM instance as SYSASM, you can use the combination of CREATE USER and GRANT SQL statements to create a user who has the SYSASM privilege. You also can revoke the SYSASM privilege from a user using the REVOKE command, and you can drop a user from the password file using the DROP USER command.

NOTE
These commands update the password file for the local ASM instance only.

The following example describes how to perform these SQL operations for the user identified as new_user:

```
REM create a new user, then grant the SYSASM privilege
SQL> CREATE USER marlie IDENTIFIED by marlie_passwd;
SQL> GRANT SYSASM TO marlie;
```

```
REM connect the user to the ASM instance
SQL> CONNECT marlie AS SYSASM;
Enter password:

REM revoke the SYSASM privilege, then drop the user
SQL> REVOKE SYSASM FROM marlie;
SQL> DROP USER marlie;
```

When you revoke the last privilege of a user in an ASM password file, the user is not automatically deleted, as is done in the Oracle Database password file. You need to run DROP USER to delete a user with no privileges in an ASM password file.

Operating System Authentication for ASM

Membership in the operating system group designated as the OSASM group provides operating system authentication for the SYSASM system privilege. OSASM is provided exclusively for ASM. Initially, only the user who installs ASM is a member of the OSASM group, if you use a separate operating system group for that privilege. However, you can add other users. Members of the OSASM group are authorized to connect using the SYSASM privilege and have full access to ASM, including administrative access to all disk groups managed by that ASM instance.

On Linux and UNIX systems, dba is the default operating system group designated as OSASM, OSOPER, and OSDBA for ASM. On Windows systems, ora_dba is the default name designated as OSASM, OSOPER, and OSDBA.

SQL*Plus commands, ASMCMD commands, and ASMCA use operating system authentication.

Password File Authentication for ASM

Password file authentication for ASM can work both locally and remotely. To enable password file authentication, you must create a password file for ASM. A password file is also required to enable Oracle Enterprise Manager to connect to ASM remotely.

If you select the ASM storage option, then ASMCA creates a password file for ASM with initial users (SYS and ASMSNMP) when it configures the ASM disk groups. To add other users to the password file, you can use the CREATE USER and GRANT commands, as described previously in "About Privileges for ASM."

If you configure an ASM instance without using ASMCA, you must manually create a password file and grant the SYSASM privilege to user SYS.

SQL*Plus commands and Oracle Enterprise Manager use password file authentication.

ASM and ASM SPFILE

Starting with Grid Infrastructure 11*g*R2, the ASM server parameter file (SPFILE) can now be stored in an ASM disk group. The key advantage of storing the SPFILE in ASM is simplicity and ease of management. This is particularly important for clustered

ASM configurations, where raw storage space (raw LUNs) is needed for storing the SPFILE. When Oracle Universal Installer (OUI) installs the Grid Infrastructure stack, the ASM server parameter file is automatically created and stored in the default disk group. Because the ASM SPFILE is stored in ASM, and ASM needs the SPFILE to start, it poses an interesting "chicken and egg" paradigm. The Grid Plug and Play (GPnP) profile plays a key role in discovering the ASM SPFILE on ASM bootstrap. This is shown in the output of the following ASM log:

```
Starting ORACLE instance (normal)
LICENSE_MAX_SESSION = 0
LICENSE_SESSIONS_WARNING = 0
Interface type 1 eth3 192.168.3.0 configured from GPnP Profile for use as a
  cluster interconnect  ← ASM reads GPnP profile to get this information
Interface type 1 eth0 10.146.88.0 configured from GPnP Profile for use as a
public interface
Picked latch-free SCN scheme 2
Using LOG_ARCHIVE_DEST_1 parameter default value as /u01/app/11.2.0/grid/dbs/arch

Autotune of undo retention is turned on.
LICENSE_MAX_USERS = 0
SYS auditing is disabled
NOTE: Volume support  enabled
Starting up:
Oracle Database 11g Enterprise Edition Release 11.2.0.1.0 - Production
With the Real Application Clusters and Automatic Storage Management options.
Using parameter settings in server-side spfile ← spfile discovered here
+CRSDATA/myclust/asmparameterfile/registry.253.701260937
System parameters with non-default values:
  large_pool_size        = 12M
  instance_type          = "asm"
  remote_login_passwordfile= "EXCLUSIVE"
  asm_diskstring         = "/dev/mapper/mpath*"
  asm_diskgroups         = "RECOV"
  asm_diskgroups         = "TESTDG"
  asm_power_limit        = 1
  diagnostic_dest        = "/u01/app/grid"
Cluster communication is configured to use the following interface(s) for
this instance
  192.168.3.6
cluster interconnect IPC version:Oracle UDP/IP (generic)
IPC Vendor 1 proto 2
Fri Apr 09 11:58:25 2010
PMON started with pid=2, OS id=12236
Fri Apr 09 11:58:25 2010
VKTM started with pid=3, OS id=12238 at elevated priority
VKTM running at (10)millisec precision with DBRM quantum (100)ms
Fri Apr 09 11:58:25 2010
```

```
.
.
LMS0 started with pid=11, OS id=12261 at elevated priority ← LMS put in RT class
.
.
lmon registered with NM - instance number 2 (internal mem no 1)
Reconfiguration started (old inc 0, new inc 28)
ASM instance
List of instances:  ← This new instance joined the cluster

 1 2 (myinst: 2)

Fri Apr 09 11:58:32 2010
```

The GPnP profile is stored in $CRS_HOME/gpnp/peer/profile/profile.xml. The ASM disk string is listed in the GPnP profile.xml. The location of the initialization parameter file is specified in the GPnP profile. During startup, ASM will obtain the ASM disk string by parsing the GPnP profile. The disk header information will show whether this disk contains the SPFILE and which allocation unit is the SPFILE. ASM reads the disk headers to find a disk with an SPFILE extent and read that extent into memory. The SPFILE is small and thus wholly contained in an Allocation Unit (AU). ASM reads the SPFILE and starts the instance. If the location has not been set in the GPnP profile, the search order changes to the following:

- SPFILE in the Oracle ASM instance home

  For example, the SPFILE for Oracle ASM has the following default path in the Oracle Grid Infrastructure home in a Linux environment: $ORACLE_HOME/dbs/spfile+ASM.ora

- PFILE in the Oracle ASM instance home

Managing the ASM SPFILE

It is recommended that you place the ASM SPFILE in the DATA disk group along with the Clusterware files. To store the SPFILE in an ASM disk group, the COMPATIBLE .ASM disk group attribute must be set to 11.2 or greater for the disk group. Once this is set, you can create, copy, or move an ASM SPFILE into the disk group. You can also use the SQL CREATE SPFILE statement to create an ASM SPFILE when connected to the ASM instance.

ASMCMD has been enhanced to support the manageability of SPFILE. For example, ASMCMD can be used to back up (spbackup), copy (spcopy), or move (spmove) an ASM SPFILE.

The spcopy and spmove commands can be used to copy/move files between ASM disk groups—from OS to ASM or from ASM to OS. Note that spbackup creates a backup copy (version) of the SPFILE. This backup copy file is treated as a standard ASM file; that is, it is not identified as an SPFILE and therefore cannot be managed by the spmove and spcopy commands. Only the ASMCMD cp command can process this backup SPFILE.

If the SPFILE is copied or moved, the ASM instance must be restarted to pick up the SPFILE or PFILE from the new location. Note that you cannot drop a disk group that contains the SPFILE. The SPFILE must be moved to another location before the disk group is dropped.

The spcopy/spmove commands are very handy after upgrading an ASM instance from 11*g* Release 1 to 11*g* Release 2. The following example illustrates this. This example assumes an ASM 11*g* Release 2 instance was upgraded from 11.1.

To create an SPFILE in a disk group, perform the following steps:

1. Connect to the ASM instance. Here's an example:

   ```
   $ sqlplus / as sysasm
   ```

2. Set the COMPATIBLE.ASM attribute to 11.2. This is covered in Chapter 4.

3. Create the SPFILE in ASM using the SQL CREATE SPFILE statement. For example, create an Oracle ASM SPFILE from the existing PFILE:

   ```
   SQL> CREATE SPFILE = '+DATA/asmspfile.ora'
   FROM PFILE = '$ORACLE_HOME/dbs/asmspfile.ora';
   ```

   If an SPFILE already exists from the previous version, use spcopy to copy the SPFILE in the ASM disk group:

   ```
   ASMCMD> spcopy -u /u01/oracle/dbs/spfile+ASM.ora +DATA/spfileASM.ora
   ```

   Both the CREATE SPFILE statement and the spcopy command (using the –u flag) update the Grid Plug and Play (GPnP) profile. You can check the location of the ASM SPFILE in the GPnP profile with the ASMCMD spget command:

   ```
   ASMCMD [+] > spget

   +DATA/spfileasm.ora
   ```

4. Restart the Oracle ASM instance so that the instance reads the SPFILE in the new location.

ASM Background Processes

Once the ASM instance is started, all the basic background processes, as well as some that are specific to the operation of ASM, are started. Notice that all the ASM processes begin with asm, whereas the RDBMS instance processes begin with ora. On UNIX, the ASM processes can be listed using the following command:

```
[grid]$ ps -ef|grep asm
grid     11200    1    0 Jan20 ?        00:03:56 asm_pmon_+ASM2
grid     11202    1    0 Jan20 ?        00:00:01 asm_vktm_+ASM2
grid     11206    1    0 Jan20 ?        00:00:00 asm_gen0_+ASM2
grid     11208    1    0 Jan20 ?        00:00:21 asm_diag_+ASM2
grid     11210    1    0 Jan20 ?        00:02:42 asm_ping_+ASM2
grid     11212    1    0 Jan20 ?        00:00:01 asm_psp0_+ASM2
grid     11214    1    0 Jan20 ?        00:48:54 asm_dia0_+ASM2
grid     11216    1    0 Jan20 ?        00:27:31 asm_lmon_+ASM2
grid     11218    1    0 Jan20 ?        00:31:29 asm_lmd0_+ASM2
grid     11223    1    0 Jan20 ?        00:00:03 asm_lms0_+ASM2
grid     11227    1    0 Jan20 ?        00:00:00 asm_lmhb_+ASM2
grid     11229    1    0 Jan20 ?        00:00:00 asm_mman_+ASM2
grid     11231    1    0 Jan20 ?        00:00:00 asm_dbw0_+ASM2
grid     11233    1    0 Jan20 ?        00:00:00 asm_lgwr_+ASM2
grid     11235    1    0 Jan20 ?        00:00:00 asm_ckpt_+ASM2
grid     11237    1    0 Jan20 ?        00:00:00 asm_smon_+ASM2
grid     11239    1    0 Jan20 ?        00:21:01 asm_rbal_+ASM2
grid     11241    1    0 Jan20 ?        00:34:02 asm_gmon_+ASM2
grid     11243    1    0 Jan20 ?        00:00:02 asm_mmon_+ASM2
grid     11245    1    0 Jan20 ?        00:00:02 asm_mmnl_+ASM2
grid     11252    1    0 Jan20 ?        00:00:02 asm_lck0_+ASM2
grid     11263    1    0 Jan20 ?        00:00:00 asm_vbg0_+ASM2
grid     11265    1    0 Jan20 ?        00:00:09 asm_acfs_+ASM2
grid     11348    1    0 Jan20 ?        00:00:46 asm_asmb_+ASM2
```

Here are some of the more important ASM background processes:

■ **ARBx**   These are the slave processes that perform the rebalance activity (where x is a number).

■ **CKPT**   The CKPT process manages cross-instance calls (in RAC).

■ **DBWR**   This process manages the SGA buffer cache in the ASM instance. DBWR writes out dirty buffers (changed metadata buffers) from the ASM buffer cache to disk.

■ **GMON**   This process is responsible for managing the disk-level activities (drop/offline) and advancing disk group compatibility.

■ **LGWR**   The LGWR process maintains the ASM Active Change Directory (ACD) buffers from the ASM instance and flushes ACD change records to disk.

■ **MARK** The Mark Allocation Unit (AU) for the Resync Koordinator (MARK) process actually runs from the RDBMS instance as well as the ASM instance. It is listed here because it is a key process in the coordination of updates to the Staleness Registry when the disks go offline (in ASM redundancy disk groups).

■ **PMON** This manages processes and process death in the ASM instance.

■ **PSP0** This process spawner process is responsible for creating and managing other Oracle processes.

■ **PZ9***x* These processes are parallel slave processes (where *x* is a number), used in fetching data on behalf of GV$ queries.

■ **RBAL** This opens all device files as part of discovery and coordinates the rebalance activity.

■ **SMON** This process is the system monitor and also acts as a liaison to the Cluster Synchronization Services (CSS) process (in Oracle Clusterware) for node monitoring.

ASM SGA and Parameter Sizing

This section discusses the parameters typically used in the ASM instance, and explains how to set the appropriate values for these parameters based on best practices. Note that the size and workload of the database does not affect or influence the sizing of the ASM instance.

As stated earlier, ASM has a limited number of parameters that can be set. The following are allowable parameters; however, the majority of these parameters do not need to be set:

Disk Group–Related Parameters

■ ASM_DISKGROUPS

■ ASM_DISKSTRING

■ ASM_POWER_LIMIT

■ ASM_PREFERRED_READ_FAILURE_GROUPS

Memory and Instance–Related Parameters

■ DB_CACHE_SIZE

■ INSTANCE_TYPE

■ LARGE_POOL_SIZE

- SHARED_POOL_SIZE
- MEMORY_TARGET
- MEMORY_MAX_TARGET

Instance Management–Related Parameters

- PROCESSES
- DIAGNOSTIC_DEST
- REMOTE_LOGIN_PASSWORDFILE

Just like the database instance, the ASM instance also uses its own SGA structure. The following shows the components that make up the ASM SGA:

- **DB_CACHE_SIZE**   This value determines the size of the ASM buffer cache, which is used to cache ASM metadata blocks. DB_CACHE_SIZE is based on a metadata block size of 4K. This block size is the buffer page size of the cached metadata and has no bearing or impact on the database block size.

- **SHARED_POOL**   This is used for standard memory usage (control structures and so on) to manage the instance. The value is also used to store open file extent maps.

- **LARGE_POOL**   The LARGE_POOL value is used for large page allocations, but typically is not used if SHARED_POOL is set.

Once the appropriate SGA values are set for the ASM instance, they can be checked using the following SQL*Plus command:

```
SQL> SHOW SGA
Total System Global Area 351682560 bytes
Fixed Size 1331588 bytes
Variable Size 283242108 bytes
ASM Cache 67108864 bytes
```

As of Oracle Database 11g, ASM can leverage the Automatic Memory Management (AMM) feature using the init.ora parameters MEMORY_TARGET and MEMORY_MAX_TARGET. Setting these two new parameters automatically manages and tunes all Oracle-related memory for the ASM instance. AMM tunes memory to the target memory size, redistributing and reallocating memory as needed between the instance's SGA and its program global area (PGA). However, because ASM instances have fairly static memory needs, it is an ASM best practice not to set any

Oracle memory parameters. The default value 256MB for MEMORY_TARGET suits most configurations. Thus, even the MEMORY_TARGET init.ora parameter does not need to be set.

NOTE
The number of disk groups, files, or disks doesn't really affect ASM SGA size significantly. However, the number of nodes in the cluster (via GES resources/enqueues) and the number of active databases connecting to ASM (via the ASM Processes parameter) have the most influence on the ASM SGA.

The ASM Processes parameter directly affects the amount of database consolidation and impacts the ASM instance's SGA size. The ASM Processes init.ora parameter limits the number of processes that can start in the ASM instance; therefore, you may need to modify this parameter from its default if you are implementing a database consolidation configuration whereby numerous databases will be leveraging ASM. The following are the recommendations for setting the ASM Processes parameter (for RAC and non-RAC systems).

For 11.2.0.2 ASM configurations:

For fewer than 10 database instances connecting to ASM per node, use:

50 * (DB instances per node + 1)

For 10 or more database instances connecting to ASM per node, use:

{50 * MIN (# db instances per node +1, 11)} + {10 * MAX (# db instance per node − 10, 0)}

In 11.2.0.3, the ASM Processes parameter will default to CPU cores * 80 + 40. The CPU cores value is the number messaged back to ASM, when polled. The default MEMORY_TARGET will be automatically derived.

To prevent "memory_target is too small" errors in ASM during an upgrade from 11.2.0.2 to 11.2.0.3, customers should unset MEMORY_TARGET so that ASM will derive the appropriate default value. However, if MEMORY_TARGET is explicitly set, you should ensure that it is large enough to prevent the errors.

If customers want to set the MEMORY_TARGET value manually, the following guidelines should be used:

- If PROCESSES is explicitly set, MEMORY_TARGET should be set to no less than:
  256M + PROCESSES * 132K (64-bit) or
  256M + PROCESSES * 120K (32-bit)

- If PROCESSES is not set, MEMORY_TARGET should be set to no less than:
  256M + (available_cpu_cores * 80 + 40) * 132K (64-bit) or
  256M + (available_cpu_cores * 80 + 40) * 120K (32-bit)

To set the value of MEMORY_TARGET, use the following command:

```
SQL>ALTER SYSTEM SET MEMORY_TARGET=500M;
```

You can also increase MEMORY_TARGET dynamically, up to the value of the MEMORY_MAX_TARGET parameter, just as you can do for the database instance.

NOTE
AMM and Linux HugePages are not compatible. It is generally considered a best practice to use HugePages for the database. However, for ASM it is recommended to continue using AMM.

ASM Health Check Monitor

In 11*g* Release 1, the Health Monitor was introduced as part of the Oracle Diagnosability Framework. This Health Monitor includes checks for ASM instance health, or more specifically the health of the metadata associated with the disk groups and ASM instance. The health checks collect enough diagnostics on first incident failures. This information is recorded in a Health Monitor finding payload for consumption by the Enterprise Manager. Additionally, the v$hm_finding view is populated when the health checker event is triggered, with specific information including description and damage description fields.

The health checkers get triggered when specific errors are encountered. These checkers monitor the following:

- **Allocation failure due to out-of-space errors** The Out of Space reactive health checker is triggered when ASM encounters a space shortage for a particular disk group. This out-of-space condition is indicated by the Oracle error message ORA-15041. The reactive health checker is triggered when this message is generated for a disk group.

- **Mount failure due to missing disks** The Missing Disks reactive health checker is triggered when ASM fails to locate one or more of a disk group's member disks during a disk group mount operation. This Missing Disk condition is indicated by the Oracle error message ORA-15042, and the reactive health checker is triggered when this message is generated during a disk group mount. When the reactive checker is triggered, it runs a query to determine the known member disks for this disk group and extracts the pathname of the missing disk. This information is used to generate a Health Monitor finding for consumption by the Enterprise Manager. Note that if this is a single instance configuration or the first node in the cluster to mount this disk group, the health checker will be unable to determine the pathname of the missing disk because this functionality depends on the disk group already being successfully mounted on another node.

■ **Add/Online disk failure due to cluster-wide visibility issues**   The Disk Visibility reactive health checker is triggered when the user attempts to add a disk to a disk group, and the disk is not visible to all nodes that currently have the disk group mounted. This is indicated by the Oracle error message ORA-15075. When the reactive checker is triggered, it runs a query to determine the discovery sets for all active ASM instances. A Health Monitor finding is generated with the name of the trace file containing the list of discovered disks.

■ **Client file drop fails**   The File Drop reactive health checker is triggered when the user attempts to drop an ASM file that is currently being accessed by one or more clients. This File Drop failure due to access conflict is indicated by the Oracle error message ORA-15028. When the reactive checker is triggered, it runs a query to determine which database instances are currently connected to the ASM instance and on which ones the error was encountered.

■ **Mount failure due to insufficient disks**   The Insufficient Disks reactive health checker is triggered when ASM fails to locate enough of a disk group's member disks during a disk group mount operation. This disk condition is indicated by the Oracle error message ORA-15063. When the reactive checker is triggered, it performs a disk discovery and writes the discovery information to a trace file. A Health Monitor finding is generated that provides the name of the trace file.

■ **Mount failure due to too many offline disks**   The Missing Disks reactive health checker is triggered when ASM fails to locate one or more of a disk group's member disks during a disk group mount operation. The too-many-offline-disks condition is indicated by the Oracle error message ORA-15066. The reactive health checker is triggered when this message is generated during a disk group mount. When the reactive checker is triggered, it performs disk discovery and loads Partner and Status Table information. The list of discovered disks is written to the trace file, along with the list of the partner disks of each discovered disk. This should enable support to determine the precise reason for the error. A Health Monitor finding is generated that provides the name of the trace file.

The following is an example of v$hm_finding based on a Health Check trigger. In this example, the event is a "mount failure due to missing disk," which is triggered by ORA-15042:

```
SQL> select time_detected, description, damage_description from v$hm_finding;
TIME_DETECTED
-----------------------------------------------------------------------------
DESCRIPTION
-----------------------------------------------------------------------------
DAMAGE_DESCRIPTION
-----------------------------------------------------------------------------
14-DEC-10 01.50.22.767000 PM
Disk missing from the disk group. Disk number: 0 Name: NA Path: NA.
See trace file main311_m000_3943.
ASM disk group mount failure can result in failure mounting Oracle database.
```

If another instance in the cluster has successfully mounted this disk group, the checker will have queried gv$asm_disk and dumped the list of disks to the trace file, along with a good guess as to which one is missing on the local instance, based on the disk number.

Summary

The ASM metadata is managed by an ASM instance. An ASM instance is similar to any Oracle instance in that it has an SGA and most of the normal background processes. It can use the same executable as the database instances. ASM instances do not mount databases, but instead mount disk groups. An ASM instance manages the metadata needed to make ASM files available to database instances. Both ASM instances and database instances must have access to all the ASM disks. The ASM instance provides an extent map to the database instance when a file is opened or created. Database instances read and write the disks directly based on the extent map. The ASM instance is not in the I/O path.

CHAPTER
4

ASM Disks and
Disk Groups

T he first task in building the ASM infrastructure is to discover and place disks under ASM management. This step is best done with the coordination of storage and system administrators. In storage area network (SAN) environments, it is assumed that the disks are identified and configured correctly—that is, they are appropriately zoned or "LUN masked" within the SAN fabric and can be seen by the operating system (OS). Although the concepts in this chapter are platform generic, we specifically show examples using the Linux or Solaris platforms.

ASM Storage Provisioning

Before disks can be added to ASM, the storage administrator needs to identify a set of disks or logical devices from a storage array. Note that the term *disk* is used loosely because a disk can be any of the following:

- An entire disk spindle

- A partition of a physical disk spindle

- An aggregation of several disk partitions across several disks

- A logical device carved from a RAID (redundant array of independent drives) group set

- A file created from an NFS file system

Once the preceding devices are created, they are deemed logical unit numbers (LUNs). These LUNs are then presented to the OS as logical disks.

In this book, we refer generically to LUNs or disks presented to the OS as simply *disks*. The terms *LUN* and *disk* may be used interchangeably.

DBAs and system administrators are often in doubt as to the maximum LUN size they can use without performance degradation, or as to the LUN size that will give the best performance. For example, will 1TB- or 2TB-sized LUNs perform the same as 100GB- or 200GB-sized LUNs?

Size alone should not affect the performance of an LUN. The underlying hardware, the number of disks that compose an LUN, and the read-ahead and write-back caching policy defined on the LUN all, in turn, affect the speed of the LUN. There is no magic number for the LUN size or the number of ASM disks in the disk group.

Seek the advice of the storage vendor for the best storage configuration for performance and availability, because this may vary between vendors.

Given the database size and storage hardware available, the best practice is to create larger LUNs (to reduce LUN management) and, if possible, generate LUNs from a separate set of storage array RAID sets so that the LUNs do not share drives. If the storage array is a low-end commodity storage unit and storage RAID will not be used, then it is best to employ ASM redundancy and use entire drives as ASM disks. Additionally, the ASM disk size is the minimal increment by which a disk group's size can change.

> **NOTE**
> *The maximum disk size for an ASM disk in pre-12c configurations is 2TB, and the minimum disk size is 4MB.*

Users should create ASM disks with sizes less than 2TB in pre-12c environments. A message such as the following will be thrown if users specify ASM candidate disks that are greater than 2TB:

```
SQL> create diskgroup DATA EXTERNAL REDUNDANCY
DISK
'/dev/sdg1' NAME asmdisk1,
ATTRIBUTE 'au_size'='4M',
  'compatible.asm' = '11.2',
  'compatible.rdbms'
create diskgroup DATA EXTERNAL REDUNDANCY
*
ERROR at line 1:
ORA-15018: diskgroup cannot be created
ORA-15099: disk '/dev/asm_dsk1' is larger than maximum size of
2097152 MBs
```

ASM Storage Device Configuration

This section details the steps and considerations involved in configuring storage devices presented to the operating system that were provisioned in the earlier section. This function is typically performed by the system administrator or an ASM administrator (that is, someone with root privileges).

Typically, disks presented to the OS can be seen in the /dev directory on Unix/ Linux systems. Note that each OS has its unique representation of small computer system interface (SCSI) disk naming. For example, on Solaris systems, disks usually have the SCSI name format *cwtxdysz*, where *c* is the controller number, *t* is the target, *d* is the LUN/disk number, and *s* is the partition. Creating a partition serves three purposes:

- To skip the OS label/VTOC (volume table of contents). Different operating systems have varying requirements for the OS label—that is, some may require an OS label before it is used, whereas others do not. For example, on a Solaris system, it is a best practice to create a partition on the disk, such as partition 4 or 6, that skips the first 1MB into the disk.

- To create a placeholder to identify that the disk is being used because an unpartitioned disk could be accidentally misused or overwritten.

- To preserve alignment between ASM striping and storage array internal striping.

The goal is to align the ASM file extent boundaries with any striping that may be done in the storage array. The Oracle database does a lot of 1MB input/outputs (I/Os) that are aligned to 1MB offsets in the data files. It is slightly less efficient to misalign these I/Os with the stripes in the storage array, because misalignment can cause one extra disk to be involved in the I/O. Although this misalignment may not affect the latency of that particular I/O, it reduces the overall throughput of the system by increasing the number of disk seeks. This misalignment is independent of the operating system. However, some operating systems may make it more difficult to control the alignment or may add more offsets to block 0 of the ASM disk.

The disk partition used for an ASM disk is best aligned at 1MB within the LUN, as presented to the OS by the storage. ASM uses the first allocation unit of a disk for metadata, which includes the disk header. The ASM disk header itself is in block 0 of the disk given to ASM as an ASM disk.

Aligning ASM disk extent boundaries to storage array striping only makes sense if the storage array striping is a power of 2; otherwise, it is not much of a concern.

The alignment issue would be solved if we could start the ASM disk at block 0 of the LUN, but that does not work on some operating systems (Solaris, in particular). On Linux, you could start the ASM disk at block 0, but then there is a chance an administrator would run fdisk on the LUN and destroy the ASM disk header. Therefore, we always recommend using a partition rather than starting the ASM disk at block 0 of the LUN.

ASM Disk Device Discovery

Once the disks are presented to the OS, ASM needs to discover them. This requires that the disk devices (Unix filenames) have their ownership changed from root to the software owner of Grid Infrastructure stack. The system administrator usually makes this change. In our example, disks c3t19d5s4, c3t19d16s4, c3t19d17s4, and c3t19d18s4 are identified, and their ownership set to the oracle:dba. Now ASM must be configured to discover these disks. This is done by defining the ASM init.ora parameter ASM_DISKSTRING. In our example, we will use the following wildcard setting:

```
*.asm_diskstring='/dev/rdsk/c3t19d*s4'
```

An alternative to using standard SCSI names (such as c*w*t*x*d*y*s*z* or /dev/sdda) is to use special files. This option is useful when establishing standard naming conventions and for easily identifying ASM disks, such as asmdisk1. This option requires creating special files using the mknod or udev generated names on Linux command.

The following is a use case example of mknod. To create a special file called asmdisk1 for a preexisting device partition called c3t19d7s4, you can determine the OS major number and minor number as follows:

```
[root@racnode1]# ls -lL c3t19d7s4
crw-r----- 1 root sys 32, 20 Feb 24 07:14 c3t19d7s4
```

NOTE
Major and minor numbers are associated with the device special files in the /dev directory and are used by the operating system to determine the actual driver and device to be accessed by the user-level request for the special device file.

The preceding example shows that the major and minor device numbers for this device are 32 and 20, respectively. The *c* at the beginning indicates that this is a character (raw) file.

After obtaining the major and minor numbers, use the mknod command to create the character and block special files that will be associated with c3t19d7s4. A special file called /dev/asmdisk can be created under the /dev directory, as shown:

```
[root@racnode1]# mkdir /dev/asmdisk
[root@racnode1]# cd /dev/asmdisk
[root@racnode1]# mknod asmdisk1 c 32 20
```

Listing the special file shows the following:

```
[root@racnode1]# ls -l
crw-r--r-- 1 root other 32, 20 May 7 07:50 asmdisk1
```

Notice that this device has the same major and minor numbers as the native device c3t19d7s4.

For this partition (or *slice)* to be accessible to the ASM instance, change the permissions on this special file to the appropriate oracle user permissions:

```
[root@racnode1]# chown grid:asmadmin disk1
[root@racnode1]# ls -l /dev/disk
crw-r--r-- 1 grid asmadmin 32, 20 May 7 07:50 disk1
```

Repeat this step for all the required disks that will be discovered by ASM. Now the slice is accessible by the ASM instance. The ASM_DISKSTRING can be set to /dev/asmdisk/*. Once discovered, the disk can be used as an ASM disk.

NOTE
It is not recommended that you create mknod devices in the /dev/asm directory because the /dev/asm path is reserved for ACFS to place ACFS configuration files and ADVM volumes. During 11gR2 Clusterware installation or upgrade, the root.sh or rootupgrade.sh script may remove and re-create the /dev/asm directory, causing the original mknod devices to be deleted. Be sure to use a different directory instead, such as /dev/asmdisk.

ASM discovers all the required disks that make up the disk group using "on-disk" headers and its search criteria (ASM_DISKSTRING). ASM scans only for disks that match that ASM search string. There are two forms of ASM disk discovery: shallow and deep. For shallow discovery, ASM simply scans the disks that are eligible to be opened. This is equivalent to executing "ls -l" on all the disk devices that have the appropriate permissions. For deep discovery, ASM opens each of those eligible disk devices. In most cases, ASM discoveries are deep, the exception being when the *_STAT tables are queried instead of the standard tables.

NOTE
For ASM in clustered environments, it is not necessary to have the same pathname or major or minor device numbers across all nodes. For example, node1 could access a disk pointed to by path /dev/rdsk/c3t1d4s4, whereas node2 could present /dev/rdsk/c4t1d4s4 for the same device. Although ASM does not require that the disks have the same names on every node, it does require that the same disks be visible to each ASM instance via that instance's discovery string. In the event that pathnames differ between ASM nodes, the only necessary action is to modify the ASM_DISKSTRING to match the search path. This is a non-issue on Linux systems that use ASMLIB, because ASMLIB handles the disk search and scan process.

Upon successful discovery, the V$ASM_DISK view on the ASM instance reflects which disks were discovered. Note that henceforth all views, unless otherwise stated, are queried from the ASM instance and not from the RDBMS instance.

The following example shows the disks that were discovered using the defined ASM_DISKSTRING. Notice that the NAME column is empty and the

GROUP_NUMBER is set to 0. This is because disks were discovered that are not yet associated with a disk group. Therefore, they have a null name and a group number of 0.

```
SQL> SELECT NAME,PATH,GROUP_NUMBER FROM V$ASM_DISK
NAME                              PATH              GROUP_NUMBER
------------------------------    ---------------   ------------
                                  /dev/rdsk/c3t19d5s4        0
                                  /dev/rdsk/c3t19d16s4       0
                                  /dev/rdsk/c3t19d17s4       0
                                  /dev/rdsk/c3t19d18s4       0
```

In an Exadata environment, the physical disks on the storage cells are called *cell disks*. Grid disks are created from the cell disks and are presented to ASM via the LIBCELL interface; they are used to create disk groups in Exadata. The default value for ASM_DISKSTRING in Exadata is 'o/*/*'.

Note that these Exadata disks as presented by LIBCELL are not presented to the OS as block devices, but rather as internal network devices; they are not visible at the OS level. However, the kfod tool can be used to verify ASM disk discovery. The following shows kfod output of grid disks:

```
$ kfod disk=all
--------------------------------------------------------------------------------
Disk          Size Path                                        User      Group
================================================================================
   1:   1501184 Mb o/192.168.10.3/DATA_EXAD_CD_00_exadcel01 <unknown> <unknown>
   2:   1501184 Mb o/192.168.10.3/DATA_EXAD_CD_01_exadcel01 <unknown> <unknown>
   3:   1501184 Mb o/192.168.10.3/DATA_EXAD_CD_02_exadcel01 <unknown> <unknown>
   4:   1501184 Mb o/192.168.10.3/DATA_EXAD_CD_03_exadcel01 <unknown> <unknown>
   5:   1501184 Mb o/192.168.10.3/DATA_EXAD_CD_04_exadcel01 <unknown> <unknown>
   6:   1501184 Mb o/192.168.10.3/DATA_EXAD_CD_05_exadcel01 <unknown> <unknown>
   7:   1501184 Mb o/192.168.10.3/DATA_EXAD_CD_06_exadcel01 <unknown> <unknown>
   8:   1501184 Mb o/192.168.10.3/DATA_EXAD_CD_07_exadcel01 <unknown> <unknown>
   9:   1501184 Mb o/192.168.10.3/DATA_EXAD_CD_08_exadcel01 <unknown> <unknown>
  10:   1501184 Mb o/192.168.10.3/DATA_EXAD_CD_09_exadcel01 <unknown> <unknown>
  11:   1501184 Mb o/192.168.10.3/DATA_EXAD_CD_10_exadcel01 <unknown> <unknown>
  12:   1501184 Mb o/192.168.10.3/DATA_EXAD_CD_11_exadcel01 <unknown> <unknown>
  13:     29808 Mb o/192.168.10.3/DBFS_DG_CD_02_exadcel01   <unknown> <unknown>
  14:     29808 Mb o/192.168.10.3/DBFS_DG_CD_03_exadcel01   <unknown> <unknown>
  15:     29808 Mb o/192.168.10.3/DBFS_DG_CD_04_exadcel01   <unknown> <unknown>
  16:     29808 Mb o/192.168.10.3/DBFS_DG_CD_05_exadcel01   <unknown> <unknown>
  17:     29808 Mb o/192.168.10.3/DBFS_DG_CD_06_exadcel01   <unknown> <unknown>
  18:     29808 Mb o/192.168.10.3/DBFS_DG_CD_07_exadcel01   <unknown> <unknown>
  19:     29808 Mb o/192.168.10.3/DBFS_DG_CD_08_exadcel01   <unknown> <unknown>
  20:     29808 Mb o/192.168.10.3/DBFS_DG_CD_09_exadcel01   <unknown> <unknown>
  21:     29808 Mb o/192.168.10.3/DBFS_DG_CD_10_exadcel01   <unknown> <unknown>
  22:     29808 Mb o/192.168.10.3/DBFS_DG_CD_11_exadcel01   <unknown> <unknown>
  23:    375344 Mb o/192.168.10.3/RECO_EXAD_CD_00_exadcel01 <unknown> <unknown>
  24:    375344 Mb o/192.168.10.3/RECO_EXAD_CD_01_exadcel01 <unknown> <unknown>
  25:    375344 Mb o/192.168.10.3/RECO_EXAD_CD_02_exadcel01 <unknown> <unknown>
  26:    375344 Mb o/192.168.10.3/RECO_EXAD_CD_03_exadcel01 <unknown> <unknown>
```

```
27:     375344 Mb o/192.168.10.3/RECO_EXAD_CD_04_exadcel01 <unknown> <unknown>
28:     375344 Mb o/192.168.10.3/RECO_EXAD_CD_05_exadcel01 <unknown> <unknown>
------------------------------------------------------------------------------
ORACLE_SID ORACLE_HOME
==============================================================================
   +ASM2 /u01/app/11.2.0.3/grid
   +ASM1 /u01/app/11.2.0.3/grid
```

The preceding output shows the following:

■ The grid disks are presented from three storage cells (192.168.10.12, 192.168.10.13, and 192.168.10.14).

Disks have various header statuses that reflect their membership state with a disk group. Disks can have the following header statuses:

■ **FORMER** This state declares that the disk was formerly part of a disk group.

■ **CANDIDATE** A disk in this state is available to be added to a disk group.

■ **MEMBER** This state indicates that a disk is already part of a disk group. Note that the disk group may or may not be mounted.

■ **PROVISIONED** This state is similar to CANDIDATE, in that it is available to be added to disk groups. However, the provisioned state indicates that this disk has been configured or made available using ASMLIB.

Note that ASM does not ever mark disks as CANDIDATE. Disks with a HEADER_STATUS of CANDIDATE is the outcome of the evaluation of ASM disk discovery. If a disk is dropped by ASM via a normal DROP DISK, the header status would become listed as FORMER. Moreover, if a disk is taken offline and subsequently force dropped, the HEADER_STATUS would remain as MEMBER.

The following is a useful query to run to view the status of disks in the ASM system:

```
SQL>SELECT NAME, PATH, HEADER_STATUS, MODE_STATUS FROM V$ASM_DISK;
```

The views V$ASM_DISK_STAT and V$ASM_DISKGROUP_STAT are identical to V$ASM_DISK and V$ASM_DISKGROUP. However, the $ASM_DISK_STAT and V$ASM_DISKGROUP_STAT views are polled from memory and are based on the last deep disk discovery. Because these new views provide efficient lightweight access, Enterprise Manager (EM) can periodically query performance statistics at the disk level and aggregate space usage statistics at the disk group level without incurring significant overhead.

Third-Party Volume Managers and ASM

Although it is not a recommended practice, host volume managers such as Veritas VxVM and IBM LVM can sit below ASM. For example, a logical volume manager (LVM) can create raw logical volumes and present these as disks to ASM. However, the third-party LVM should not use any host-based mirroring or striping. ASM algorithms are based on the assumption that I/Os to different disks are relatively independent and can proceed in parallel. If any of the volume manager virtualization features are used beneath ASM, the configuration becomes too complex and confusing and can needlessly incur overhead, such as the maintenance of a dirty region log (DRL). DRL is discussed in greater detail later in this chapter.

In a clustered environment, such a configuration can be particularly expensive. ASM does a better job of providing this configuration's functionality for database files. Additionally, in RAC environments, if ASM were to run over third-party volume managers, the volume managers must be cluster-aware—that is, they must be cluster volume managers (CVMs).

However, it may make sense in certain cases to have a volume manager under ASM (for example, when Sysadmins need a simplified management and tracking of disk assignments is needed).

If a volume manager is used to create logical volumes as ASM disks, the logical volumes should not use any LVM RAID functionality.

Preparing ASM Disks on NFS

ASM supports Network File System (NFS) files as ASM disks. To prepare NFS for ASM storage, the NAS NFS file system must be made accessible to the server where ASM is running.

The following steps can be used to set up and configure ASM disks using the NFS file system:

1. On the NAS server, create the file system. Depending on the NAS server, this will require creating LUNs, creating RAID groups out of the LUNs, and finally creating a file system from the block devices.

2. Export the NAS file system so that it's accessible to the host server running ASM. This mechanism will differ based on the filer or NFS server being used. Typically this requires the /etc/exports file to specify the NFS file system to be remotely mounted.

3. On the host server, create the mount point where the NFS file system will be mounted:

```
#mkdir /oradata/asmdisks
#chown -R grid:asmadmin  /oradata/asmdisks
```

4. Update /etc/fstab with the following entry:

```
nfssrv1:/u01/asmdisks  /oradata/asmdisks  nfs
rw,bg,hard,nointr,tcp,vers=3,timeo=600,rsize=32768,
wsize=32768,actimeo=0   0 0
```

5. Mount the NFS file system on the host server using the mount –a command.

6. Initialize the NFS file system files so they can be used as ASM disks:

```
$ dd if=/dev/zero of=/oradata/asmdisks/asm_dsk1
bs=1M count=1000000
```

This step should be repeated to configure the appropriate number of disks.

7. Ensure that ASM can discover the newly created disk files (that is, check that the permissions are grid:asmadmin).

8. Set the ASM disk string appropriately when prompted in OUI for the ASM configuration.

It is very important to have the correct NFS mount options set. If wrong mount options are set, an exception will be thrown on file open. This is shown in the following listing. RAC and Clusterware code uses the O_DIRECT flag for write calls, so the data writes bypass the cache and go directly to the NFS server (thus avoiding possible corruptions by an extra caching layer).

File system files that are opened as read-only by all nodes (such as shared libraries) or files that are accessed by a single node (such as trace files) can be on a mount point with the mount option actimeo set to greater than 0. Only files that are concurrently written and read by multiple nodes (such as database files, application output files, and natively compiled libraries shared among nodes) need to be on a mount point with actimeo set to 0. This not only saves on network round trips for stat() calls, but the calls also don't have to wait for writes to complete. This could be a significant speedup, especially for files being read and written by a single node.

```
WARNING:NFS file system /nfs_data2 mounted with incorrect options
(rw,vers=3,rsize=32768,wsize=32768,hard,proto=tcp,timeo=600,retrans=2,
sec=sys,addr=strracnfs01-p)
WARNING:Expected NFS mount options: rsize>=32768,wsize>=32768,hard,no
ac/actimeo=0
Errors in file /u01/app/oracle/diag/rdbms/yoda/yoda1/trace/ORCL1_
dbw0_260693.trc:
```

Direct NFS

Oracle Database has built-in support for the Network File System (NFS) client via Direct NFS (dNFS). dNFS, an Oracle-optimized NFS client introduced in Oracle Database 11*g*R1, is built directly into the database kernel.

dNFS provides faster performance than the native OS NFS client driver because it bypasses the OS. Additionally, once dNFS is enabled, very little user configuration or tuning is required. Data is cached just once in user space, so there's no second copy in kernel space. dNFS also provides implicit network interface load balancing. ASM supports the dNFS client that integrates the NFS client functionality directly in the Oracle Database software stack. If you are using dNFS for RAC configurations, some special considerations need to be made. dNFS cannot be used to store (actually access) voting files. The reason for this lies in how voting files are accessed. CSS is a multi-threaded process and dNFS (in its current state) is not thread safe. OCR files and other cluster files (including database files) are accessed using ASM file I/O operations.

Note that ASM Dynamic Volume Manager (Oracle ADVM) does not currently support NFS-based ASM files.

Preparing ASM Disks on OS Platforms

This section illustrates the specific tasks needed to configure ASM for the specific operating systems and environments.

Linux

On Intel-based systems such as Linux/Windows, the first 63 blocks have been reserved for the master boot record (MBR). Therefore, the first data partition starts with offset at 31.5KB (that is, 63 times 512 bytes equals 31.5KB).

This offset can cause misalignment on many storage arrays' memory cache or RAID configurations, causing performance degradation due to overlapping I/Os. This performance impact is especially evident for large block I/O workloads, such as parallel query processing and full table scans.

The following shows how to manually perform the alignment using sfdisk against an EMC Powerpath device. Note that this procedure is applicable to any OS device that needs to be partitioned aligned.

```
Create partition alignment of 1M
$ cat sfdisk_alignment.txt
# --
# -- Partition alignment of Data / FRA disks with 1MB offset
# Repeat lines for each device to be passed to ASM/ASMLIB
echo "2048,," | sfdisk -uS /dev/emcpowerb
```

Here's an example output:
```
# echo "2048,," | sfdisk -uS /dev/emcpowerb
```

```
Checking that no-one is using this disk right now ...
OK
Disk /dev/emcpowerb: 1018 cylinders, 166 heads, 62 sectors/track
Old situation:
No partitions found
New situation:
Units = sectors of 512 bytes, counting from 0
    Device Boot        Start      End    #sectors   Id  System
/dev/emcpowerb1         2048  10477255   10475208   83  Linux
/dev/emcpowerb2            0        -           0    0  Empty
/dev/emcpowerb3            0        -           0    0  Empty
/dev/emcpowerb4            0        -           0    0  Empty
Warning: no primary partition is marked bootable (active)
This does not matter for LILO, but the DOS MBR will not boot this disk.
Successfully wrote the new partition table
Re-reading the partition table ...
```

To check on the partition alignment
```
# cat  check_alignment.txt
sfdisk -uS -l /dev/emcpowerb

[root@ljtcdb157 work]# ./check_alignment.txt

Disk /dev/emcpowerb: 1018 cylinders, 166 heads, 62 sectors/track
Units = sectors of 512 bytes, counting from 0

    Device Boot        Start      End    #sectors   Id  System
/dev/emcpowerb1         2048  10477255   10475208   83  Linux
/dev/emcpowerb2            0        -           0    0  Empty
/dev/emcpowerb3            0        -           0    0  Empty
/dev/emcpowerb4            0        -           0    0  Empty
```

Check that partitions exist
```
# /sbin/fdisk -l /dev/emcpowerb

Disk /dev/emcpowerb: 5368 MB, 5368709120 bytes
166 heads, 62 sectors/track, 1018 cylinders
Units = cylinders of 10292 * 512 = 5269504 bytes

Device Boot            Start        End      Blocks   Id  System
/dev/emcpowerb1            1       1018     5237604   83  Linux
```

cat /proc/partitions
```
 120    16    5242880 emcpowerb
 120    17    5237604 emcpowerb1
...
```

Solaris

This section covers some of the nuances of creating disk devices in a Solaris environment. The Solaris format command is used to create OS slices. Note that slices 0 and 2 (for SMI labels) cannot be used as ASM disks because these slices include the Solaris VTOC. An example of the format command output (partition map) for the device follows:

```
/dev/rdsk/c2t12d29.
Current partition table (original):
Total disk cylinders available: 18412 + 2 (reserved cylinders)
Part      Tag    Flag     Cylinders        Size            Blocks
  0 unassigned    wm       0               0          (0/0/0)            0
  1 unassigned    wm       0               0          (0/0/0)            0
  2     backup    wu       0 - 18411       8.43GB     (18412/0/0) 17675520
  3          -    wu       0 -     2       1.41MB     (3/0/0)         2880
  4          -    wu       4 - 18411       8.43GB     (18408/0/0) 17671680
  5 unassigned    wm       0               0          (0/0/0)            0
  6 unassigned    wm       0               0          (0/0/0)            0
  7 unassigned    wm       0               0          (0/0/0)            0
```

Notice that slice 4 is created and that it skips four cylinders, thus offsetting past the VTOC.

Use the logical character device as listed in the /dev/rdsk directory. Devices in this directory are symbolic links to the physical device files. Here's an example:

```
[root@racnode1]# ls -l /dev/rdsk/c0t2d0s4
lrwxrwxrwx 1 root root 45 Feb 24 07:14 c0t2d0s4 -> ../../devices/
pci@1f,4000/scsi@3/sd@2,0:e,raw
```

To change the permission on these devices, do the following:

```
[root@racnode1]# chown oracle:dba ../../devices/pci@1f,4000/scsi@3/
sd@2,0:e,raw
```

Now the ASM instance can access the slice. Set the ASM_DISKSTRING to /dev/rdsk/c*s4. Note that the actual disk string differs in each environment.

AIX

This section describes how to configure ASM disks for AIX. It also recommends some precautions that are necessary when using AIX disks.

In AIX, a disk is assigned a physical volume identifier (PVID) when it is first assigned to a volume group or when it is manually set using the AIX chdev command. When the PVID is assigned, it is stored on the physical disk and in the AIX server's system object database, called *Object Data Manager (ODM)*. The PVID resides in the first 4KB of the disk and is displayed using the AIX lspv command. In the following listing, the first two disks have PVIDs assigned and the others do not:

```
lspv
hdisk11    000f0d8dea7df87c    None
hdisk12    000f0d8dea7a6940    None
hdisk15    none                None
hdisk16    none                None
hdisk17    none                None
```

If a PVID-assigned disk is incorporated into an ASM disk group, ASM will write an ASM disk header on the first 40 bytes of the disk, thus overwriting the PVID. Although initially no problems may arise, on the subsequent reboot the OS, in coordination with the ODM database, will restore the PVID onto the disk, thus destroying the ASM disk and potentially resulting in data loss.

Therefore, it is a best practice on AIX not to include a PVID on any disk that ASM will use. If a PVID does exist and ASM has not used the disk yet, you can clear the PVID by using the AIX chdev command.

Functionality was added to AIX to help prevent corruption such as this. AIX commands that write to the LVM information block have special checking added to determine if the disk is already in use by ASM. This mechanism is used to prevent these disks from being assigned to the LVM, which would result in the Oracle data becoming corrupted. Table 4-1 lists the command and the corresponding AIX version where this checking is done.

AIX 6.1 and AIX 7.1 LVM commands contain new functionality that can be used to better manage AIX devices used by Oracle. This new functionality includes commands to better identify shared disks across multiple nodes, the ability to assign

AIX Command	AIX 5.3	AIX 6.1	AIX 7.1	Description
mkvg	TL07 or newer	All	All	Prevents reassigning a disk used by Oracle
extendvg	TL07 or newer	All	All	Prevents reassigning a disk used by Oracle
chdev … -a pv=yes chdev … -a pv=clear	–	–	–	No checking

TABLE 4-1. *AIX Version Where This PVID Checking Is Implemented*

a meaningful name to a device, and a locking mechanism that the system administrator can use when the disk is assigned to ASM to help prevent the accidental reuse of a disk at a later time. This new functionality is listed in Table 4-2, along with the minimum AIX level providing that functionality. Note that these manageability commands do not exist for AIX 5.3.

The following illustrates the disk-locking and -checking functionality:

```
SQL> select name, path, mode_status, state from v$asm_disk order by name;
NAME                 PATH                 MODE_STATUS      STATE
---------------- -------------------- ---------------- ----------------
DATA_0000            /dev/rhdiskASMd001   ONLINE           NORMAL
...
```

Lock every raw disk used by ASM Lock to protect the disk. This can be done while Oracle RAC is active on the cluster:

```
root@racnode1# lkdev -l hdiskASMd001 -a
hdiskASMd001 locked
```

Then use the lspv command to check the status of the disks.

```
root@racnode1# lspv
    hdiskASMd001     00c1892c11ce6578                        None            locked
```

AIX Command	AIX 5.3	AIX 6.1	AIX 7.1	Description
lspv	N/A	TL07	TL01	The new AIX lspv command option "-u" provides additional identification and state information.
lkdev	N/A	TL07	TL01	This new command can lock a device so that any attempt to modify the device characteristics will fail.
rendev	N/A	TL06	TL00	This new command is used to rename the device and to provide consistency across RAC nodes.

TABLE 4-2. *Existing AIX Commands That Have Been Updated Used to Better Identify ASM Devices*

ASM and Multipathing

An I/O path generally consists of an initiator port, fabric port, target port, and LUN. Each permutation of this I/O path is considered an independent path. For example, in a high-availability scenario where each node has two host bus adapter (HBA) ports connected to two separate switch ports to two target ports on the back-end storage to a LUN, eight paths are visible to that LUN from the OS perspective (two HBA ports times two switch ports times two target ports times one LUN equals eight paths).

Path managers discover multiple paths to a device by issuing a SCSI inquiry command (SCSI_INQUIRY) to each operating system device. For example, on Linux the scsi_id call queries a SCSI device via the SCSI_INQUIRY command and leverages the vital product data (VPD) page 0x80 or 0x83. A disk or LUN responds to the SCSI_INQUIRY command with information about itself, including vendor and product identifiers and a unique serial number. The output from this query is used to generate a value that is unique across all SCSI devices that properly support pages 0x80 or 0x83.

Typically devices that respond to the SCSI_INQUIRY with the same serial number are considered to be accessible from multiple paths.

Path manager software also provides multipath software drivers. Most multipathing drivers support multipath services for fibre channel–attached SCSI-3 devices. These drivers receive naming and transport services from one or more physical HBA devices. To support multipathing, a physical HBA driver must comply with the multipathing services provided by this driver. Multipathing tools provide the following benefits:

- They provide a single block device interface for a multipathed LUN.

- They detect any component failures in the I/O path, including the fabric port, channel adapter, or HBA.

- When a loss of path occurs, such tools ensure that I/Os are rerouted to the available paths, with no process disruption.

- They reconfigure the multipaths automatically when events occur.

- They ensure that failed paths get revalidated as soon as possible and provide auto-failback capabilities.

- They configure the multipaths to maximize performance using various load-balancing methods, such as round robin, least I/Os queued, and least service time.

When a given disk has several paths defined, each one will be presented as a unique pathname at the OS level, although they all reference the same physical

LUN; for example, the LUNs /dev/rdsk/c3t19d1s4 and /dev/rdsk/c7t22d1s4 could be pointing to the same disk device. The multipath abstraction provides I/O load balancing across the HBAs as well as nondisruptive failovers on I/O path failures.

ASM, however, can tolerate the discovery of only one unique device path per disk. For example, if the ASM_DISKSTRING is /dev/rdsk/*, then several paths to the same device will be discovered and ASM will produce an error message stating this. A multipath driver, which generally sits above this SCSI-block layer, usually produces a pseudo device that virtualizes the subpaths. For example, in the case of EMC's PowerPath, you can use the ASM_DISKSTRING setting of /dev/rdsk/ emcpower*. When I/O is issued to this disk device, the multipath driver intercepts it and provides the necessary load balancing to the underlying subpaths.

Examples of multipathing software include Linux Device Mapper, EMC PowerPath, Veritas Dynamic Multipathing (DMP), Oracle Sun Traffic Manager, Hitachi Dynamic Link Manager (HDLM), Windows MPIO, and IBM Subsystem Device Driver Path Control Module (SDDPCM).

Additionally, some HBA vendors, such as QLogic, also provide multipathing solutions.

NOTE
Users are advised to verify the vendor certification of ASM/ASMLIB with their multipathing drivers, because Oracle does not certify or qualify these multipathing tools. Although ASM does not provide multipathing capabilities, it does leverage multipathing tools as long as the path or device that they produce brings back a successful return code from an fstat system call. Metalink Note 294869.1 provides more details on ASM and multipathing.

Linux Device Mapper
Device mapper provides a kernel framework of allowing multiple device drivers to be stacked on top of each other. This section will describe the details of device mapper as it relates to ASM and ASMLIB or Udev, as these components all are heavily used together. This section will provide a high-level overview of Linux Device Mapper and Udev, in order to support ASM more effectively.

Linux device mapper's subsystem is the core component of the Linux multipath chain. The component provides the following high-level functionality:

■ A single logical device node for multiple paths to a single storage device.

■ I/O gets rerouted to the available paths when a path loss occurs and there is no disruption at the upper (user) layers because of this.

Device mapper is configured by using the library libdevmapper. This library is used by multiple modules such as dmsetup, LVM2, multipath tools, and kpartx, as shown in Figure 4-1.

Device mapper provides the kernel resident mechanisms that support the creation of different combinations of stacked target drivers for different block devices. At the highest level of the stack is a single mapped device. This mapped device is configured in the device mapper by passing map information about the target devices to the device mapper via the libdevmapper library interfaces. This role is performed by the multipath configuration tool (discussed later). Each mapped segment consists of a start sector and length and a target driver–specific number of target driver parameters.

Here's an example of a mapping table for a multipath device with two underneath block devices:

```
0 1172123568 multipath 0 0 2 1 round-robin 0 1 1 65:208 1000
round-robin 0 1 1 65:16 1000
```

The preceding indicates that the starting sector is 0, the length is 1172123558, and the driver is multipath followed by multipathing parameters. Two devices are associated with this map, 65:208 and 65:16 (major:minor). The parameter 1000 indicates that after 1,000 I/Os the second path will be used in a round-robin fashion.

Here's an example of a mapping table for a logical volume (LVM2) device with one underneath block device:

```
0 209715200 linear 9:1 188744064
```

This indicates that the starting sector is 0 and the length is 209715200 with a linear driver for device 9:1 (major:minor).

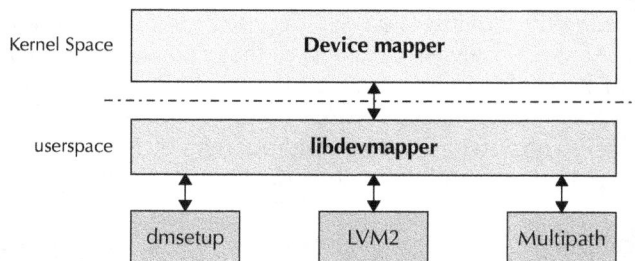

FIGURE 4-1.   *Device mapper topology*

Udev

In the previous versions of Linux, all the devices were statically created in the dev-FS (/dev) file system at installation time. This created a huge list of entries in /dev, most of which were useless because most of the devices were not actually connected to the system. The other problem with this approach was that the same device could be named differently when connected to the system because the kernel assigned the devices on a first-come basis, so the first SCSI device discovered was named /dev/sda, the second one /dev/sdb, and so on. Udev resolves this problem by managing the device nodes on demand. Also, name-to-device mappings are not based on the order in which the devices are detected but on a system of predefined rules. Udev relies on the kernel hot-plug mechanism to create device files in user space.

The discovery of the current configuration is done by probing block device nodes created in Sysfs. This file system presents to the user space kernel objects such as block devices, busses, drivers, and so on in a hierarchical manner. A device node is created by Udev in reaction to a hot-plug event generated when a block device's request queue is registered with the kernel's block subsystem.

As shown in Figure 4-2, in the context of multipath implementation, Udev performs the following tasks:

- The addition and suppression of paths are listened to by the multipath user space daemon. This ensures that the multipath device maps are always up to date with the physical topology.

- The user space callbacks after path addition or suppression also call the user space tool kpartx to create maps for device partitions.

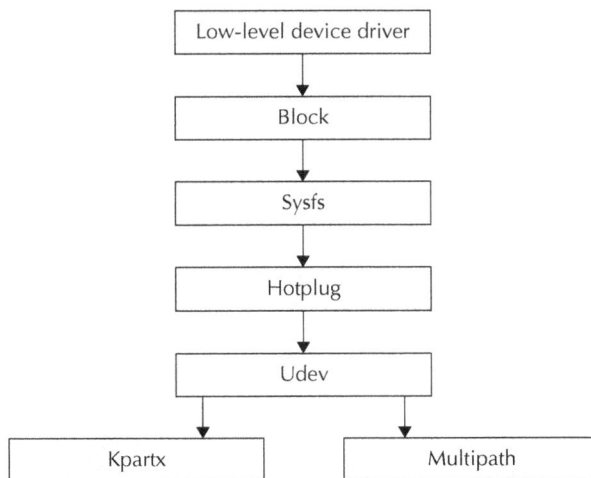

FIGURE 4-2. *Udev topology*

Many users use symbolic links to point to ASM disks instead of using Udev. A common question we get is, is there a difference (advantages/disadvantages) between using symbolic links versus mknod devices with respect to aliasing a device?

Neither one provides persistent naming. In other words, if you use a mknod device, you have a new alias to the major/minor number. However, if the device changes its major/minor number for any reason, your mknod device will be stale, just like the symlink will be stale. The only way to obtain persistence is by using ASMLIB, ASM, or Udev. For example, in Udev, you can create either an mknod/block/char device or a SYMLINK using that keyword. Here's an example:

```
KERNEL=="sd*", BUS=="scsi", PROGRAM=="/sbin/scsi_id -g -u -s %p",
RESULT=="360a98000686f6375575a542d6a677744", NAME="asmdisk1",
OWNER="root",
GROUP="root", MODE="0640"
## SYMLINK Will ADD link called 'name_u_give'pointing to 'sdg':
KERNEL=="sd*", BUS=="scsi", PROGRAM=="/sbin/scsi_id -g -u -s %p",
RESULT=="360a98000686f6375575a542d6a677744", SYMLINK+="asmdisk1",
OWNER="root", GROUP="root", MODE="0640"
```

The first example will modify a sd device to be called "asmdisk1". The second example will leave the sd device alone and create a new symlink called "asmdisk1" pointing to the sd device. Both methods keep pointing to the right device as given by the UUID; obviously you should use only one method or the other.

Multipath Configuration

Now that we've talked about the various tools and modules involved in making Linux multipathing work, this section discusses the configuration steps required to make it operational.

The main configuration file that drives the Linux multipathing is /etc/multipath.conf. The configuration file is composed of the following sections:

- **Defaults** The default values of attributes are used whenever no specific device setting is given.

- **Blacklist** Devices that should be excluded from the multipath discovery.

- **Blacklist_exceptions** Devices that should be included in the multipath discovery despite being listed in the blacklist section. This section is generally for when you use wildcards in the blacklist section to remove many disks and want to manually use a few of them.

- **Multipaths** This is the main section that defines the multipath topology. The values are indexed by the worldwide identifier (WWID) of the device.

- **Devices** Device-specific settings.

Following are some commonly used configuration parameters in the multipath .conf file (for a complete listing, refer to the man pages on your system):

- **Path_grouping_policy**   This parameter defines the path grouping policy. Here are the possible values:

    - **Failover**   There is one active path. This is equivalent to active/passive configuration.

    - **Multibus**   All the paths are in one priority group and are used in a load-balancing configuration. This is the default value.

    - **Group_by_serial/group_by_prio/group_by_node_name**   The paths are grouped based on serial number or priority, as defined by a usercallout program or based on target node names.

- **Prio_callout**   The default program and arguments to call out to obtain a path priority value.

- **path_checker**   The method used to determine the path's state.

- **user_friendly_names**   The names assigned to the multipath devices will be in the form of mpath<*n*>, if not defined in the multipaths section.

- **no_path_retry**   Used to specify the number of retries until queuing is disabled, or issue fail I/O for immediate failure (in this case no queuing). Default is 0.

Here's an example of a configuration file that is used for RAC cluster configurations:

```
blacklist {
   devnode "^asm/*"
   devnode "ofsctl"
   wwid SATA_SEAGATE_ST950009SP19KZT_
   wwid SATA_SEAGATE_ST950009SP122XT_
}

defaults {
user_friendly_names  yes
path_grouping_policy failover
failback manual
no_path_retry fail
}

multipaths {
    multipath {
       wwid 35000c500399d69e7
       alias HDD__966617575
```

```
      mode 660
      uid 1000
      gid 1006
  }
   multipath {
      wwid 35000c50033c3cb17
      alias HDD__868469527
      mode 660
      uid 1000
      gid 1006
   }
}
```

The first section blacklists the asm and ofsctl (ACFS) devices. It also specifically blacklists the two disks with specific WWIDs, which in the context of the sample setup were the OS disks. The defaults section provides generic parameters that are applicable in this setup. Finally, the multipaths section lists two WWIDs and corresponding aliases to be assigned to the devices. The mode, uid, and gid provide the created device permissions, user ID, and group ID, respectively, after creation.

Setting Up the Configuration

To create the multipath device mappings after configuring the multipath.conf file, use the /sbin/multipath command:

```
#/sbin/multipath -v2

HDD__966617575 (35000c500399cd73f) dm-24 SEAGATE,ST360057SSUN600
[size=559G] [features=0] [hwhandler=0] [rw]
\_ round-robin 0 [prio=0] [active]
 \_ 7:0:21:0 sdau 66:224 [active] [undef]
\_ round-robin 0 [prio=0] [enabled]
 \_ 6:0:8:0  sdk  8:160  [active] [undef]

HDD__868469527 (35000c50033c3e66b) dm-13 SEAGATE,ST360057SSUN600
[size=559G] [features=0] [hwhandler=0] [rw]
\_ round-robin 0 [prio=0] [active]
 \_ 7:0:9:0  sdaj 66:48  [active] [undef]
\_ round-robin 0 [prio=0] [enabled]
 \_ 6:0:22:0 sdx  65:112 [active] [undef]

# ls -l /dev/mapper
brw-rw---- 1 grid asmadmin 253,  8 Oct 29 03:19 HDD__868469527
brw-rw---- 1 grid asmadmin 253,  8 Oct 29 03:19 HDD__966617575

#kpartx -a /dev/mapper/ HDD__868469527
#kpartx -a /dev/mapper/ HDD__966617575
```

```
# ls -l /dev/mapper
brw-rw---- 1 grid asmadmin 253,  8 Oct 29 03:19 HDD__868469527
brw-rw---- 1 grid asmadmin 253,  8 Oct 29 03:19 HDD__868469527p1
brw-rw---- 1 grid asmadmin 253,  8 Oct 29 03:19 HDD__868469527p2
brw-rw---- 1 grid asmadmin 253,  8 Oct 29 03:19 HDD__966617575
brw-rw---- 1 grid asmadmin 253,  8 Oct 29 03:19 HDD__966617575p1
brw-rw---- 1 grid asmadmin 253,  8 Oct 29 03:19 HDD__966617575p2
```

In this example, two multipath devices are created in failover configuration. The first priority group is the active paths: The device /dev/sdau is the active path for HDD__966617575 and /dev/sdk is the passive (standby) path. The path is visible in the /dev/mapper folder. Furthermore, the partition mappings for the devices can be created on the device using the kpartx tool.

After these settings have completed, the devices can be used by ASM or other applications on the server.

Disk Group

The primary component of ASM is the disk group, which is the highest-level data structure in ASM (see Figure 4-3). A disk group is essentially a container that consists of a logical grouping of disks that are managed together as a unit. The disk group is comparable to a logical volume manager's (LVM's) volume group.

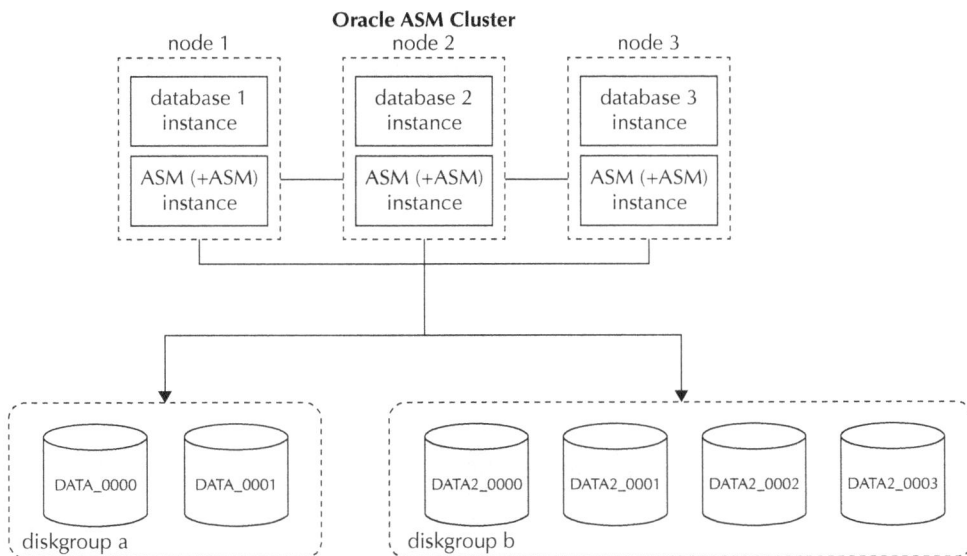

FIGURE 4-3. *ASM layer*

A disk group can contain files from many different Oracle databases. Allowing multiple databases to share a disk group provides greater potential for improved disk utilization and greater overall throughput. The Oracle database may also store its files in multiple disk groups managed by the same ASM instance. Note that a database file can only be part of one disk group.

ASM disk groups differ from typical LVM volume groups in that ASM disk groups have inherent automatic file-level striping and mirroring capabilities. A database file created within an ASM disk group is distributed equally across all disks in the disk group, which provides an even input/output (I/O) load.

Disk Group Management

ASM has three disk groups types: external redundancy, normal redundancy, and high redundancy. The disk group type, which is defined at disk group creation time, determines the default level of mirroring performed by ASM. An external redundancy disk group indicates stripping will be done by ASM and the mirroring will be handled and managed by the storage array. For example, a user may create an external redundancy disk group where the storage array (SAN) is an EMC VMAX or Hitachi USP series. Because the core competency of these high-end arrays is mirroring, external redundancy is well suited for them. A common question is, does ASM stripping conflict with the stripping performed by the SAN? The answer is no. ASM stripping is complementary to the SAN stripping.

With ASM redundancy, ASM performs and manages the mirroring. ASM redundancy is the core deployment strategy used in Oracle's Engineered Solutions, such as Oracle Exadata, Oracle SuperCluster, and Oracle Database Appliance. ASM redundancy is also used with low-cost commodity storage or when deploying stretch clusters. For details on ASM redundancy, see the "ASM Redundancy and Failure Groups" section later in this chapter. The next section focuses on creating disk groups in an external redundancy environment.

Creating Disk Groups

The creation of a disk group involves validation of the disks to be added. The disks must have the following attributes:

- They cannot already be in use by another disk group.

- They must not have a preexisting valid ASM header. The FORCE option must be used to override this.

- They cannot have an Oracle file header (for example, from any file created by the RDBMS). The FORCE option must be used to override this. Trying to create an ASM disk using a raw device data file results in the following error:

```
SQL> CREATE DISKGROUP DATA DISK '/dev/sdd3';
create diskgroup data disk '/dev/sdd3'
```

```
ERROR at line 1:
ORA-15032: not all alterations performed
ORA-15201: disk /dev/sda3 contains a valid RDBMS file
```

The disk header validation prevents ASM from destroying any data device already in use. Only disks with a header status of CANDIDATE, FORMER, or PROVISIONED are allowed to be included in disk group creation. To add disks to a disk group with a header status of MEMBER or FOREIGN, use the FORCE option in the disk group creation. To prevent gratuitous use of the FORCE option, ASM allows it only when using the NOFORCE option would fail. An attempt to use FORCE when it is not required results in an ORA-15034 error (disk '%s' does not require the FORCE option). Use the FORCE option with extreme caution, because it overwrites the data on the disk that was previously used as an ASM disk or database file.

A disk without a recognizable header is considered a CANDIDATE. There is no persistent header status called "candidate."

Once ASM has discovered the disks, they can be used to create a disk group. To reduce the complexity of managing ASM and its disk groups, Oracle recommends that generally no more than two disk groups be maintained and managed per RAC cluster or single ASM instance. The following are typical disk groups that are created by customers:

- **DATA disk group** This is where active database files such as data files, control files, online redo logs, and change-tracking files used in incremental backups are stored.

- **Fast Recovery Area (FRA) disk group** This is where recovery-related files are created, such as multiplexed copies of the current control file and online redo logs, archived redo logs, backup sets, and flashback log files.

Having one DATA disk group means there's only one place to store all your database files, and it obviates the need to juggle around data files or having to decide where to place a new tablespace, like in traditional file system configurations. Having one disk group for all your files also means better storage utilization, thus making the IT director and storage teams very happy. If more storage capacity or I/O capacity is needed, just add an ASM disk and ensure that this storage pool container houses enough spindles to accommodate the I/O rate of all the database objects.

To provide higher availability for the database, when a Fast Recovery Area is chosen at database creation time, an active copy of the control file and one member set of the redo log group are stored in the Fast Recovery Area. Note that additional copies of the control file or extra log files can be created and placed in either disk group, as desired.

RAC users can optionally create a CRSDATA disk group to store Oracle Clusterware files (for example, voting disks and the Oracle Cluster registry) or the ASM spfile.

When deploying the CRSDATA disk group for this purpose, you should minimally use ASM normal redundancy with three failure groups. This is generally done to provide added redundancy for the Clusterware files. See Chapter 2 for more details.

Note that creating additional disk groups for storing database data does not necessarily improve performance. However, additional disk groups may be added to support tiered storage classes in Information Lifecycle Management (ILM) or Hierarchical Storage Management (HSM) deployments. For example, a separate disk group can be created for archived or retired data (or partitions), and these partitioned tablespaces can be migrated or initially placed on a disk group based on Tier2 storage (RAID5), whereas Tier1 storage (RAID10) can be used for the DATA disk group.

ASM provides out-of-the-box enablement of redundancy and optimal performance. However, the following items should be considered to increase performance and/or availability:

- Implement multiple access paths to the storage array using two or more HBAs or initiators.

- Deploy multipathing software over these multiple HBAs to provide I/O load-balancing and failover capabilities.

- Use disk groups with similarly sized and performing disks. A disk group containing a large number of disks provides a wide distribution of data extents, thus allowing greater concurrency for I/O and reducing the occurrences of hotspots. Because a large disk group can easily sustain various I/O characteristics and workloads, a single DATA disk group can be used to house database files, log files, and control files.

- Use disk groups with four or more disks, making sure these disks span several back-end disk adapters. As stated earlier, Oracle generally recommends no more than two to three disk groups. For example, a common deployment can be four or more disks in a DATA disk group spanning all back-end disk adapters/directors, and eight to ten disks for the FRA disk group. The size of the FRA will depend on what is stored and how much (that is, full database backups, incremental backups, flashback database logs, and archive logs). Note that an active copy of the control file and one member of each of the redo log group are stored in the FRA.

A disk group can be created using SQL, Enterprise Manager (EM), ASMCMD commands, or ASMCA. In the following example, a DATA disk group is created using four disks that reside in a storage array, with the redundancy being handled externally by the storage array. The following query lists the available disks that will be used in the disk group:

```
SQL> SELECT NAME, PATH, HEADER_STATUS, STATE FROM V$ASM_DISK;

NAME          PATH                     HEADER_STATU     STATE
------------  ----------------------   ------------     ------
              /dev/rdsk/c3t19d5s4      CANDIDATE        NORMAL
              /dev/rdsk/c3t19d16s4     CANDIDATE        NORMAL
              /dev/rdsk/c3t19d17s4     CANDIDATE        NORMAL
              /dev/rdsk/c3t19d18s4     CANDIDATE        NORMAL
              /dev/rdsk/c3t19d19s4     FORMER           NORMAL
```

Notice that one of the disks, c3t19d19s4, was dropped from a disk group and thus shows a status of FORMER.

```
SQL> CREATE DISKGROUP DATA EXTERNAL REDUNDANCY DISK
'/dev/rdsk/c3t19d5s4',
'/dev/rdsk/c3t19d16s4',
'/dev/rdsk/c3t19d17s4',
'/dev/rdsk/c3t19d18s4';
```

The output from V$ASM_DISGROUP shows the newly created disk group:

```
SQL> SELECT NAME, STATE, TYPE, TOTAL_MB, FREE_MB FROM V$ASM_DISKGROUP;
NAME                              STATE       TYPE    TOTAL_MB    FREE_MB
-------------------------------   ---------   ------  ----------  ----------
DATA                              MOUNTED     EXTERN     34512       34101
```

The output from V$ASM_DISK shows the status disks once the disk group is created:

```
SQL> SELECT NAME, PATH, HEADER_STATUS, STATE FROM V$ASM_DISK;

NAME          PATH                     HEADER_STATU     STATE
------------  ----------------------   ------------     ------
DATA_0000     /dev/rdsk/c3t19d5s4      MEMBER           NORMAL
DATA_0001     /dev/rdsk/c3t19d16s4     MEMBER           NORMAL
DATA_0002     /dev/rdsk/c3t19d17s4     MEMBER           NORMAL
DATA_0003     /dev/rdsk/c3t19d18s4     MEMBER           NORMAL
              /dev/rdsk/c3t19d19s4     FORMER           NORMAL
```

After the disk group is successfully created, metadata information, which includes creation date, disk group name, and redundancy type, is stored in the System Global Area (SGA) and on each disk (in the disk header) within the disk group. Although it possible to mount disk groups only on specific nodes of the cluster, this is generally not recommended because it may potentially obstruct CRS resource startup modeling.

Once these disks are under ASM management, all subsequent mounts of the disk group reread and validate the ASM disk headers. The following output shows how the V$ASM_DISK view reflects the disk state change after the disk is incorporated into the disk group:

```
SQL> SELECT NAME, PATH, MODE_STATUS, STATE, DISK_NUMBER FROM V$ASM_DISK;

NAME            PATH                   MODE_ST STATE     DISK_NUMBER
------------    --------------------   ------- --------  -----------
DATA_0000       /dev/rdsk/c3t19d5s4    ONLINE  NORMAL              0
DATA_0001       /dev/rdsk/c3t19d16s4   ONLINE  NORMAL              1
DATA_0002       /dev/rdsk/c3t19d17s4   ONLINE  NORMAL              2
DATA_0003       /dev/rdsk/c3t19d18s4   ONLINE  NORMAL              3
```

The output that follows shows entries from the ASM alert log reflecting the creation of the disk group and the assignment of the disk names:

```
SQL> CREATE DISKGROUP DATA EXTERNAL REDUNDANCY DISK
'/dev/rdsk/c3t19d5s4',  '/dev/rdsk/c3t19d16s4',  '/dev/rdsk/c3t19d17s4',
'/dev/rdsk/c3t19d18s4'
NOTE: Assigning number (1,0) to disk (/dev/rdsk/c3t19d5s4)
NOTE: Assigning number (1,1) to disk (/dev/rdsk/c3t19d16s4)
NOTE: Assigning number (1,2) to disk (/dev/rdsk/c3t19d17s4)
NOTE: Assigning number (1,3) to disk (/dev/rdsk/c3t19d18s4)
NOTE: initializing header on grp 1 disk DATA_0000
NOTE: initializing header on grp 1 disk DATA_0001
NOTE: initializing header on grp 1 disk DATA_0002
NOTE: initializing header on grp 1 disk DATA_0003
NOTE: initiating PST update: grp = 1
Wed May 15 03:26:00 2012
NOTE: group DATA: initial PST location: disk 0000 (PST copy 0)
NOTE: group DATA: initial PST location: disk 0001 (PST copy 1)
NOTE: group DATA: initial PST location: disk 0001 (PST copy 3)
NOTE: group DATA: initial PST location: disk 0001 (PST copy 4)
NOTE: PST update grp = 1 completed successfully
NOTE: cache registered group DATA number=1 incarn=0xa311b052
NOTE: cache opening disk 0 of grp 1: DATA_0000 path: /dev/rdsk/c3t19d5s4
NOTE: cache opening disk 1 of grp 1: DATA_0001 path: /dev/rdsk/c3t19d16s4
NOTE: cache opening disk 2 of grp 1: DATA_0002 path: /dev/rdsk/c3t19d17s4
NOTE: cache opening disk 3 of grp 1: DATA_0003 path: /dev/rdsk/c3t19d18s4
```

When you're mounting disk groups, either at ASM startup or for subsequent mounts, it is advisable to mount all required disk groups at once. This minimizes the overhead of multiple ASM disk discovery scans. With Grid Infrastructure, agents will automatically mount any disk group needed by a database.

ASM Disk Names

ASM disk names are assigned by default based on the disk group name and disk number, but names can be defined by the user either during ASM disk group creation or when disks are added. The following example illustrates how to create a disk group where disk names are defined by the user:

```
SQL> CREATE DISKGROUP DATA EXTERNAL REDUNDANCY DISK
'/dev/rdsk/c3t19d5s4' name VMAX_disk1,
'/dev/rdsk/c3t19d16s4' name VMAX_disk2,
'/dev/rdsk/c3t19d17s4' name VMAX_disk3,
'/dev/rdsk/c3t19d18s4' name VMAX_disk4;
```

If disk names are not provided, ASM dynamically assigns a disk name with a sequence number to each disk added to the disk group:

```
SQL> CREATE DISKGROUP DATA EXTERNAL REDUNDANCY DISK
'/dev/rdsk/c3t19d5s4',
'/dev/rdsk/c3t19d16s4',
'/dev/rdsk/c3t19d17s4',
'/dev/rdsk/c3t19d18s4';
```

The ASM disk name is used when performing disk management activities, such as DROP, ONLINE, OFFLINE, and RESIZE DISK.

The ASM disk name is different from the small computer system interface (SCSI) address. ASM disk names are stored persistently in the ASM header, and they persist even if the SCSI address name changes. Persistent names also allow for consistent naming across Real Application Clusters (RAC) nodes. SCSI address name changes occur due to array reconfigurations and/or after OS reboots. There is no persistent binding of disk numbers to pathnames used by ASM to access the storage.

Disk Group Numbers

The lowest nonzero available disk group number is assigned on the first mount of a disk group in a cluster. However, in an ASM cluster, even if the disk groups are mounted in a different order between cluster nodes, the disk group numbers will still be consistent across the cluster (for a given disk group) but the disk group name never changes. For example, if node 1 has dgA as group number 1 and dgB as group number 2, then if node 2 mounts only dgB, it will be group number 2, even though 1 is not in use in node 2.

NOTE
Disk group numbers are never recorded persistently, so there is no disk group number in a disk header. Only the disk group name is recorded in the disk header.

Disk Numbers

Although disk group numbers are never recorded persistently, disk numbers are recorded on the disk headers. When an ASM instance starts up, it discovers all the devices matching the pattern specified in the initialization parameter ASM_DISKSTRING and for which it has read/write access. If it sees an ASM disk header, it knows the ASM disk number.

Also, disks that are discovered but are not part of any mounted disk group are reported in disk group 0. A disk that is not part of any mounted disk group will be in disk group 0 until it is added to a disk group or mounted. When the disk is added to a disk group, it will be associated with the correct disk group.

ASM Redundancy and Failure Groups

For systems that do not use external redundancy, ASM provides its own redundancy mechanism. This redundancy, as stated earlier, is used extensively in Exadata and Oracle Database Appliance systems. These Engineered Solutions are covered in Chapter 12.

A disk group is divided into failure groups, and each disk is in exactly one failure group. A failure group (FG) is a collection of disks that can become unavailable due to the failure of one of its associated components. Possible failing components could be any of the following:

- Storage array controllers

- Host bus adapters (HBAs)

- Fibre Channel (FC) switches

- Disks

- Entire arrays, such as NFS filers

Thus, disks in two separate failure groups (for a given disk group) must not share a common failure component. If you define failure groups for your disk group, ASM can tolerate the simultaneous failure of multiple disks in at least one failure group or two FGs in a high-redundancy disk group.

ASM uses a unique mirroring algorithm. ASM does not mirror disks; rather, it mirrors extents. When ASM allocates a primary extent of a file to one disk in a failure group, it allocates a mirror copy of that extent to another disk in another failure group. Thus, ASM ensures that a primary extent and its mirror copy never reside in the same failure group.

Each file can have a different level of mirroring (redundancy) in the same disk group. For example, in a normal redundancy disk group, with at least three failure groups, we can have one file with (default) normal redundancy, another file with no redundancy, and yet another file with high redundancy (triple mirroring).

Unlike other volume managers, ASM has no concept of a primary disk or a mirrored disk. As a result, to provide continued protection in the event of failure, your disk group requires only spare capacity; a hot spare disk is unnecessary. Redundancy for disk groups can be either *normal* (the default), where files are two-way mirrored (requiring at least two failure groups), or *high*, which provides a higher degree of protection using three-way mirroring (requiring at least three failure groups). After you create a disk group, you cannot change its redundancy level. If you want a different redundancy, you must create another disk group with the desired redundancy and then move the data files (using Recovery Manager [RMAN] restore, the ASMCMD copy command, or DBMS_FILE_TRANSFER) from the original disk group to the newly created disk group.

NOTE
Disk group metadata is always triple mirrored with normal or high redundancy.

Additionally, after you assign a disk to a failure group, you cannot reassign it to another failure group. If you want to move it to another failure group, you must first drop it from the current failure group and then add it to the desired failure group. However, because the hardware configuration usually dictates the choice of a failure group, users generally do not need to reassign a disk to another failure group unless it is physically moved.

Creating ASM Redundancy Disk Groups

The following simple example shows how to create a normal redundancy disk group using two failure groups over a NetApp filer:

```
SQL> CREATE DISKGROUP DATA_NRML NORMAL REDUNDANCY
FAILGROUP F1GRP1 DISK '/dev/rdsk/c3t19d3s4','/dev/rdsk/c3t19d4s4',
'/dev/rdsk/c3t19d5s4', '/dev/rdsk/c3t19d6s4','/dev/rdsk/c4t20d3s4',
'/dev/rdsk/c4t20d4s4', '/dev/rdsk/c4t20d5s4', '/dev/rdsk/c4t20d6s4'
FAILGROUP FLGRP2 DISK  '/dev/rdsk/c5t21d3s4','/dev/rdsk/c5t21d4s4',
'/dev/rdsk/c5t21d5s4', '/dev/rdsk/c5t21d6s4','/dev/rdsk/c6t22d3s4',
'/dev/rdsk/c6t22d4s4', '/dev/rdsk/c6t22d5s4', '/dev/rdsk/c6t22d6s4';
```

The same create diskgroup command can be executed using wildcard syntax:

```
SQL> CREATE DISKGROUP DATA_NRML NORMAL REDUNDANCY
FAILGROUP FL1GRP1 DISK  '/dev/rdsk/c[34]*'
FAILGROUP FLGRP2 DISK '/dev/rdsk/c[56]*';
```

In this following example, ASM normal redundancy is being deployed over a low-cost commodity storage array. This storage array has four internal trays, with each tray having four disks. Because the failing component to isolate is the storage tray, the failure group boundary is set for the storage tray—that is, each storage tray is associated with a failure group:

```
SQL> CREATE DISKGROUP DATA_NRML NORMAL REDUNDANCY
FAILGROUP FLGRP1 DISK  '/dev/rdsk/c3t19d3s4','/dev/rdsk/c3t19d4s4',
'/dev/rdsk/c3t19d5s4', '/dev/rdsk/c3t19d6s4'
FAILGROUP FLGRP2 DISK '/dev/rdsk/c4t20d3s4','/dev/rdsk/c4t20d4s4',
'/dev/rdsk/c4t20d5s4', '/dev/rdsk/c4t20d6s4'
FAILGROUP FLGRP3 DISK '/dev/rdsk/c5t21d3s4','/dev/rdsk/c5t21d4s4',
'/dev/rdsk/c5t21d5s4', '/dev/rdsk/c5t21d6s4'
FAILGROUP FLGRP4 DISK  /dev/rdsk/c6t22d3s4','/dev/rdsk/c6t22d4s4',
'/dev/rdsk/c6t22d5s4', '/dev/rdsk/c6t22d6s4';
```

ASM and Intelligent Data Placement

Short stroking (along with RAID 0 striping) is a technique that storage administrators typically use to minimize the performance impact of head repositioning delays. This technique reduces seek times by limiting the actuator's range of motion and increases the media transfer rate. This effectively improves overall disk throughput. Short stroking is implemented by formatting a drive so that only the outer sectors of the disk platter (which have the highest track densities) are used to store heavily accessed data, thus providing the best overall throughput. However, short stroking a disk limits the drive's capacity by using a subset of the available tracks, resulting in reduced usable capacity.

Intelligent Data Placement (IDP), a feature introduced in Oracle Database version 11 Release 2, emulates the short stroking technique without sacrificing usable capacity or redundancy.

IDP automatically defines disk region boundaries on ASM disks for best performance. Using the disk region settings of a disk group, you can place frequently accessed data on the outermost (hot) tracks. In addition, files with similar access patterns are located physically close, thus reducing latency. IDP also enables the placement of primary and mirror extents into different hot or cold regions.

The IDP feature primarily works on JBOD (just a bunch of disks) storage or disk storage that has not been partitioned (for example, using RAID techniques) by the array. Although IDP can be used with external redundancy, it can only be effective if you know that certain files are frequently accessed while other files are rarely accessed and if the lower numbered blocks perform better than the higher numbered blocks. IDP on external redundancy may not be highly beneficial. Moreover, IDP over external redundancy is not a tested configuration in Oracle internal labs.

The default region of IDP is COLD so that all data is allocated on the lowest disk addresses, which are on the outer edge of physical disks. When the disk region settings are modified for an existing file, only new file extensions are affected. Existing file extents are not affected until a rebalance operation is initiated. It is recommended that you manually initiate an ASM rebalance when a significant number of IDP file policies (for existing files) are modified. Note that a rebalance may affect system throughput, so it should be a planned change management activity.

IDP settings can be specified for a file or by using disk group templates. The disk region settings can be modified after the disk group has been created. IDP is most effective for the following workloads and access patterns:

- For databases with data files that are accessed at different rates. A database that accesses all data files in the same way is unlikely to benefit from IDP.

- For ASM disk groups that are sufficiently populated with usable data. As a best-practice recommendation, the disk group should be more than 25-percent full. With lesser populated disk groups, the IDP management overhead may minimize the IDP benefits.

- For disks that have better performance at the beginning of the media relative to the end. Because Intelligent Data Placement leverages the geometry of the disk, it is well suited to JBOD (just a bunch of disks). In contrast, a storage array with LUNs composed of concatenated volumes masks the geometry from ASM.

To implement IDP, the COMPATIBLE.ASM and COMPATIBLE.RDBMS disk group attributes must be set to 11.2 or higher. IDP can be implemented and managed using ASMCA or the following SQL commands:

- ALTER DISKGROUP ADD or MODIFY TEMPLATE

- ALTER DISKGROUP TEMPLATE SQL or MODIFY FILE

These commands include the disk region clause for setting hot/mirrorhot or cold/mirrorcold regions in a template:

```
ALTER DISKGROUP data ADD TEMPLATE userdata_hot
    ATTRIBUTE (
      HOT
      MIRRORHOT);


ALTER DISKGROUP data MODIFY FILE '+data/yoda/datafile/users.271.689156907'
    ATTRIBUTE (
      HOT
      MIRRORHOT);
```

IDP is also applicable for ADVM volumes. When creating ADVM volumes, you can specify the region location for primary and secondary extents:

```
volcreate  -G DATA -s 10G --primary hot  --secondary cold  ACFS_OH
```

Designing for ASM Redundancy Disk Groups

Note that with ASM redundancy, you are not restricted to having two failure groups for normal redundancy and three for high redundancy. In the preceding example, four failure groups are created to ensure that disk partners are not allocated from the same storage tray. Another such example can be found in Exadata. In a full-frame Exadata, there are 14 failure groups.

There may be cases where users want to protect against storage area network (SAN) array failures. This can be accomplished by putting each array in a separate failure group. For example, a configuration may include two NetApp filers and the deployment of ASM normal redundancy such that each filer—that is, all logical unit numbers (LUNs) presented through the filer—is part of an ASM failure group. In this scenario, ASM mirrors the extent between the two filers.

If the database administrator (DBA) does not specify a failure group in the CREATE DISKGROUP command, a failure group is automatically constructed for each disk. This method of placing every disk in its own failure group works well for most customers. In fact, in Oracle Database Appliance, all disks are assigned in this manner.

In case of Exadata, the storage grid disks are presented with extra information to the database server nodes, so these servers know exactly how to configure the failure groups without user intervention.

The choice of failure groups depends on the kinds of failures that need to be tolerated without the loss of data availability. For small numbers of disks (for example, fewer than 20), it is usually best to put every disk in its own failure group. Nonetheless, this is also beneficial for large numbers of disks when the main concern is spindle failure. To protect against the simultaneous loss of multiple disk drives due to a single component failure, an explicit failure group specification should be used. For example, a disk group may be constructed from several small modular disk arrays. If the system needs to continue operation when an entire modular array fails, each failure group should consist of all the disks in one module. If one module fails, all the data on that module is relocated to other modules to restore redundancy. Disks should be placed in the same failure group if they depend on a common piece of hardware whose unavailability or failure needs to be tolerated.

It is much better to have several failure groups as long as the data is still protected against the necessary component failures. Having additional failure groups provides better odds of tolerating multiple failures. Failure groups of uneven capacity can lead to allocation problems that prevent full utilization of all available storage. Moreover, having failure groups of different sizes can waste disk space. There may be enough room to allocate primary extents, but no space available for secondary extents. For example, in a disk group with six disks and three failure groups, if two disks are in their own individual failure groups and the other four are in one common failure group, the allocation will be very unequal. All the secondary extents from the big failure group can be placed on only two of the six disks. The disks in the individual failure groups fill up with secondary extents and block additional allocation even though plenty of space is left in the large failure group. This also places an uneven read and write load on the two disks that are full because they contain more secondary extents that are accessed only for writes or if the disk with the primary extent fails.

Allocating ASM Extent Sets

With ASM redundancy, the first file extent allocated is chosen as the primary extent, and the mirrored extent is called the secondary extent. In the case of high redundancy, there will be two secondary extents. This logical grouping of primary and secondary extents is called an *extent set*. Each disk in a disk group contains nearly the same number of primary and secondary extents. This provides an even distribution of read I/O activity across all the disks.

   All the extents in an extent set always contain the exact same data because they are mirrored versions of each other. When a block is read from disk, it is always read from the primary extent, unless the primary extent cannot be read. The preferred read feature allows the database to read the secondary extent first instead of reading the primary extent. This is especially important for RAC Extended Cluster implementations. See the section "ASM and Extended Clusters," later in this chapter, for more details on this feature.

   When a block is to be written to a file, each extent in the extent set is written in parallel. This requires that all writes complete before acknowledging the write to the client. Otherwise, the unwritten side could be read before it is written. If one write I/O fails, that side of the mirror must be made unavailable for reads before the write can be acknowledged.

Disk Partnering

In ASM redundancy disk groups, ASM protects against a double-disk failure (which can lead to data loss) by mirroring copies of data on disks that are partners of the disk containing the primary data extent. A *disk partnership* is a symmetric relationship between two disks in a high- or normal-redundancy disk group, and ASM automatically creates and maintains these relationships. ASM selects partners for a disk from failure groups other than the failure group to which the disk belongs. This ensures that a disk with a copy of the lost disk's data will be available following the failure of the shared resource associated with the failure group. ASM limits the number of disk partners to eight for any single disk.

Note that ASM did not choose partner disks from its own failure group (FLGRP1); rather, eight partners were chosen from the other three failure groups. Disk partnerships are only changed when there is a loss or addition of an ASM disk. These partnerships are not modified when disks are placed offline. Disk partnership is detailed in Chapter 9.

Recovering Failure Groups

Let's now return to the example in the previous CREATE DISKGROUP DATA_NRML command. In the event of a disk failure in failure group FLGRP1, which will induce a rebalance, the contents (data extents) of the failed disk are reconstructed using the redundant copies of the extents from partner disks. These partner disks are from failure group FLGRP2, FLGRP3, or both. If the database instance needs to access an extent whose primary extent was on the failed disk, the database will read the mirror copy from the appropriate disk. After the rebalance is complete and the disk contents are fully reconstructed, the database instance returns to reading primary copies only.

ASM and Extended Clusters

An extended cluster—also called a *stretch cluster, geocluster, campus cluster,* or *metro-cluster*—is essentially a RAC environment deployed across two data center locations. Many customers implement extended RAC to marry disaster recovery with the benefits of RAC, all in an effort to provide higher availability. Within Oracle, the term *extended clusters* is used to refer to all of the stretch cluster implementations.

The distance for extended RAC can be anywhere between several meters to several hundred kilometers. Because Cluster Ready Services (CRS)–RAC cluster group membership is based on the ability to communicate effectively across the interconnect, extended cluster deployment requires a low-latency network infrastructure. For close proximity, users typically use Fibre Channel, whereas for large distances Dark Fiber is used.

For normal-redundancy disk groups in extended RAC, there should be only one failure group on each site of the extended cluster. High-redundancy disk groups should not be used in extended cluster configurations unless there are three sites. In this scenario, there should one failure group at each site. Note that you must name the failure groups explicitly based on the site name.

NOTE
If a disk group contains an asymmetrical configuration, such that there are more failure groups on one site than another, then an extent could get mirrored to the same site and not to the remote failure group. This could cause the loss of access to the entire disk group if the site containing more than one failure group fails.

In Oracle Clusterware 11*g* Release 2, the concept of a quorum failgroup was introduced. Regular failgroup is the default. A quorum failure group is a special type of failure group that is used to house a single CSS quorum file, along with ASM metadata. Therefore, this quorum failgroup only needs to be in 300MB in size. Because these failure groups do not contain user data, the quorum failure group is not considered when determining redundancy requirements. Additionally, the USABLE_FILE_MB in V$ASM_DISKGROUP does not consider any free space that is present in QUORUM disks. However, a quorum failure group counts when mounting a disk group. Chapter 1 contains details on creating disk groups with a quorum failgroup.

ASM Preferred Read

As stated earlier, ASM always reads the primary copy of a mirrored extent set. Thus, a read for a specific block may require a read of the primary extent at the remote site across the interconnect. Accessing a remote disk through a metropolitan area or wide area storage network is substantially slower than accessing a local disk. This can tax the interconnect as well as result in high I/O and network latency.

To assuage this, a feature called *preferred reads* enables ASM administrators to specify a failure group for local reads—that is, provide preferred reads. In a normal- or high-redundancy disk group, with an extent set that has a preferred disk, a read is always satisfied by the preferred disk if it is online. This feature is especially beneficial for extended cluster configurations.

The ASM_PREFERRED_READ_FAILURE_GROUPS initialization parameter is used to specify a list of failure group names that will provide local reads for each node in a cluster. The format of the ASM_PREFERRED_READ_FAILURE_GROUPS is as follows:

```
ASM_PREFERRED_READ_FAILURE_GROUPS = DISKGROUP_NAME.FAILUREGROUP_NAME,...
```

Each entry is composed of *DISKGROUP_NAME,* which is the name of the disk group, and *FAILUREGROUP_NAME,* which is the name of the failure group within that disk group, with a period separating these two variables. Multiple entries can be specified using commas as separators. This parameter can be dynamically changed.

The Preferred Read feature can also be useful in mixed storage configurations. For example, in read-mostly workloads, SSD storage can be created in one failgroup and standard disk drives can be included in a second failgroup. This mixed configuration is beneficial when the SSD storage is in limited supply (in the array) or for economic reasons. The ASM_PREFERRED_READ_FAILURE_GROUPS parameter can be set to the SSD failgroup. Note that writes will occur on both failgroups.

In an extended cluster, the failure groups that you specify with settings for the ASM_PREFERRED_READ_FAILURE_GROUPS parameter should contain only disks that are local to the instance. V$ASM_DISK indicates the preferred disks with a Y in the PREFERRED_READ column.

The following example shows how to deploy the preferred read feature and demonstrates some of its inherent benefits. This example illustrates I/O patterns when the ASM_PREFERRED_READ_FAILURE_GROUPS parameter is not set, and then demonstrates how changing the parameter affects I/O:

1. Create a disk group with two failure groups:

```
CREATE DISKGROUP MYDATA NORMAL REDUNDANCY
-- these disks are local access from node1/remote from node2
FAILGROUP FG1 DISK '/dev/sda1','/dev/sdb1', '/dev/sdc1'
-- these disks are local access from node2/remote from node 1
FAILGROUP FG2 DISK '/dev/sdf1', '/dev/sdg1','/dev/sdh1';
```

2. The I/Os are evenly distributed across all disks—that is, these are non-localized I/Os.

3. The following query displays the balanced IO, default for ASM configurations:

```
SQL> SELECT INST_ID, FAILGROUP, SUM(READS), SUM(WRITES) FROM
GV$ASM_DISK WHERE FAILGROUP IN ('FG1','FG2') GROUP BY INST_ID,
FAILGROUP;


INST_ID FAILGROUP                           SUM(READS) SUM(WRITES)
---------- ------------------------------ ---------- -----------
        1 FG1                                   3796        2040
        1 FG2                                   5538        2040
        2 FG1                                   4205        1874
        2 FG2                                   5480        1874
```

NOTE
V$ASM_DISK includes I/Os that are performed by the ASM instance for ASM metadata. The V$ASM_DISK_IOSTAT tracks I/O on a per-database basis. This view can be used to verify that the RDBMS instance does not perform any I/O to a nonpreferred disk.

4. Now set the appropriate ASM parameters for the preferred read. Note that you need not dismount or remount the disk group because this parameter is dynamic.

Enter the following for Node1 (site1):

```
+ASM1.asm_preferred_read_failure_groups=MYDATA.FG1
```

Enter this code for Node2 (site2):

```
+ASM2.asm_preferred_read_failure_groups='MYDATA.FG2'
```

5. Verify that the parameter took effect by querying GV$ASM_DISK. From Node1, observe the following:

```
SELECT INST_ID, FAILGROUP, NAME, PREFERRED_READ FROM G$ASM_DISK
ORDER BY INST_ID, FAILGROUP;
   INST_ID FAILGROUP      NAME          PREFERRED_READ
---------- ------------ ------------ --------------
         1 FG1            MYDATA_0000   Y
         1 FG1            MYDATA_0001   Y
         1 FG1            MYDATA_0004   Y
         1 FG2            MYDATA_0002   N
         1 FG2            MYDATA_0003   N
         1 FG2            MYDATA_0005   N
         2 FG1            MYDATA_0000   N
         2 FG1            MYDATA_0001   N
         2 FG1            MYDATA_0004   N
         2 FG2            MYDATA_0002   Y
         2 FG2            MYDATA_0003   Y
         2 FG2            MYDATA_0005   Y
```

Keep in mind that disks MYDATA_0000, MYDATA_0001, and MYDATA_0004 are part of the FG1 failure group, and disks MYDATA_0002, MYDATA_0003, and MYDATA_0005 are in failure group FG2.

6. Put a load on the system and check I/O calls via EM or using V$ASM_DISK_IOSTAT. Notice in the "Reads-Total" column that reads have a strong affinity to the disks in FG1. This is because FG1 is local to Node1 where +ASM1 is running. The remote disks in FG2 have very few reads.

7. Notice the small number of reads that instance 1 is making to FG2 and the small number of reads that instance 2 is making to FG1:

```
SQL> SELECT INST_ID, FAILGROUP, SUM(READS), SUM(WRITES) FROM
GV$ASM_DISK WHERE FAILGROUP ING ('FG1','FG2') GROUP BY INST_ID,
FAILGROUP;

   INST_ID FAILGROUP                         SUM(READS) SUM(WRITES)
---------- ------------------------------- ---------- -----------
         1 FG1                                    8513        3373
         1 FG2                                     118        3373
         2 FG1                                      72        1756
         2 FG2                                    5731        1756
```

Recovering from Transient and Permanent Disk Failures

This section reviews how ASM handles transient and permanent disk failures in normal- and high-redundancy disk groups.

Recovering from Disk Failures: Fast Disk Resync

The ASM Fast Disk Resync feature significantly reduces the time to recover from transient disk failures in failure groups. The feature accomplishes this speedy recovery by quickly resynchronizing the failed disk with its partnered disks.

With Fast Disk Resync, the repair time is proportional to the number of extents that have been written or modified since the failure. This feature can significantly reduce the time that it takes to repair a failed disk group from hours to minutes.

The Fast Disk Resync feature allows the user a grace period to repair the failed disk and return it online. This time allotment is dictated by the ASM disk group attribute DISK_REPAIR_TIME. This attribute dictates maximum time of the disk outage that ASM can tolerate before dropping the disk. If the disk is repaired before this time is exceeded, then ASM resynchronizes the repaired disk when the user places the disk online. The command ALTER DISKGROUP DISK ONLINE is used to place the repaired disk online and initiate disk resynchronization.

Taking disks offline does not change any partnerships. Repartnering occurs when the disks are dropped at the end of the expiration period.

Fast Disk Resync requires that the COMPATIBLE.ASM and COMPATIBLE.RDBMS attributes of the ASM disk group be set to at least 11.1.0.0.

In the following example, the current ASM 11*g*R2 disk group has a compatibility of 11.1.0.0 and is modified to 11.2.0.3. To validate the attribute change, the V$ASM_ATTRIBUTE view is queried:

```
SQL> SELECT NAME, COMPATIBILITY, DATABASE_COMPATIBILITY FROM
V$ASM_DISKGROUP_STAT;
NAME    COMPATIBILITY    DATABASE_COMPATIBILITY
------  ---------------------------------------------
DATA    11.1.0.0.0       11.1.0.0.0
SQL> ALTER DISKGROUP DATA SET ATTRIBUTE 'COMPATIBLE.ASM' = '11.2.0.3';
SQL> ALTER DISKGROUP DATA SET ATTRIBUTE 'COMPATIBLE.RDBMS' ='11.2.0.3';
SQL> SELECT NAME, VALUE FROM V$ASM_ATTRIBUTE;
NAME             VALUE
-------------    -------------------------------------
disk_repair_time 12960
compatible.asm   11.2.0.3.0
compatible.rdbms 11.2.0.3.0
```

After you correctly set the compatibility to Oracle Database version 11.2.0.3, you can set the DISK_REPAIR_TIME attribute accordingly. Notice that the default repair time is 12,960 seconds, or 3.6 hours. The best practice is to set DISK_REPAIR_ TIME to a value depending on the operational logistics of the site; in other words, it should be set to the mean time to detect and repair the disk.

If the value of DISK_REPAIR_TIME needs to be changed, you can enter the following command:

```
ALTER DISKGROUP DATA SET ATTRIBUTE 'DISK_REPAIR_TIME' = '4 H'
```

If the DISK_REPAIR_TIME parameter is not 0 and an ASM disk fails, that disk is taken offline but not dropped. During this outage, ASM tracks any modified extents using a bitmap that is stored in disk group metadata. (See Chapter 9 for more details on the algorithms used for resynchronization.)

ASM's GMON process will periodically inspect (every three seconds) all mounted disk groups for offline disks. If GMON finds any, it sends a message to a slave process to increment their timer values (by three seconds) and initiate a drop for the offline disks when the timer expires. This timer display is shown in the REPAIR_TIMER column of V$ASM_DISK.

The ALTER DISKGROUP DISK OFFLINE SQL command or the EM ASM Target page can also be used to take the ASM disks offline manually for preventative maintenance. The following describes this scenario using SQL*Plus:

```
SQL> ALTER DISKGROUP DATA OFFLINE DISK DATA_0000 DROP AFTER 20 m;

SQL> SELECT NAME, HEADER_STATUS, MOUNT_STATUS, MODE_STATUS, STATE,
REPAIR_TIMER FROM V$ASM_DISK WHERE GROUP_NUMBER=1;

NAME          HEADER_STATU  MOUNT_S   MODE_ST   STATE     REPAIR_TIMER
-----------   ------------  -------   -------   --------  ------------
DATA_0003     MEMBER        CACHED    ONLINE    NORMAL               0
DATA_0002     MEMBER        CACHED    ONLINE    NORMAL               0
DATA_0001     MEMBER        CACHED    ONLINE    NORMAL               0
DATA_0000     UNKNOWN       MISSING   OFFLINE   NORMAL             840
```

Notice that the offline disk's MOUNT_STATUS and MODE_STATUS are set to the MISSING and OFFLINE states, and also that the REPAIR_TIMER begins to decrement from the drop timer.

Disks Are Offline

After the maintenance is completed, you can use the DISKGROUP DATA ONLINE command to bring the disk(s) online:

```
SQL> ALTER DISKGROUP DATA ONLINE DISK DATA_0000;
```

or

```
SQL> ALTER DISKGROUP DATA ONLINE ALL;
```

This statement brings all the offline disks back online to bring the stale contents up to date and to enable new contents. See Chapter 9 for more details on how to implement resynchronization.

The following is an excerpt from the ASM alert log showing a disk being brought offline and online:

```
SQL> ALTER DISKGROUP DATA OFFLINE DISK DATA_0000
NOTE: DRTimer CodCreate: of disk group 2 disks  0
WARNING: initiating offline of disk 0.3915947593 (DATA_0000) with mask 0x7e
NOTE: initiating PST update: grp = 2, dsk = 0, mode = 0x15
NOTE: PST update grp = 2 completed successfully
NOTE: initiating PST update: grp = 2, dsk = 0, mode = 0x1
NOTE: PST update grp = 2 completed successfully
Tue May 15 08:15:37 2012
NOTE: cache closing disk 0 of grp 2: DATA_0000
Tue May 15 08:17:50 2012
GMON SlaveB: Deferred DG Ops completed.
Tue May 15 08:19:06 2012
......
```

After fixing the disk, you can bring it online using the following command:

```
SQL> ALTER DISKGROUP DATA ONLINE DISK DATA_0000;
SQL> SELECT NAME, HEADER_STATUS, MOUNT_STATUS, MODE_STATUS, STATE,
REPAIR_TIMER FROM V$ASM_DISK WHERE GROUP_NUMBER=1;


NAME          HEADER_STATU  MOUNT_S  MODE_ST  STATE     REPAIR_TIMER
------------- ------------- -------  -------  --------  ------------
DATA_0003     MEMBER        CACHED   ONLINE   NORMAL               0
DATA_0002     MEMBER        CACHED   ONLINE   NORMAL               0
DATA_0001     MEMBER        CACHED   ONLINE   NORMAL               0
DATA_0000     MEMBER        CACHED   ONLINE   NORMAL               0


SQL> ALTER DISKGROUP DATA ONLINE disk DATA_0000
Tue May 15 08:29:06 2012
NOTE: initiating online of disk group 2 disks 0
NOTE: initiating PST update: grp = 2, dsk = 0, mode = 0x19
NOTE: disk validation pending for group 2/0x62087046 (DATA)
NOTE: cache opening disk 0 of grp 2: DATA_0000 path:/u01/ASM/1/DISK7
SUCCESS: validated disks for 2/0x62087046 (DATA)
NOTE: initiating PST update: grp = 2, dsk = 0, mode = 0x1d
NOTE: PST update grp = 2 completed successfully
NOTE: initiating PST update: grp = 2, dsk = 0, mode = 0x5d
NOTE: PST update grp = 2 completed successfully
NOTE: initiating PST update: grp = 2, dsk = 0, mode = 0x7d
NOTE: PST update grp = 2 completed successfully
Tue May 15 08:29:17 2012
NOTE: initiating PST update: grp = 2, dsk = 0, mode = 0x7f
```

```
NOTE: PST update grp = 2 completed successfully
NOTE: completed online of disk group 2 disks 0
```

Once the disk is brought back online, the REPAIR_TIMER is reset to 0 and the MODE_STATUS is set to ONLINE.

At first glance, the Fast Disk Resync feature may seem to be a substitute for Dirty Region Logging (DRL), which several logical volume managers implement. However, Fast Disk Resync and DRL are distinctly different.

DRL is a mechanism to track blocks that have writes in flight. A mirrored write cannot be issued unless a bit in the DRL is set to indicate there may be a write in flight. Because DRL itself is on disk and also mirrored, it may require two DRL writes before issuing the normal mirrored write. This is mitigated by having each DRL bit cover a range of data blocks such that setting one bit will cover multiple mirrored block writes. There is also some overhead for I/O to clear DRL bits for blocks that are no longer being written. You can often clear these bits while setting another bit in DRL.

If a host dies while it has mirrored writes in flight, it is possible that one side of the mirror is written and the other is not. Most applications require that they get the same data every time if they read a block multiple times without writing it. If one side was written but not the other, then different reads may get different data. DRL mitigates this by constructing a set of blocks that must be copied from one side to the other to ensure that all blocks are the same on both sides of the mirror. Usually this set of blocks is much larger than those that were being written at the time of the crash, and it takes a while to create the copies.

During the copy, the storage is unavailable, which increases overall recovery times. Additionally, it is possible that the failure caused a partial write to one side, resulting in a corrupt logical block. The copying may write the bad data over the good data because the volume manager has no way of knowing which side is good.

Fortunately, ASM does not need to maintain a DRL. ASM clients manage resilvering ASM clients, which includes the Oracle database and ACFS, and know how to recover their data so that the mirror sides are the same for the cases that matter; in other words, it is a client-side implementation. It is not always necessary to make the mirror sides the same. For example, if a file is being initialized before it is part of the database, it will be reinitialized after a failure, so that file does not matter for the recovery process. For data that does matter, Oracle must always have a means of tolerating a write that was started but that might not have been completed. The redo log is an example of one such mechanism in Oracle. Because Oracle already has to reconstruct such interrupted writes, it is simple to rewrite both sides of the mirror even if it looks like the write completed successfully. The number of extra writes can be small, because Oracle is excellent at determining exactly which blocks need recovery.

Another benefit of not using a DRL is that a corrupt block, which does not report an I/O error on read, can be recovered from the good side of the mirror. When a block corruption is discovered, each side of the mirror is read to determine whether one of them is valid. If the sides are different and one is valid, then the valid copy is used and rewritten to both sides. This can repair a partial write at host death. This mechanism is used all the time, not just for recovery reads. Thus, an external corruption that affects only one side of an ASM mirrored block can also be recovered.

ASM and I/O Error Failure Management

Whereas the previous section covers ASM handling of transient and permanent disk failures in ASM redundancy disk groups, this section discusses how ASM processes I/O errors, such as read and write errors, and also discusses in general how to handle I/O failures in external redundancy disk groups.

General Disk Failure Overview

Disk drives are mechanical devices and thus tend to fail. As drives begin to fail or have sporadic I/O errors, database failures become more likely.

The ability to detect and resolve device path failures is a core component of path managers as well as HBAs. A disk device can be in the following states or have the following issues:

- **Media sense errors** These include hard read errors and unrecoverable positioning errors. In this situation, the disk device is still functioning and responds to SCSI_INQUIRY requests.

- **Device too busy** A disk device can become so overwhelmed with I/O requests that it will not respond to the SCSI_INQUIRY within a reasonable amount of time.

- **Failed device** In this case, the disk has actually failed and will not respond to a SCSI_INQUIRY request, and when the SCSI_INQUIRY timeout occurs, the disk and path will be taken offline.

- **Path failure** The disk device may be intact, but a path component—such as a port or a fiber adapter—has failed.

In general, I/O requests can time out because either the SCSI driver device is unable to respond to a host message within the allotted time or the path on which a message was sent has failed. To detect this path failure, HBAs typically enable a timer each time a message is received from the SCSI driver. A link failure is thrown if the timer exceeds the link-down timeout without receiving the I/O acknowledgment. After the link-down event occurs, the Path Manager determines that the path is dead and evaluates whether to reroute queued I/O requests to alternate paths.

ASM and I/O Failures

The method that ASM uses to handle I/O failures depends on the context in which the I/O failure occurred. If the I/O failure occurs in the database instance, then it notifies ASM, and ASM decides whether to take the disk offline. ASM takes whatever action is appropriate based on the redundancy of the disk group and the number of disks that are already offline.

If the I/O error occurs while ASM is trying to mount a disk group, the behavior depends on the release. In Oracle Database 10g Release 2, if the instance is not the first to mount the disk group in the cluster, it will not attempt to take any disks offline that are online in the disk group mounted by other instances. If none of the disks can be found, the mount will fail. The rationale here is that if the disk in question has truly failed, the running instances will very quickly take the disk offline. If the instance is the "first to mount," it will offline the missing disks because it has no other instance to consult regarding the well-being of the missing disks.

If the error is local and you want to mount the disk group on the instance that cannot access the disk, you need to drop the disk from a node that mounted the disk group. Note that a drop force command will allow the mount immediately. Often in such scenarios, the disk cannot be found on a particular node because of errors in the ASM_DISKSTRING or the permissions on the node.

In Oracle Database 11g, these two behaviors are still valid, but rather than choosing one or the other based on whether the instance is first to mount the disk group, the behavior is based on how it was mounted. For example, if the disk group MOUNT [NOFORCE] command is used, which is the default, this requires that all online disks in the disk group be found at mount time. If any disks are missing (or have I/O errors), the mount will fail. A disk group MOUNT FORCE attempts to take disks offline as necessary, but allows the mount to complete. Note that to discourage the excessive use of FORCE, MOUNT FORCE succeeds only if a disk needs to be taken offline.

In 11.2.0.3, MOUNT [NOFORCE] will succeed in Exadata and Oracle Database Appliance as long as the result leaves more than one failgroup for normal redundancy or more than two failgroups for high-redundancy disk groups.

ASM, as well as the database, takes proactive measures to handle I/O failures or data corruptions.

When the database reads a data block from disk, it validates the checksum, the block number, and some other fields. If the block fails the consistency checks, then an attempt is made to reread the block to get a valid block read. A reread is meant to handle potential transient issues with the I/O subsystem. Oracle can read individual mirror sides to resolve corruptions. For corrupt blocks in data files, the database code reads each side of the mirror and looks for a good copy. If it finds a good copy, the read succeeds and the good copy is written back to disk to repair the corruption, assuming that the database is holding the appropriate locks to perform a write. If the mirroring is done in a storage array (external redundancy), there is no interface to select mirror sides for reading. In that case, the RDBMS simply rereads the same block and hopes for the best; however, with a storage array, this process will most likely return the same data from the array cache unless the original read was corrupted. If the RDBMS cannot find good data, an error is signaled. The corrupt block is kept in buffer cache (if it is a cache-managed block) to avoid repeated attempts to reread the block and to avoid excessive error reporting. Note that the handling of corruption is different for each file type and for each piece of code that accesses the file. For example, the handling of data file corruption during an RMAN backup is different from that described in this section, and the handling of archive log file corruption.

ASM, like most volume managers, does not do any proactive polling of the hardware looking for faults. Servers usually have enough I/O activity to make such polling unnecessary. Moreover, ASM cannot tell whether an I/O error is due to a cable being pulled or a disk failing. It is up to the operating system (OS) to decide when to return an error or continue waiting for an I/O completion. ASM has no control over how the OS handles I/O completions. The OS signals a permanent I/O error to the caller (the Oracle I/O process) after several retries in the device driver.

NOTE
Starting with Oracle Database 11g, in the event of a disk failure, ASM polls disk partners and the other disks in the failure group of the failed disk. This is done to efficiently detect a pathological problem that may exist in the failure group.

ASM takes disks offline from the disk group only on a write operation I/O error, not for read operations. For example, in Oracle Database 10g, if a permanent disk I/O error is incurred during an Oracle write I/O operation, ASM takes the affected disk offline and immediately drops it from the disk group, thus preventing stale data reads. In Oracle Database 11g, if the DISK_REPAIR_TIMER attribute is enabled, ASM takes the disk offline but does not drop it. However, ASM does drop the disk if the DISK_REPAIR_TIMER expires. This feature is covered in the section "Recovering from Disk Failures: Fast Disk Resync," earlier in this chapter.

In Oracle Database 11g, ASM (in ASM redundancy disk groups) attempts to remap bad blocks if a read fails. This remapping can lead to a write, which could lead to ASM taking the disk offline. For read errors, the block is read from the secondary extents (only for normal or high redundancy). If the loss of a disk would result in data loss, as in the case where a disk's partner disk is also offline, ASM automatically dismounts the disk group to protect the integrity of the disk group data.

NOTE
Read failures from disk header and other unmirrored, physically addressed reads also cause ASM to take the disk offline.

In 11*g*, before taking a disk offline, ASM checks the disk headers of all remaining disks in that failure group to proactively check their liveliness. For offline efficiency, if all remaining disks in that same failure group show signs of failure, ASM will proactively offline the entire failure group.

ASM dismounts a disk group rather than taking some disks offline and then dismounting the disk group in case of apparent failures of disks in multiple failure groups. Also, ASM takes disks in a failure group offline all at once to allow for more efficient repartnering.

If the heartbeat cannot be written to a copy of the Partnership Status Table (PST) in a normal- or high-redundancy disk group, ASM takes the disk containing the PST copy offline and moves the PST to another disk in the same disk group. In an external redundancy disk group, the disk group is dismounted if the heartbeat write fails. At mount time, it is read twice, at least six seconds apart, to determine whether an instance outside the local cluster mounts the disk group. If the two reads show different contents, the disk group has mounted in an unseen instance.

After the disk group is mounted, ASM will reread the heartbeat every hundredth I/O that it is written. This is done to address two issues: One, to catch any potential race condition that mount time check did not catch, and, two, to check if a disk group got accidently mounted into two different clusters, with both of them heartbeating against the PST.

In the following example, ASM detects I/O failures as shown from the alert log:

```
Wed May 10 08:13:47 2006
NOTE: cache initiating offline of disk 1  group 1
WARNING: offlining mode 3 of disk 1/0x0 (DATA_1_0001)
NOTE: halting all I/Os to diskgroup DATA_1
NOTE: active pin found: 0x0x546d24cc
Wed May 10 08:13:52 2006
ERROR: PST-initiated MANDATORY DISMOUNT of group DATA_1
```

The following warning indicates that ASM detected an I/O error on a particular disk:

```
WARNING: offlining mode 3 of disk 1/0x0 (DATA_1_0001)
```

This error message alerts the user that trying to take the disk offline would cause data loss, so ASM is dismounting the disk group instead:

```
ERROR: PST-initiated MANDATORY DISMOUNT of group DATA_1
```

Messages should also appear in the OS log indicating problems with this same disk (`DATA_1_0001`).

Many users want to simulate corruption in an ASM file in order to test failure and recovery. Two types of failure-injection tests that customers induce are block corruption and disk failure. Unfortunately, overwriting an ASM disk simulates corruption, *not* a disk failure. Note further that overwriting the disk will corrupt ASM metadata as well as database files. This may not be the user's intended fault-injection testing. You must be cognizant of the redundancy type deployed before deciding on the suite of tests run in fault-injection testing. In cases where a block or set of blocks is physically corrupted, ASM (in ASM redundancy disk groups) attempts to reread all mirror copies of a corrupt block to find one copy that is not corrupt.

Redundancy and the source of corruption does matter when recovering a corrupt block. If data is written to disk in an ASM external redundancy disk group through external means, then these writes will go to all copies of the storage array mirror. An example of this is that corruption could occur if the Unix/Linux dd command is inadvertently used to write to an in-use ASM disk.

Space Management Views for ASM Redundancy

Two V$ ASM views provide more accurate information on free space usage: USABLE_FREE_SPACE and REQUIRED_MB_FREE.

In Oracle Database 10g Release 2, the column USABLE_FILE_MB in V$ASM_DISKGROUP indicates the amount of free space that can be "safely" utilized taking mirroring into account. The column provides a more accurate view of usable space in the disk group. Note that for external redundancy, the column FREE_MB is equal to USABLE_FREE_SPACE.

Along with USABLE_FREE_SPACE, the REQUIRED_MB_FREE column, in V$ASM_DISKGROUP is used to indicate more accurately the amount of space that is required to be available in a given disk group to restore redundancy after one or more disk failures. The amount of space displayed in this column takes mirroring into account. The following discussion describes how REQUIRED_MB_FREE is computed.

REQUIRED_MB_FREE indicates the amount of space that must be available in a disk group to restore full redundancy after the worst failure that can be tolerated by the disk group without adding additional storage, where the worst failure refers to permanent disk failures and disks become dropped. The purpose of this requirement is to ensure that there is sufficient space in the failure groups to restore redundancy. However, the computed value depends on the type of ASM redundancy deployed:

■ For a normal-redundancy disk group with more than two failure groups, the value is the total raw space for all of the disks in the largest failure group. The largest failure group is the one with the largest total raw capacity. For example, if each disk is in its own failure group, the value would be the size of the largest capacity disk. In the case where there are only two failure groups in a normal redundancy, the size of the largest disk in the disk group is used to compute the REQUIRED_MB_FREE.

■ For a high-redundancy disk group with more than three failure groups, the value is the total raw space for all the disks in the two largest failure groups.

If disks are of different sizes across the failure groups, this further complicates the REQUIRED_MB_FREE calculation. Therefore, it is highly recommended that disk groups have disks of equal size.

Be careful of cases where USABLE_FILE_MB has negative values in V$ASM_DISKGROUP due to the relationship among FREE_MB, REQUIRED_MIRROR_FREE_MB, and USABLE_FILE_MB. If USABLE_FILE_MB is a negative value, you do not have sufficient space to reconstruct the mirror of all extents in certain disk failure scenarios. For example, in a normal-redundancy disk group with two failure groups, USABLE_FILE_MB goes negative if you do not have sufficient space to tolerate the loss of a single disk. In this situation, you could gain more usable space, at the expense of losing all redundancy, by force-dropping the remaining disks in the failure group containing the failed disk.

Negative values in USABLE_FILE_MB could mean that depending on the value of FREE_MB, you may not be able to create new files. The next failure may result in files with reduced redundancy or can result in an out-of-space condition, which can hang the database. If USABLE_FILE_MB becomes negative, it is strongly recommended that you add more space to the disk group as soon as possible.

Disk Groups and Attributes

Oracle Database 11*g* introduced the concept of ASM attributes. Unlike initialization parameters, which are instance specific but apply to all disk groups, ASM attributes are disk group specific and apply to all instances.

Attributes Overview

The ASM disk group attributes are shown in the V$ASM_ATTRIBUTES view. However, this view is not populated until the disk group compatibility—that is, COMPATIBLE.ASM—is set to 11.1.0. In Clusterware Database 11*g* Release 2, the following attributes can be set:

Compatibility

- **COMPATIBLE.ASM**   This attribute determines the minimum software version for an Oracle ASM instance that can mount the disk group. This setting also affects the format of the data structures for the ASM metadata on the disk. If the SQL CREATE DISKGROUP statement, the ASMCMD mkdg command, or Oracle Enterprise Manager is used to create disk groups, the default value for the COMPATIBLE.ASM attribute is 10.1.

- **COMPATIBLE.RDBMS**   This attribute determines the minimum COMPATIBLE database initialization parameter setting for any database instance that is allowed to use (open) the disk group. Ensure that the values for the COMPATIBLE initialization parameter for all of the databases that access the disk group are set to at least the value of the new setting for COMPATIBLE.RDBMS. As with the COMPATIBLE.ASM attribute, the default value is 10.1. The COMPATIBLE

.ASM will always be greater than or equal to COMPATIBLE.RDBMS. This topic is covered in more detail later in this section.

■ **COMPATIBLE.ADVM**   This attribute determines whether the disk group can contain ADVM volumes. The value can only be set to 11.2 or higher. The default value of the COMPATIBLE.ADVM attribute is empty until set. However, before the COMPATIBLE.ADVM is advanced, the COMPATIBLE .ASM attribute must already be set to 11.2 or higher and the ADVM volume drivers must be loaded. The COMPATIBLE.ASM attribute will always be greater than or equal to COMPATIBLE.ADVM. Also, there is no relation between COMPATIBLE.ADVM and COMPATIBLE.RDBMS.

ASM Disk Group Management

■ **DISK_REPAIR_TIME**   This attribute defines the delay in the drop disk operation by specifying a time interval to repair the disk and bring it back online. The time can be specified in units of minutes (m or M) or hours (h or H). This topic is covered in the "Recovering from Disk Failures: Fast Disk Resync" section.

■ **AU_SIZE**   This attribute defines the disk group allocation unit size.

■ **SECTOR_SIZE**   This attribute specifies the default sector size of the disk contained in the disk group. The SECTOR_SIZE disk group attribute can be set only during disk group creation, and the possible values are 512, 4096, and 4K. The COMPATIBLE.ASM and COMPATIBLE.RDBMS disk group attributes must be set to 11.2 or higher to set the sector size to a value other than the default value.

Exadata Systems

■ **CONTENT.TYPE**   This new attribute was introduced in 11gR2 specifically and is valid only for Exadata systems. The COMPATIBLE.ASM attribute must be set to 11.2.0.3 or higher to enable the CONTENT.TYPE attribute for the disk group. The CONTENT.TYPE attribute identifies the disk group type, and implicitly dictates disk partnering specifically for that specific disk group. The option type can be DATA, Recovery, or System. Setting this parameter determines the distance to the nearest neighbor disk in the failure group where ASM mirrors copies of the data. Keep the following points in mind:

  ■ The default value is DATA, which specifies a distance of 1 to the nearest neighbor disk.

  ■ A value of RECOVERY specifies a distance of 3 to the nearest neighbor disk.

  ■ A value of SYSTEM specifies a distance of 5.

- **STORAGE.TYPE**   This attribute identifies the type of disks in the disk group and allows users to enable Hybrid Columnar Compression (HCC) on that hardware. The possible values are AXIOM, PILLAR, ZFSSA, and OTHER. The AXIOM and ZFSSA values reflect the Oracle Sun Pillar Axiom storage platform and the Oracle SUN ZFSSA storage appliance, respectively. If the attribute is set to OTHER, any types of disks can be in the disk group. The STORAGE.TYPE attribute can only be set when creating a disk group or when altering a disk group. The attribute cannot be set when clients are connected to the disk group.

- **IDP.TYPE**   This attribute is related to the Intelligent Data Placement feature and influences data placement on disk.

- **CELL.SMART_SCAN_CAPABLE**   When set, this attribute enables Smart Scan capabilities in Exadata.

File Access Control

- **ACCESS_CONTROL.ENABLED**   This attribute, when set, enables the facility for File Access Control. This attribute can only be set when altering a disk group, with possible values of TRUE and FALSE.

- **ACCESS_CONTROL.UMASK**   This attribute specifies which permissions are masked on the creation of an ASM file for the user that owns the file, for users in the same user group and others not in the user group. The semantics of ASM umask settings are similar to Unix/Linux umask. This attribute applies to all files on a disk group, with possible values in the combinations of three digits: {0|2|6} {0|2|6} {0|2|6}. The default is 066. This attribute can only be set when altering a disk group.

This is just a placeholder for real output as well as a table for the features enabled by the disk group compatibility attribute settings:

```
Diskgroup  Attribute                    Value
---------- ---------------------------- --------------------
DATA       access_control.enabled       FALSE
DATA       access_control.umask         066
DATA       au_size                      4194304
DATA       cell.smart_scan_capable      FALSE
DATA       compatible.asm               11.2.0.2.0
DATA       compatible.rdbms             11.2.0.2.0
DATA       disk_repair_time              3.6h
DATA       idp.boundary                 auto
DATA       idp.type                     dynamic
DATA       sector_size                  512
```

Disk Group Compatibility Attributes

The disk group attributes can be set at disk group creation or by using the ALTER DISKGROUP command. For example, a disk group can be created with 10.1 disk group compatibility and then advanced to 11.2 by setting the COMPATIBLE.ASM attribute to 11.2. The discussion on compatibility attributes is covered in the next section.

The following example shows a CREATE DISKGROUP command that results in a disk group with 10.1 compatibility (the default):

```
SQL> CREATE DISKGROUP DATA DISK '/dev/rdsk/c3t19d16s4',
'/dev/rdsk/c3t19d17s4' ;
```

This disk group can then be advanced to 11.2 using the following command:

```
SQL> ALTER DISKGROUP DATA SET ATTRIBUTE 'compatible.asm' =
'11.2.0.0.0';
```

On successful advancing of the disk group, the following message appears:

```
SUCCESS: Advancing ASM compatibility to 11.2.0.0.0 for grp 1
```

In another example, the AU_SIZE attribute, which dictates the allocation unit size, and the COMPATIBLE.ASM attributes are specified at disk group creation. Note that the AU_SIZE attribute can only be specified at disk group creation and cannot be altered using the ALTER DISKGROUP command:

```
SQL> CREATE DISKGROUP FLASH DISK '/dev/raw/raw15', '/dev/raw/raw16',
'/dev/raw/raw17' ATTRIBUTE 'au_size' = '4M', 'compatible.asm' = '11.2';
```

The V$ASM_ATTRIBUTE view can be queried to get the DATA disk group attributes:

```
SQL> SELECT NAME, VALUE FROM V$ASM_ATTRIBUTE WHERE GROUP_NUMBER=1;
  NAME                VALUE
  ------------------  ----------
  disk_repair_time    3.6 H
  compatible.asm      11.2.0.0.0
  compatible.rdbms    11.1.0.0.0
```

In the previous example, the COMPATIBLE.ASM attribute was advanced; this next example advances the COMPATIBLE.RDBMS attribute. Notice that the version is set to simply 11.2, which is equivalent to 11.2.0.0.0.

```
SQL> ALTER DISKGROUP DATA SET ATTRIBUTE 'COMPATIBLE.RDBMS' = '11.2';
  NAME                VALUE
  ------------------  ----------
  disk_repair_time    4 H
  compatible.asm      11.2.0.0.0
  compatible.rdbms    11.2.0.0.0
```

Database Compatibility

When a database instance first connects to an ASM instance, it negotiates the highest Oracle version that can be supported between the instances. There are two types of compatibility settings between ASM and the RDBMS: instance-level software compatibility settings and disk group–specific settings.

Instance-level software compatibility is defined using the init.ora parameter COMPATIBLE. This COMPATIBLE parameter, which can be set to 11.2, 11.1, 10.2, or 10.1 at the ASM or database instance level, defines what software features are available to the instance. Setting the COMPATIBLE parameter in the ASM instance is not allowed. Using lower values of the COMPATIBLE parameter for an ASM instance is not useful, because ASM is compatible with multiple database versions. Note that the COMPATIBLE.ASM value must be greater than or equal to that of COMPATIBLE .RDBMS.

The other compatibility settings are specific to a disk group and control which attributes are available to the ASM disk group and which are available to the database. This is defined by the ASM compatibility (COMPATIBLE.ASM) and RDBMS compatibility (COMPATIBLE.RDBMS) attributes, respectively. These compatibility attributes are persistently stored in the disk group metadata.

RDBMS Compatibility

RDBMS disk group compatibility is defined by the COMPATIBLE.RDBMS attribute. This attribute, which defaults to 10.1 in Oracle Database 11*g,* is the minimum COMPATIBLE version setting of a database that can mount the disk group. After the disk group attribute of COMPATIBLE.RDBMS is advanced to 11.2, it cannot be reversed.

ASM Compatibility

ASM disk group compatibility, as defined by COMPATIBLE.ASM, controls the persistent format of the on-disk ASM metadata structures. The ASM compatibility defaults to 10.1 and must always be greater than or equal to the RDBMS compatibility level. After the compatibility is advanced to 11.2, it cannot be reset to lower versions. Any value up to the current software version can be set and will be enforced. The compatibility attributes have quantized values, so not all five parts of the version number have to be specified.

COMPATIBLE.RDBMS and COMPATIBLE.ASM together control the persistent format of the on-disk ASM metadata structures. The combination of the compatibility parameter setting of the database, the software version of the database, and the RDBMS compatibility setting of a disk group determines whether a database instance is permitted to mount a given disk group. The compatibility setting also determines which ASM features are available for a disk group.

The following query shows an ASM instance that was recently upgraded from Oracle Database 10g to Oracle Clusterware 11gR2:

```
SQL> SELECT NAME, BLOCK_SIZE, ALLOCATION_UNIT_SIZE "AU_SIZE", STATE,
COMPATIBILITY "ASM COMP",DATABASE_COMPATIBILITY "DB COMP" FROM V$ASM_DISKGROUP;
NAME  BLOCK_SIZE AU_SIZE STATE  ASM_COMP   DB_COMP
----- ---------- ------- ----- --------   ----------
DATA  4096       1048576 MOUNTED 10.1.0.0.0 10.1.0.0.0
```

Notice that the ASM compatibility and RDBMS compatibility are still at the default (for upgraded instances) of 10.1. The 10.1 setting is the lowest attribute supported by ASM.

NOTE
An ASM instance can support different RDBMS clients with different compatibility settings, as long as the database COMPATIBLE init.ora parameter setting of each database instance is greater than or equal to the RDBMS compatibility of all disk groups.

See the section "Disk Groups and Attributes," earlier in this chapter, for examples on advancing the compatibility.

The ASM compatibility of a disk group can be set to 11.0, whereas its RDBMS compatibility could be 10.1, as in the following example:

```
SQL> SELECT DB_NAME, STATUS,SOFTWARE_VERSION,COMPATIBLE_VERSION FROM
V$ASM_CLIENT;
DB_NAME  STATUS       SOFTWARE_V COMPATIBLE
-------- ------------ ---------- ----------
YODA     CONNECTED    11.1.0.7.0 11.1.0.0.0

SQL> SELECT NAME,COMPATIBILITY "COMPATIBLE",DATABASE_COMPATIBILITY
 "DATABASE_COMP" FROM V$ASM_DISKGROUP
NAME                            COMPATIBILE DATABASE_COMP
------------------------------- ----------- -------------
DATA                            10.1.0.0.0  10.1.0.0.0
```

This implies that the disk group can be managed only by ASM software version 11.0 or higher, whereas any database software version must be 10.1 or higher.

Summary

An ASM disk is the unit of persistent storage given to a disk group. A disk can be added to or dropped from a disk group. When a disk is added to a disk group, it is given a disk name either automatically or by the administrator. This is different from the OS name that is used to access the disk through the operating system. In a RAC environment, the same disk may be accessed by different OS names on different nodes. ASM accesses disks through the standard OS interfaces used by Oracle to access any file (unless an ASMLIB is used). Typically an ASM disk is a partition of an LUN seen by the OS. An ASM disk can be any device that can be opened through the OS open system call, except for a local file system file—that is, the LUN could be a single physical disk spindle or it could be a virtual LUN managed by a highly redundant storage array.

A disk group is the fundamental object managed by ASM. It is composed of multiple ASM disks. Each disk group is self-describing—that is, all the metadata about the usage of the space in the disk group is completely contained within the disk group. If ASM can find all the disks in a disk group, it can provide access to the disk group without any additional metadata.

A given ASM file is completely contained within a single disk group. However, a disk group may contain files belonging to several databases, and a single database may use files from multiple disk groups. Most installations include only a small number of disk groups—usually two, and rarely more than three.

CHAPTER
5

Managing
Databases in ASM

I n the chapters so far, we have discussed the various components of ASM and how they all work together to provide a solid storage management solution, taking advantage of Oracle metadata and providing performance benefits by storing data the way that Oracle databases need them. But how do the relational database management system (RDBMS) and the new storage manager work together? At this point, every reader must be wondering about the answer to this important question. In this chapter, let's discuss the interaction between ASM and the RDBMS. We will also discuss the various interfaces to the ASM instance and how to migrate data into and from ASM storage.

ASM supports both a single-instance version of the Oracle Database and a clustered version. Although from a strategic point of view ASM best fits a clustered configuration such as Real Application Clusters (RAC), it is not short of any features when it comes to implementing ASM in a single-instance database. So in this chapter, unless otherwise mentioned, all discussions apply to both types of configurations.

Interaction Between ASM and Database

An RDBMS instance is the standard Oracle instance and is the client of the ASM instance. The RDBMS-to-ASM communications are always intranode—that is, the RDBMS will not contact the remote ASM instance (in case of RAC) for servicing disk group requests. This is true until 12c ASM. See Chapter 14 for details.

It is important to note that RDBMS instances do not pass an I/O request to the ASM instance—that is, RDBMS instances do not proxy the I/O request through ASM. When an RDBMS instance opens an ASM file such as the system tablespace data file, ASM ships the file's extent map to the RDBMS instance, which stores the extent's map in its System Global Area (SGA). Given that the RDBMS instance has the extent map for the ASM file cached in the SGA, the RDBMS instance can process reads/writes directly from the disk without further intervention from the ASM instance. As is the case with raw devices, the I/O request size is dictated by the RDBMS instance, not by ASM. Therefore, if the RDBMS needs to read or flush an 8KB database block, it will issue an 8KB I/O, not a 1MB I/O.

Users often ask whether there is any dependency between Automatic Segment Space Management (ASSM)–based data files and ASM. There is no dependency between ASM and ASSM (although their acronyms only differ by one extra letter). ASM manages how data files are laid out across disks (among other things) without looking at the data stored in those data files. ASSM deals with empty blocks that exist within a single segment (it replaces freelists and freelist groups). ASM does not care if the data files contain segments that are freelist-managed or autospace-segment-managed via Bitmap Managed Block (BMB), so no conversion of internal structures takes place.

An active RDBMS instance that uses ASM storage can operate just like a typical database instance. All file access is directly performed with minimal ASM intervention. When a file is opened or created, the ASM instance sends the file layout to the RDBMS instance and all subsequent inputs/outputs (I/Os) are done using the extent map stored in the RDBMS instance.

All ASM file access can only be done via the RDBMS instance and its utilities. For example, database backups of ASM files can be performed only with RMAN. Note that utilities such as the Unix dd command are not recommended for backing up or restoring ASM disk groups.

Database instances usually interact with the ASM instance when files are created, resized, deleted, or opened. ASM and RDBMS instances also interact if the storage configuration changes, such as when disks are added, are dropped or fail.

From a user perspective, the database-file-level access (read/write) of ASM files is similar to non-ASM, except that any database filename that begins with a plus sign (+) will automatically be handled and managed using the ASM code path. However, with ASM files, the database file access inherently has the characteristics of raw devices—that is, unbuffered (direct I/O) with kernelized asynchronous I/O (KAIO). Because the RDBMS instance issues I/Os against raw devices, there is no need to set the database parameter FILESYSTEMIO_OPTION unless network file system (NFS) volumes are used as ASM disks. Additionally, because ASYNCIO is enabled by default, no additional parameters are needed to leverage ASM. In fact, from database side, no database init.ora parameters are mandatory to support ASM.

Cloning ASM and Database Homes

As of Oracle Database 11*g* Release 2, ASM is now part of the Grid Infrastructure (GI) stack and no longer part of the database software stack. In this section, we review how to clone the ASM and database software stack for non-RAC environments. To start the ASM software cloning process, the software stack should be archived with the tar or zip command as root. Savvy Unix folks can take advantage of the tar command and redirect the files to the ssh command and thus extract the files in a single command on the target server. Here's an example of the single command that can be leveraged as root from the /u01/app/oracle/product/11.2.0 directory:

```
tar cvf - grid |ssh target_host "cd /u01/app/oracle/product/11.2.0; tar xvf -"
```

Note that grid is the Grid Infrastructure HOME software directory. This single command will archive the complete subdirectory of the grid directory, copy the contents to the target host, and extract it, preserving all the permissions. The tar command is the preferred option because symbolic links will be preserved.

A golden copy of the non-RAC Grid Infrastructure Home should be maintained to clone to other servers. Certain directories that contain log files can be cleaned up prior to establishing a golden image copy of the ASM software stack.

Once the software is copied to the target server, we can start the cloning process. To clone the GI stack, change your directory to the $ORACLE_HOME/clone/bin directory and execute the Perl cloning script with the following options:

```
# --
# -- Clone Grid Infrastructure
# --
viscosity01:/home/oracle/workasm - oracle: cat clone_grid.txt
export ORACLE_HOME=/u01/app/oracle/product/11.2.0/grid
sudo chmod 770 $ORACLE_HOME
cd $ORACLE_HOME/clone/bin
$ORACLE_HOME/perl/bin/perl clone.pl ORACLE_BASE="/u01/app/oracle"
ORACLE_HOME="/u01/app/oracle/product/11.2.0/grid" OSDBA_GROUP=oinstall
OSOPER_GROUP=oinstall ORACLE_HOME_NAME=Ora11g_gridinfrahome1
INVENTORY_LOCATION=/u01/app/oraInventory
$sudo chmod 750 $ORACLE_HOME
```

Executing the shell script will result in an output that looks like this:

```
$asm - oracle: ksh clone_grid.txt
./runInstaller -clone -waitForCompletion  "ORACLE_BASE=/u01/app/oracle"
"ORACLE_HOME=/u01/app/oracle/product/11.2.0/grid"
"oracle_install_OSDBA=oinstall" "oracle_install_OSOPER=oinstall"
"ORACLE_HOME_NAME=Ora11g_gridinfrahome1"
"INVENTORY_LOCATION=/u01/app/oraInventory" -silent -noConfig -nowait
Starting Oracle Universal Installer...
Checking swap space: must be greater than 500 MB.  Actual 32767 MB  Passed
Preparing to launch Oracle Universal Installer from
/tmp/OraInstall2011-06-11_10-06-13AM. Please wait ...
Oracle Universal Installer, Version 11.2.0.2.0 Production
Copyright (C) 1999, 2010, Oracle. All rights reserved.

You can find the log of this install session at:
 /u01/app/oraInventory/logs/cloneActions2011-06-11_10-06-13AM.log
..............................................................................
......................... 100% Done.



Installation in progress (Saturday, June 11, 2011 10:06:20 AM CDT)
............................................................. 72% Done.
Install successful

Linking in progress (Saturday, June 11, 2011 10:06:22 AM CDT)
Link successful

Setup in progress (Saturday, June 11, 2011 10:06:42 AM CDT)
................ 100% Done.
Setup successful

End of install phases.(Saturday, June 11, 2011 10:06:43 AM CDT)
WARNING: A new inventory has been created in this session. However, it has
not yet been registered as the central inventory of this system.
To register the new inventory please run the script
'/u01/app/oraInventory/orainstRoot.sh' with root privileges.
If you do not register the inventory, you may not be able to update
```

```
or patch the products you installed.
The following configuration scripts need to be executed as the "root" user.
/u01/app/oraInventory/orainstRoot.sh
/u01/app/oracle/product/11.2.0/grid/root.sh
To execute the configuration scripts:
     1. Open a terminal window
     2. Log in as "root"
     3. Run the scripts

Run the script on the local node.
The cloning of Ora11g_gridinfrahome1 was successful.
Please check '/u01/app/oraInventory/logs/cloneActions2011-06-11_10-06-13AM.log'
for more details.
```

As root, execute the orainstRoot.sh script to register the new GI Home with the central inventory located in the /u01/app/oraInventory subdirectory. The location of oraInventory can be identified by perusing the contents of the /etc/oraInst.loc file. Executing the orainstaRoot.sh script produces the following result:

```
viscosity01:/home/oracle/work
$asm - oracle: sudo /u01/app/oraInventory/orainstRoot.sh
Changing permissions of /u01/app/oraInventory.
Adding read,write permissions for group.
Removing read,write,execute permissions for world.

Changing groupname of /u01/app/oraInventory to oinstall.
The execution of the script is complete.
viscosity01:/home/oracle/work
```

As instructed, execute the root.sh script:

```
asm - oracle: sudo /u01/app/oracle/product/11.2.0/grid/root.sh
Check /u01/app/oracle/product/11.2.0/grid/install/
root_viscosity01.viscosityna.com_2011-06-11_10-07-33.log
for the output of root script
viscosity01:/home/oracle/work
asm - oracle: cat  /u01/app/oracle/product/11.2.0/grid/install/
root_viscosity01.viscosityna.com_2011-06-11_10-07-33.log

Running Oracle 11g root script...

The following environment variables are set as:
    ORACLE_OWNER= oracle
    ORACLE_HOME=  /u01/app/oracle/product/11.2.0/grid

Creating /etc/oratab file...
Entries will be added to the /etc/oratab file as needed by
Database Configuration Assistant when a database is created
Finished running generic part of root script.
Now product-specific root actions will be performed.
```

```
To configure Grid Infrastructure for a Stand-Alone Server run the following
command as the root user:
/u01/app/oracle/product/11.2.0/grid/perl/bin/perl -
I/u01/app/oracle/product/11.2.0/grid/perl/lib -
I/u01/app/oracle/product/11.2.0/grid/crs/install
/u01/app/oracle/product/11.2.0/grid/crs/install/roothas.pl

To configure Grid Infrastructure for a Cluster execute the following command:
/u01/app/oracle/product/11.2.0/grid/crs/config/config.sh
This command launches the Grid Infrastructure Configuration Wizard.
The wizard also supports silent operation, and the parameters can be passed
through the response file that is available in the installation media.
```

As the final step of the cloning process, execute the Perl script again, invoking the roothas.pl script:

```
$asm - oracle: sudo /u01/app/oracle/product/11.2.0/grid/perl/bin/perl -
I/u01/app/oracle/product/11.2.0/grid/perl/lib -
I/u01/app/oracle/product/11.2.0/grid/crs/install
/u01/app/oracle/product/11.2.0/grid/crs/install/roothas.pl
[sudo] password for oracle:
Using configuration parameter file:
/u01/app/oracle/product/11.2.0/grid/crs/install/crsconfig_params
LOCAL ADD MODE
Creating OCR keys for user 'oracle', privgrp 'oinstall'..
Operation successful.
LOCAL ONLY MODE
Successfully accumulated necessary OCR keys.
Creating OCR keys for user 'root', privgrp 'root'..
Operation successful.
CRS-4664: Node viscosity01 successfully pinned.
Adding daemon to inittab
ACFS-9300: ADVM/ACFS distribution files found.
ACFS-9307: Installing requested ADVM/ACFS software.
ACFS-9308: Loading installed ADVM/ACFS drivers.
ACFS-9321: Creating udev for ADVM/ACFS.
ACFS-9323: Creating module dependencies - this may take some time.
ACFS-9327: Verifying ADVM/ACFS devices.
ACFS-9309: ADVM/ACFS installation correctness verified.
viscosity01    2011/06/11 10:13:12    /u01/app/oracle/product/11.2.0/grid/
cdata/viscosity01/
backup_20110611_101312.olr
Successfully configured Oracle Grid Infrastructure for a Standalone Server
```

We now have successfully configured the GI stack with ASM for the standalone server. The next step will be to create the ASM disk groups. There are several ways to create the ASM disk groups. ASMCA (ASM Configuration Assistant) and SQL*Plus (with the create diskgroup command) are two such options. In this chapter, we introduce the asmcmd mkdg command:

```
asmcmd mkdg DATA.xml
asmcmd mkdg FRA.xml
```

If the server is configured with ASMLIB, the ASMLIB disk names can be retrieved with the /etc/init.d/oracleasm listdisks command. Simply replace the "ORCL:" disk names with the ASMLIB disk names retrieved from the listdisks command. The contents of the sample DATA.xml and FRA.xml files are shown here:

```
DATA.xml
<dg name="DATA" redundancy="external">
    <dsk string="ORCL:DATA_DISK1" />
    <dsk string="ORCL:DATA_DISK2" />
    <dsk string="ORCL:DATA_DISK3" />
    <dsk string="ORCL:DATA_DISK4" />
  <a name="compatible.asm" value="11.2"/>
  <a name="compatible.rdbms" value="11.2"/>
  <a name="compatible.advm" value="11.2"/>
  <a name="au_size" value="4M"/>
</dg>

FRA.xml
<dg name="FRA" redundancy="external">
    <dsk string="ORCL:FRA_DISK1" />
  <a name="compatible.asm" value="11.2"/>
  <a name="compatible.rdbms" value="11.2"/>
  <a name="compatible.advm" value="11.2"/>
  <a name="au_size" value="4M"/>
</dg>
```

Create Database in Command-Line Mode

Now that the ASM disk groups are created, our next step is to clone over the database software stack. The database software cloning process is similar to the GI stack. With the database software stack, we also issue the clone.pl script and pass the following arguments for ORACLE_BASE, ORACLE_HOME, OSDBA_GROUP, OSOPER_GROUP, ORACLE_HOME_NAME, and INVENTORY_LOCATION:

```
viscosity01:/home/oracle/work
 - oracle: cat clone_db.txt
export ORACLE_HOME=/u01/app/oracle/product/11.2.0/DB
cd $ORACLE_HOME/clone/bin
$ORACLE_HOME/perl/bin/perl clone.pl ORACLE_BASE="/u01/app/oracle"
ORACLE_HOME="/u01/app/oracle/product/11.2.0/DB" OSDBA_GROUP=oinstall
OSOPER_GROUP=oinstall ORACLE_HOME_NAME=OraDb11g_home1
INVENTORY_LOCATION=/u01/app/oraInventory
```

Standardization is crucial for effective and rapid Oracle GI and database software provisioning. If all the DBAs were standardized with the same directory structures for ORACLE_HOME, ORACLE_BASE, and INVENTORY_LOCATION, we could leverage the same cloning scripts to clone the database home software from one server to another. We could realistically provision a fully functional database(s) in a matter of hours instead of days or even weeks. The biggest benefit of cloning the GI and database software stack is that we do not need to configure X-Windows or vncserver on the database server or deal with the X-Windows client or vncviewer on our desktops.

Executing the clone_db.txt script yields the following results:

```
viscosity01:/home/oracle/work
 - oracle: ksh clone_db.txt
./runInstaller -clone -waitForCompletion  "ORACLE_BASE=/u01/app/oracle"
"ORACLE_HOME=/u01/app/oracle/product/11.2.0/DB"
"oracle_install_OSDBA=oinstall" "oracle_install_OSOPER=oinstall"
"ORACLE_HOME_NAME=OraDb11g_home1" "INVENTORY_LOCATION=/u01/app/oraInventory"
-silent -noConfig -nowait
Starting Oracle Universal Installer...

Checking swap space: must be greater than 500 MB.  Actual 32767 MB  Passed
Preparing to launch Oracle Universal Installer from
/tmp/OraInstall2011-06-11_10-33-15AM. Please wait ...
Oracle Universal Installer, Version 11.2.0.2.0 Production
Copyright (C) 1999, 2010, Oracle. All rights reserved.

You can find the log of this install session at:
 /u01/app/oraInventory/logs/cloneActions2011-06-11_10-33-15AM.log
.................................................................................
...................... 100% Done.

Installation in progress (Saturday, June 11, 2011 10:33:23 AM CDT)
.................................................................................
78% Done.
Install successful

Linking in progress (Saturday, June 11, 2011 10:33:27 AM CDT)
Link successful

Setup in progress (Saturday, June 11, 2011 10:33:55 AM CDT)
Setup successful

End of install phases.(Saturday, June 11, 2011 10:33:57 AM CDT)
WARNING:
The following configuration scripts need to be executed as the "root" user.
/u01/app/oracle/product/11.2.0/DB/root.sh
To execute the configuration scripts:
    1. Open a terminal window
    2. Log in as "root"
    3. Run the scripts

The cloning of OraDb11g_home1 was successful.
Please check '/u01/app/oraInventory/logs/cloneActions2011-06-11_10-33-15AM.log'
for more details.
```

As instructed, execute the root.sh script:

```
viscosity01:/u01/app/oracle/product/11.2.0/DB
 - oracle: sudo /u01/app/oracle/product/11.2.0/DB/root.sh
Check /u01/app/oracle/product/11.2.0/DB/install/
root_viscosity01.viscosity.com_2011-06-11_10-34-40.log
for the output of root script
```

Even the root.sh shell script is executed in silent mode. As a final review, check the suggested log file to see the output of root.sh:

```
 - oracle: cat /u01/app/oracle/product/11.2.0/DB/install/
root_viscosity01.viscosity.com_2011-06-11_10-34-40.log

Running Oracle 11g root script...

The following environment variables are set as:
    ORACLE_OWNER= oracle
    ORACLE_HOME=  /u01/app/oracle/product/11.2.0/DB
Entries will be added to the /etc/oratab file as needed by
Database Configuration Assistant when a database is created
Finished running generic part of root script.
Now product-specific root actions will be performed.
Finished product-specific root actions.
```

We have successfully cloned over the GI and database software stack; now the last step is to create the database. Of course, our goal is also to create the database in silent mode with DBCA for a standalone server (in the upcoming sections, we will review the other options for creating a database). In the following example, we create a database called RMANPOC on the DATA disk group with 300MB redo logs:

```
db - oracle: cat cr_rmanpoc.txt
dbca -silent                             \
     -createDatabase                     \
     -templateName General_Purpose.dbc   \
     -gdbName RMANPOC                     \
     -sid RMANPOC \
     -SysPassword oracle123 \
     -SystemPassword oracle123 \
     -emConfiguration NONE               \
     -redoLogFileSize 300 \
     -recoveryAreaDestination FRA \
     -storageType ASM                    \
       -asmSysPassword Only4dba \
       -diskGroupName DATA       \
     -characterSet AL32UTF8            \
     -nationalCharacterSet AL16UTF16 \
     -totalMemory 2400 \
```

```
-databaseType MULTIPURPOSE \
-nodelist viscosity01  \
-initparams db_recovery_file_dest=+FRA \
-initparams db_recovery_file_dest_size=521876275200 \
-initparams compatible=11.2.0.3
```

Executing dbca in silent mode with the options just specified will produce the following output:

```
viscosity01:/home/oracle/work
db - oracle: ksh cr_rmanpoc.txt
Copying database files
1% complete
3% complete
35% complete
Creating and starting Oracle instance
37% complete
42% complete
47% complete
52% complete
53% complete
56% complete
58% complete
Registering database with Oracle Restart
64% complete
Completing Database Creation
68% complete
71% complete
75% complete
85% complete
96% complete
100% complete
Look at the log file "/apps/oracle/cfgtoollogs/dbca/RMANPOC/RMANPOC.log"
for further details.
```

As suggested in the dbca output, you should review the log file for additional details. For RAC databases, the syntax for dbca will be similar except that the –nodelist options will include all the nodes of the RAC cluster. The following example was produced to create the DBFSPRD database on the half RACK Exadata:

```
dbca -silent                         \
     -createDatabase                 \
     -templateName General_Purpose.dbc \
     -gdbName DBFSPRD                   \
     -sid DBFSPRD                       \
     -SysPassword exadata135 \
     -SystemPassword exadata135 \
     -emConfiguration LOCAL             \
```

```
-redoLogFileSize 1000 \
-recoveryAreaDestination RECO_DG \
-storageType ASM                   \
  -asmSysPassword oracle123 \
  -diskGroupName DBFS_DG      \
-characterSet AL32UTF8           \
-nationalCharacterSet AL16UTF16 \
-totalMemory 8192 \
-databaseType MULTIPURPOSE \
-nodelist exapdb01,exapdb02,exapdb03,exapdb04 \
-initparams db_recovery_file_dest=+RECO_DG \
-initparams db_recovery_file_dest_size=521876275200 \
-initparams compatible=11.2.0.3
```

One note of caution: We cannot enable archivelog mode leveraging dbca in silent mode unless we create a template database. Just like we create a golden image for our GI and database software stack, we should also create a golden image template database that has all of our security policies in place, the correct redo log sizes and number, standby redo logs, monitoring schemas, custom profiles, custom password management, and so on. After we establish our golden image database with all of our standards intact, we can leverage DBCA to create a golden image template database that can be leveraged to easily create new databases. Creating a golden image template from DBCA will essentially shut down the database and perform a cold backup of the database. Once the golden image database is created, all new databases we create will automatically inherit all the changes that were incorporated into the golden image database.

Unfortunately, creating the golden image template database is outside the scope of this book. For advanced examples on leveraging DBCA in silent mode, visit the http://dbaexpert.com/blog website.

As an alternative approach, we can create the database in the old traditional mode with SQL*Plus. This method is no longer a recommended option because we have the DBCA with the silent option, but a few of the proud still prefer this approach. To create a database with SQL*Plus, the following script can be leveraged:

```
spool /tmp/create_database_CLIDBA.log
startup nomount

create database  CLIDBA
user sys identified by oracle123
user system identified by oracle123
  maxdatafiles  1021
    maxinstances  4
    maxlogfiles   16
    character set WE8MSWIN1252
    national character set AL16UTF16
```

```
     datafile '+DATA'       size 1000M autoextend off extent management local
     sysaux datafile '+DATA' size 1000m
     default temporary tablespace temp tempfile '+DATA'
     size 1000m uniform size 1m
     undo tablespace undo_rbs datafile '+DATA' size 1000m
     logfile
          ('+DATA','+FRA')           size 300M,
          ('+DATA','+FRA')           size 300M,
          ('+DATA','+FRA')           size 300M,
          ('+DATA','+FRA')           size 300M;

REM - Creates data dictionary views.
@?/rdbms/admin/catalog.sql

REM - Scripts for procedural option
@?/rdbms/admin/catproc.sql

REM - Scripts for export/import -
@?/rdbms/admin/catexp.sql

create tablespace TOOLS;
create tablespace USERS;

alter user sys temporary tablespace temp;
alter user system default tablespace tools temporary tablespace temp;
alter user system quota unlimited on tools;
alter user system quota 0 on system;

connect system/oracle123
@?/rdbms/admin/catdbsyn.sql
@?/sqlplus/admin/pupbld.sql
create user ops$oracle identified externally default tablespace tools
  temporary tablespace temp;
grant dba to ops$oracle;
spool off
```

In this example, we are creating a database called CLIDBA in the DATA disk group. The redo logs are multiplexed to the DATA and FRA disk groups with a size of 300MB per member. This script assumes that all the necessary directories under $ORACLE_BASE/admin/$ORACLE_SID are created and the initialization parameters (or spfile) are already established under $ORACLE_HOME/dbs. For old-time veterans, this approach may still be a preferred method. After we create the database, we execute the standard set of scripts: catalog.sql, catproc.sql, catexp .sql, and catdbsyn.sql. If you create a custom database with DBCA, the database is created similar to this approach, and these scripts are also executed behind the scenes.

Database Interaction with ASM

DBAs predominantly choose the DBCA in GUI mode as their tool of choice, which is provided with the product. As shown in preceding examples, DBCA can also be invoked in silent mode (nongraphical approach). Creating a database using the GUI requires you to have some sort of X Server or a VNC Server running to export your display to. This also implies that you have to forward your X packets using putty or SecrureCRT. This section highlights key screens in the DBCA as they relate to ASM and RAC.

The creation of a Real Application Clusters (RAC) database is different from the regular standalone configuration because a RAC configuration consists of one database and two or more instances.

In the past, we preferred the GUI simply because there are fewer steps to remember. When you use DBCA, the steps are predefined and based on the selected template, and the type of database is automatically created, sized, and configured. However, the script approach has an advantage over the GUI approach in the sense that the user can see what is happening during the creation process and physically monitor the process. Another advantage of this option is that you can create the script based on the needs of the enterprise.

DBCA helps in the creation of the database. It follows the standard naming and placement conventions defined in the Optimal Flexible Architecture (OFA) standards.

DBCA can be launched automatically as part of the Oracle installation process or manually by directly executing the dbca command from the $ORACLE_HOME/ bin directory. From this screen, the type of database to be created is selected. The screen provides two choices: Oracle Real Application Clusters (RAC) database and Oracle single instance database. Figure 5-1 shows the DBCA Welcome screen. Note that RAC One is a RAC database on a single node. The steps needed to configure RAC One and regular RAC are the same.

Configuration of the database using either option should be similar. For the purposes of our discussions, we will use the RAC option. Therefore, select the Oracle Real Application Clusters (RAC) database option and then click Next.

NOTE
The Oracle Real Application Clusters database option is visible only if the Clusterware is configured. If this option is not shown on this screen, the database administrator (DBA) should cancel the configuration process and verify that the Clusterware and ASM are running before proceeding.

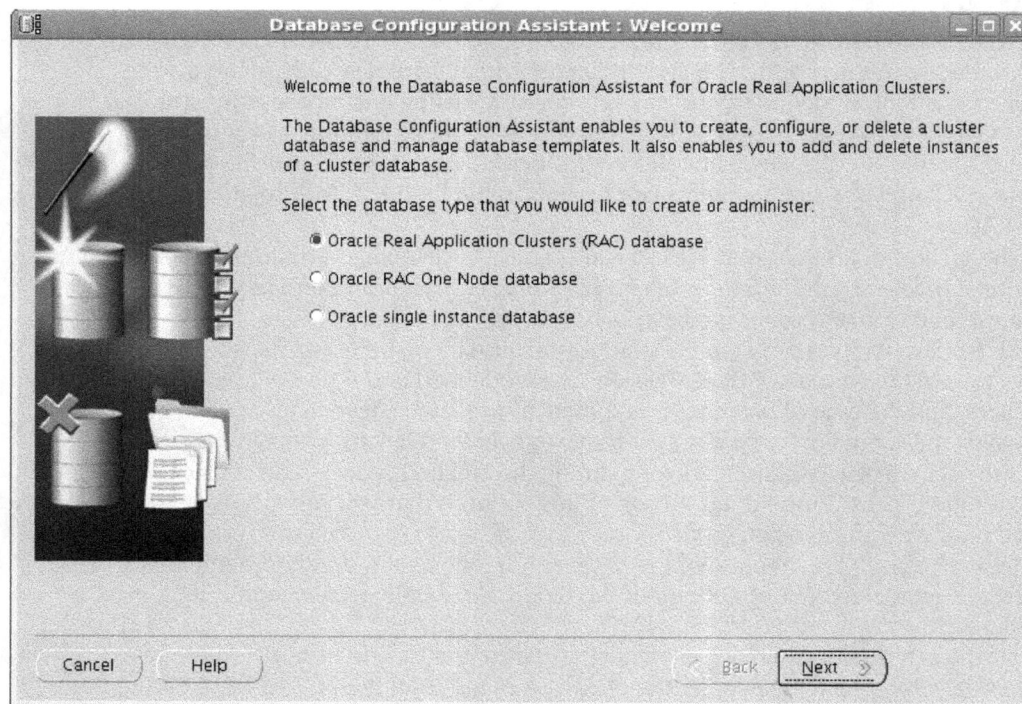

FIGURE 5-1. *The DBCA's Welcome screen enables you to select the database type.*

The third screen defines how the database is configured in the cluster (see Figure 5-2). In this example, we will choose Admin-Managed over Policy-Managed because the cluster size is only three nodes. As a general rule, policy-managed databases make the most sense with four or more nodes. On this same screen is the node selection window, and the appropriate node where RAC needs to be configured is selected. Because the Oracle Universal Installer (OUI) copies the required files to all nodes participating in the cluster, it is advisable to select all nodes listed and then click Next.

On DBCA step 6, shown in Figure 5-3, the database file storage location choices are listed. For 11*g*R2 RAC, only two choices are offered: ASM and Clustered Filesystem (raw is no longer supported). Choose ASM, select the Use Oracle-Managed Files option, and indicate the default disk group location. Oracle-managed files are detailed in Chapter 7.

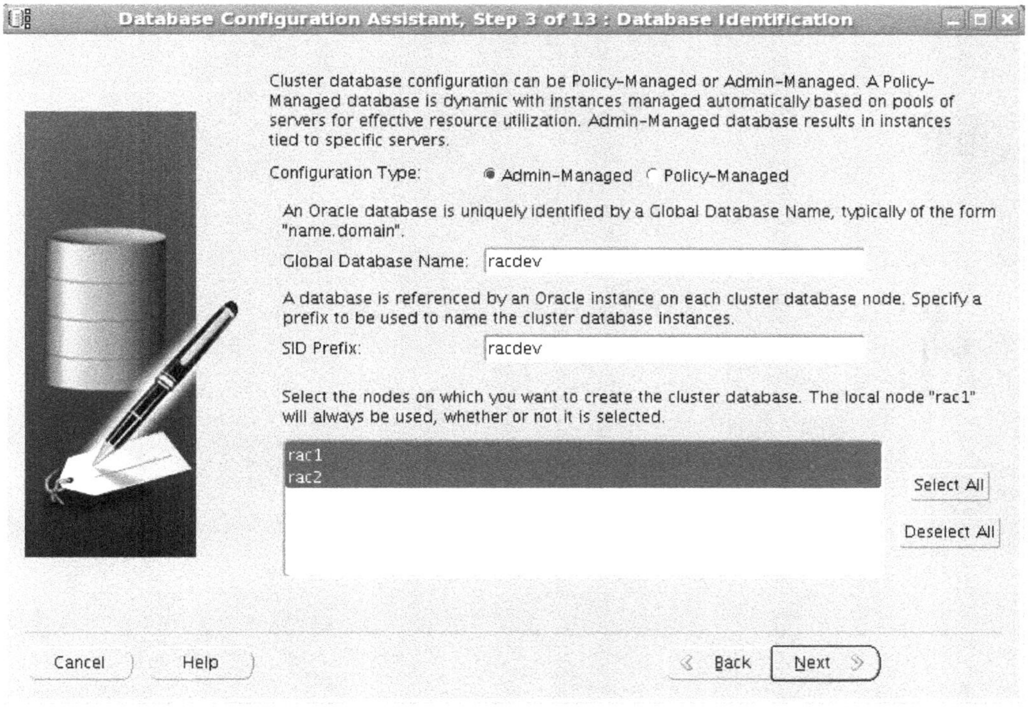

FIGURE 5-2.   *The DBCA's Database Identification screen*

As Figure 5-4 shows, when ASM is chosen as the storage type, a pop-up screen appears that requires the user to specify the ASMSNMP password.

When Oracle Clusterware is initially installed, the ASMSNMP user is generated by the ASM Configuration Assistant (ASMCA) when an ASM instance is created. During this process, the user is also prompted for the ASMSNMP password. ASMSNMP is primarily used by Oracle Enterprise Manager to monitor ASM instances. This account is granted the SYSDBA privilege.

The next screen, shown in Figure 5-5, is the Recovery Configuration screen. In this screen, the DBA has the option to create a fast recovery area (FRA) and enable archiving. For easy sharing of recovery data among the various nodes participating in the cluster, it is a requirement that these areas are located on shared storage. OUI has options to select the appropriate location by browsing through a list.

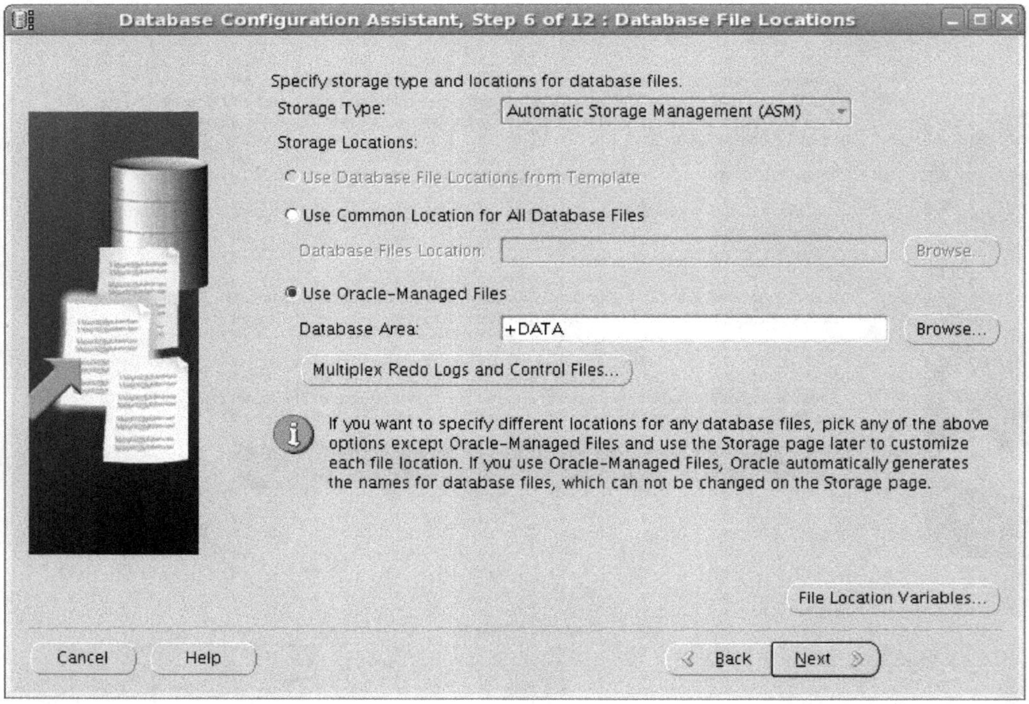

FIGURE 5-3. *Selecting the settings in the Database File Locations screen*

Both the archive log files and FRA are to be configured on the same type of storage.

The next several screens (steps 8–11 in the DBCA process, and not shown here) present the option to create sample schemas when the database is configured, and they allow the DBA to select various instance-specific information such as memory allocation (for example, shared pool and buffer cache), sizing (such as processes), character modes (for example, UTF8), and the connection methods (dedicated, for instance). The DBA defines these parameters by selecting the respective tabs on the screen.

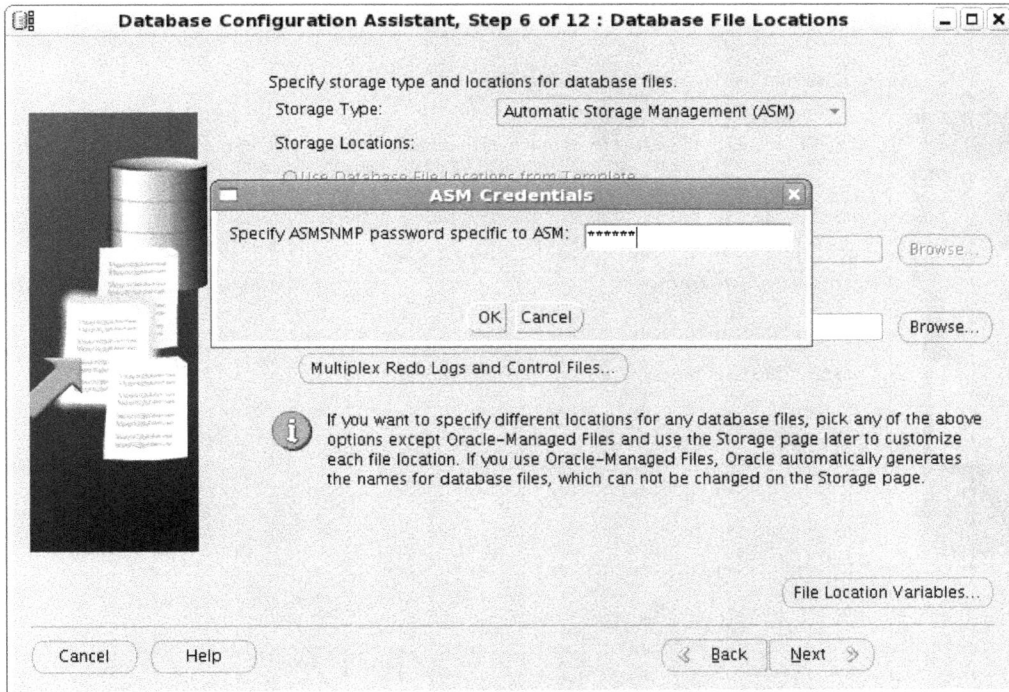

FIGURE 5-4.   *The ASM Credentials screen*

The last screen shows the database creation options. In this screen, the DBCA provides the option to generate the database creation scripts or to create the database. The DBA can select both the options, in which case OUI generates the scripts and subsequently creates the database automatically. Alternatively, users can allow DBCA to generate the scripts and execute them manually. Ensure that the Create Database check box is selected and then click Finish.

When the DBA selects the Finish option, the DBCA begins creating the database. When the process has finished, a new database and the required database instances are created.

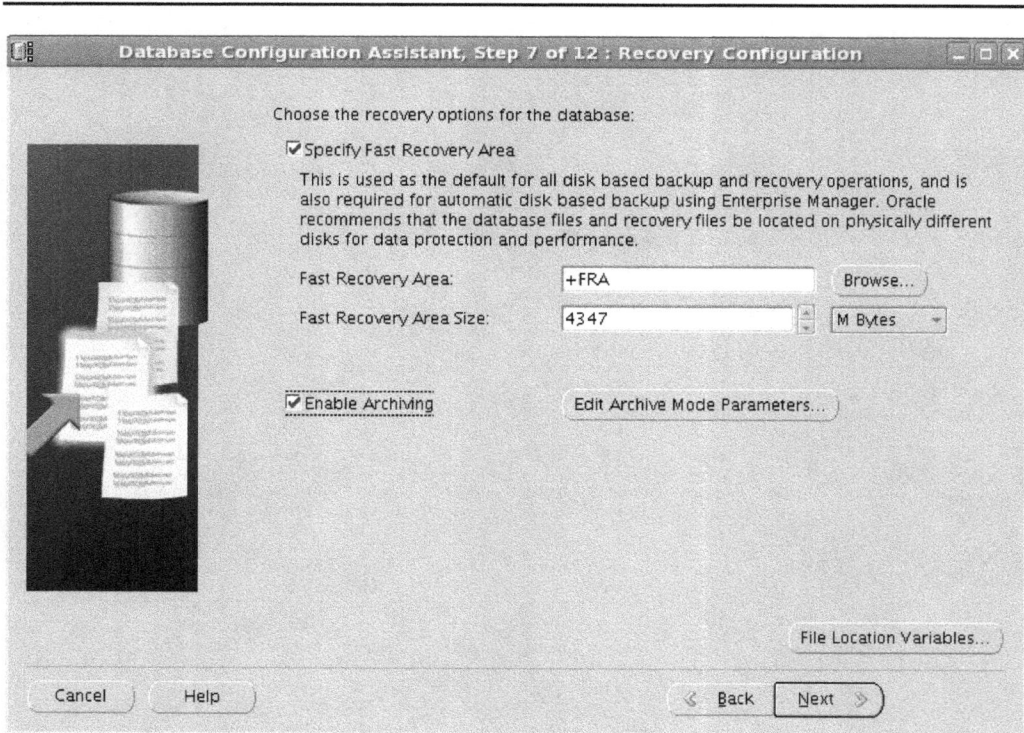

FIGURE 5-5. *The DBCA's Recovery Configuration screen*

Based on the database configuration specified, the progress screen shows the various stages of the installation process. After all the stages of the installation are complete, the DBCA starts the instances on the respective nodes. Finally, the OCR is updated with the new database information and its dependencies, such as ASM disk groups, ACFS mount points, and the listener.

Disk Groups and Databases

A disk group can contain files from many different Oracle databases. These databases can be from the same server or they can reside on different servers. However, a disk and a database file can be part of only one disk group. Furthermore, one Oracle Database may also store its files in multiple disk groups managed by the same ASM instance. Allowing multiple databases to share a disk group provides greater potential for improved disk utilization and greater overall throughput.

To reduce the complexity of managing ASM and its disk groups, it is recommended that you maintain and manage two ASM disk groups per RAC cluster. Additional disk groups may be added to support tiered storage classes in information lifecycle management (ILM) or hierarchical storage management (HSM) deployments. Another variation of this model deployed by customers is where a third disk group is created and used to house the temporary tablespaces. In these cases, the temporary tablespace disk group is usually on less-expensive storage.

The two primary disk groups are used for the database map to the following areas:

- **Database area**   This area stores active database files such as data files, control files, online redo logs, and change-tracking files used in incremental backups.

- **Fast recovery area**   This is where recovery-related files are created, such as multiplexed copies of the current control file and online redo logs, archived redo logs, backup sets, and flashback log files.

If chosen at database creation time (via DBCA), an FRA stores an active copy of the control file and one member set of the redo log group to provide higher availability for the database. Note that additional copies of the control file or extra log files can be created and placed in either disk group.

NOTE
When using multiple control files in different disk groups, all the disk groups need to be available before the database can be started. The dependency between database and ASM disk groups maintained by CRS ensures that all necessary disk groups are mounted correctly.

What about cases where there are several databases on the server, each one with differing recovery point objectives (RPOs) and recovery time objectives (RTOs)? One solution is to create a single large disk group for all the database areas and (possibly) a separate FRA for each database. This caters to environments where the database growth can be contained and where disk utilization is of great importance. There are many other alternatives, such as grouping databases together into a single DATA disk group and a single FRA disk group. The main point here is not to create too many disk groups or to mimic a file system environment. This just ends up producing "islands of storage pools" and becomes highly unmanageable.

An additional scenario is where multiple single-instance databases share disk groups managed by ASM in a clustered environment. In such situations, the primary objective is database consolidation.

Transportable Tablespaces and ASM

This section describes the method for creating transportable tablespaces (TTSs), where the source and destination databases are ASM based. This method uses standard utilities such as Datapump and the database package DBMS_FILE_TRANSFER. This package is used to transfer the Datapump metadata and data files to the remote database server. For completeness, the command CONVERT DATABASE is covered in the last subsection.

We will examine a working example of creating and plugging in transportable tablespaces. In the example, two servers (host1 and host2) are in disparate locations, with each one on an independent Hitachi storage array. Server host1 is the source database and will house the database named db1. The server host2, which is deemed the target server and will subscribe to the transportable tables, will house the database SSKYDB.

Performing the Preliminary Steps to Set Up the TTSs

Before setting up the TTSs, you need to take the following steps:

1. Create or use two existing tablespaces on the source database:

    ```
    SQL> SHOW PARAMETER DB_CREATE_FILE_DEST
    NAME TYPE VALUE
    -------------------- ----------- ------------------------------
    db_create_file_dest string +DATA
    SQL> CREATE TABLESPACE TTS_1;
    SQL> CREATE TABLESPACE TTS_2;
    ```

    Although having two tablespaces is not necessary in all cases, we will need them for this example to demonstrate object dependency.

    NOTE
    OMF is being employed in this example, so set the init.ora parameter DB_CREATE_FILE_DEST to the appropriate disk group name.

2. Create a table in TTS_1 and an index in TTS_2 to ensure that the tablespaces have object dependencies:

    ```
    SQL> CONNECT scott/tiger
    Connected.
    SQL> CREATE TABLE EMP_COPY TABLESPACE TTS_1 AS SELECT * FROM EMP;
    SQL> SELECT COUNT(*) FROM EMP_COPY;
    10 rows returned
    SQL> CREATE INDEX EMP_COPY_I ON EMP_COPY (EMPNO);
    2 TABLESPACE TTS_2;
    ```

3. Check to make sure you have a self-contained transportable set. Oracle provides a PL/SQL package that aids in this check:

```
SQL> EXECUTE DBMS_TTS.TRANSPORT_SET_CHECK ('TTS_1, TTS_2' TRUE);
```

4. Query the TRANSPORT_SET_VIOLATIONS view to see whether any dependency violations exist:

```
SQL> SELECT * FROM TRANSPORT_SET_VIOLATIONS;
No rows returned
```

5. Create a new service names entry, which will point to the destination database to which the tablespaces will be transported. For example, add the following lines to tnsnames.ora:

```
SSKYDB =
DESCRIPTION =
ADDRESS_LIST =
ADDRESS = (PROTOCOL = TCP)(HOST = host2)(PORT = 1521))
)
CONNECT_DATA =
SERVICE_NAME = host2.us.oracle.com)
INSTANCE_NAME = SSKYDB)
)
)
```

6. As SYSTEM, create a database link between the two databases. This is needed because you will be using the DBMS_FILE_TRANSFER package to move metadata between the two databases:

```
SQL> CREATE DATABASE LINK SSKYDB CONNECT TO SYSTEM IDENTIFIED
BY MANAGER1 USING 'SSKYDB';
```

7. Create a directory object in the source database db1 to hold the dump file. Because we are using ASM, this needs to be an ASM object; make sure that the directory path ends with a slash (/):

```
SQL> CREATE DIRECTORY TTS_DUMP AS '+DATA/';
```

8. Create another directory object in the source database that points to an operating system path for the log file:

```
SQL> CREATE DIRECTORY TTS_DUMP_LOG AS '/export/home/tts_log/';
```

9. Create a directory object in the source database that points to the data files:

```
SQL> CREATE DIRECTORY TTS_DATAFILE AS '+DATA/db1/datafile/';
```

10. Grant read/write access to the user you will perform the export as (you need only perform this step if you are using a nonprivileged user):

```
SQL> GRANT READ, WRITE ON DIRECTORY TTS_DUMP TO SYSTEM;
SQL> GRANT READ, WRITE ON DIRECTORY TTS_DUMP_LOG TO SYSTEM;
SQL> GRANT READ, WRITE ON DIRECTORY TTS_DUMP_DATAFILE TO SYSTEM;
```

11. Repeat steps 7 through 10 for the target database SSKYDB as well.

12. Set all tablespaces in the transportable set to read-only:

```
SQL> ALTER TABLESPACE tts_1 READ ONLY;
SQL> ALTER TABLESPACE tts_2 READ ONLY;
```

13. Check the status of the tablespaces on the source database:

```
SQL> SELECT TABLESPACE_NAME, STATUS FROM DBA_TABLESPACES;
TABLESPACE_NAME                          STATUS
------------------------------- ---------
SYSTEM                                   ONLINE
UNDOTBS1                                 ONLINE
SYSAUX                                   ONLINE
TEMP                                     ONLINE
USERS                                    ONLINE
UNDOTBS2                                 ONLINE
TTS_1                                    READ ONLY
TTS_2                                    READ ONLY
Export metadata
```

14. Export the metadata for the two tablespaces:

```
[ora10g@host1]$ expdp system/manager1 directory=
tts_dump dumpfile=tts1_db1.dmp
logfile=tts_dump_log:tts.log
transport_tablespaces=tts_1,tts_2 transport_full_check=y
Starting "SYSTEM"."SYS_EXPORT_TRANSPORTABLE_02":
system/********
directory=tts_datafile dumpfile=tts1.dmp
logfile=tts_dump_log:tts.log transport
_tablespaces=tts_1,tts_2 transport_full_check=y
Processing object type TRANSPORTABLE_EXPORT/PLUGTS_BLK
Processing object type TRANSPORTABLE_EXPORT/TABLE
Processing object type TRANSPORTABLE_EXPORT/INDEX
Processing object type TRANSPORTABLE_EXPORT/INDEX_STATISTICS
Processing object type TRANSPORTABLE_EXPORT/TABLE_STATISTICS
Processing object type TRANSPORTABLE_EXPORT/POST_INSTANCE/
PLUGTS_BLK
Master table "SYSTEM"."SYS_EXPORT_TRANSPORTABLE_02"
successfully loaded/unloaded
*******************************************************************
Dump file set for SYSTEM.SYS_EXPORT_TRANSPORTABLE_02 is:
+DATA/tts1.dmp
Job "SYSTEM"."SYS_EXPORT_TRANSPORTABLE_02"
successfully completed at 14:00:34
```

15. Use DBMS_FILE_TRANSFER to send the dump file across to the target. Alternatively, asmcmd copy could also be used.

```
[ora10g@host1]$ sqlplus system/manager
SQL> BEGIN
2 DBMS_FILE_TRANSFER.PUT_FILE
3 (SOURCE_DIRECTORY_OBJECT => 'TTS_DUMP',
4 SOURCE_FILE_NAME => 'tts1.db1.dmp',
5 DESTINATION_DIRECTORY_OBJECT => 'TTS_DUMP',
6 DESTINATION_FILE_NAME => 'tts1.db1.dmp',
7 DESTINATION_DATABASE => 'SSKYDB');
8 END;
9 /
```

16. Check the filenames on the source database for the two tablespaces being transported:

```
SQL> SELECT FILE_NAME FROM DBA_DATA_FILES
2 WHERE TABLESPACE_NAME LIKE 'TTS%';
FILE_NAME
------------------------------------------------
+DATA/sskydb/datafile/tts_1.294.590721319
+DATA/sskydb/datafile/tts_2.295.586721335
```

17. Transfer the two data files to the target database using DBMS_FILE_TRANSFER:

```
TTS1 datafile
SQL> BEGIN
2 DBMS_FILE_TRANSFER.PUT_FILE
3 (SOURCE_DIRECTORY_OBJECT => 'TTS_DATAFILE',
4 SOURCE_FILE_NAME => 'tts_1.294.570721319',
5 DESTINATION_DIRECTORY_OBJECT => 'TTS_DATAFILE',
6 DESTINATION_FILE_NAME => 'tts1.db1.dbf',
7 DESTINATION_DATABASE => 'SSKYDB');
8 END;
9 /
TTS2 datafile
SQL> BEGIN
2 DBMS_FILE_TRANSFER.PUT_FILE
3 (SOURCE_DIRECTORY_OBJECT => 'TTS_DATAFILE',
4 SOURCE_FILE_NAME => 'tts_2.295.586721335',
5 DESTINATION_DIRECTORY_OBJECT => 'TTS_DATAFILE',
6 DESTINATION_FILE_NAME => 'tts2.db1.dbf',
7 DESTINATION_DATABASE => 'SSKYDB');
8 END;
9 /
```

18. On host2 (the target server), import the data file metadata using Datapump:

```
imp.par has the following contents:
DIRECTORY=TTS_DUMP
DUMPFILE=TTS1_DB1.DMP
LOGFILE=TTS_DUMP_LOG:TTS1.LOG
TRANSPORT_DATAFILES='+DATA1/tts1_db1.dbf','+DATA1/tts2_db1.dbf'
KEEP_MASTER=y

[ora10g@host2]$ impdp system/oracle parfile=imp.par
Master table "SYSTEM"."SYS_IMPORT_TRANSPORTABLE_03" successfully
loaded/unloaded
Starting "SYSTEM"."SYS_IMPORT_TRANSPORTABLE_03": system/********
parfile=impdp.par
Processing object type TRANSPORTABLE_EXPORT/PLUGTS_BLK
Processing object type TRANSPORTABLE_EXPORT/TABLE
Processing object type TRANSPORTABLE_EXPORT/INDEX
Processing object type TRANSPORTABLE_EXPORT/INDEX_STATISTICS
Processing object type TRANSPORTABLE_EXPORT/TABLE_STATISTICS
Processing object type TRANSPORTABLE_EXPORT/POST_INSTANCE/
PLUGTS_BLK
Job "SYSTEM"."SYS_IMPORT_TRANSPORTABLE_03" successfully
completed at 15:05:00
```

NOTE
For the TRANSPORT_DATAFILES parameter, you can either use the alias names (filenames in the DBMS_FILE_TRANSFER) or use the names generated by DBMS_FILE_TRANSFER (these start with the name File_Transfer.xxxx.xxxxxx). To determine the latter system-generated names, use the asmcmd line tool by simply entering cd +DATA/sskydb/datafile followed by the ls –l command.

19. Switch the tablespaces back to read/write mode:

```
SQL> ALTER TABLESPACE tts_1 READ WRITE;
SQL> ALTER TABLESPACE tts_2 READ WRITE;
```

20. Verify that the data files are successfully plugged in:

```
SQL> SELECT NAME FROM V$DATAFILE;
NAME
--------------------------------------------------
+DATA/sskydb/datafile/system.271.599658207
+DATA/sskydb/datafile/undotbs1.268.599658207
```

```
+DATA/sskydb/datafile/sysaux.270.599658207
+DATA/sskydb/datafile/users.267.599658209
+DATA/sskydb/datafile/example.262.599658459
+DATA/sskydb/datafile/tts2_db1.dbf
+DATA/sskydb/datafile/tts1_db1.dbf
```

21. To validate that the data was imported, select the required tables:

```
SQL> CREATE TABLE EMP_COPY TABLESPACE TTS_1 AS SELECT * FROM
EMP;
SQL> SELECT COUNT(*) FROM EMP_COPY;
10 rows returned
```

Alert Log Monitoring

Monitoring the ASM instance is no different than any other database and starts with scrutinizing the alert log file. The ASM instance alert log file is located in the $DIAG_DEST/asm/+asm/+ASM1/trace directory for the +ASM1 instance, in the $DIAG_DEST/asm/+asm/+ASM2/trace directory for the +ASM2 instance, and so on. The DIAG_DEST is defined as an initialization parameter and defaults to $ORACLE_BASE.

The following function in bash or ksh shell can easily help you change your directory to the ASM trace directory:

```
function trace {
export ASMDB=$1
# DB = The sed command strips off the last character of ORACLE_SID off
export DB1=$ORACLE_SID
export DB=$(echo $ORACLE_SID|tr '[A-Z]' '[a-z]' |sed -e '$s/.$//')
export DBLOWER=$(echo $ORACLE_SID|tr '[A-Z]' '[a-z]')
[ "$ASMDB" = "" ] && export ASMDB=rdbms
if [ -d "$ORACLE_BASE/diag/$ASMDB/$DB/$ORACLE_SID/trace" ]; then cd
$ORACLE_BASE/diag/$ASMDB/$DB/$ORACLE_SID/trace; fi
if [ -d "$ORACLE_BASE/diag/$ASMDB/$DB1/$ORACLE_SID/trace" ]; then cd
$ORACLE_BASE/diag/$ASMDB/$DB1/$ORACLE_SID/trace; fi
if [ -d "$ORACLE_BASE/diag/$ASMDB/$DBLOWER/$ORACLE_SID/trace" ]; then
cd $ORACLE_BASE/diag/$ASMDB/$DBLOWER/$ORACLE_SID/trace; fi
}
```

This function interprets the current ORACLE_SID and changes your directory to the trace subdirectory for your current ORACLE_SID. For non-ASM ORACLE_SIDs, simply type the word **trace** and press ENTER. You will instantly be changed to the trace subdirectory of the $DIAG_DEST directory. For ASM ORACLE_SIDs, you will need to pass the parameter of asm, as shown here:

```
+ASM1 - oracle: trace asm
exaddb01:/u01/app/oracle/diag/asm/+asm/+ASM1/trace
```

We can monitor the ASM alert log with the following Perl script. The entire premise of the alert log monitoring script is to capture all the ORA- messages in the alert_+ASM[i].log, where *i* represents the ASM instance ORACLE_SID number. Efficiency is the key to the alert log monitoring script, so we capture and store the last line number at the end of the alert log file. A subsequent scan of the alert starts from the last stored line number and scans to the end of the file for ORA- messages. At the end of the file, the line number is stored again to be used as the beginning point for the next scan.

```perl
$ cat alertlog.pl
#!/usr/bin/perl
#Name: alertlog.pl
#
sub counterSet{
  open(OUT,">$idFile");
  printf(OUT "%d",$currCount);
  close(OUT);
}

# --
# Define Variables
# --------------------------
#
$obase="/u01/app/oracle";
$SH_TOP="/home/oracle/general/sh";
$SID="$ARGV[0]";
$idFile="$SH_TOP/log/alert_${SID}.id";
if (! -f $idFile){
  open(OUT,">$idFile");
  printf(OUT "%s\n",1);
  close(OUT);
}

$alertFile="${obase}/admin/${SID}/bdump/alert_${SID}.log";
$errFile="$SH_TOP/err${SID}.txt";

$cmd="head -1 $idFile";
$preCount=qx/$cmd/;
chomp($preCount);
$cmd="wc -l $alertFile | awk '{print \$1}'";
$currCount=qx/$cmd/;
printf("$preCount:$currCount\n");

# -- Modified tail +preCount with tail -minusCount for Linux Compliance
$minusCount=$currCount-$preCount;
$cmd="tail -$minusCount $alertFile| grep \"ORA\-\" | /bin/egrep -v -f
$SH_TOP/errLogAlert.dat | sort -u> $errFile";
printf("$cmd \n");
```

```
system($cmd);
$size=-s $errFile;
if ($size > 1){
  printf("Sending Alert for $SID \n");
  $cmd="$SH_TOP/alert_notification_db.ksh -s \"Alert Log Error\" -d
$SID
-h 'hostname' -f $errFile";
  printf("$cmd \n");
  system($cmd);
}

&counterSet;
```

As a prerequisite, we should create a bdump in the $ORACLE_BASE/admin/$ORACLE_SID directory as /u01/app/oracle/admin/+ASM/bdump. In addition, we need to create a symbolic link in the bdump directory that points to the alert_+ASM[i].log in the trace directory. Here's an example of the alert log symbolic link:

```
exaddb01:/u01/app/oracle/admin/+ASM/bdump
+ASM1 - oracle: ls -ltr
total 0
lrwxrwxrwx 1 oracle dba 57 Nov 13  2011 alert_+ASM.log ->
/u01/app/oracle/diag/asm/+asm/+ASM1/trace/alert_+ASM1.log
```

In this particular example, the symbolic link is created as alert_+ASM.log (without the ASM instance name) that points to the alert_+ASM1.log file. We do this intentionally so that our cron jobs can be the same on every database server, regardless of whether the server is a standalone server or a RAC node. Here's what the cron job should look like:

```
# -----------------------------------------------------------------
# -- Monitor Alert Logs
# -----------------------------------------------------------------
0,10,20,30,40,50 * * * * /home/oracle/general/sh/alertlog.pl +ASM
>/tmp/alertlog_+ASM.log 2>&1
```

SH_TOP, listed in the alertlog.pl file, defines where the Perl script is being executed from. Underneath the SH_TOP directory, the last line number of the alert log will be placed in the log subdirectory. The log subdirectory should be created as part of the alert log file monitoring configuration:

```
exaddb01:/home/oracle/general/sh/log
TOOLSDEV1 - oracle: cat alert_+ASM.id
191126
```

If, for some reason, you want the alert log mining to start from the beginning, you can simply change the contents of the alert_+ASM.id file to 0.

The alert_notification_db.ksh line of the Perl script can be replaced with mail or mailx. In our example, each ORA- message detected in the alert log file is uploaded to an Oracle table for future analytics.

Just like the database alert log, the ASM alert log also needs to be purged and archived:

```
exaddb01:/home/oracle/general/sh
+ASM1 - oracle: cat rotate_asm.ksh
export CONF=/tmp/asm1.conf
cat <<!! >$CONF
/u01/app/oracle/diag/asm/+asm/+ASM1/trace/alert_+ASM1.log {
weekly
copytruncate
rotate 4
compress
}
!!

logrotate -s $SH/log_rotate_asm1 -f $CONF-s $SH/log_rotate_listener_scan1
-f $CONF
```

The –s option specifies the alternative state file for the logrotate utility. In order for the oracle or grid unix account to execute logrotate, the –s option must be specified because the default state file is /var/lib/logrotate.status. Typically, only the root account has access to write to this file. The –f option specifies the force option to rotate the file with a vengeance, even if the logrotate utility does not think that the rotate is necessary. The last option for the log rotate script is to indicate the configuration file, where we can specify the following:

- The location of the log file to rotate and options for log rotation

- The frequency of the rotation

- The number of files to keep

- Whether to compress or not compress

After we execute the log rotate script for the first time, we can see that the old alert log is compressed and the new file has a file size of zero bytes:

```
exaddb01:/u01/app/oracle/diag/asm/+asm/+ASM1/trace
+ASM1 - oracle: ls -l alert_+ASM*
-rw-r----- 1 oracle dba       0 Dec 11 14:55 alert_+ASM1.log
-rw-r----- 1 oracle dba 643647 Dec 11 14:55 alert_+ASM1.log.1.gz
```

Monitoring the ASM Disk Group

The ASM disk group can easily be remotely monitored from any server on your network. All that is required is SQL*Plus, access to the database, and SELECT privileges against the V$ASM_DISKGROUP_STAT dictionary view. The shell script and all the ancillary scripts shown in this section can be downloaded from http://viscosityna.com/asmbook/.

Instead of querying V$ASM_DISKGROUP_STAT from the ASM instance, we can query the underlying database. In most environments, we should be able to query a single database to get ASM disk group free space information for the server. This shell script accepts two parameters:

- The paging threshold

- The TNS alias listed in the TNSNAMES.ORA file

The script sends an alert if the free space threshold drops below the $PAGER_THRESHOLD parameter for the specified database $DB as the TNS ALIAS in the TNSNAMES.ORA file.

The shell script also logs into the database as the RODBA schema, which stands for *read-only DBA,* and only has select dictionary privileges against the database:

```ksh
#!/bin/ksh
. $HOME/.ORACLE_BASE
setup_oracle;

export PAGER_THRESHOLD=$1
export DB=$2
export FN='echo $0 | sed s/\.*[/]//'

export ORACLE_BASE='grep -i ^oracle: /etc/passwd | cut -d: -f6'
. $HOME/general/sh/functions.ksh

set_basics;
# ---------------------
# CONFIGURATION SECTION
# ---------------------
# Ksh version issue
# So enter it again here
#-----------------------------------------------
export FILENAME=$(basename $0 |awk -F"." {'print $1'})
export CONFIG_FILE="${SH}"/"${FILENAME}".conf
export CONTROL_FILE="${SH}"/"${FILENAME}".ctl
source_config_file;
```

```
#--------------------------------------------------------------------
# Setup the Oracle Environment and pass the ORACLE_SID
#--------------------------------------------------------------------
[ -d /var/opt/oracle/bin ] && export BINDIR=/var/opt/oracle/bin || export
BINDIR=$HOME/general/sh/bin
. $BINDIR/oracle_setup.ksh '$BINDIR/getsid.ksh'

function get_server_name
{
  SRVRNM='tnsping $DB |grep "HOST" |awk -F"HOST" '{print $2}'
|awk '{print $2}' |awk -F")" '{print $1}''
  echo "SRVRNM=$SRVRNM"
}

function chk_dbstatus
{
  DBCONN='echo "select dummy||'OK' from dual;" | sqlplus-s $CONNECT_STRING'
  if [ 'echo $DBCONN | grep -c "ORA-01017"' -ne 0 ]; then
     echo "Invalid username/password used! Exiting..."
     exit 1
  elif [ 'echo $DBCONN | grep -c "ORA-01034"' -ne 0 ]; then
     echo "Database is not up! Exiting..."
     exit 1
  else
     echo "DB connection passed..."
  fi
}

function show_debug_parameters
{
echo "Max Number of Alerts: $MAX_NUMBER_ALERTS"
echo "Log Directory: $LOGDIR"
echo "COUNTER: $COUNTER"
}

#++++++++++++++++++++++++++++++++++++++++++++++++++++++++
#  MAIN LOGIC
#++++++++++++++++++++++++++++++++++++++++++++++++++++++++

# Quit if DB is not up...
get_rodba_prefix;
export CONNECT_STRING=rodba/${RODBA_PREFIX}@${DB}
#echo "Connect String:  $CONNECT_STRING"
chk_dbstatus;


#----------------------------------------------
# Parameters from the ${0}.conf file
# And define error and log files
#----------------------------------------------
[ "$TMPDIR" = "" ] && TMPDIR=/tmp/dba
```

```
LOGDIR=${TMPDIR}
[ ! -d $LOGDIR ] && mkdir $LOGDIR
LOGFILE=${LOGDIR}/${FILENAME}_${DB}.alert
[ "$MAX_NUMBER_ALERTS" = "" ] && MAX_NUMBER_ALERTS=5

if [ -f "$LOGFILE" ]; then
   rm $LOGFILE
fi


#-------------------------------------------------------------------
# Count the number of error files (LOGFILE) in the LOGDIR directory
#-------------------------------------------------------------------
if [ -f ${LOGFILE}.* ]; then
   export COUNTER=$(ls ${LOGFILE}.* |wc -l)
else
   COUNTER=0
fi

show_debug_parameters;

sqlplus -s $CONNECT_STRING 2>&1 <<__ENDSQL
  whenever sqlerror exit sql.sqlcode;

  set pages 60
  set lines 90
  set verif off
  set trims on

  col Total_GB for 999,999,999.9  hea 'Total|(GB)'
  col free_mb  for 999,999,999.9  hea 'Free|(MB)'
  col pct_free for 999.9 hea 'FREE|(%)'

  define PAGE_THRESHOLD=$PAGER_THRESHOLD

  spool $LOGFILE

  select name DG_NAME, total_mb/1024 Total_GB, free_mb, round(free_mb/
total_mb,2)*100 pct_free
  from v\$asm_diskgroup_stat
  where round(free_mb/total_mb,2)*100 < &PAGE_THRESHOLD
    and total_mb > 0
  order by pct_free;

  spool off

  set pages 14
  set lines 80
  set verif on
__ENDSQL
```

```
grep "DG_NAME" $LOGFILE
export RC1=$?

grep ORA-00257 $LOGFILE
export RC2=$?

if [[ "$RC1" -eq 0 || "$RC2" -eq 0 ]]
then
   if [ "$COUNTER" -ge "$MAX_NUMBER_ALERTS" ]; then
      echo "Exceeded Max number of Alerts:  $MAX_NUMBER_ALERTS"
   else
      (( EMAIL_COUNTER = ${COUNTER} + 1 ))
      # Set ALERT_COUNTER to be used by alert_notification.ksh
      export ALERT_COUNTER=$EMAIL_COUNTER
      get_server_name;

      echo "Sending dgmon alert ... $ALERT_COUNTER for $DB ;
sending logfile: $LOGFILE"

      $SH/alert_notification.ksh $FN 'hostname' $DB ""
"Disk Group Free on Server $SRVRNM < $PAGER_THRESHOLD percent!" $LOGFILE

      # Increment the counter by one and append it to the LOGFILE filename
      (( COUNTER = ${COUNTER} + 1 ))
      echo $COUNTER
      mv ${LOGFILE} ${LOGFILE}.${COUNTER}
   fi
else # i.e. if problem has been resolved, then reset the counter...
   [ -f ${LOGFILE}.* ] && rm ${LOGFILE}.*
fi
```

This shell script is unique in the way it sends all alerts by calling the alert_notification.ksh shell script. The alert_notification.ksh shell script is set up to handle mailx, Tivoli alerts integrated with wpostemsg, and even HP Openview alerts with opcmsg. The alert_notification.ksh shell script can also be downloaded from http://viscosityna.com/asmbook/.

Issues DBAs Encounter with ASM

Many DBAs struggle with the same set of problems inside of ASM because they normally don't encounter these problems in the file system world. In particular, several distinct areas can cause additional production outages if DBAs do not know the correct procedures for navigating inside of ASM. We want to bring these common problems to the surface so that everyone can easily tackle them and mitigate any kind of unnecessary outages.

Spfile with an Incorrect Initialization Parameter

What do you do if you cannot start up the instance because of an incorrect initialization parameter and your spfile is inside ASM? You will not even be able to start up the nomount database. As a general rule, always create a backup of the spfile into a pfile before you issue any alter system commands and commit the changes to the spfile:

```
create pfile='/tmp/init[DB_NAME].ora' from spfile;
```

However, if you happen to get stuck in a situation where you cannot bring up a database instance due to an incorrect syntax in the initialization parameter, you can change your environment to the ASM instance and create the pfile. First, determine where your spfile is located with the srvctl command:

```
$ srvctl config database -d PROD |grep -i spfile
Spfile: +DATA_EXAD/PROD/spfileprod.ora
```

Then, from the ASM instance, create a copy of the spfile from asmcmd:

```
+ASM1 - oracle: asmcmd
ASMCMD [+] > cp +DATA_EXAD/prod/spfileprod.ora /tmp/spfilebkup.ora
copying +DATA_EXAD/prod/spfileprod.ora -> /tmp/spfilebkup.ora
```

You can invoke the native Unix strings command to pull out the contents of the spfile to a text file:

```
exaddb01:/tmp
+ASM1 - oracle: strings spfilebkup.ora  > init.ora
```

You will have to do some manual massaging of the file because some lines will overlap and some lines will be cut off. You can take this opportunity to fix the erroneous initialization parameter entry that caused this issue to start. Once you get your golden initialization parameter, you can replace your old spfile. You can proactively remove the existing DATA_EXAD/prod/spfileprod.ora file first. Once you start your database instance in nomount mode, you can create the spfile from pfile using the following syntax and then restart the database:

```
create spfile='+DATA_EXAD/prod/spfileprod.ora' from pfile='/tmp/init.ora';
shutdown immediate;
srvctl start database -d $DB
```

Archiver Is Stuck

What do you do when your archive destination (in this case, the FRA disk group) hits 100-percent utilization? Every now and then, we encounter the following dreaded Oracle error message:

```
ORA-00257: archiver error. Connect internal only, until freed.
```

DBAs never want to see this message. Often, it is not because we ran of space in the ASM FRA disk group but rather because our initialization parameter db_recovery_file_dest_size is not sized adequately. We can fix this easily by modifying the db_recovery_file_dest_size parameter to a value that is significantly higher. For example, we can set the db_recovery_file_dest_size to 5TB, like so:

```
ALTER SYSTEM SET db_recovery_file_dest_size='5000G' SCOPE=BOTH SID='*';
```

However, if the FRA disk group runs out of space and becomes 100-percent utilized, you can end up in a situation where you have to perform some heroics to get out of the situation. When the FRA disk group reaches 100-percent full, you will want to perform one of these tasks:

- Remove old archive logs (if possible).

- Back up and delete archive logs.

- Add more storage to FRA by adding new disks. See Chapter 4 for details on how to add storage to a given disk group.

To remove old archive logs, log into asmcmd as the grid user. Often the grid user is oracle; in the Exadata world, the grid user is oracle. After logging in as the grid user, source your environment so that you can successfully invoke the asmcmd command. After sourcing your environment, launch asmcmd. Within asmcmd, change your directory to the FRA directory, followed by the database name, followed by the archive log directory, as demonstrated here:

```
+ASM1 - oracle: asmcmd
ASMCMD [+] > cd +RECO_EXAD/TOOLSDEV/archivelog
ASMCMD [+RECO_EXAD/TOOLSDEV/archivelog] > ls -l
Type  Redund  Striped  Time        Sys  Name
                                    Y    2012_09_19/
                                    Y    2012_11_07/
                                    Y    2012_11_08/
                                    Y    2012_12_10/
                                    Y    2012_12_11/
                                    Y    2012_12_12/
```

The easiest way would be to remove the oldest directory. In this scenario, we can safely remove the 2012_09_19/, 2012_11_07/, and 2012_11_08/ subdirectories with the following command:

```
rm -rf 2012_09_19 2012_11_07 2012_11_08
```

If you are pressed for space and do not have the luxury of removing days of archive logs, you can back up the archive logs first to the file system and then remove the older backups. The best way to back up and remove archive logs is by using RMAN with the following command:

```
run
{
allocate channel d1 type disk format '/u01/app/oracle/admin/PROD/
bkup1/%d.%s.%p.%t.ARC';
set limit channel d1 kbytes = 8000000;
allocate channel d2 type disk format '/u01/app/oracle/admin/PROD/
bkup2/%d.%s.%p.%t.ARC';
set limit channel d2 kbytes = 8000000;
allocate channel d3 type disk format '/u01/app/oracle/admin/PROD/
bkup3/%d.%s.%p.%t.ARC';
set limit channel d3 kbytes = 8000000;

backup filesperset 5 skip inaccessible (archivelog all delete input);

release channel d1;
release channel d2;
release channel d3;
}
```

This will simply back up all the archive logs and delete them. You will immediately start noticing available space in the FRA because this command will back up and delete five archive logs at a time. Another option is to simply delete the old archive logs from RMAN as well:

```
delete noprompt archivelog until time 'sysdate - 2' backed up 2 times
to device type disk;
```

Moving the Control Files to ASM

DBAs often struggle trying to move control files from the file system to the ASM disk groups. The first thing to be aware of is that the database should be in nomount mode when the activities occur. Second, there should be at least one control file copy per ASM disk group. Some DBAs often make the mistake of creating three control files in the DATA disk group and forget to create a control file copy for the FRA disk group. Instead of creating three control files for the DATA disk group, the recommended architecture will be to place one control file in the DATA disk group and the second copy of the control file in the FRA disk group. To move the control file to ASM, you can do one of two things:

- Copy the control file using the asmcmd cp command from the file system to the ASM disk groups.

- Restore the control files to the ASM disk groups using RMAN.

As a preliminary step, restore the control file from the file system to the ASM disk groups. You should issue the restore command to each of the disk groups:

```
RMAN> restore controlfile to '+dba_pd101/dbatools/controlfile/control01.ctl'
from '/data/oracle/bkup/DBATOOLS/control01.ctl';

Starting restore at 15-JUN-11
using target database control file instead of recovery catalog
allocated channel: ORA_DISK_1
channel ORA_DISK_1: SID=189 device type=DISK

channel ORA_DISK_1: copied control file copy
Finished restore at 15-JUN-11
```

Repeat the restore step for the FRA disk group (in our example, +dba_pf101):

```
RMAN> restore controlfile to '+dba_pf101/dbatools/controlfile/control02.ctl'
from '/data/oracle/bkup/DBATOOLS/control01.ctl';
```

As an alternative option, starting with Oracle Database 11g Release 2, we can take advantage of the asmcmd command in lieu of the RMAN restore command and copy (cp) the files from the file system to the ASM disk group:

```
ASMCMD [+] > cp /data/oracle/bkup/DBATOOLS/control01.ctl
+dba_pd101/dbatools/controlfile/control01.ctl
ASMCMD [+] > cp /data/oracle/bkup/DBATOOLS/control01.ctl
+dba_pf101/dbatools/controlfile/control01.ctl
```

As the final step, change the control_files initialization parameter with the new location in ASM where these files should be placed with the alter system command:

```
SQL> alter system set control_files='+dba_pd101/dbatools/controlfile/control01.ctl',
'+dba_pd101/dbatools/controlfile/control02.ctl' scope=spfile;
```

In the preceding examples, we restored the control files and specified the target location in our RMAN command. Instead, we can modify the location target of the control files in our CONTROL_FILES initialization parameter and simply issue the following command:

```
RMAN> restore controlfile from '/data/oracle/bkup/DBATOOLS/control01.ctl';
```

This command will restore the control files to all the locations specified in the initialization parameters.

As a final step, you will need to shut down and restart the database with the new control files in ASM.

Starting with Oracle Database 11g Release 2, the control file backup and snapshot control file need to be located on shared storage. Shared storage can be in the ASM disk group, NFS, or ACFS. In a RAC configuration, any instance in the cluster can write to the snapshot control file. For this reason, the snapshot control file needs to be visible to all instances. You will encounter an "ORA-00245: control file backup failed; target is likely on a local file system" error while backing up the control file using SQL*Plus/RMAN, if an auto-backup of the control file is configured on nonshared location. You need to move the snapshot control file to an ASM disk group:

```
CONFIGURE SNAPSHOT CONTROLFILE NAME TO '+RECO_EXAD/snapcf_DEV.f';
```

You also need to back up the control file to shared storage. To back up the control file to the FRA disk group (+RECO_EXAD on Exadata), issue the following command:

```
RMAN> backup tag control_to_ASM format '+RECO_EXAD' (current controlfile);

Starting backup at 17-DEC-12 06:49:10
using target database control file instead of recovery catalog
allocated channel: ORA_DISK_1
… handle=+RECO_EXAD/dev/backupset/2012_12_17/
ncnnf0_control_to_asm_0.37182.802248557 tag=CONTROL_TO_ASM comment=NONE
channel ORA_DISK_1: backup set complete, elapsed time: 00:00:01
Finished backup at 17-DEC-12 06:49:18
```

Notice that the backup control file's name includes the tag specified in the control file backup.

Use Cases for DBAs

This section describes how various use-case scenarios affect DBAs who manage ASM configurations as well as illustrates some specific tasks when ASM comes into the picture.

Impact of DB_UNIQUE_NAME for the ASM Directory Structure

The DB_UNIQUE_NAME plays a vital role in the ASM directory structure. By default, the DB_NAME and DB_UNIQUE_NAME initialization parameters are the same. The DB_UNIQUE_NAME dictates the directory name used after the +DATA and +FRA disk group name. The following directory structures are created below the DB_UNIQUE_NAME directory:

- +DATA/DB_UNIQUE_NAME/datafile
- +DATA/DB_UNIQUE_NAME/controlfile
- +DATA/DB_UNIQUE_NAME/parameterfile

- +DATA/DB_UNIQUE_NAME/onlinelog

- +DATA/DB_UNIQUE_NAME/changetracking

- +DATA/DB_UNIQUE_NAME/tempfile

- +FRA/DB_UNIQUE_NAME/archivelog

- +FRA/DB_UNIQUE_NAME/backupset

- +FRA/DB_UNIQUE_NAME/controlfile

- +FRA/DB_UNIQUE_NAME/onlinelog

So you ask, why is this important? This allows you to create a physical standby database with a different directory structure than the primary database. The DB_UNIQUE_NAME also plays a critical role when we are manually cloning a database. If we want to clone the PROD database to QA, we keep the DB_NAME as PROD but change the DB_UNIQUE_NAME to QA during the RMAN restore process. Once the database restore and recovery are complete, we rename the PROD database to QA. At this point, we change the initialization parameters for DB_NAME to match DB_UNIQUE_NAME and rebuild the control file.

Backing Up the Database to the FRA Disk Group

OK, you have backed up your database to the +FRA disk group. You do not own a license of the media management layer (MML), nor do you ever plan to purchase a license. So what do you do now? Let's start by reviewing our backup script to perform a full database backup:

```
RMAN> backup database format '+reco_exad' tag FULL_DB_BACKUP;
```

By querying the RMAN repository, we can collect high-level information about the backup that was performed:

```
RMAN> list backupset summary;
List of Backups
===============
Key     TY LV S Device Type Completion Time     #Pieces #Copies Compressed Tag
------- -- -- - ----------- ------------------- ------- ------- ---------- ---
...
946     B  F  A DISK        17-DEC-12 13:28:12 1     1       NO         FULL_DB_BACKUP
947     B  F  A DISK        17-DEC-12 13:28:17 1     1       NO         FULL_DB_BACKUP
948     B  F  A DISK        17-DEC-12 13:28:19 1     1       NO         FULL_DB_BACKUP
949     B  F  A DISK        17-DEC-12 13:29:06 1     1       NO         FULL_DB_BACKUP
950     B  F  A DISK        17-DEC-12 13:29:24 1     1       NO         FULL_DB_BACKUP
```

Taking advantage of the tag from the full database backup, we recognize that the FULL_DB_BACKUP backup set includes the primary keys 946, 947, 948, 949, and 950. Leveraging the primary keys of the backup set, we can perform a backup of the backup set to the file system. You can perform a copy of the backup set or the image copy to the backup file system using this command:

```
RMAN> backup backupset 946,947,948,949,950 format
'/u01/app/oracle/admin/DEV/bkups/%d.%s.%p.%t.L1.DB';
```

A more preferable approach would be to leverage the tag again to perform the backup of the backup set to the file system:

```
RMAN> backup backupset from tag FULL_DB_BACKUP format
'/u01/app/oracle/admin/DEV/bkups/%d.%s.%p.%t.L1_b.DB';
```

As you will notice throughout this chapter, RMAN tags are heavily utilized to assist and simplify our backup and restore infrastructure. The same logic applies to image copies that we apply to the FRA disk group. To copy database images from the FRA disk group to the file system, issue the following RMAN command:

```
RMAN> backup TAG "IMAGE_COPY_QUARTERLY_BACKUP" copy of database format
'/u01/app/oracle/admin/DEV/bkups/%d.%s.%p.%t.L1.DB';
```

Specifying Default Locations for Data Files and Redo Logs

The db_create_file_dest parameter should always be set to the DATA disk group, where the database data/temp files reside. Instead of specifying a location of the database file during tablespace creation or adding a data file to a tablespace, we can leverage the default location for all newly created data files. The db_create_online_log_dest_1 and db_create_online_log_dest_2 parameters refer to redo logs and play an important role as well. Here are the three initialization parameters being investigated:

```
db_create_file_dest                   string       +DATA_EXAD
db_create_online_log_dest_1           string       +DATA_EXAD
db_create_online_log_dest_2           string       +RECO_EXAD
```

Because we have our db_create_file_dest parameter set, we can issue a simple command to create a tablespace:

```
create tablespace asm_default_test;
```

Notice that no location option was specified. Automatically, the asm_default_test tablespace will be created in the DATA disk group (+DATA_EXAD) with a 100MB data file. Because auto-extend is automatically enabled, this newly created data file will be able to auto-extend to approximately 32GB.

Adding a data file to a tablespace has never been so easy. We simply issue the following command:

```
alter tablespace asm_default_test add datafile;
```

Again, a 100MB data file will be created in the location specified in the db_create_file_dest parameter. Like everyone else who manages large database, you want to be able to specify 32GB data files. The syntax is extremely simple for that, too:

```
alter tablespace asm_default_test add datafile size 32g;
```

Not only does the db_create_file_dest parameter save time in creating/altering tablespaces, it can also mitigate potential fat-fingering during the tablespace growth process. If the + sign is left out accidentally during a tablespace growth process, the new data file would locate itself in the $ORACLE_HOME/dbs directory, as shown here:

```
SQL> alter tablespace asm_default_test add datafile 'data_exad' size 32000m;
Tablespace altered.

1* select file_name from dba_data_files
where tablespace_name='ASM_DEFAULT_TEST';
FILE_NAME
--------------------------------------------------------------------------
+DATA_EXAD/dev/datafile/asm_default_test.586.802253035
+DATA_EXAD/dev/datafile/asm_default_test.585.802253061
+DATA_EXAD/dev/datafile/asm_default_test.584.802253075
/u01/app/oracle/product/11.2.0/dbhome_1/dbs/data_exad
```

Other RAC instances will report foul play on the newly created data file because it will not be able to read/write to the data file. To get yourself out of this situation, you can copy the data file from the file system back to ASM with either RMAN or asmcmd after offlining the data file. Once the data file is copied into ASM, you can switch the data file to copy and initiate a data file recovery. Once data file recovery completes, you can online the data file for production usage.

So far we have covered default locations for data files. The two parameters, db_create_online_log_dest_1 and db_create_online_dest_2, specify the default locations for online redo logs. For the RAC instance, we can create another redo log group with the size 250MB:

```
SQL> alter database add logfile thread 2 group 30 size 250m;

Database altered.
```

Once the redo log is created in our +DATA_EXAD and +RECO_EXAD disk groups, we can issue a query against the v$logfile and v$log views to retrieve the location of our redo log group:

```
1   select b.sequence#, b.thread#, b.group#, a.member,
      b.bytes/1024/1024 mb, b.status
2   from v$logfile a, v$log b
```

```
   3  where a.group#=b.group#
   4* order by 2,3
SQL> /

  SEQUENCE#     THREAD#     GROUP# MEMBER
MB STATUS
---------- ---------- ---------- -----------------------------------------------------
-------- --------
       972          1         11 +DATA_EXAD/toolsdev/onlinelog/group_11.328.764042893
250 CURRENT
       972          1         11 +RECO_EXAD/toolsdev/onlinelog/group_11.302.764042893
250 CURRENT
...

...
         0          2         30 +DATA_EXAD/toolsdev/onlinelog/group_30.584.802253661
250 UNUSED
         0          2         30 +RECO_EXAD/toolsdev/onlinelog/gro
up_30.32009.802253663                    250 UNUSED
```

As you can see, redo log group 30 was successfully created in the +DATA_EXAD and +RECO_EXAD disk groups. The default locations for the redo logs will come in extremely handy as we clone databases with RMAN. When we issue the "alter database open resetlogs" command, all the redo logs will be created in the db_ create_online_log_dest_1 and db_create_online_dest_2 disk groups.

Copying Files from One ASM Instance to Another

What do you do if you need to ship archive logs from the primary database to the standby database? What do you do if you need to ship the backups from the primary RAC cluster on the primary data center to the disaster recovery data center physical standby RAC cluster and you do not have a file system to stage your backups? Oracle Database 11g Release 1 provided the feature to copy files from an ASM disk group to another ASM disk group with the asmcmd cp command. We can leverage this technique, but for a majority of DBAs, an easier approach would be to copy the archivelog backups from source to target destination using the standard OS scp command.

The classic problem that a lot of companies face today is that larger companies have multiterabyte databases or even databases that are hundreds of terabytes. Obviously, if you have a multiterabyte database, you can't copy that over the network, especially over a WAN. In this case, you will be backing up to tape and restoring the backup. If you happen to own the Media Management Layer (MML) license, you can restore directly to ASM. If you do not, ASM Clustered File System (ACFS) plays a vital role in this scenario. Like a local file system or a network file system, ACFS can be used as the destination for disk-to-disk backup. You can ask the system administrators to sweep the ACFS file system to tape. On the target Data Guard server, the system administrator can restore the backup taken from the primary data center to the ACFS or local file system.

Lot of companies have spare space on the ASM disk groups. We can easily carve a volume out of an ASM disk group and instantly create an ACFS file system on demand as needed. With ACFS, you can dynamically resize an ACFS file system as needed to meet your space requirements. For larger companies, the time to perform the backup to tape, collect and ship the tapes to the disaster recovery site, add the tapes to the tape array, and restore the tape content to the ACFS file system can take days. During this time, we need to manually ship the archive logs from the primary data center to the disaster recovery data center. To make the process simpler, we want to ship archive logs from the primary data center FRA ASM disk group (+ASM1 instance) to the disaster recovery site FRA ASM disk group (+ASM1). The tedious tasks of performing RMAN backups of the archive logs to the ACFS, copying the archive logs to the ACFS file system on the disaster recovery site, and restoring the archive logs will overburden most of the DBAs. We need a much simpler approach to transferring the archive log from the primary data center to the disaster recovery data center.

We can copy Oracle-related files from one ASM instance to another ASM instance using the asmcmd cp command. The syntax to perform the copy command is as follows:

```
usage: cp [-i] [-f] [connect_str:]src_file [connect_str:]tgt_file
```

If you are pushing archive logs, you will want to push increments, either by the day or incrementally throughout the day, of the delta archive logs that were generated since the last push of the archive log files. The following script does exactly that:

```
export ORACLE_SID=+ASM1
export ORAENV_ASK=NO
. oraenv

export ARCH_DATE=2012_11_26
# Date example: 2012_11_19

# -- Get Password
#export push_passwd=$(cat .push_arch_asm.passwd |grep -v ^# |head -1)
export push_passwd=peanutbutter123

#  -- Get the last file name and derive the new file name
#  --
#  -- File names are derived from # of files of the same prefix
#from the file system
export PUSH_FILELIST=push_arch_asm.list
export PUSH_FILELIST_COUNT=$(ls ${PUSH_FILELIST}.* |wc -l|sed -e "s/ //g")
(( NEXT_FILELIST_COUNT = ${PUSH_FILELIST_COUNT} + 1 ))

echo "Number of Files: $PUSH_FILELIST_COUNT - Next: $NEXT_FILELIST_COUNT"

# -- Execute asmcmd and compose full list of archivelogs for the day
# --
```

```
asmcmd ls +FRA/prod_db/ARCHIVELOG/${ARCH_DATE} >${PUSH_FILELIST}.${NEXT_FILELIST_
COUNT}

# -- Perform a diff of the last file derived and newly generated file listing
# --
# -- Parse through file listing and generate the syntax to push the
#archivelogs from ASM to ASM
diff ${PUSH_FILELIST}.${PUSH_FILELIST_COUNT} ${PUSH_FILELIST}.${NEXT_FILELIST_COUNT}
|grep \> |sed -e "s/ //g" -e "s#>##g" | \
    awk {'print "echo \"_ASM_PASSWORD_\"|asmcmd cp +FRA/PROD/ARCHIVELOG/_ARCHDATE_/'
$1 " dgmenu@dr_db-vip.+ASM1:+FRA/ARCH/PROD/" $1'} | \
    sed -e "s/_ARCHDATE_/${ARCH_DATE}/g" -e "s/_ASM_PASSWORD_/${push_passwd}/g" |cut
-d. -f1-4
```

In this script example, replace the ARCH_DATE using the format YYYY_MM_DD with the actual date for the archive logs we are interested in transferring. The push_passwd variable represents the password for the user account called dgmenu. Instead of using the SYS account, we created a user account called dgmenu with the proper sysasm privileges on the ASM instance. The logic behind this decision is to drop or disable the dgmenu account after the archivelog propagation exercise is complete. The shell script generates a file called push_arch_asm.list.[i] that houses the list of archive log names that match for the day. The following output only lists the first three archive logs in question:

```
> cat push_arch_asm.list.2 |head -3
thread_1_seq_3819.8679.800334247
thread_1_seq_3820.8681.800334247
thread_1_seq_3821.8682.800334247
```

Once the script identifies the archive logs to push by listing out the directory contents, it composes the remainder of the syntax. Because this script has the requirements of copying the deltas of the archive logs since the last push, it performs a diff between the current push_arch_asm.list file and the latest file it detects. You will also notice that the password for the privileged user account with the sysasm privilege is hard-coded in the script. The passwords are not echoed back during the execution asmcmd cp command.

```
echo "peanutbutter123"|asmcmd cp +FRA/PROD/ARCHIVELOG/2012_11_26/
thread_1_seq_3819.8679.800334247
dgmenu@dr_db-vip.+ASM1:+FRA/ARCH/PROD/thread_1_seq_3819
echo "peanutbutter123"|asmcmd cp
+FRA/PROD/ARCHIVELOG/2012_11_26/thread_1_seq_3820.8681.800334247
dgmenu@dr_db-vip.+ASM1:+FRA/ARCH/PROD/thread_1_seq_3820
echo "peanutbutter123"|asmcmd cp
+FRA/PROD/ARCHIVELOG/2012_11_26/thread_1_seq_3821.8682.800334247
dgmenu@dr_db-vip.+ASM1:+FRA/ARCH/PROD/thread_1_seq_3821
```

Prior to starting to send the archive logs to the disaster recovery site, you will need to manually create the directory structures on the ASM +FRA disk group. From the asmcmd command prompt, cd to +FRA and then mkdir ARCH; from the ARCH directory, mkdir PROD. This will complete the setup required on the target ASM instance. Obviously, the directory structure can be different and most likely will be different in your environment.

Capture the output of the preceding shell script, redirect the output to another shell script, and execute the shell script in no-hang-up mode (nohup) in the background. Executing the new captured shell script will yield the following output:

```
prod_db:/home/oracle/work > cat PROD_1126.log
nohup: ignoring input
Enter password: ***************
copying +FRA/PROD/ARCHIVELOG/2012_11_26/thread_1_seq_3819.8679.800334247 ->
dr_db-vip:+FRA/ARCH/PROD/thread_1_seq_3819
Enter password: ***************
copying +FRA/PROD/ARCHIVELOG/2012_11_26/thread_1_seq_3820.8681.800334247 ->
dr_db-vip:+FRA/ARCH/PROD/thread_1_seq_3820
Enter password: ***************
copying +FRA/PROD/ARCHIVELOG/2012_11_26/thread_1_seq_3821.8682.800334247 ->
dr_db-vip:+FRA/ARCH/PROD/thread_1_seq_3821
Enter password: ***************
copying +FRA/PROD/ARCHIVELOG/2012_11_26/thread_1_seq_3822.8684.800334331 ->
dr_db-vip:+FRA/ARCH/PROD/thread_1_seq_3822
```

As the archive logs are being shipped, you can check the +FRA/ARCH/PROD directory and issue the du command to see space consumption increase on the directory. One very important thing to note is that we intentionally do not fully qualify the target filename; we cannot provide the file.incarnation file/incarnation pair, which is used to ensure uniqueness. If the target filename is fully qualified, you will encounter an ASMCMD-8016 error. The cp command will fail if you fully qualify the target filename because the ASM filename is not a single-file creation form that can be used to create a single file. The filename should not contain the file number/incarnation:

```
prdb3:/home/grid/work > echo "peanutbutter123"|asmcmd cp
+FRA/NRSP/ARCHIVELOG/2012_12_13/thread_2_seq_2455.5196.801911871
dgmenu@drdb3-vip.+ASM1:+FRA/ARCH/NRSP/thread_2_seq_2455.5196.801911871
Enter password: ***************
copying +FRA/NRSP/ARCHIVELOG/2012_12_13/thread_2_
seq_2455.5196.801911871 ->
drdb3-vip:+FRA/ARCH/NRSP/thread_2_seq_2455.5196.801911871
ASMCMD-8016: copy source->'+FRA/NRSP/ARCHIVELOG/2012_12_13/thread_2_
seq_2455.5196.801911871' and target->'+FRA/ARCH/NRSP/thread_2_
seq_2455.5196.801911871' failed
```

Another important piece of information to mention is that the target filename generates an alias rather than using the system-generated filename. Notice the filename alias for thread_2_seq_2455:

```
ASMCMD> ls -l thread_2_seq_2455
Type        Redund  Striped  Time                 Sys  Name
                                                  N    thread_2_seq_2455 =>
+FRA/ASM/ARCHIVELOG/thread_2_seq_2455.12363.801929873
```

How to Migrate from File System to ASM with Minimal Downtime

You can use a couple of clever techniques to move a database from file system to ASM with minimal downtime. One out-of-the-box solution is to leverage Data Guard in the equation and simply perform a switchover to the database on ASM. Another option is to leverage RMAN image copies with forever incremental updates. In this section, we cover the option to perform incremental updates to image copy backups.

Because we can perform our due diligence and prepare our ASM environment ahead of time, we can significantly reduce our outage window. No matter what the size of the database is—500GB, 5TB, or even 50TB—we can cut our downtime to be less than 30 minutes moving the even largest databases out there.

With the Data Guard approach, we have to worry about the database being in force logging mode. If the database is not in force logging mode, we will have to go back to development and business to investigate batch jobs, scheduled maintenance, and any specific tasks executed in unrecoverable or nologging mode. If we identify any jobs running in nologging mode, we will have to modify the jobs or come to a realization that we cannot force logging mode quite yet. On the other hand, the Data Guard option does provide an added advantage because we can switch back over to the file system if the storage on the ASM does not meet the IOPs and throughput requirements of the database workload.

To start our migration to the ASM, we must first perform an RMAN image copy of the database to the Data disk group. This step will be the longest-running step of the process. We can expect to see about 1TB an hour for the RMAN image copy to ASM. For performance considerations, you can increase the number of RMAN channels from six to eight. To perform an RMAN image copy of the database to ASM, execute the following command:

```
backup as copy incremental level 0 tag=TO_ASM_NOV2012 format '+DATA'
(database) ;
```

Notice the "tag=" embedded in the syntax to identify the backup. Tags are crucial to the forever incremental update strategy. If we do not specify a user-friendly tag, RMAN will generate a tag automatically and assign it to the backup.

Another tidbit to add is that the RMAN image copy is an exact copy of the database files. The size of the RMAN image copy will be identical to the size of the database. You cannot perform a compressed RMAN image copy.

The RMAN image copy can be taken a week prior to cutover, several days prior to cutover, or even the night before cutover. You will have to make the decision based on how long it takes and how comfortable you are with the process. The closer you take the RMAN image copy to the cutover date, the fewer incremental backups and updates you will have to perform. Once we have successfully performed our level 0 image copy, we can proceed with performing the level 1 incremental backup:

```
Step #2:
BACKUP INCREMENTAL LEVEL 1 FOR RECOVER OF COPY WITH TAG 'TO_ASM_NOV2012'
format '/u01/app/oracle/admin/DBATOOLS/bkups/%d.%s.%p.%t.L1.4R.DB' DATABASE;
```

In the level 1 incremental backup, notice that we specify that it is to be used to recover our level 0 image copy backup. Also, pay particular attention to the tag being used. The tag is the same one we specified in our level 0 image copy backup. For backup simplicity purposes, we are placing the level 1 incremental backups in the file system. Next, we perform the incremental update, which is really a recovery to our database image copy to bring the database to a state that's current with the production database. Once the update process is complete, we can perform our incremental backup again. This is the process we will repeat, thus the marketing term "forever incrementals." Let's see what the syntax for the update image copy process looks like:

```
Step #3:
recover copy of database with tag 'TO_ASM_NOV2012';
```

Notice that the tag is referenced again in the recovery process as well. We will need to repeat steps 2 and 3 until cutover time. Furthermore, we will want to repeat steps 2 and 3 as much as possible, at a minimum of once per day. On the day of cutover, we will want to repeat steps 2 and 3 often. As we near the cutover window, we will want to perform another incremental update to the database image copy. At the time of cutover, we will want to shut down the database and bring it back up in mount mode. As the last step, we will perform the final incremental update:

```
RMAN> shutdown immediate;
RMAN> startup mount;
RMAN> BACKUP INCREMENTAL LEVEL 1 FOR RECOVER OF COPY WITH TAG 'TO_ASM_NOV2012'
format '/u01/app/oracle/admin/DBATOOLS/bkups/%d.%s.%p.%t.L1.4R.DB' DATABASE;
RMAN> recover copy of database with tag 'TO_ASM_NOV2012';
```

Now we are ready to switch our database to the image copy. Old-timers would spend time generating the script to alter the database rename file from source to

target for each data file. We can rename data files for the entire database with a
single switch database command:

```
RMAN> startup mount;
RMAN> switch database to copy;
```

We are almost there. We need to issue the recover database command to get our
database on ASM to be completely consistent and then open the database:

```
RMAN> recover database;
RMAN> alter database open;
```

We still have some cleanup to do. We still need to move the redo logs (really,
create new groups and drop old groups) to ASM, move the control files to ASM,
move the spfile to ASM, and move our temporary tablespace to ASM. Of the steps
listed earlier, the control file and spfile relocation efforts need an outage window.
All other activities can be done while the database is online. We encourage you to
perform the redo log activity prior to the cutover weekend. The same logic applies
for the temp tablespace move to ASM as well. Because we can easily ping pong
back and forth between ASM and the file system, you should reduce the stress
during the cutover weekend and perform these two tasks beforehand. Oracle fully
supports a hybrid ASM and file system database placement configuration. The
cookbook approach to moving the redo logs and temporary tablespaces to ASM is
available in the subsequent sections of this chapter.

How to Move the Temporary Tablespace to ASM

The temporary tablespace also needs to be moved from file system to ASM.
Remember that RMAN does not back up the temporary tablespace. The easiest way
to move the temporary tablespace to ASM is to create a new tablespace and move
all the database accounts to use the new temporary tablespace:

```
create temporary tablespace temp_asm tempfile '+DATA' size 4g autoextend on
maxsize 32000m;'
alter database default temporary tablespace temp_asm;
```

If a database account was created specifying the temporary tablespace explicitly,
you will have to modify these accounts to the newly created temporary tablespace.
In the following example, we are relocating the system account's default tablespace
to the new temporary tablespace:

```
alter user system temporary tablespace temp_asm;
```

As the final step, we need to drop the previous temporary tablespace. If the drop
of the temporary tablespace takes too long, you can query the V$SORT_USAGE
view for consumers of the temporary tablespace.

Alternatively, we can add the new temp files to ASM and drop the old temp files. First, we will query the V$TEMPFILE dictionary view to identify the temp file we want to drop from the file system:

```
SQL> select * from v$tempfile;
     FILE# CREATION_CHANGE# CREATION_        TS#      RFILE# STATUS  ENABLED
---------- ---------------- --------- ---------- ---------- ------- ----------
     BYTES       BLOCKS CREATE_BYTES BLOCK_SIZE
---------- ---------- ------------ ----------
NAME
--------------------------------------------------------------------------------
         2          2274361 23-SEP-11          3          2 ONLINE  READ WRITE
1.7180E+10    2097152  1.7180E+10       8192
/zfs/dev/tempfile/temp01.dbf
```

In this example, we will add another temp file to the +DATA_EXAD disk group and drop the old temp file that existed on the file system:

```
SQL> alter tablespace temp add tempfile '+DATA_EXAD' size 8g;
Tablespace altered.

SQL> alter tablespace temp drop tempfile 2;
Tablespace altered.
```

How to Move the Spfile to ASM

Moving the spfile to ASM is a simple process. We can leverage several techniques to achieve our end goal. We can create the spfile from pfile and specify the location inside ASM, restore the spfile from our last backup to ASM, or copy the spfile with asmcmd to the DATA disk group. The easiest way is to leverage asmcmd:

```
+ASM1 - oracle: asmcmd cp
/u01/app/oracle/product/11.2.0/dbhome_1/dbs/spfiledev.ora
+DBFS_DG/toolsdev/spfiletoolsdev.ora
```

Once you copy the spfile from the file system to ASM, you need to update the contents of the OCR to reflect the new location:

```
srvctl modify database -d DEV -p +DATA_EXAD/dev/spfiledev.ora
```

As a precautionary measure, you can shut down and restart the database to make sure you are able to restart the database with the spfile inside of ASM:

```
srvctl stop database -d DEV
srvctl start database -d DEV
```

As a general rule, you may want to consider creating a backup pfile to a file system before touching the spfile.

How to Move a Tablespace from One Disk Group to Another

Often we have to move a tablespace or data file from one disk group to another because we either ran out of space in the existing disk group or the existing disk group does not provide the level of IOPs and throughput necessary for the database workload.

To move a tablespace from one disk group to another, we must take tablespaces offline, copy the data files from one disk group to the other, rename the data files for the tablespace, and bring the tablespace back online. For large tablespaces, the amount of downtime required to copy data files from one disk group to another can take hours or even days. We can introduce tablespace recovery in the equation to reduce the downtime. We can copy the tablespace from one disk group to another, rename the data files for the tablespace, and as the final step recover the tablespace to forward the System Change Number (SCN) to be consistent with the database. Again, for small tablespaces, this approach is perfectly acceptable because the amount of downtime will be minimal. The amount of downtime to perform the final recovery step can be excessive when we talking about rolling forward a half day or a full day's worth of database activity.

As DBAs working with ASM, especially working in the RAC world, we should have high availability and minimal downtime in mind with everything we do. To move a tablespace with minimal downtime, we need to introduce incremental backups to reduce the downtime. In our test case, we expose four sets of scripts: r1.sql, r2.rman, r3.rman, and rf.rman. Here are the steps:

1. r1.rman performs the image copy of the tablespace.

2. r2.rman performs the incremental backup for the tablespace.

3. r3.rman performs the incremental update (recovery) in the new tablespace on the new disk group. We can perform steps r2.rman and r3.rman as many times as we need to reduce our downtime needed for rf.rman.

4. rf.rman, which stands for RMAN final, executes the final step, where we take the tablespace offline, switch the tablespace to copy, recover the new tablespace on the new disk group, and bring the tablespace back online.

In the r1.rman script, we simply copy the tablespace called ck as an image copy from the DATA disk group to the RECO disk group:

```
r1.rman
backup as copy incremental level 0 tag=MOVE_RECO format '+RECO_EXAD'
tablespace ck;
```

As a second step, we will perform an incremental backup for the tablespace. In our test case, we perform the incremental backup to the file system on /u01. The bkups subdirectory is a symbolic link that points to the NFS mount point. Alternatively, we can perform the backup to an ASM disk group:

r2.rman

```
BACKUP INCREMENTAL LEVEL 1 FOR RECOVER OF COPY WITH TAG 'MOVE_RECO' format
'/u01/app/oracle/admin/TOOLSDEV/bkups/%d.%s.%p.%t.L1.4R.DB' tablespace ck;
```

As a third step, we perform our incremental update to the new ck tablespace in the new disk group. Tags are instrumental in performing incremental updates.

r3.rman

```
recover copy of tablespace ck with tag 'MOVE_RECO';
```

We can repeat steps r2.rman and r3.rman as often as we need to keep the newly copied tablespace as current as possible. When we can get a brief outage window or when we can quiesce the tablespace, we can perform the rf.rman final step. As you can see next, the final step takes the tablespace offline, switches the tablespace to the copy image that we have been recovering, recovers the new tablespace, and brings the new tablespace on the new disk group online:

```
-- Final Steps (rf=rman final)
TOOLSDEV1 - oracle: cat rf.rman
sql "alter tablespace ck offline";
switch tablespace ck to copy;
recover tablespace ck;
sql "alter tablespace ck online";
```

Executing the rf.rman final step yields the following output:

```
sql statement: alter tablespace ck offline
sql "alter tablespace ck offline";
switch tablespace ck to copy;

switch tablespace ck to copy;

using target database control file instead of recovery catalog
datafile 11 switched to datafile copy "+RECO_EXAD/toolsdev/datafile/
ck.19624.778149277"

RMAN> sql "alter tablespace ck online";

sql statement: alter tablespace ck online
RMAN-00571: ===========================================================
RMAN-00569: =============== ERROR MESSAGE STACK FOLLOWS ===============
RMAN-00571: ===========================================================
RMAN-03009: failure of sql command on default channel at 03/17/2012
```

```
08:41:50
RMAN-11003: failure during parse/execution of SQL statement:
alter tablespace ck online
ORA-01113: file 11 needs media recovery
ORA-01110: data file 11: '+RECO_EXAD/toolsdev/datafile/
ck.19624.778149277'

RMAN> recover tablespace ck;

Starting recover at 17-MAR-12 08:41:59
allocated channel: ORA_DISK_1
channel ORA_DISK_1: SID=136 instance=TOOLSDEV1 device type=DISK
...
...
allocated channel: ORA_DISK_6
channel ORA_DISK_6: SID=169 instance=TOOLSDEV1 device type=DISK

starting media recovery
media recovery complete, elapsed time: 00:00:02
Finished recover at 17-MAR-12 08:42:02

RMAN> sql "alter tablespace ck online";
sql statement: alter tablespace ck online
```

After we execute rf.rman as the final step, the tablespace is now running from the new disk group. You can leverage this same technique to do the following:

■ Move a data file from one ASM disk group to another disk group

■ Move a tablespace from file system to an ASM disk group

■ Move a data file from file system to an ASM disk group

Create Multiplexed Redo Logs

From time to time, DBAs need to resize redo logs for optimal performance. The size of online redo log files depends on the amount of redo the database generates. As a general rule, we should not see a log switch more than once every 20 minutes. If you have excessive redo log switches (greater than three to four in an hour), you should consider creating new redo groups and drop the old redo groups. Unfortunately, we cannot resize online redo logs. It is reasonable to see a redo log in the range of a hundred megabytes to several gigabytes in size. To create new redo logs, you can leverage the alter database add logfile command:

```
> ck_add_redo 1000m
set echo on
alter database add logfile thread 1 group 11 ('+data02','+fra02') size 1000m;
```

```
alter database add logfile thread 1 group 12 ('+data02','+fra02') size 1000m;
alter database add logfile thread 1 group 13 ('+data02','+fra02') size 1000m;
alter database add logfile thread 1 group 14 ('+data02','+fra02') size 1000m;

alter database add logfile thread 2 group 21 ('+data02','+fra02') size 1000m;
alter database add logfile thread 2 group 22 ('+data02','+fra02') size 1000m;
alter database add logfile thread 2 group 23 ('+data02','+fra02') size 1000m;
alter database add logfile thread 2 group 24 ('+data02','+fra02') size 1000m;
...
Continue for each RAC instance
```

As a best practice, we should multiplex redo log groups with one member in the DATA and FRA disk groups; we should also at a minimum have at least four groups for each thread.

For standby redo logs (SRL), we do not need to multiplex them. We just need to have one SRL more than the total number of redo groups for the entire database. An SRL should be created on the fastest disk group possible; it does not need to belong to a specific thread. SRLs should be created on both the primary and standby databases. As a best practice, SRLs should be created on the primary database prior to the Data Guard instantiation process. SRLs will automatically be copied to the physical standby. The syntax to create an SRL looks like this:

```
alter database add standby logfile group 31 ('+data') size 2048m;
alter database add standby logfile group 32 ('+data') size 2048m;
alter database add standby logfile group 33 ('+data') size 2048m;
...
alter database add standby logfile group 39 ('+data') size 2048m;
```

Dropping existing redo log groups is a little more tricky. You just need to make sure that the redo group you are dropping is not current or active. If it is not active, you can drop the redo log group with the following command:

```
alter database drop logfile group #;
```

To switch between redo logs, you can consider leveraging one of these three commands:

```
alter system switch logfile;
alter system archivelog current;
alter system checkpoint global;
```

Summary

ASM is a storage management solution from Oracle Corporation that has made the storage management layer more suitable and flexible. In this chapter, we discussed this technology and you learned how the ASM storage management solution differs from other solutions available on the market as well as how ASM complements RAC.

This chapter covered using ASM with an RDBMS instance, starting with the basic installation and configuration through maintenance administration and performance monitoring. While configuring the RDBMS instance using DBCA, we followed the best practice of using two disk groups—one for data and the other for FRA. Regardless of whether the database is a clustered solution or a single instance, the configuration and deployment of ASM are no different. We covered the various methods in which data can be migrated from a non-ASM-based Oracle database into ASM. Finally, we looked into the monitoring options.

CHAPTER

6

ASMLIB Concepts and Overview

Early in the design of ASM, Oracle decided that an alternative to the standard operating system interface for device management, disk discovery, and provisioning was necessary and that this mechanism needed to be easily integrated into ASM. The core concept was to produce a storage management interface called ASMLIB. ASMLIB is not required to run ASM; it is instead an add-on module that simplifies the management and discovery of ASM disks.

This chapter covers the ASMLIB layers and their corresponding benefits.

Benefits of ASMLIB

The objective of ASMLIB is to provide a more efficient mechanism for managing disks and input/output (I/O) processing of ASM storage. ASMLIB provides a set of interdependent functions that are implemented in a layered fashion. From an implementation perspective, these functions are grouped into two sets of functions:

- Device discovery
- I/O processing

Each function group is dependent on the existence of the lower-level group. For example, device discovery functions are the lowest-layer functions.

Device Discovery

Device discovery identifies and names the storage devices that are operated on by higher-level functions. The discovery function makes the characteristics of the disk available to ASM. Disks discovered through ASMLIB do not need to be available through normal operating system interfaces.

The device discovery function takes a discovery string as input from the user and then performs a disk discovery. The output from this procedure is a set of all qualified disks. In a Real Application Clusters (RAC) environment, the discover procedure executes the discovery function on the node where the procedure was issued.

Disk Management and Discovery

ASMLIB automatically takes the ASM disk name from the name that the ASMLIB administrative tool provides. This simplifies adding disks and correlating OS names with ASM names; also, pre-naming disks eliminates erroneous disk management activities. The user can manually change the name by using the NAME clause while issuing a CREATE DISKGROUP or ADD DISK statement. The default discovery string for ASM is NULL, so with ASMLIB in place, all disks are automatically discovered if NULL is kept as the discovery string. Because the user does not even need to modify the ASM_DISKSTRING, this makes disk discovery much more straightforward.

The ASMLIB permissions are persistent across reboot, and in the event of major/minor number changes, ASMLIB will continue to find its labeled disks. In RAC environments, the disk identification and discovery process is similar to that of a single-instance environment. Once the disks are labeled on one node, the other clustered nodes simply use the default disk discovery string, and discovery is seamless.

I/O Processing

The current standard I/O model (one where ASMLIB is not implemented) imposes OS central processing unit (CPU) overhead partly because of mode and context switches. The deployment of ASMLIB reduces the number of state transitions from kernel-to-user mode by employing a more efficient I/O scheduling and call processing mechanism. A single call to ASMLIB can submit and reap multiple I/Os. This dramatically reduces the number of calls to the operating system when performing I/O. Additionally, all the processes in an instance can use one I/O handle to access the same disk. This eliminates multiple open calls and multiple file descriptors.

The ASMLIB I/O processing function, which is implemented as a device driver within the operating system kernel, provides an optimized asynchronous interface for scheduling I/O operations and managing I/O operation completion events. These functions, in effect, extend the operating system interface. Consequently, the I/O processing functions must be implemented as a device driver within the operating system kernel.

NOTE
ASMLIB does not use the kernel asynchronous (async) I/O calls, such as the standard io_submit(2) and io_getevents(2) system calls. In fact, it does not use kioctx types at all. ASMLIB uses the interface provided by the ASMLIB kernel driver. Async I/O is automatically used with ASMLIB.

Reduced Overhead

ASMLIB provides the capability for a process (ASM RBAL) to perform a global open/close on the disks that are being dropped or closed. Every file and device currently open on the system has an open file descriptor, and the system has a finite number (defined at the system level) of these file descriptors. ASMLIB reduces the number of open file descriptors on the system, thus making it less likely that the system will run out of global file descriptors. Also, the open and close operations are reduced, ensuring orderly cleanup of file descriptors when storage configurations change. A side benefit of this capability is that the database starts up faster. Without ASMLIB, file descriptors often cannot be cleaned up for dropped disks until ASM instances are shut down. This is because idle database foreground processes, which have open file descriptors, never get around to closing file descriptors.

ASMLIB performance benefits are evident when the CPU usage on the server is very high (85 to 90 percent); this is when ASMLIB's reduced context switches and efficient reaping of I/Os really help to minimize CPU overhead. Also, for very big databases with a large number of open data files, ASMLIB efficiently handles file descriptors and thus reduces the number of open file descriptors on the system, making it less likely to run out of global file descriptors. Also, the open and close operations are reduced, ensuring orderly cleanup of file descriptors when the storage configuration changes.

Although it helps reduce CPU overhead, ASMLIB is foremost a device management tool used to simplify ASM disk administration. This is especially evident when large clusters of four or more nodes are being deployed. Once ASMLIB is used to mark the ASM disks one node, the remaining nodes in the cluster only need to scan and discover the devices. The repetitive administrative and error-prone tasks needed to manage OS devices for RAC are significantly minimized.

ASMLIB Implementation

This section will cover the essentials of ASMLIB packaging and implementation.
ASMLIB consists of two main components:

- **ASMLib** This consists of a userspace library with config tools. Since the userspace library contains Oracle header files, it is distributed as a binary-only module.

- **oracleasm.ko** A kernel module that implements the asm device for the asm device via /dev/oracleasm.

Note that there is only one asm library for the various Linux platforms, and this library is opened by ASM and Oracle Database processes. This library also interacts with the OS through the /dev/oracleasm. Further note that the userspace library is opaque to the underlying OS version; however, the kernel module and device driver are kernel and OS dependent

ASMLIB Installation

Oracle's ASMLIB software is available from the Oracle Technology Network (OTN) at http://otn.oracle.com. Users are encouraged to go to the ASMLIB site to download the appropriate Linux rpm files for their platform.

Three ASMLIB packages are available for each Linux platform. For example, the following three packages are for the Intel (x86_64) architecture (as of this writing):

Package	Description
oracleasm-support-2.1.7-1.el5.x86_64.rpm	This package contains the command-line utilities.
oracleasmlib-2.0.4-1.el5.x86_64.rpm	This is the core ASMLIB library.
oracleasm-2.6.18-274.7.1.el5-2.0.5-1.el5.x86_64.rpm	This is the kernel driver and is kernel dependent.

Choose the correct kernel driver rpm file based on the uname –r command on the system to be installed. For example, if the OS is Red Hat Enterprise Linux 5 AS and the kernel is 2.6.18-274.7.1.el5, then accordingly choose the suite of packages associated with this kernel:

- oracleasm-2.6.18-274.7.1.el5-2.0.5-1.el5.x86_64.rpm

- oracleasm-2.6.18-274.7.1.el5xen-2.0.5-1.el5.x86_64.rpm

- oracleasm-2.6.18-274.7.1.el5debug-2.0.5-1.el5.x86_64.rpm

- oracleasm-2.6.18-274.7.1.el5-debuginfo-2.0.5-1.el5.x86_64.rpm

The ASMLib kernel driver is included in the Unbreakable Enterprise Kernel, thus no driver package needs to be installed when using this kernel. However, the oracleasm-support and oracleasmlib packages still need to be installed. These can be obtained through the Oracle Unbreakable Linux Network (ULN), available at the following location:

www.oracle.com/technetwork/server-storage/linux/uln-095759.html

Note that the version number listed in the ASMLib kernel package is the Linux kernel version that was used to compile the driver. Install the required rpm files using the rpm –Uvh command. For example, if the platform is the Intel x86_64 architecture and the kernel is 2.6.18-274.7.1-el, then the following would need to be installed:

```
[root@racnode1]# rpm –Uvh oracleasm-support-2.1.7-1.el5.x86_64.rpm \
oracleasmlib-2.0.4-1.el5.x86_64.rpm  \
oracleasm-2.6.18-274.7.1.el5-2.0.5-1.el5.x86_64.rpm
```

Installing ASMLIB for Unbreakable Linux Network

For systems registered with Oracle's Unbreakable Linux Network, all the ASMLIB software can be downloaded directly from ULN. This greatly simplifies ASMLIB installation and upgrades.

The ASMLIB rpm file is part of the Oracle Software for Enterprise Linux channel. A system must be added to this channel to install the library package. This requires that users log in at the ULN website, https://linux.oracle.com, and select the Systems tag. This brings up a list of systems registered with ULN. Select the system that will install the ASMLIB package. Then, select the Subscribe button under the Oracle Software for Enterprise Linux link. The system is now able to download the ASMLIB rpm file.

Once the system is registered with ULN, it will automatically download (and optionally installs) the new upgrade versions of all the ASMLIB packages via the up2date –u command. Log in as root and run the following:

```
# up2date -i oracleasm-support oracleasmlib oracleasm-'uname -r'
```

Upgrading ASMLIB

In certain cases the Linux kernel needs to upgraded. When this occurs, the ASMLIB kernel driver needs to be upgraded as well. The oracleasm update-driver command can be used to download and install the latest ASMLib driver for the installed kernel. This program, which is a front end for linkoracleasm:oracleasm-update-driver, queries the Oracle Technology Network. It supports drivers available via the Unbreakable Linux Network and on the Oracle Technology Network. If no kernel version is specified for the command, it will update the currently running kernel. If multiple kernels are installed, this command can be used to update multiple kernel versions.

To upgrade ASMLIB, the system administrator can take the following steps. Note that this is strictly a software upgrade and no disk labels are manipulated. Also, this is a local node upgrade; therefore, for RAC environments, each individual node should be upgraded.

1. Shut down ASM.

2. Execute /usr/sbin/oracleasm stop.

3. Execute /usr/sbin/oracleasm update-driver, as follows:

```
[root@racnode1 ~]# /usr/sbin/oracleasm update-driver
Kernel:        2.6.18-194.8.1.0.1.el5 x86_64
Driver name:   oracleasm-2.6.18-194.8.1.0.1.el5

Fetching Obsoletes list for channel: el5_x86_64_latest...
########################################

Fetching rpm headers...
########################################

Name                                 Version       Rel
---------------------------------------------------------------
oracleasm-2.6.18-194.8.1.0.1.el5     2.0.5         1.el5        x86_64

Testing package set / solving RPM inter-dependencies...
########################################
oracleasm-2.6.18-194.8.1.0.       ################ Done.
Preparing              ############################# [100%]

Installing...
1:oracleasm-2.6.18-194.8.########################## [100%]
```

4. Execute /usr/sbin/oracleasm start.

5. Start up ASM.

Setting Up and Configuring ASMLIB

Once the appropriate Linux rpm files are installed, the ASMLIB installation places a utility in the /usr/sbin and /etc/init.d directory called oracleasm. As a best practice, the /etc/init.d/oracleasm utility should be used only to configure, enable, and disable ASMLIB. The /usr/sbin utility should be used as the front-end tool to perform all device management activities, such as to create, delete, list, and scan disks. The next step is to set up and configure ASMLIB. Typically, a system administrator with root access performs this step.

Execute the /etc/init.d/oracleasm script with the configure option. This sets up and configures ASMLIB for the system. You must execute this command on each node of RAC cluster. In our example, ASM is running as the grid user and the asmadmin group:

```
[root@racnode1]# /usr/init.d/oracleasm configure
Configuring the Oracle ASM library driver.
This will configure the on-boot properties of the Oracle ASM library driver.
The following questions will determine whether the driver is loaded on boot
and what permissions it will have. The current values will be shown in
brackets ('[]'). Hitting without typing an answer will keep that current
value. Ctrl-C will abort.
Default user to own the driver interface: grid
Default group to own the driver interface []: asmadmin
Start Oracle ASM library driver on boot (y/n) [n]: y
Fix permissions of Oracle ASM disks on boot (y/n) [y]: y
Writing Oracle ASM library driver configuration [ OK ]: OK
Creating /dev/oracleasm
mount point [ OK ]
 Loading module "oracleasm" [ OK ]
 Mounting ASMLIB driver filesystem [ OK ]
 Scanning system for ASM disks [ OK ]
```

At the end of this configuration, a virtual file system (specific to ASMLIB) called /dev/oraclesasm is created and mounted. This file system has two subdirectories called disks and iid. The disks subdirectory lists the ASMLIB scanned and present on the system. The iid directory contains metadata information about all instances (ASM and databases) that registered with the ASMLIB. These directories are for internal use only, and should not be manipulated in any way by users.

Finally, the configuration will load the oracleasm.o driver module and mount the ASM driver file system because the on-boot load of the module was selected during the configuration.

Now that ASMLIB is installed, the automatic startup of ASMLIB can be enabled or disabled manually with the enable and disable options. Using the /etc/init.d/ oracleasm utility, the process runs as follows:

```
[root@racnode1]# /etc/init.d/oracleasm enable
 Writing Oracle ASM library driver configuration [ OK ]
 Loading module "oracleasm" [ OK ]
 Mounting ASMLIB driver filesystem [ OK ]
 Scanning system for ASM disks [ OK ]
```

Managing Disks in ASMLIB

After the storage administrator provides disk devices to the server, they become available to the server and can be seen in the /proc/partitions virtual file on Linux.

The oracleasm requires that disks have a disk partition defined. However, oracleasm has a whitelist of the devices that do not need to be partitioned. Devices in this whitelist include RAM disks and device mapper (DM) devices.

Creating ASMLIB Disks

Once the system administrator appropriately partitions the disk devices using the Linux fdisk utility, each disk device is ready to be configured as an ASMLIB disk (in other words, the system administrator creates an ASMLIB disk). The administrator does this using the oracleasm createdisk command. The createdisk command takes two input parameters—the user-defined disk name followed by the device name—as follows:

```
[root@racnode1]#/usr/sbin/oracleasm createdisk VOL1 /dev/sdg1
 Creating Oracle ASM disk "VOL1" [ OK ]
```

Disk names are limited to 24 characters. They must start with a letter but may otherwise consist of any ASCII characters, including capital letters, numbers, and underscores.

Each disk successfully created is considered a *marked* ASMLIB disk and is listed in the oracleasm file system, /dev/oracleasm/disks.

You can query disk devices to determine whether they are valid ASMLIB disks. To do so, use the following oracleasm querydisk commands. The querydisk command is applicable to both the raw device and the ASMLIB disk. The oracleasm querydisk command has two options: the -d and -p options. The -d option displays the device number of the queried disk. The -p option attempts to locate matching device paths if the blkid(8) tool is installed.

```
[root@racnode1]# /usr/sbin/oracleasm querydisk /dev/sdg1
 Checking if device "/dev/sdg" is an Oracle ASM disk [ OK ]
```

```
[root@racnode1]# /usr/sbin/oracleasm querydisk VOL1
 Checking for ASM disk "VOL1" [ OK ]
```

Alternatively, all the disks marked and created using ASMLIB can be listed using the following oracleasm listdisks command:

```
[root@racnode1]# /usr/sbin/oracleasm listdisks
 VOL1
 VOL2
 VOL3
```

If a disk device is not an ASMLIB, the following is displayed:

```
[root@racnode1]# /usr/sbin/oracleasm querydisk /dev/sdh1
 Checking if device "/dev/sdh1" is an Oracle ASM disk [FAILED]
```

Disks that are no longer needed by ASM can be unmarked and deleted using the oracleasm deletedisk command:

```
[root@racnode1]# /usr/sbin/oracleasm deletedisk VOL1
 Deleting Oracle ASM disk "VOL1" [ OK ]
```

When ASMLIB is deployed in a RAC environment, the shared disk architecture of RAC allows the createdisk command to be run on only one node; all other nodes of the RAC cluster simply need to pick up the disk list via an ASMLIB scan command. For example, in a two-node RAC cluster, node 1 can mark an ASMLIB disk and node 2 can then execute a scan of the ASMLIB disks to discover the marked ASMLIB disks. This process mitigates the need to discover and set up the disks manually on each node and provides each disk with a unique clusterwide name.

```
[root@racnode1]# /usr/sbin/oracleasm createdisk VOL1 /dev/sdg1
 Creating Oracle ASM disk "VOL1" [ OK ]
[root@racnode2]# /usr/sbin/oracleasm scandisks
 Scanning system for ASM disks [ OK ]
```

NOTE
The ASMLIB scandisks command should not be used against devices that are currently open and in use (that is, are part of an open disk group). Running this command against open disks will close and reopen them, which causes the disk group to be dismounted and any database using the disk group to abort. Users should instead run oracleasm scandisks specifically for any newly configured or modified disks (for example, oracleasm scandisk /dev/sdxx).

After the appropriate ASMLIB disks are created, the ASM init.ora parameter ASM_DISKSTRING can either be left with the default (NULL) or set to 'ORCL:*'. Once this is set, ASM will discover the disks as follows:

```
SQL> SELECT NAME, LIBRARY, PATH FROM V$ASM_DISK;
  NAME           LIBRARY                     PATH
  -----------    ------------------------    ------------------------
  VOL1           ASM Library Generic Linux   ORCL:VOL1
  VOL2           ASM Library Generic Linux   ORCL:VOL2
  VOL3           ASM Library Generic Linux   ORCL:VOL3
```

Note that if ASMLIB is not being used, then the preceding query returns "System" under the LIBRARY column. See the "Troubleshooting ASMLIB" section in this chapter for more details.

Renaming Disks

The renamedisk command is used for changing the label of an existing member without losing data. Note that the modification of the disk must be done while ASM is not accessing the disk. Therefore, the disk group must be dismounted, and in an RAC environment, all ASM nodes in the cluster must have dismounted the disk group as well. Corruption may result if a renamedisk operation is done while any ASM instance is accessing the disk to be relabeled. Because this renamedisk command is dangerous, ASM indicates this by printing out a gentle message after the command is executed:

```
[root@racnode1]# /usr/sbin/oracleasm renamedisk /dev/sdb3  VOL1
WARNING: Changing the label of an disk marked for ASM is a very dangerous
operation. If this is really what you mean to do, you must ensure that all
Oracle and ASM instances have ceased using this disk.  Otherwise, you may
LOSE DATA. If you are really sure you wish to change the label and are sure
that all of your Oracle and ASM instances have ceased using the disk, rerun
this command with the '-f' option.
```

The renamedisk command takes two parameters: the raw device name followed by the ASM disk name.

Discovering Disks

The command /usr/sbin/oracleasm-discover is a simple utility that determines which devices Oracle's Linux ASMLIB sees during discovery. This command is more of a debugging tool to validate that the discovery is listing all the required disks. This command also lists the maximum I/O size (maxio) per disk—that is, the maximum I/O, in sectors, that ASMLIB can send to the device as one command.

```
[root@racnode1]#/usr/sbin/oracleasm-discover 'ORCL:*'
Using ASMLib from /opt/oracle/extapi/32/asm/orcl/1/libasm.so
```

```
[ASM Library - Generic Linux, version 2.0.0 (KABI_V1)]
Discovered disk: ORCL:VOL1 [819200 blocks (419430400 bytes), maxio 512]
Discovered disk: ORCL:VOL2 [1955808 blocks (1001373696 bytes), maxio 512]
```

The maximum I/O size comes from the small computer system interface (SCSI) host bus adapter (HBA) driver and anything else in the disk device chain. In the preceding case, maxio equals 512—that is, 512 byte sectors, or 256K. If maxio shows low values, such as 128, then it is possible that intermediary components, such as multipathing drivers or HBA drivers, may be the limiting factor.

The following script is useful to map ASMLIB devices to OS devices:

```
#!/bin/bash
 for asmlibdisk in 'ls /dev/oracleasm/disks/*'
  do
   echo "ASMLIB disk name: $asmlibdisk"
   asmdisk='kfed read $asmlibdisk | grep dskname | tr -s ' '| cut -f2 -d' ''
   echo "ASM disk name: $asmdisk"
   majorminor='ls -l $asmlibdisk | tr -s ' ' | cut -f5,6 -d' ''
   device='ls -l /dev | tr -s ' ' | grep "$majorminor" | cut -f10 -d' ''
   echo "Device path: /dev/$device"
   done
```

Migrating to ASMLIB

There may be cases where you need to convert a "member" ASM raw disk to an ASMLIB disk; for example, you may need to do so when installing ASMLIB after the ASM infrastructure is in place. Conversely, if you're de-installing ASMLIB, you can convert an ASMLIB disk to a standard ASM disk. All this can be done without destroying the data on the disk. However, the disk group must be dismounted before the conversion because ASM cannot be actively using the disk.

This conversion works without destroying data because of the structures on the disk and what ASM reads on disk open. ASM reads the header off of the disk and recognizes the disk group to which it belongs. When a disk is added to a disk group, ASM writes several things on disk. Two of the most important items are the disk marker (or tag) and the ASMLIB label. All ASM disks have the tag ORCLDISK stamped on them. If the tag already exists, the disk is either currently or was formerly in use by ASM. This tag can be created by ASM or ASMLIB. For example, when ASM initially uses a disk as a raw device via disk group creation, ASM automatically adds the tag. Conversely, ASMLIB adds this tag when a disk is configured by the ASMLIB command /usr/sbin/oracleasm createdisk. Regardless of which tool creates the tag, once this tag is added, the disk is considered "marked."

The second part of the disk header that is relevant to ASMLIB is the ASMLIB label. This string of 24 characters allotted for ASMLIB is used to identify the disk. When the disk is configured by ASMLIB using the /usr/sbin/oracleasm createdisk command, the associated label is written to the device. Note that ASM preserves the disk's contents, but it does write to this section reserved for ASMLIB.

The following is a sample dump of an ASM disk (without ASMLIB) that was incorporated into a disk group. Notice the ASM disk name in the header, DATA_0002:

```
[root@racnode1]# dd if=/dev/asmdisk17 bs=128 count=1 |od -a
0000000 soh stx soh soh nul nul nul nul stx nul nul nul    : stx   " dc4
0000020 nul nul nul nul nul nul nul nul nul nul nul nul nul nul nul nul
0000040  O   R   C   L   D   I   S   K nul nul nul nul nul nul nul nul
0000060 nul nul nul nul nul nul nul nul nul nul nul nul nul nul nul nul
0000100 nul nul dle  nl stx nul soh etx  D   A   T   A   _   0   0   0
0000120  2 nul nul nul nul nul nul nul nul nul nul nul nul nul nul nul
0000140 nul nul nul nul nul nul nul nul  D   A   T   A nul nul nul nul
```

The following is a sample dump of an ASMLIB disk created using the following /usr/sbin/oracleasm createdisk command. Notice that VOL1 is appended to the ORCLDISK label:

```
[root@racnode1]# /usr/sbin/oracleasm createdisk VOL1 /dev/sdc3
Dump of disk header after ASMLIB, via oracleasm createdisk VOL1 /dev/
asmdisk26.
[usupport@jfrac2 bin]$ dd if=/dev/asmdisk26 bs=128 count=1 |od -a
0000000 nul nul nul nul nul nul nul nul nul nul nul nul  V   O   N   5
0000020 nul nul nul nul nul nul nul nul nul nul nul nul nul nul nul nul
0000040  O   R   C   L   D   I   S   K   V   O   L   1 nul nul nul nul
0000060 nul nul nul nul nul nul nul nul nul nul nul nul nul nul nul nul
0000100 nul nul dle  nl stx nul soh etx  D   A   T   A   _   0   0   0
0000120  2 nul nul nul nul nul nul nul nul nul nul nul nul nul nul nul
0000140 nul nul nul nul nul nul nul nul  D   A   T   A nul nul nul nul
```

In this example, the tag ORCLDISK and the label VOL1 are stamped to the disk. The next time that ASMLIB scans for disks, it will see the tag ORCLDISK and the label VOL1 and create an ASMLIB disk-to-device mapping using the name VOL1. Subsequently, ASM will discover this disk via the ASMLIB driver. If the disk were not initially managed by ASMLIB—that is, if it were instead managed by ASM's block device (non-ASMLIB) access—then when ASM discovers the disk, it would detect that no ASMLIB label exists, bypass this section of the header, and open the device as a native (non-ASMLIB) ASM disk. This is why a disk can move from ASMLIB access to raw device access with no problems.

Using ASMLIB and Multipathing Utilities

As was stated in Chapter 4, multipathing drivers generally virtualize subpaths using pseudo devices. During disk discovery, ASMLIB uses the pseudo file /proc/partitions. This is a Linux file that records all the devices and partitions presented to the machine. To function correctly with multipathing, ASMLIB must operate only on the pseudo devices. Thus, the behavior of the ASMLIB discovery must be altered to leverage the pseudo devices. You can configure this behavior in the file /etc/sysconfig/oracleasm by changing two parameters:

- **ORACLEASM_SCANORDER**   Dictates the ASMLIB scan order of the devices, using the generic prefix

- **ORACLEASM_SCANEXCLUDE**   Indicates which devices should not be discovered by ASMLIB

For example, if you are configuring ASMLIB with EMC's PowerPath, you can use the following setup:

```
ORACLEASM_SCANEXCLUDE=sd
ORACLEASM_SCANORDER=emcpower
```

In this example, ASMLIB scans EMC PowerPath disks identified under /dev/emcpower* and excludes all the devices in /dev/sd*. Consult your multipathing vendor for details and a support matrix.

The following is an example of an /etc/sysconfig/oracleasm file:

```
# This is a configuration file for automatic loading of the Oracle
# Automatic Storage Management library kernel driver.  It is generated
# By running /usr/sbin/oracleasm configure.  Please use that method
# to modify this file
# ORACLEASM_ENABELED: 'true' means to load the driver on boot.
ORACLEASM_ENABLED=true
#
# ORACLEASM_UID: Default user owning the /dev/oracleasm mount point.
ORACLEASM_UID=grid
#
# ORACLEASM_GID: Default group owning the /dev/oracleasm mount point.
ORACLEASM_GID=asmadmin
#
# ORACLEASM_SCANBOOT: 'true' means fix disk perms on boot
ORACLEASM_SCANBOOT=true
#
# ORACLEASM_CLEARBOOT: 'true' means clean old disk perms on boot
ORACLEASM_CLEARBOOT=true
#
# ORACLEASM_SCANORDER: Matching patterns to order disk scanning
ORACLEASM_SCANEXCLUDE=sd
ORACLEASM_SCANORDER=emcpower
```

Using ASMLIB and Device Mapper

I/O multipathing is the ability to access storage block devices via multiple paths from the host computer. To have high availability in storage access, you must make use of the I/O multipathing solution, which provides failover between I/O paths. Many of the multipathing solutions also provide load balancing of I/O between the I/O paths, which gives better performance. The path can be thought of a connection between a port on the host to a port on the target storage device. Many multipathing solutions are provided by various vendors. In this section, we are mainly going to talk about Linux multipathing based on Linux Device Mapper. Linux Device Mapper–based multipathing provides path failover and path load sharing capability on the redundant paths to the block device from the host. The block device could be of any type—SCSI, IDE, and so on.

User Case Scenario

A customer configures ASMLIB on Linux Device Mapper. There are three locations where device mapper devices exists. Which device should be used for ASMLIB?

- /dev/dm-*

- /dev/mpath/mpathN

- /dev/mapper/mpathN

ASMLib currently acknowledges devices only listed in /proc/partition. The only device mapper devices listed in /proc/partitions are the /dev/dm-* devices. However, these are not generated by default. In order to generate /dev/dm-* names appropriately, users will need to comment out the line in /etc/udev/rules.d/50-udev.rules that reads

```
KERNEL=="dm-[0-9]*", ACTION=="add", OPTIONS+="ignore_device"
```

like this:

```
# KERNEL=="dm-[0-9]*", ACTION=="add", OPTIONS+="ignore_device"
```

NOTE
The /dev/dm- devices are not named consistently across nodes in a cluster. For this reason, users should create ASMLib devices using the /dev/ mapper names. However, users do not need to change any permissions because ASMLib handles permissions for you.*

Troubleshooting ASMLIB

The section provides a top-down list of items to review and validate that ASMLIB is installed and working correctly.

1. Use the current release of ASMLIB. Verify the software versions. ASMLIB requires a driver exactly matching the running kernel, thus matching the oracleasm kernel package with the output of the uname –r command:

```
[rpm -qa | grep oracleasm
oracleasm-2.6.18-128.1.1.0.1.el5xen-2.0.5-1.el5
oracleasmlib-2.0.4-1.el5
oracleasm-support-2.1.2-1.el5
rpm -q oracleasm-'uname -r'
oracleasm-2.6.18-128.1.1.0.1.el5xen-2.0.5-1.el5
# uname -r
2.6.18-128.1.1.0.1.el5xen
```

Verify the ASMLIB installation as indicated in the installation documentation.

2. Make sure that the oracleasm configure command ran properly. Confirm this configuration as follows:

   a. Execute the lsmod command (as root) to show the loaded oracleasm module. The oracleasm module should be listed with a "Used by" column setting of 1.

   ```
   [root@racnode1]# lsmod |grep asm
   Module                Size  Used by    Not tainted
   oracleasm            16384   1
   ```

   b. Execute the command cat /proc/filesystems, and make sure that an entry named oracleasmfs exists in this file system listing.

   ```
   [oracle@racnode1]$ cat /proc/filesystems|grep oracleasm
   nodev    oracleasmfs
   ```

   c. Execute the command df –ha. This should show you that oracleasmfs is mounted on /dev/oracleasm:

   ```
   [oracle@racnode1]$ df -ha |grep oracleasm
   Filesystem       Size  Used  Avail Use%  Mounted on
   oracleasmfs         0     0      0    -   /dev/oracleasm
   ```

   d. Make sure that oracleasm createdisk was properly run for the candidate disks. To be used for ASM, a disk must be marked by the createdisk command. When a disk is "marked," a signature is written to the header of the disk—that is, the disk is stamped for ASM use. You can validate this by using the following commands:

■ Execute the oracleasm listdisks command. This command displays marked ASMLIB disks. This command will list all marked disks.

■ Execute the oracleasm querydisk command for each disk marked to ensure that each is marked.

3. Execute ls -l /dev/oracleasm/disks to ensure the ownership and permissions are grid:asmadmin (that is, the user and group used in the configure oracleasm configure command) for each disk name that was created using the oracleasm createdisk command:

```
[oracle@racnode1]$ ls -l /dev/oracleasm/disks
total 0
brw-rw----    1 grid    asmadmin    8,  32 Apr  9 16:09 VOL1
brw-rw----    1 grid    asmadmin    8,  48 Apr  9 16:09 VOL2
brw-rw----    1 grid    asmadmin    8,  64 Apr  9 16:09 VOL3
brw-rw----    1 grid    asmadmin    8,  80 Apr  9 16:10 VOL4
```

4. Verify that the ASMLIB discovery string (either at the ASM Configuration Assistant [ASMCA] prompt or in the ASM init.ora ASM_DISKSTRING parameter) is set to ORCL:* or to NULL. Also, if the ASM instance is active, check the ASM alert log to see whether the correct string is being used.

5. Use the Unix grep command against the ASM alert log to see whether ASM is displaying any messages regarding discovery. A successfully loaded ASMLIB will display the following general message (depending on the version):

```
Loaded ASM Library - Generic Linux, version 2.0.2 library
for ASMLIB interface
```

The following query shows disks that ASMLIB properly discovered:

```
SQL> SELECT LIBRARY, PATH FROM V$ASM_DISK;

LIBRARY                                         PATH
----------------------------------------------- -------------
ASM Library - Generic Linux, version 2.0.0.1   ORCL:VOL1
ASM Library - Generic Linux, version 2.0.0.1   ORCL:VOL2
ASM Library - Generic Linux, version 2.0.0.1   ORCL:VOL3
```

NOTE
If the query shows SYSTEM under the Library column, then the ASM_DISKSTRING is not set correctly—that is, ASMLIB is not used to access the disks. ASMLIB needs to access the disks through the diskstring ORCL:. Check ASM_DISKSTRING and verify that it is set to ORCL:* or to NULL:*

```
SQL> SELECT LIBRARY, PATH FROM V$ASM_DISK;

LIBRARY         PATH
--------------  -------------------------------------------
System          /dev/oracleasm/disks/DATA1D1
System          /dev/oracleasm/disks/DATA1D2
System          /dev/oracleasm/disks/DATA1D3
```

6. Look for errors:

   a. Use /usr/sbin/oracleasm-discover 'ORCL:*' to discover devices or watch for the following error messages in the ASM alert log:

   ```
   ORA-15186: ASMLIB error function = [asm_open],
   error = [1],  mesg = [Operation not permitted]
   ```

   This message usually means that the ASMLIB configuration permissions were incorrectly specified during the /usr/sbin/oracleasm configure stage.

NOTE
In its current implementation, ASMLIB creates devices in /dev/oracleasm/disks/. Setting a discovery string to /dev/oracleasm/disks/ causes ASM to use standard OS system calls to access the devices. It is not guaranteed that future versions of ASMLIB will continue to create entries in this location. Users should not set the ASM_DISKSTRING to /dev/oracleasm/disks/*.*

   b. Use strace to debug the command /usr/sbin/oracleasm-discover 'ORCL:*':

   ```
   strace -f -o asm_discover.out /usr/sbin/oracleasm-discover
   'ORCL:*'
   ```

   Check for the reference to library libasm.so:

   ```
   open("/opt/oracle/extapi/32/asm/orcl/1/libasm.so",
   O_RDONLY) = 3
   ```

   If you get

   ```
    open("/opt/oracle/extapi/32/asm/orcl/1/libasm.so",
   O_RDONLY) = -1 EACCES (Permission denied)
   ```

   check if the library exists or if the permissions are correct (755). Also validate that the directories in the path also have the correct permissions (755).

   ASM instance report errors ORA-604, ORA-15183, and ORA-15180 after deleting file libasm.so.

When all the files under /opt/oracle/extapi path are deleted, if ASMLIB is used, the following errors will be reported when mounting disk groups:

```
ORA-00604 : error occurred at recursive SQL level 2
ORA-15183 : ASMLIB initialization error [/opt/oracle/
extapi/64/asm/orcl/1/libasm.so]
```

c. ASMLIB provides additional logging for the following functional areas:

- **ENTRY** Function func call entry

- **EXIT** Function call exit

- **DISK** Disk information

- **REQUEST** I/O requests

- **BIO** BIOS backing I/O

- **IOC** ASM_IOCS

- **ABI** ABI entry points

The settings are recorded in the file /proc/fs/oracleasm. The following are the default values:

```
ENTRY deny
EXIT deny
DISK off
REQUEST off
BIO off
IOC off
ABI off
ERROR allow
```

The three possible values are deny, off, and allow.

You can change the logging by executing the following (note that this does not require the oracleasm service to be restarted):

```
echo "xxxx allow" > /proc/fs/oracleasm/log_mask
```

Here, xxxx is the function listed previously.

Typically, when users have problems accessing devices via the ASMLIB discovery string or cannot list ASMLIB disks, this is the result of a failure to install the right version of one of the three packages in the current Linux ASMLIB implementation, or due to missing or inability to access the library /opt/oracle/extapi/64/asm/orcl/1/ libasm.so. Also, if you're using a 32-bit Linux installation, you need to verify the permissions of the ASMLIB library file in /opt/oracle/extapi/32/asm/orcl/1/libasm.so.

Summary

ASMLIB is the support library for the ASM. ASMLIB provides an Oracle database using ASM with more efficient access to disk groups. The purpose of ASMLIB, which is an add-on to ASM, is to provide an alternative interface to identify and access block devices. These features provide benefits such as improved manageability and performance as well as greater integrity.

CHAPTER
7

ASM Files, Aliases, and Security

When an ASM disk group is created, a hierarchical file system structure is created. This hierarchical layout is very similar to the Unix or Windows file system hierarchy. ASM files, stored within this file system structure, are the objects that RDBMS instances access. They come in the form of data files, control files, spfiles, and redo log files, and several other file types. The RDBMS treats ASM-based database files just like standard file system files.

ASM Filenames

When you create a database file (using the create tablespace, add datafile, or add logfile command) or even an archive log file, ASM explicitly creates the ASM file in the disk group specified. The following example illustrates how database files can be created in an ASM disk group:

```
SQL> CREATE TABLESPACE ISHAN DATAFILE '+DATA' SIZE 10GB;
```

This command creates a data file in the DATA disk group. ASM filenames are derived from and generated upon the successful creation of a data file. Once the file is created, the file becomes visible to the user via the standard RDBMS views, such as the V$DATAFILE view. Note that the ASM filename syntax is different from that of the typical naming standards; ASM filenames use the following format:

+diskgroup_name/database_name/database file type/tag_name.file_number
.incarnation

For example, the ASM filename of +DATA/yoda/datafile/ishan.259.616618501 for the tablespace named ISHAN can be dissected as follows:

- **+DATA**   This is the name of the disk group where this file was created.

- **yoda**   This specifies the name of the database that contains this file.

- **datafile**   This is the database file type—in this case, *datafile*. There are over 20 file types in Oracle 11*g*.

- **ISHAN.259.616618501**   This portion of the filename is the suffix of the full filename, and is composed of the tag name, file number, and incarnation number. The tag name in the data file name corresponds to the tablespace name. In this example, the tag is the tablespace named ISHAN. For redo log files, the tag name is the group number (for example, group_3.264.54632413). The ASM file number for the ISHAN tablespace is 259. The file number in the ASM instance can be used to correlate filenames in database instance. The incarnation number is 616618501. The incarnation number, which has been derived from a timestamp, is used to provide uniqueness. Note that once the file has been created, the incarnation number does not change. The incarnation number distinguishes between a new file that has been created using the same file number and another file that has been deleted.

For best practice, every database should implement the Oracle Managed File (OMF) feature to simplify Oracle database file administration. Here are some key benefits of OMF:

- **Simplified Oracle file management**   All files are automatically created in a default location with system-generated names, thus a consistent file standard is inherently in place.

- **Space usage optimization**   Files are deleted automatically when the tablespaces are dropped.

- **Reduction of Oracle file management errors**   OMF minimizes errant file creation and deletion, and also mitigates file corruption due to inadvertent file reuse.

- **Enforcement of Optimal Flexible Architecture (OFA) standards**   OMF complies with the OFA standards for filename and file locations.

You can enable OMF by setting the DB_CREATE_FILE_DEST and DB_ RECOVERY_FILE_DEST parameters. Note that other *_DEST variables can be used for other file types. When the DB_CREATE_FILE_DEST parameter is set to +DATA, the default file location for tablespace data files becomes +DATA. Moreover, you need not even specify the disk group location in the tablespace creation statement. In fact, when the DB_CREATE_FILE_DEST and DB_RECOVERY_FILE_DEST parameters are set, the create database command can be simplified to the following statement:

```
SQL> CREATE DATABASE;
```

You can use the following command to create a tablespace:

```
SQL> CREATE TABLESPACE ISHAN;
```

This command simply creates a data file in the ISHAN tablespace under the +DATA disk group using the default data file size of 100MB. However, this file size can be overridden and still leverage the OMF name, as in the following example:

```
SQL> CREATE TABLESPACE ISHAN DATAFILE '+DATA' SIZE 10GB;
```

NOTE
OMF is not enabled for a file when the filename is explicitly specified in "create/alter tablespace add datafile" commands. For example, the following is not considered an OMF file because it specifies an explicit filename and path:
```
SQL> CREATE TABLESPACE ISHAN DATAFILE
'+DATA/YODA/ISHAN_01.DBF';
```
However, the following is considered an OMF file:
```
SQL> CREATE TABLESPACE ISHAN DATAFILE
'+DATA';
```

The following listing shows the relationship between the RDBMS files and the ASM file. Note that the file number from V$ASM_FILE is embedded in the filename. The first query is executed from the ASM instance and the second query is executed from the RDBMS instance:

```
ASM_SQL> SELECT FILE_NUMBER, SUM(BYTES)/1024*1024) FROM V$ASM_FILE GROUP BY
FILE_NUMBER;

FILE_NUMBER SUM(BYTES)/(1024*1024)
----------- ----------------------
        256             360.007813
        257              35.0078125
        259              35.0078125
        261              .002441406
        262             450.007813
        263              23.0078125
        264              10.0004883
        265               5.0078125
        266              10.0004883
        267              10.0004883
        268               2.2109375
        269              23.0078125
        270              28.0078125
        273              28.0078125

RDBMS_SQL> SELECT NAME FROM V$DATAFILE;
NAME
-----------------------------------------
+DATA/yoda/datafile/system.256.589462555
+DATA/yoda/datafile/sysaux.257.621507965
+DATA/yoda/datafile/undotbs1.258.621507965
+DATA/yoda/datafile/ishan.259.616618501
+DATA/yoda/datafile/undotbs2.262.621508063
+DATA/yoda/datafile/nitin.263.621507963
+DATA/yoda/datafile/kiran.269.689507964
```

```
+DATA/yoda/datafile/anya.270.689804549
+DATA/yoda/datafile/naveen.273.698804847
```

/u01/oradata/yoda/nisha01.dbf

```
SQL> SELECT MEMBER FROM V$LOGFILE;
MEMBER
------------------------------------
+DATA/yoda/onlinelog/group_3.264.3
+DATA/yoda/onlinelog/group_2.266.3
+DATA/yoda/onlinelog/group_1.267.3
```

Observe that this database contains ASM files and a non-ASM file named NISHA01 .dbf. The NISHA tablespace is stored in a Unix file system called /u01/oradata—that is, it is not an ASM-managed file. Because the NISHA01.dbf file is a Unix file system file rather than an ASM file, the ASM file list from the SQL output does not include it. This illustrates an important point: An Oracle database can have files that reside on file systems, raw devices, and ASM, simultaneously. However, in RAC environments, they must all be on shared storage and accessible by all nodes in the cluster.

ASM Directories

ASM provides the capability to create user-defined directories using the ADD DIRECTORY clause of the ALTER DISKGROUP statement. User-defined directories can be created to support user-defined ASM aliases (discussed later). ASM directories must start with a plus sign (+) and valid disk group name, followed by any user-specified subdirectory names. The only restriction is that the parent directory must exist before you attempt to create a subdirectory or alias in that directory. For example, both of the following are valid ASM directories:

```
SQL> ALTER DISKGROUP DATA ADD DIRECTORY '+DATA/yoda/oradata';
ASMCMD> mkdir +DATA/yoda/oradata
```

However, the following ASM directory cannot be created because the parent directory of data files (oradata) does not exist:

```
SQL> ALTER DISKGROUP DATA ADD DIRECTORY '+DATA/oradata/datafiles';
```

Although system directories such as +DATA/yoda cannot be manipulated, user-defined directories, such as the one successfully created in the previous example, can be renamed or dropped. The following examples illustrate this:

```
SQL> ALTER DISKGROUP DATA RENAME DIRECTORY '+DATA/yoda/oradata' to
'+DATA/yoda/oradata_old';
ASMCMD> mv +DATA/yoda/oradata  +DATA/yoda/oradata_old
SQL> ALTER DISKGROUP DATA DROP DIRECTORY '+DATA/yoda/oradata;
ASMCMD> rm +DATA/yoda/oradata_old
```

ASM Aliases

The filename notation described thus far (+*diskgroup_name/database_name/ database file type/tag_name.file_number.incarnation*) is called the fully qualified filename notation (FQFN). An ASM alias can be used to make filenaming conventions easier to remember.

Note that whenever a file is created, a system alias is also automatically created for that file. The system aliases are created in a hierarchical directory structure that takes the following syntax:

<db_unique_name>/<file_type>/<alias name>

When the files are removed, the <alias name> is deleted but the hierarchical directory structure remains.

ASM aliases are essentially in hierarchical directory format, similar to the filesystem hierarchy (*/u01/oradata/dbname/datafile_name*) and are used to reference a system-generated filename such as +DATA/yoda/datafile/system.256.589462555.

Alias names specify a disk group name, but instead of using a file and incarnation number, they take a user-defined string name. Alias ASM filenames are distinguished from fully qualified or numeric names because they do not end in a dotted pair of numbers. Note that there is a limit of one alias per ASM file. The following examples show how to create an ASM alias:

```
SQL> CREATE TABLESPACE ISHAN DATAFILE '+DATA/YODA/ORADATA/ISHAN_01.DBF';
```

Note, as stated earlier, that OMF is not enabled when file aliases are explicitly specified in "create/alter tablespace add datafile" commands (as in the previous example).

Aliases are particularly useful when dealing with control files and spfiles—that is, an ASM alias filename is normally used in the CONTROL_FILES and SPFILE initialization parameters. In the following example, the SPFILE and CONTROL_FILES parameters are set to the alias, and the DB_CREATE_FILE_DEST and DB_RECOVERY_FILE_DEST parameters are set to the appropriate OMF destinations:

```
SPFILE                  = +DATA/yoda/spfileorcl.ora
CONTROL_FILES           = +DATA/yoda/controlfile/control_01.ctl
DB_CREATE_FILE_DEST     = +DATA
DB_RECOVERY_FILE_DEST   = +FLASH
```

To show the hierarchical tree of files stored in the disk group, use the following connect by clause SQL to generate the full path. However, a more efficient way to browse the hierarchy is to use the ASMCMD ls command or Enterprise Manager.

```
Select connect ('+'||gname,sys_connect_by_path(aname, '/'))
full_alias_path from (select g.name gname, a.parent_index pindex,
a.name aname, a.reference_index rindex from v$asm_alias a,
```

```
v$asm_diskgroup g where a.group_number=g.group_number) start with
(mod(pindex,
power(2,24))) = 0 connect by prior rindex = pindex;
FULL_ALIAS_PATH
----------------------------------------------------------------------
+DATA/YODA
+DATA/YODA/spfilered.ora
+DATA/YODA/CONTROLFILE
+DATA/YODA/CONTROLFILE/Current.260.629979753
+DATA/YODA/ONLINELOG
+DATA/YODA/ONLINELOG/group_1.261.629979755
+DATA/YODA/ONLINELOG/group_2.262.629979775
+DATA/YODA/ONLINELOG/group_3.265.629979903
+DATA/YODA/ONLINELOG/group_4.266.629979921
+DATA/YODA/TEMPFILE
+DATA/YODA/TEMPFILE/TEMP.263.629979811
+DATA/YODA/PARAMETERFILE
+DATA/YODA/PARAMETERFILE/spfile.267.629979939
+DATA/YODA/DATAFILE
+DATA/YODA/DATAFILE/SYSTEM.256.629979635
+DATA/YODA/DATAFILE/SYSAUX.257.629979639
+DATA/YODA/DATAFILE/UNDOTBS1.258.629979641
+DATA/YODA/DATAFILE/USERS.259.629979643
+DATA/YODA/DATAFILE/UNDOTBS2.264.629979829
```

Templates

ASM file templates are named collections of attributes applied to files during file creation. Templates are used to set file-level redundancy (mirror, high, or unprotected) and striping attributes (fine or coarse) of files created in an ASM disk group.

Templates simplify file creation by housing complex file attribute specifications. When a disk group is created, ASM establishes a set of initial system default templates associated with that disk group. These templates contain the default attributes for the various Oracle database file types. When a file is created, the redundancy and striping attributes are set for that file, where the attributes are based on the system template that is the default template for the file type or an explicitly named template.

The following query lists the ASM files, redundancy, and striping size for a sample database.

```
SQL> select name, redundancy, striped from v$asm_alias a, v$asm_file b
       where a.file_number=b.file_number and a.group_number=b.group_number
       order by name;


NAME                                    REDUNDANCY STRIPE
------------------------------------    ---------- -------
Current.260.616618829                   HIGH       FINE
EXAMPLE.264.616618877                   MIRROR     COARSE
```

```
ISHAN.259.616618501                    UNPROTECTED   COARSE
NITIN.269.617736951                    MIRROR        COARSE
SYSAUX.257.616618501                   MIRROR        COARSE
SYSTEM.256.589462555                   MIRROR        COARSE
TEMP.263.616618871                     MIRROR        COARSE
KIRAN.269.689507964                    MIRROR        COARSE
ANYA.270.689804549                     MIRROR        COARSE
UNDOTBS1.258.616618501                 MIRROR        COARSE
UNDOTBS2.265.616619119                 MIRROR        COARSE
GROUP_1.261.616618835                  MIRROR        COARSE
GROUP_2.262.616618849                  MIRROR        COARSE
GROUP_3.266.616619217                  MIRROR        COARSE
GROUP_4.267.616619231                  MIRROR        COARSE
spfile.268.616619243                   MIRROR        COARSE
spfileorcl.ora                         MIRROR        COARSE
```

The administrator can change attributes of the default templates if required. However, system default templates cannot be deleted. Additionally, administrators can add their own unique templates, as needed. The following SQL command illustrates how to create user templates (performed on the ASM instance) and then apply them to a new tablespace data file (performed on the RDBMS):

```
ASM_SQL> alter diskgroup DATA add template noncritical_files attributes
(unprotected);
ASMCMD [+] > mktmpl -G data --redundancy unprotected noncritical_files
```

Once a template is created, you can apply it when creating the new tablespace:

```
RDBMS_SQL> create tablespace ISHAN datafile
'+DATA/ishan(noncritical_files)' size 200M;
```

Using the ALTER DISKGROUP command, you can modify a template or drop the template using the DROP TEMPLATE clause. The following commands illustrate this:

```
ASM_SQL> ALTER DISKGROUP DATA ALTER TEMPLATE NONCRITICAL_FILES ATTRIBUTES
(COARSE);
ASMCMD [+] > chtmpl -G data --striping coarse noncritical_files
ASM_SQL> ALTER DISKGROUP DATA DROP TEMPLATE NONCRITICAL_FILES;
ASMCMD [+] > rmtmpl -G noncritical_files
```

If you need to change an ASM file attribute after the file has been created, the file must be copied into a new file with the new attributes. This is the only method of changing a file's attributes.

```
ASMCMD [+] > lstmpl -l -G data
Group_Name Group_Num Name          Stripe Sys Redund PriReg MirrReg
DATA                 1 ARCHIVELOG   COARSE Y          MIRROR COLD
COLD
```

```
DATA                1 ASMPARAMETERFILE COARSE Y MIRROR COLD COLD
DATA                1 AUTOBACKUP      COARSE Y MIRROR COLD COLD
DATA                1 BACKUPSET COARSE Y MIRROR COLD COLD
DATA 1 CHANGETRACKING COARSE Y MIRROR COLD COLD
DATA 1 CONTROLFILE FINE Y HIGH COLD COLD
DATA 1 DATAFILE COARSE Y MIRROR COLD COLD
DATA 1 DATAGUARDCONFIG COARSE Y MIRROR COLD COLD
DATA 1 DUMPSET COARSE Y MIRROR COLD COLD
DATA 1 FLASHBACK COARSE Y MIRROR COLD COLD
DATA 1 FLASHFILE COARSE Y MIRROR COLD COLD
DATA 1 MYTEMPLATE FINE N HIGH COLD COLD
DATA 1 OCRFILE COARSE Y MIRROR COLD COLD
DATA 1 ONLINELOG COARSE Y MIRROR COLD COLD
DATA 1 PARAMETERFILE COARSE Y MIRROR COLD COLD
DATA 1 TEMPFILE COARSE Y MIRROR COLD COLD
DATA 1 XTRANSPORT COARSE Y MIRROR COLD COLD
```

V$ASM_TEMPLATE

Query the V$ASM_TEMPLATE view for information about templates. Here is an example for one of the disk groups:

```
SQL> SELECT name "Template Name", redundancy "Redundancy", stripe "Striping",
system "System" FROM v$asm_template WHERE group_number=1;
```

Template Name	Redundancy	Striping	System
PARAMETERFILE	MIRROR	COARSE	Y
ASMPARAMETERFILE	MIRROR	COARSE	Y
DUMPSET	MIRROR	COARSE	Y
CONTROLFILE	HIGH	FINE	Y
FLASHFILE	MIRROR	COARSE	Y
ARCHIVELOG	MIRROR	COARSE	Y
ONLINELOG	MIRROR	COARSE	Y
DATAFILE	MIRROR	COARSE	Y
TEMPFILE	MIRROR	COARSE	Y
BACKUPSET	MIRROR	COARSE	Y
AUTOBACKUP	MIRROR	COARSE	Y
XTRANSPORT	MIRROR	COARSE	Y
CHANGETRACKING	MIRROR	COARSE	Y
FLASHBACK	MIRROR	COARSE	Y
DATAGUARDCONFIG	MIRROR	COARSE	Y
OCRFILE	MIRROR	COARSE	Y

ASM File Access Control

In 11gR2, a new feature called ASM File Access Control was introduced to restrict file access to specific database instance users who connect as SYSDBA. ASM File Access Control uses the user ID that owns the database instance home.

ASM ACL Overview

ASM uses File Access Control to determine the additional privileges that are given to a database that has been authenticated as SYSDBA on the ASM instance. These additional privileges include the ability to modify and delete certain files, aliases, and user groups. Cloud DBAs can set up "user groups" to specify the list of databases that share the same access permissions to ASM files. User groups are lists of databases, and any database that authenticates as SYSDBA can create a user group.

Just as in Unix/Linux file permissions, each ASM file has three categories of privileges: owner, group, and other. Each category can have read-only permission, read-write permission, or no permission. The file owner is usually the creator of the file and can assign permissions for the file in any of the owner, group, and other categories. The owner can also change the group associated with the file. Note that only the creator of a group can delete it or modify its membership list.

When administering ASM File Access Control, it is recommended that you connect as SYSDBA to the database instance that is the owner of the files in the disk group.

To set up ASM File Access Control for files in a disk group, ensure the COMPATIBLE.ASM and COMPATIBLE.RDBMS disk group attributes are set to 11.2 or higher.

Create a new (or alter an existing) disk group with the following ASM File Access Control disk group attributes: ACCESS_CONTROL.ENABLED and ACCESS_CONTROL.UMASK. Before setting the ACCESS_CONTROL.UMASK disk group attribute, you must set the ACCESS_CONTROL.ENABLED attribute to true to enable ASM File Access Control.

The ACCESS_CONTROL.ENABLED attribute determines whether Oracle ASM File Access Control is enabled for a disk group. The value can be true or false.

The ACCESS_CONTROL.UMASK attribute determines which permissions are masked out on the creation of an ASM file for the user who owns the file, users in the same user group, and others not in the user group. This attribute applies to all files on a disk group. The values can be combinations of three digits: {0|2|6} {0|2|6} {0|2|6}. The default is 066. Setting the attribute to 0 masks out nothing. Setting it to 2 masks out write permission. Setting it to 6 masks out both read and write permissions.

The upcoming example in the next section shows how to enable ASM File Access Control for a disk group with a permissions setting of 026, which enables read-write access for the owner, read access for users in the group, and no access to others not in the group. Optionally, you can create user groups that are groups of database users who share the same access permissions to ASM files. Here are some File Access Control list considerations:

- For files that exist in a disk group, before setting the ASM File Access Control disk group attributes, you must explicitly set the permissions and ownership on those existing files. Additionally, the files must be closed before setting the ownership or permissions.

■ When you set up File Access Control on an existing disk group, the files previously created remain accessible by everyone, unless you run the set permissions to restrict access.

■ Ensure that the user exists before setting ownership or permissions on a file.

■ File Access Control, including permission management, can be performed using SQL*Plus, ASCMD, or Enterprise Manager (but using Enterprise Manager or ASMCMD is the easiest method).

ASM ACL Setup Example

To illustrate ASM File Access Control, we start with three OS users:

```
$ id oracle
uid=500(oracle) gid=501(dba) groups=501(dba),502(oinstall)

$ id oragrid
uid=600(oragrid) gid=506(oradba) groups=506(oradba),502(oinstall),
503(asmadmin),504(asmdba),505(asmoper)

$ id oradb
uid=601(oradb) gid=506(oradba) groups=506(oradba),502(oinstall),
504(asmdba)
```

In the ASM instance, prepare the disk group for File Access Control:

```
SQL> alter diskgroup DATA set attribute 'access_control.enabled' = 'TRUE';

ASMCMD [+] > setattr -G data access_control.enabled true

SQL> alter diskgroup DATA set attribute 'access_control.umask' = '026';

ASMCMD [+] > setattr -G data access_control.umask 026
```

Next, add two ASM groups:

```
SQL> alter diskgroup DATA add usergroup 'DBUSERS' with member 'oracle', 'oradb';

ASMCMD [+] > mkgrp data dbusers oradb

SQL> alter diskgroup DATA add usergroup 'GRIDUSERS' with member 'oragrid';

ASMCMD [+] > mkgrp data gridusers oragrid



SQL> select group_number, usergroup_number, name from v$asm_usergroup;
```

```
GROUP_NUMBER USERGROUP_NUMBER NAME
------------ ---------------- --------------------------------
           1                1 DBUSERS
           1                2 GRIDUSERS


SQL> select group_number, user_number, os_id, os_name from v$asm_user;

GROUP_NUMBER USER_NUMBER OS_ID            OS_NAME
------------ ----------- ---------------- ----------------
           1           1 600              oragrid
           1           2 500              oracle
           1           3 601              oradb


ASMCMD [+] > lsusr -G data
User_Num    OS_ID       OS_Name
       1    600         oragrid
       2    500         oracle
       3    601         oradb
```

Set File Access Control for the data file '+DATA/yoda/datafile/
marlie.283.702218775':

```
SQL> select a.name, f.permissions, f.user_number, f.usergroup_number
from v$asm_alias a, v$asm_file f
where a.file_number = f.file_number and f.file_number=283;

NAME                PERMISSIONS     USER_NUMBER     USERGROUP_NUMBER
------------------- --------------- --------------- -----------------
MARLIE.283.702218775 rw-rw-rw-                    0                0
```

Ownership cannot be changed for an open file, so we need to take the file
offline in the database instance:

```
SQL> alter tablespace MARLIE offline;

Tablespace altered.
```

We can now set file ownership in the ASM instance:

```
SQL> alter diskgroup DATA set ownership owner='oradb', group='dbusers' for
file '+DATA/yoda/datafile/marlie.283.702218775';

ASMCMD [+] > chown oradb:dbusers
  '+DATA/yoda/datafile/marlie.283.702218775'
```

Default permissions are unchanged:

```
SQL> select a.name, f.permissions, f.user_number, f.usergroup_number
from v$asm_alias a, v$asm_file f
where a.file_number = f.file_number and f.file_number=283;

NAME                PERMISSIONS     USER_NUMBER USERGROUP_NUMBER
------------------- ----------- --------------- -----------------
MARLIE.283.702218775 rw-rw-rw-                 3                1
```

Now set the file permissions in the ASM instance:

```
SQL> alter diskgroup DATA set permission other = none for file '+DATA/yoda/datafile/
marlie.283.702218775';

ASMCMD [+] > chmod ug+rw '+DATA/yoda/datafile/marlie.283.702218775'

SQL> select a.name, f.permissions, f.user_number, f.usergroup_number
from v$asm_alias a, v$asm_file f
where a.file_number = f.file_number and f.file_number=283;

NAME                  PERMISSIONS      USER_NUMBER      USERGROUP_NUMBER
------------------    ---------------  ---------------  -----------------
MARLIE.283.702218775 rw-rw----                      3                 1
```

This example illustrates that the Grid Infrastructure owner (ASM owner) cannot copy files (in this case, RMAN backups) out of the disk group if they are protected by ASM File Access Control.

First, create an RMAN backup:

```
[oracle@node1 ~]$ rman target /
Recovery Manager: Release 11.2.0.3.0 - Production on Mon Feb 20 12:21:41 2012
Copyright (c) 1982, 2011, Oracle and/or its affiliates.  All rights reserved.
connected to target database: BR (DBID=1068878239)

RMAN> backup database;

Starting backup at 20-FEB-12
using target database control file instead of recovery catalog
allocated channel: ORA_DISK_1
channel ORA_DISK_1: SID=40 device type=DISK
channel ORA_DISK_1: starting full datafile backup set
channel ORA_DISK_1: specifying datafile(s) in backup set
input datafile file number=00001 name=+DATA/yoda/datafile/system.256.769030243
input datafile file number=00002 name=+DATA/yoda/datafile/sysaux.257.769030245
input datafile file number=00005 name=+DATA/yoda/datafile/example.269.769030517

input datafile file number=00003 name=+DATA/yoda/datafile/undotbs1.258.769030245
input datafile file number=00006 name=+DATA/yoda/datafile/priya.274.77210220
input datafile file number=00010 name=+RECO/yoda/datafile/bane.256.772409591
input datafile file number=00011 name=+RECO/yoda/datafile/aneesh.257.772409891
input datafile file number=00004 name=+DATA/yoda/datafile/users.259.769030245
input datafile file number=00007 name=+DATA/yoda/datafile/naveen.271.771793293
input datafile file number=00008 name=+DATA/yoda/datafile/nishan.272.771794469
input datafile file number=00009 name=+DATA/yoda/datafile/marlie.283.771795255
channel ORA_DISK_1: starting piece 1 at 20-FEB-12
channel ORA_DISK_1: finished piece 1 at 20-FEB-12
piece handle=+DATA/yoda/backupset/2012_02_20/nnndf0_tag20120220t122152_0.276.775743713
tag=TAG20120220T122152 comment=NONE
channel ORA_DISK_1: backup set complete, elapsed time: 00:03:55
channel ORA_DISK_1: starting full datafile backup set
channel ORA_DISK_1: specifying datafile(s) in backup set
including current control file in backup set
including current SPFILE in backup set
channel ORA_DISK_1: starting piece 1 at 20-FEB-12
channel ORA_DISK_1: finished piece 1 at 20-FEB-12
```

```
piece handle=+DATA/yoda/backupset/2012_02_20/ncsnf0_tag20120220t122152_0.277.775743951
tag=TAG20120220T122152 comment=NONE
channel ORA_DISK_1: backup set complete, elapsed time: 00:00:07
Finished backup at 20-FEB-12

RMAN> list backup;
List of Backup Sets
===================
BS Key  Type LV Size       Device Type Elapsed Time Completion Time
------- ---- -- ---------- ----------- ------------ ---------------
1       Full    9.36M       DISK         00:00:08    20-FEB-12
        BP Key: 1   Status: AVAILABLE  Compressed: NO  Tag: TAG20120220T122026
        Piece Name: +DATA/yoda/backupset/2012_02_20/ncsnf0_tag2012022
0t122026_0.275.775743631
  SPFILE Included: Modification time: 20-FEB-12
  SPFILE db_unique_name: YODA
  Control File Included: Ckp SCN: 2025472      Ckp time: 20-FEB-12

BS Key  Type LV Size       Device Type Elapsed Time Completion Time
------- ---- -- ---------- ----------- ------------ ---------------
2       Full    1.12G       DISK         00:03:50    20-FEB-12
        BP Key: 2   Status: AVAILABLE  Compressed: NO  Tag: TAG20120220T122152
        Piece Name: +DATA/yoda/backupset/2012_02_20/nnndf0_tag2012022
0t122152_0.276.775743713
  List of Datafiles in backup set 2
  File LV Type Ckp SCN    Ckp Time  Name

BS Key  Type LV Size       Device Type Elapsed Time Completion Time
------- ---- -- ---------- ----------- ------------ ---------------
3       Full    9.36M       DISK         00:00:06    20-FEB-12
        BP Key: 3   Status: AVAILABLE  Compressed: NO  Tag: TAG20120220T122152
        Piece Name: +DATA/yoda/backupset/2012_02_20/ncsnf0_tag2012022
0t122152_0.277.775743951
  SPFILE Included: Modification time: 20-FEB-12
  SPFILE db_unique_name: YODA
  Control File Included: Ckp SCN: 2026216      Ckp time: 20-FEB-12
```

Now, using the grid users, we'll try to copy those backup pieces to the OS file system (recall that the backup files were created using the oracle user). File Access Control should prevent the copy operation and throw an "ORA-15260: permission denied on ASM disk group":

```
[grid@node1 ~]$ asmcmd ls +DATA/YODA/BACKUPSET/2012_02_20/
ncsnf0_TAG20120220T122026_0.275.775743631
ncsnf0_TAG20120220T122152_0.277.775743951
nnndf0_TAG20120220T122152_0.276.775743713

[grid@node1~]$ asmcmd cp +DATA/YODA/BACKUPSET/2012_02_20/ncsnf0_TAG2012022
0T122026_0.275.775743631
/u01/rman/ncsnf0_TAG20120220T122026_0.dbf
```

```
copying +DATA/YODA/BACKUPSET/2012_02_20/ncsnf0_TAG20120220T122026_0.275.775743631 -> /
u01/rman/ncsnf0_TAG20120220T122026_0.dbf
ASMCMD-8016: copy source->'+DATA/YODA/BACKUPSET/2012_02_20/ncsnf0_TAG2012022
0T122026_0.275.775743631' and target->'/u01/rman/ncsnf0_TAG20120220T122026_0.dbf' failed
ORA-19505: failed to identify file
"+DATA/YODA/BACKUPSET/2012_02_20/ncsnf0_TAG20120220T122026_0.275.775743631"
ORA-17503: ksfdopn:2 Failed to open file
+DATA/YODA/BACKUPSET/2012_02_20/ncsnf0_TAG20120220T122026_0.275.775743631
ORA-15260: permission denied on ASM disk group
ORA-06512: at "SYS.X$DBMS_DISKGROUP", line 413
ORA-06512: at line 3 (DBD ERROR: OCIStmtExecute)
```

To be able to copy files from the disk group (DATA) to the file system, either disable access control or add an OS user grid to the correct ASM user group.

Check the user and user groups setup in ASM:

```
SQL> SELECT u.group_number "Disk group#",
  u.os_id "OS ID",
  u.os_name "OS user",
  u.user_number "ASM user#",
  g.usergroup_number "ASM group#",
  g.name "ASM user group"
FROM v$asm_user u, v$asm_usergroup g, v$asm_usergroup_member m
WHERE u.group_number=g.group_number and u.group_number=m.group_number
  and u.user_number=m.member_number
  and g.usergroup_number=m.usergroup_number
  ORDER BY 1, 2;

Disk group# OS ID OS user ASM user# ASM group# ASM user group
----------- ----- ------- --------- ---------- --------------
          1 1101  oracle          2          1 DBATEAM1

- This shows that the Grid Infrastructure owner (OS user grid) is not a
member of DBATEAM1 ASM user group.

- I then disabled access control (temporary):

SQL> alter diskgroup DATA set attribute 'access_control.enabled' = 'false';

Diskgroup altered.

- And I was then able to copy the file(s) out of the disk group:

[grid@pixel142 ~]$ asmcmd cp +DATA/YODA/BACKUPSET/2012_02_20/ncsnf0_TAG2012022
0T122026_0.275.775743631 /u01/rman/ncsnf0_TAG20120220T122026_0.dbf
copying +DATA/YODA/BACKUPSET/2012_02_20/ncsnf0_TAG20120220T122026_0.275.775743631 -> /
u01/rman/ncsnf0_TAG20120220T122026_0.dbf

[grid@pixel142 ~]$ ls -l /u01/rman
total 10652
-rw-r----- 1 grid oinstall 9830400 Feb 21 11:37 ncsnf0_TAG20120220T122026_0.dbf
...
```

Summary

Like most file systems, an ASM disk group contains a directory tree. The root directory for the disk group is always the disk group name. Every ASM file has a system-generated filename; the name is generated based on the instance that created it, the Oracle file type, the usage of the file, and the file numbers. The system-generated filename is of the form +*disk_group/db_name/file_type/usage_tag .file_number.time_stamp*. Directories are created automatically as needed to construct system-generated filenames.

A file can have one user alias and can be placed in any existing directory within the same disk group. The user alias can be used to refer to the file in any file operation where the system-generated filename could be used. When a full pathname is used to create the file, the pathname becomes the user alias. If a file is created by just using the disk group name, then no user alias is created. A user alias may be added to or removed from any file without disturbing the file.

The system-generated name is an OMF name, whereas a user alias is not an OMF name. If the system-generated name is used for a file, the system will automatically create and delete the file as needed. If the file is referred to by its user alias, the user is responsible for creating and deleting the file and any required directories.

File templates are used to specify striping (coarse or fine) and, in a normal redundancy disk group, the redundancy (unprotected, normal, or high) for a file when it is created. A default template is provided for every Oracle file type. These defaults may be edited or custom templates can be created. Changing a template only affects new file creations, not existing files. When creating a file, you can specify a template by placing the template name in parentheses after the disk group name in the file-creation name.

CHAPTER
8

ASM Space Allocation
and Rebalance

When a database is created under the constructs of ASM, it will be striped (and can be optionally mirrored) as per the Stripe and Mirror Everything (SAME) methodology. SAME is a concept that makes extensive use of striping and mirroring across large sets of disks to achieve high availability and to provide good performance with minimal tuning. ASM incorporates the SAME methodology. Using this method, ASM evenly distributes and balances input/output (I/O) load across all disks within the disk group. ASM solves one of the shortcomings of the original SAME methodology, because ASM maintains balanced data distribution even when storage configurations change.

ASM Space Allocation

This section discusses how ASM allocates space in the disk group and how clients such as the relational database management system (RDBMS) and ASM Cluster File System (ACFS) use the allocated space.

ASM Allocation Units

ASM allocates space in chunks called *allocation units (AUs)*. An AU is the most granular allocation on a per-disk basis—that is, every ASM disk is divided into AUs of the same size. For most deployments of ASM, 1MB stripe size has proved to be the best stripe depth for Oracle databases and also happens to be the largest I/O request that the RDBMS will currently issue in Oracle Database 11*g*. In large environments, it is recommended to use a larger AU size to reduce the metadata associated to describe the files in the disk group. This optimal stripe size, coupled with even distribution of extents in the disk group and the buffer cache in the RDBMS, prevents hot spots.

Unlike traditional random array of independent drives (RAID) configurations, ASM striping is not done in a round-robin basis, nor is it done at the individual disk level. ASM randomly chooses a disk for allocating the initial extent. This is done to optimize the balance of the disk group. All subsequent AUs are allocated in such a way as to distribute each file equally and evenly across all disks and to fill all disks evenly (see Figure 8-1). Thus, every disk is maintained at the same percentage full, regardless of the size of the disk.

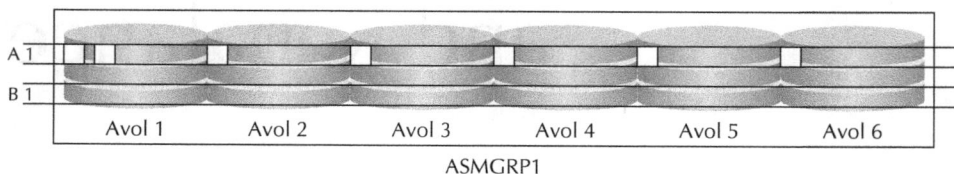

FIGURE 8-1. *ASM extents*

For example, if a disk is twice as big as the others, it will contain twice as many extents. This ensures that all disks in a disk group have the same I/O load relative to their capacity. Because ASM balances the load across all the disks in a disk group, it is not a good practice to create multiple disk partitions from different areas of the same physical disk and then allocate the partitions as members of the same disk group. However, it may make sense for multiple partitions on a physical disk to be in different disk groups. ASM is abstracted from the underlying characteristic of the storage array (LUN). For example, if the storage array presents several RAID5 LUNs to ASM as disks, ASM will allocate extents transparently across each of those LUNs.

ASM Extents

When a database file is created in an ASM disk group, it is composed of a set of ASM extents, and these extents are evenly distributed across all disks in the disk group. Each extent consists of an integral number of AUs on an ASM disk. The extent size to number of AU mapping changes with the size of the file

The following two queries display the extent distribution for a disk group (the FAST disk group) that contains four disks. The first query shows the evenness based on megabytes per disk, and the second query lists the total extents for each disk in the FAST disk group (group_number 2) using the X$KFFXP base table:

```
SQL> SELECT NAME, TOTAL_MB, FREE_MB FROM V$ASM_DISK WHERE GROUP_NUMBER=2;
NAME                                  TOTAL_MB    FREE_MB
-----------------------------------   ----------  ----------
FAST_0001                                  8628        4996
FAST_0000                                  8628        4996
FAST_0002                                  8583        4970
FAST_0003                                  8628        4996
SQL> SELECT COUNT(PXN_KFFXP), DISK_KFFXP, GROUP_KFFXP FROM X$KFFXP
WHERE GROUP_KFFXP=2 GROUP BY DISK_KFFXP, GROUP_KFFXP ORDER BY  GROUP_KFFXP,
DISK_KFFXP;
COUNT(PXN_KFFXP) DISK_KFFXP GROUP_KFFXP
---------------- ---------- -----------
            3736          0           2
            3737          1           2
            3716          2           2
            3734          3           2
```

Similarly, the following example illustrates the even distribution of ASM extents for the System tablespace across all the disks in the DATA disk group (group number 3). This tablespace contains a single 100MB data file called +DATA/yoda/datafile/system.256.589462555.

```
SQL> SELECT F.FILE#, T.NAME TBSNAME, F.NAME FILENAME, BYTES/1024/1024 MB
FROM V$DATAFILE F, V$TABLESPACE T WHERE F.TS# = T.TS#;
```

```
FILE#       TBSNAME     FILENAME                                          MB
----------  ----------  ------------------------------------------------  ------
1           SYSTEM      +DATA/yoda/datafile/system.256.589462555           100
SQL> SELECT DISK_KFFXP, COUNT (DISK_KFFXP) EXTENTS FROM X$KFFXP
WHERE GROUP_KFFXP=3 AND NUMBER_KFFXP=256 AND DISK_KFFXP <> 65534 GROUP BY
NUMBER_KFFXP,DISK_KFFXP

DISK_KFFXP   EXTENTS
----------  ----------
         0          27
         1          25
         2          25
         3          25
```

ASM Striping

There are two types of ASM file striping: coarse and fine-grained. For coarse distribution, each coarse-grained file extent is mapped to a single allocation unit.

With fine-grained distribution, each grain is interleaved 128K across groups of eight AUs. Since each AU is guaranteed to be on a different ASM disk, each strip will end up on a different physical disk. It is also used for very small files (such as control files) to ensure that they are distributed across disks. Fine-grained striping is generally not good for sequential I/O (such as full table scans) once the sequential I/O exceeds one AU. As of Oracle 11gR2, only control files are file-striped by default when the disk group is created; the users can change the template for a given file type to change the defaults.

As discussed previously, each file stored in ASM requires metadata structures to describe the file extent locations. As the file grows, the metadata associated with that file also grows as well as the memory used to store the file extent locations. Oracle 11g introduces a new feature called Variable Sized Extents to minimize the overhead of the metadata. The main objective of this feature is to enable larger file extents to reduce metadata requirements as a file grows, and as a byproduct it allows for larger file size support (file sizes up to 140PB [a petabyte is 1,024TB]). For example, if a data file is initially as small as 1GB, the file extent size used will be 1 AU. As the file grows, several size thresholds are crossed and larger extent sizes are employed at each threshold, with the maximum extent size capped at 16 AUs. Note that there are two thresholds: 20,000 extents (20GB with 1MB AUs) and 40,000 extents (100GB [20GB of 1×AU and 20,000 of 4×AU] with 1MB AUs). Finally, extents beyond 40,000 use a 16× multiplier. Valid extent sizes are 1, 4, and 16 AUs (which translate to 1MB, 4MB, and 16MB with 1MB AUs, respectively). When the file gets into multiple AU extents, the file gets striped at 1AU to maintain the coarse-grained striping granularity of the file. The database administrator (DBA) or ASM administrator need not manage variable extents; ASM handles this automatically. This feature is very similar in behavior to the Automatic Extent Allocation that the RDBMS uses.

NOTE
The RDBMS layers of the code effectively limit file size to 128TB. The ASM structures can address 140PB.

The following example demonstrates the use of Variable Sized Extents. In this example, the SYSAUX tablespace contains a data file that is approximately 32GB, which exceeds the first threshold of 20,000 extents (20GB):

```
SQL> SELECT NAME, BYTES/(1024*1024*1024) "SIZE", FILE# FROM V$DATAFILE
  WHERE BYTES/(1024*1024*1024) > 20
NAME                                        SIZE       FILE#
------------------------------------------ ---------- -----
+DATA/yoda/datafile/sysaux.263.62577323 31.9999924    263
```

Now if X$KFFXP is queried to find the ASM file that has a nondefault extent size, it should indicate that it is file number 263:

```
SQL> SELECT DISTINCT NUMBER_KFFXP, SIZE_KFFXP FROM X$KFFXP WHERE
SIZE_KFFXP = 8 GROUP BY NUMBER_KFFXP, SIZE_KFFXP
NUMBER_KFFXP SIZE_KFFXP
------------ ----------
         263          8
```

The Variable Sized Extents feature is available only for disk groups with Oracle 11*g* RDBMS and ASM compatibility. For disk groups created with Oracle Database 10*g*, the compatibility attribute must be advanced to 11.1.0. Variable extents take effect for newly created files and will not be retroactively applied to files that were created with 10*g* software.

Setting Larger AU Sizes for VLDBs

For very large databases (VLDBs)—for example, databases that are 10TB and larger—it may be beneficial to change the default AU size, for example 4MB AU size. The following are benefits of changing the default size for VLDBs:

- Reduced SGA size to manage the extent maps in the RDBMS instance

- Increased file size limits

- Reduced database open time, because VLDBs usually have many big data files

Increasing the AU size improves the time to open large databases and also reduces the amount of shared pool consumed by the extent maps. With 1MB AUs and fixed-size extents, the extent map for a 10TB database is about 90MB, which has to be read at open and then kept in memory. With 16MB AUs, this is reduced to about 5.5MB. In Oracle Database 10*g,* the entire extent map for a file is read from disk at file-open time.

Oracle Database 11*g* significantly minimizes the file-open latency issue by reading extent maps on demand for certain file types. In Oracle 10*g,* for every file open, the complete extent map is built and sent to the RDBMS instance from the ASM instance. For large files, this unnecessarily lengthens file-open time. In Oracle 11*g,* only the first 60 extents in the extent map are sent at file-open time. The rest are sent in batches as required by the database instance.

Setting Larger AU Sizes in Oracle Database 11*g*

For Oracle Database 11*g* ASM systems, the following CREATE DISKGROUP command can be executed to set the appropriate AU size:

```
SQL> CREATE DISKGROUP DATA DISK '/dev/emcpower[q-s] ATTRIBUTE 'au_size' = '4M',
'compatible.asm' = '11.2';
```

The AU attribute can be used only at the time of disk group creation; furthermore, the AU size of an existing disk group cannot be changed after the disk group has been created.

ASM Rebalance

With traditional volume managers, expanding or shrinking striped file systems has typically been difficult. With ASM, these disk changes are now seamless operations involving redistribution (rebalancing) of the striped data. Additionally, these operations can be performed online.

Any change in the storage configuration—adding, dropping, or resizing a disk— triggers a rebalance operation. ASM does not dynamically move around "hot areas" or "hot extents." Because ASM distributes extents evenly across all disks and the database buffer cache prevents small chunks of data from being hot areas on disk, it completely obviates the notion of hot disks or extents.

Rebalance Operation

The main objective of the rebalance operation is always to provide an even distribution of file extents and space usage across all disks in the disk group. The rebalance is done on a per-file basis to ensure that each file is evenly balanced across all disks. Upon completion of distributing the files evenly among all the disks in a disk group, ASM starts compacting the disks to ensure there is no fragmentation in the disk group. Fragmentation is possible only in disk groups where one or more files use variable extents. This is critical to ASM's assurance of balanced I/O load. The ASM background process, RBAL, manages this rebalance. The RBAL process examines each file extent map, and the extents are redistributed on the new storage configuration. For example, consider an eight-disk external redundancy disk group, with a data file with 40 extents (each disk will house five extents). When two new drives of same size are added, that data file is rebalanced and distributed across 10 drives, with each drive containing four extents. Only eight extents need to move to complete the rebalance—that is, a complete redistribution of extents is not necessary because only the minimum number of extents is moved to reach equal distribution.

During the compaction phase of the rebalance, each disk is examined and data is moved to the head of the disk to eliminate any holes. The rebalance estimates reported in V$ASM_OPERATIONS do not factor in the work needed to complete the compaction of the disk group as of Oracle 11*g*.

NOTE
A weighting factor, influenced by disk size and file size, affects rebalancing. A larger drive will consume more extents. This factor is used to achieve even distribution based on overall size.

The following is a typical process flow for ASM rebalancing:

1. On the ASM instance, a DBA adds (or drops) a disk to (or from) a disk group.

2. This invokes the RBAL process to create the rebalance plan and then begin coordination of the redistribution.

3. RBAL calculates the work required to perform the task and then messages the ASM Rebalance (ARB*x*) processes to handle the request. In Oracle Release 11.2.0.2 and earlier, the number of ARB*x* processes invoked is directly determined by the init.ora parameter ASM_POWER_LIMIT or the power level specified in an add, drop, or rebalance command. Post–Oracle 11.2.0.2, there is always just one ARB0 process performing the rebalance operation. The ASM_POWER_LIMIT or the power level specified in the SQL command translates to the number of extents relocated in parallel.

4. The Continuing Operations Directory (COD) is updated to reflect a rebalance activity. The COD is important when an influx rebalance fails. Recovering instances will see an outstanding COD entry for the rebalance and restart it.

5. RBAL distributes plans to the ARBs. In general, RBAL generates a plan per file; however, larger files can be split among ARBs.

6. ARB*x* performs a rebalance on these extents. Each extent is locked, relocated, and unlocked. Reads can proceed while an extent is being relocated. New writes to the locked extent are blocked while outstanding writes have to be reissued to the new location after the relocation is complete. This step is shown as Operation REBAL in V$ASM_OPERATION. The rebalance algorithm is detailed in Chapter 9.

The following is an excerpt from the ASM alert log during a rebalance operation for a drop disk command:

```
SQL> alter diskgroup reco drop disk 'ASM_NORM_DATA4' rebalance power 12
←here we issue the rebalance
NOTE: requesting all-instance membership refresh for group=2
GMON querying group 2 at 120 for pid 19, osid 19030
GMON updating for reconfiguration, group 2 at 121 for pid 19, osid 19030
NOTE: group 2 PST updated.
NOTE: membership refresh pending for group 2/0x89b87754 (RECO)
GMON querying group 2 at 122 for pid 13, osid 4000
SUCCESS: refreshed membership for 2/0x89b87754 (RECO)
NOTE: starting rebalance of group 2/0x89b87754 (RECO) at power 12 ←rebalance
internally started
Starting background process ARB0    ← ARB0 gets started for this rebalance
SUCCESS: alter diskgroup reco drop disk 'ASM_NORM_DATA4' rebalance power 12
Wed Sep 19 23:54:10 2012
ARB0 started with pid=21, OS id=19526
NOTE: assigning ARB0 to group 2/0x89b87754 (RECO) with 12 parallel I/Os ← ARB0
assigned to this
 diskgroup rebalance.  Note that it states 12 parallel I/Os
NOTE: Attempting voting file refresh on diskgroup RECO
Wed Sep 19 23:54:38 2012
NOTE: requesting all-instance membership refresh for group=2  ← first indications
that rebalance is completing
GMON updating for reconfiguration, group 2 at 123 for pid 22, osid 19609
NOTE: group 2 PST updated.
SUCCESS: grp 2 disk ASM_NORM_DATA4 emptied  ← Once rebalanced relocation phase is
complete, the disk is emptied
NOTE: erasing header on grp 2 disk ASM_NORM_DATA4  ← The emptied disk's header is
erased and set to FORMER
NOTE: process _x000_+asm (19609) initiating offline of disk 3.3915941808 (ASM_NORM_
DATA4) with mask 0x7e in group 2    ← The dropped disk is offlined
NOTE: initiating PST update: grp = 2, dsk = 3/0xe96887b0, mask = 0x6a, op = clear
GMON updating disk modes for group 2 at 124 for pid 22, osid 19609
NOTE: PST update grp = 2 completed successfully
NOTE: initiating PST update: grp = 2, dsk = 3/0xe96887b0, mask = 0x7e, op = clear
GMON updating disk modes for group 2 at 125 for pid 22, osid 19609
NOTE: cache closing disk 3 of grp 2: ASM_NORM_DATA4
NOTE: PST update grp = 2 completed successfully
GMON updating for reconfiguration, group 2 at 126 for pid 22, osid 19609
NOTE: cache closing disk 3 of grp 2: (not open) ASM_NORM_DATA4
NOTE: group 2 PST updated.
Wed Sep 19 23:54:42 2012
NOTE: membership refresh pending for group 2/0x89b87754 (RECO)
GMON querying group 2 at 127 for pid 13, osid 4000
GMON querying group 2 at 128 for pid 13, osid 4000
NOTE: Disk  in mode 0x8 marked for de-assignment
SUCCESS: refreshed membership for 2/0x89b87754 (RECO)
NOTE: Attempting voting file refresh on diskgroup RECO
Wed Sep 19 23:56:45 2012
NOTE: stopping process ARB0   ← All phases of rebalance are completed and ARB0 is
shutdown
SUCCESS: rebalance completed for group 2/0x89b87754 (RECO)  ← Rebalance marked as
complete
```

The following is an excerpt from the ASM alert log during a rebalance operation for a add disk command:

```
Starting background process ARB0
SUCCESS: alter diskgroup reco add disk 'ORCL:ASM_NORM_DATA4'  rebalance power 16
Thu Sep 20 23:08:22 2012
ARB0 started with pid=22, OS id=19415
NOTE: assigning ARB0 to group 2/0x89b87754 (RECO) with 16 parallel I/Os
Thu Sep 20 23:08:31 2012
NOTE: Attempting voting file refresh on diskgroup RECO
Thu Sep 20 23:08:46 2012
NOTE: requesting all-instance membership refresh for group=2
Thu Sep 20 23:08:49 2012
NOTE: F1X0 copy 1 relocating from 0:2 to 0:459 for diskgroup 2 (RECO)
Thu Sep 20 23:08:50 2012
GMON updating for reconfiguration, group 2 at 134 for pid 27, osid 19492
NOTE: group 2 PST updated.
Thu Sep 20 23:08:50 2012
NOTE: membership refresh pending for group 2/0x89b87754 (RECO)
NOTE: F1X0 copy 2 relocating from 1:2 to 1:500 for diskgroup 2 (RECO)
NOTE: F1X0 copy 3 relocating from 2:2 to 2:548 for diskgroup 2 (RECO)
GMON querying group 2 at 135 for pid 13, osid 4000
SUCCESS: refreshed membership for 2/0x89b87754 (RECO)
Thu Sep 20 23:09:06 2012
NOTE: Attempting voting file refresh on diskgroup RECO
Thu Sep 20 23:09:57 2012
NOTE: stopping process ARB0
SUCCESS: rebalance completed for group 2/0x89b87754 (RECO)
```

An ARB trace file is created for each ARB process involved in the rebalance operation. This ARB trace file can be found in the trace subdirectory under the DIAG directory. The following is a small excerpt from this trace file:

```
*** 2013-06-21 12:56:39.928
ARB0 relocating file +DATA.257.625774759 (120 entries)
ARB0 relocating file +DATA.257.625774759 (120 entries)
............
ARB0 relocating file +DATA.263.625773231 (120 entries)
ARB0 relocating file +DATA.263.625773231 (120 entries)
ARB0 relocating file +DATA.263.625773231 (120 entries)
```

The preceding entries are repeated for each file assigned to the ARB process.

Resizing a Physical Disk or LUN and the ASM Disk Group

When you're increasing the size of a disk group, it is a best practice to add disks of similar size. However, in some cases it is appropriate to resize disks rather than to add storage of equal size. For these cases, you should resize all the disks in the disk group (to the same size) at the same time. This section discusses how to expand or resize the logical unit number (LUN) as an ASM disk.

Disks in the storage are usually configured as a LUN and presented to the host. When a LUN runs out of space, you can expand it within the storage array by adding new disks in the back end. However, the operating system (OS) must then recognize the new space. Some operating systems require a reboot to recognize the new LUN size. On Linux systems that use Emulex drivers, for example, the following can be used:

```
echo "- - -" >/sys/class/scsi_host/host{N}/scan
```

Here, N is the SCSI port ordinal assigned to this HBA port (see the /proc/scsi/lpfc directory and look for the "port_number" files).

The first step in increasing the size of an ASM disk is to add extra storage capacity to the LUN. To use more space, the partition must be re-created. This operation is at the partition table level, and that table is stored in the first sectors of the disk. Changing the partition table does not affect the data as long as the starting offset of the partition is not changed.

The view V$ASM_DISK called OS_MB gives the actual OS size of the disk. This column can aid in appropriately resizing the disk and preventing attempts to resize disks that cannot be resized.

The general steps to resize an ASM disk are as follows:

1. Resize the LUN from storage array. This is usually a noninvasive operation.

2. Query V$ASM_DISK for the OS_MB for the disk to be resized. If the OS or ASM does not see the new size, review the steps from the host bus adapter (HBA) vendor to probe for new devices. In some cases, this may require a reboot.

Rebalance Power Management

Rebalancing involves physical movement of file extents. Its impact is usually low because the rebalance is done a few extents at a time, so there's little outstanding I/O at any given time per ARB process. This should not adversely affect online database activity. However, it is generally advisable to schedule the rebalance operation during off-peak hours.

The init.ora parameter ASM_POWER_LIMIT is used to influence the throughput and speed of the rebalance operation. For Oracle 11.2.0.1 and below, the range of values for ASM_POWER_LIMIT is 0–11, where a value of 11 is full throttle and a value of 1 (the default) is low speed. A value of 0, which turns off automatic rebalance, should be used with caution. In a Real Application Clusters (RAC) environment, the ASM_POWER_LIMIT is specific to each ASM instance. (A common question is why the maximum power limit is 11 rather than 10. Movie lovers might recall the amplifier discussion from *This is Spinal Tap.*)

For releases 11.2.0.2 and above, the ASM_POWER_LIMIT can be set up to 1024, which results in ASM relocating those many extents in parallel. Increasing the rebalance power also increases the amount of PGA memory needed during relocation. In the event the current memory settings of the ASM instance prevents allocation of the required memory, ASM dials down the power and continues with the available memory.

The power value can also be set for a specific rebalance activity using the ALTER DISKGROUP command. This value is effective only for the specific rebalance task. The following example demonstrates this:

```
"Session1 SQL"> ALTER DISKGROUP DATA ADD DISK '/dev/rdsk/c3t19d39s4'
REBALANCE POWER 11;
```

Here is an example from another session:

```
"Session2 SQL"> SELECT * FROM V$ASM_OPERATION;
OPERA  STAT POWER      ACTUAL     SOFAR    EST_WORK    EST_RATE EST_MINUTES
-----  ---- --------- ---------- ---------- ---------- ---------- ---------
1 REBAL WAIT      11          0          0          0          0          0

(time passes............)
OPERA STAT  POWER     ACTUAL     SOFAR    EST_WORK    EST_RATE EST_MINUTES
----------- ----- ---- --------- --------- ---------- ---------- ---------
1 REBAL RUN      11        11     115269    217449       6333         16
(time passes............)
```

Each rebalance step has various associated states. The following are the valid states:

- **WAIT** This indicates that currently no operations are running for the group.

- **RUN** An operation is running for the group.

- **HALT** An administrator is halting an operation.

- **ERRORS** An operation has been halted by errors.

A power value of 0 indicates that no rebalance should occur for this rebalance. This setting is particularly important when you're adding or removing storage (that has external redundancy) and then deferring the rebalance to a later scheduled time. However, a power level of 0 should be used with caution; this is especially true if the disk group is low on available space, which may result in an ORA-15041 for out-of-balance disk groups.

The power level is adjusted with the ALTER DISKGROUP REBALANCE command, which affects only the current rebalance for the specified disk group; future rebalances are not affected. If you increase the power level of the existing rebalance, it will spawn new ARB processes. If you decrease the power level, the running ARB process will finish its extent relocation and then quiesce and die off.

If you are removing or adding several disks, add or remove disks in a single ALTER DISKGROUP statement; this reduces the number of rebalance operations needed for storage changes. This behavior is more critical where normal- and high-redundancy disk groups have been configured because of disk repartnering. Executing a single disk group reconfiguration command allows ASM to figure out the ideal disk partnering and reduce excessive data movement. The following example demonstrates this storage change:

```
SQl> ALTER DISKGROUP DATA ADD DISK '/dev/rdsk/c7t19*'
DROP DATA_0012 REBALANCE POWER 8;
```

An ASM disk group rebalance is an asynchronous operation in that the control is returned immediately to the DBA after the operation executes in the background. The status of the ongoing operation can be queried from V$ASM_OPERATION. However, in some situations the disk group operation needs to be synchronous—that is, it must wait until rebalance is completed. The ASM ALTER DISKGROUP commands that result in a rebalance offer a WAIT option. This option allows for accurate (sequential) scripting that may rely on the space change from a rebalance completing before any subsequent action is taken. For instance, if you add 100GB of storage to a completely full disk group, you will not be able to use all 100GB of storage until the rebalance completes. The WAIT option ensures that the space addition is successful and is available for space allocations. If a new rebalance command is entered while one is already in progress in WAIT mode, the command will not return until the disk group is in a balanced state or the rebalance operation encounters an error.

The following SQL script demonstrates how the WAIT option can be used in SQL scripting. The script adds a new disk, /dev/sdc6, and waits until the add and rebalance operations complete, returning the control back to the script. The subsequent step adds a large tablespace.

```
#An example script to demonstrate WAIT option
#Login to ASM to add the disk
sqlplus  "/ as sysasm" << EOF
ALTER DISKGROUP data ADD DISK '/dev/sdc6' REBALANCE POWER 2 WAIT;
<< EOF
#login into database & create tablespace for the next month's Order Entry data
sqlplus  oe_dba/oe1@proddb  << EOF
 CREATE BIGFILE TABLESPACE May_OE  DATAFILE SIZE 800 G
<< EOF
```

In the event that dropping a disk results in a hung rebalance operation due to the lack of free space, ASM rejects the drop command when it is executed. Here's an example:

```
SQL> select name, total_mb, free_mb from v$asm_diskgroup;

NAME                            TOTAL_MB    FREE_MB
------------------------------- ---------- ----------
DATA                                2750        234
SQL> select name, total_mb, free_mb from v$asm_disk;

NAME                            TOTAL_MB    FREE_MB
------------------------------- ---------- ----------
```

```
DATA_0000                                      250        21
DATA_0001                                      250        20
DATA_0002                                      250        22
DATA_0003                                      250        24
DATA_0004                                      250        21
DATA_0005                                      250        21
DATA_0006                                      250        22
DATA_0007                                      250        14
DATA_0008                                      250        22
DATA_0009                                      250        22
DATA_0010                                      250        25

11 rows selected.
SQL> alter diskgroup data drop disk DATA_0000;
alter diskgroup data drop disk DATA_0000
*
ERROR at line 1:
ORA-15032: not all alterations performed
ORA-15250: insufficient diskgroup space for rebalance completion
```

Fast Rebalance

When a storage change initiates a disk group rebalance, typically all active ASM instances of an ASM cluster and their RDBMS clients are notified and become engaged in the synchronization of the extents that are being rearranged. This messaging between instances can be "chatty" and thus can increase the overall time to complete the rebalance operation.

In certain situations where the user does not need the disk group to be "user accessible" and needs rebalancing to complete as soon as possible, it is beneficial to perform the rebalance operation without the extra overhead of the ASM-to-ASM and ASM-to-RDBMS messaging. The Fast Rebalance feature eliminates this overhead by allowing a single ASM instance to rebalance the disk group without the messaging overhead. The primary goal of Fast Rebalance is to improve the overall performance of the rebalance operation. Additionally, the rebalance operation can be invoked at maximum power level (power level 11 or 1024 for 11.2.0.2 above) to provide the highest throttling, making the rebalance operation limited only by the I/O subsystem (to the degree you can saturate the I/O subsystem with maximum synchronous 1MB I/Os).

To eliminate messaging to other ASM instances, the ASM instance that performs the rebalance operation requires exclusive access to the disk group. To provide this exclusive disk group access, a new disk group mount mode, called RESTRICTED, was introduced in Oracle Database 11*g*. A disk group can be placed in RESTRICTED mode using STARTUP RESTRICT or ALTER DISKGROUP MOUNT RESTRICT.

When a disk group is mounted in RESTRICTED mode, RDBMS instances are prevented from accessing that disk group and thus databases cannot be opened. Furthermore, only one ASM instance in a cluster can mount a disk group in RESTRICTED mode. When the instance is started in RESTRICTED mode, all disk group mounts in that instance will automatically be in RESTRICTED mode. The ASM instance needs to be restarted in NORMAL mode to get it out of RESTRICTED mode.

At the end of the rebalance operation, the user must explicitly dismount the disk group and remount it in NORMAL mode to make the disk group available to RDBMS instances.

Effects of Imbalanced Disks

This section illustrates how ASM distributes extents evenly and creates a balanced disk group. Additionally, the misconceptions of disk group space balance management are covered.

The term "balanced" in the ASM world is slightly overloaded. A disk group can become imbalanced for several reasons:

■ Dissimilarly sized disks are used in a given disk group.

■ A rebalance operation was aborted.

■ A rebalance operation was halted. In this case, this state can be determined by the UNBALANCED column of the V$ASM_DISKGROUP view. Operationally, the DBA can resolve this problem by manually performing a rebalance against the specific disk group.

NOTE
The UNBALANCED column in V$ASM_DISKGROUP indicates that a rebalance is in flux—that is, either in progress or stopped. This column is not an indicator for an unbalanced disk group.

■ A disk was added to the disk group with an ASM_POWER_LIMIT or power level of 0, but the disk group was never rebalanced afterward.

This section focuses on the first reason: a disk group being imbalanced due to differently sized disks. For the other reasons, allowing the rebalance to complete will fix the imbalance automatically.

The main goal of ASM is to provide an even distribution of data extents across all disk members of a disk group. When an RDBMS instance requests a file creation, ASM allocates extents from all the disks in the specified disk group. The first disk allocation is chosen randomly, but all subsequent disks for extent allocation are chosen to evenly spread each file across all disks and to evenly fill all disks. Therefore, if all disks are equally sized, all disks should have the same number of extents and thus an even I/O load.

But what happens when a disk group contains unequally sized disks—for example, a set of 25GB disks mixed with a couple of 50GB disks? When allocating extents, ASM will place twice as many extents on each of the bigger 50GB disks as on the smaller 25GB disks. Thus, the 50GB disks will contain more data extents than their 25GB counterparts. This allocation scheme causes dissimilarly sized disks to fill at the same proportion, but will also induce unbalanced I/O across the disk group because the disk with more extents will receive more I/O requests.

The following example illustrates this scenario:

1. Note that the FAST disk group initially contains two disks that are equally sized (8.6GB):

```
SQL> SELECT NAME, TOTAL_MB, FREE_MB FROM V$ASM_DISK WHERE
GROUP_NUMBER =2;
NAME                               TOTAL_MB   FREE_MB
------------------------------ ---------- ----------
FAST_0001                              8628       1159
FAST_0000                              8628       1160
```

2. Display the extent distribution on the current disk group layout. The even extent distribution is shown by the COUNT(PXN_KFFXP) column.

```
SQL> SELECT COUNT ( PXN_KFFXP), DISK_KFFXP, GROUP_KFFXP
FROM X$KFFXP WHERE GROUP_KFFXP=2 GROUP BY DISK_KFFXP,
GROUP_KFFXP ORDER BY GROUP_KFFXP, DISK_KFFXP;
COUNT(PXN_KFFXP) DISK_KFFXP GROUP_KFFXP
---------------- ---------- -----------
            7461          0           2
            7462          1           2
```

3. Add two more 8.6GB disks to the disk group:

```
SQL> ALTER DISKGROUP FAST ADD DISK '/dev/rdsk/c2t12d13s4',
 '/dev/rdsk/c2t12d14s4' REBALANCE POWER 8 WAIT;
```

4. Use the following query to display the extent distribution after the two disks were added:

```
SQL> SELECT COUNT(PXN_KFFXP), DISK_KFFXP, GROUP_KFFXP
FROM X$KFFXP WHERE GROUP_KFFXP=2 GROUP BY DISK_KFFXP,
GROUP_KFFXP ORDER BY GROUP_KFFXP, DISK_KFFXP;
COUNT(PXN_KFFXP) DISK_KFFXP GROUP_KFFXP
---------------- ---------- -----------
            3736          0           2
            3737          1           2
            3716          2           2
            3734          3           2
```

5. Note that a 1GB disk was accidentally added:

```
sql> ALTER DISKGROUP FAST ADD DISK '/dev/rdsk/c2t12d29s4'
SIZE 1G;
```

6. Display the space usage from V$ASM_DISK. Notice the size of disk FAST_0004:

```
SQL> SELECT NAME, TOTAL_MB, FREE_MB FROM V$ASM_DISK WHERE
GROUP_NUMBER=2;
NAME                                  TOTAL_MB    FREE_MB
------------------------------------ ---------- ----------
FAST_0001                                 8628       4996
FAST_0000                                 8628       4996
FAST_0002                                 8583       4970
FAST_0003                                 8628       4996
FAST_0004                                 1024        590
```

7. The extent distribution query is rerun to display the effects of this mistake. Notice the unevenness of the extent distribution.

```
SQL> SELECT COUNT (PXN_KFFXP), DISK_KFFXP, GROUP_KFFXP
FROM X$KFFXP WHERE GROUP_KFFXP =2 GROUP BY DISK_KFFXP,
GROUP_KFFXP ORDER BY GROUP_KFFXP, DISK_KFFXP;
COUNT(PXN_KFFXP) DISK_KFFXP GROUP_KFFXP
---------------- ---------- -----------
            3628          0           2
            3628          1           2
            3609          2           2
            3626          3           2
             432          4           2
```

MYTH

Adding and dropping a disk in the same disk group requires two separate rebalance activities. In fact, some disks can be dropped and others added to a disk group with a single rebalance command. This is more efficient than separate commands.

ASM and Storage Array Migration

One of the core benefits of ASM is the ability to rebalance extents not only within disk enclosure frames (storage arrays) but also across frames. Customers have used this ability extensively when migrating between storage arrays (for example, between an EMC VNX to the VMAX storage systems) or between storage vendors (for example, from EMC arrays to Hitachi Data Systems [HDS] arrays).

The following example illustrates the simplicity of this migration. In this example, the DATA disk group will migrate from an EMC VNX storage enclosure to the EMC VMAX enclosure. A requirement for this type of storage migration is that both storage enclosures must be attached to the host during the migration and must be discovered by ASM. Once the rebalance is completed and all the data is moved from the old frame, the old frame can be "unzoned" and "uncabled" from the host(s).

```
SQl> ALTER DISKGROUP ADD DISK '/dev/rdsk/c7t19*'
DROP DISK DATA_0001, DATA_0002, DATA_0003, DATA_0004 REBALANCE POWER 8;
```

This command indicates that the disks DATA_0001 through DATA_0004 (from the current EMC VNX disks) are to be dropped and that the new VMAX disks, specified by /dev/rdsk/c7t19*, are to be added. The ADD and DROP commands can all be done in one rebalance operation. Additionally, the RDBMS instance can stay online while the rebalance is in progress. Note that migration to new storage is an exception to the general rule against mixing different size/performance disks in the same disk group. This mixture of disparate disks is transient; the configuration at the end of the rebalance will have disks of similar size and performance characteristics.

ASM and OS Migration

Customers often ask whether they can move between the same endianness systems, but different operating systems, while keeping the storage array the same. For example, suppose that a customer wants to migrate from Solaris to AIX, with the database on ASM over an EMC Clariion storage array network (SAN). The storage will be kept intact and physically reattached to the AIX server. Customers ask whether this migration is viable and/or supported.

Although ASM data structures are compatible with most OSs (except for endianness) and should not have a problem, other factors preclude this from working. In particular, the OS LUN partition has its own OS partition table format. It is unlikely that this partition table can be moved between different OSs.

Additionally, the database files themselves may have other issues, such as platform-specific structures and formats, and thus the database data will need to be converted to the target platform's format. Some viable options include the following:

- Data pump full export/import

- Cross-platform transportable tablespaces (XTTSs)

- Streams

Important Points on ASM Rebalance

The following are some important points on rebalance and extent distribution:

■   It is very important that similarly sized disks be used in a single disk group, and that failure groups are also of similar sizes. The use of dissimilar disks will cause uneven extent distribution and I/O load. If one disk lacks free space, it is impossible to do any allocation in a disk group because every file must be evenly allocated across all disks. Rebalancing and allocation should make the percentage of allocated space about the same on every disk.

■   Rebalance runs automatically only when there is a disk group configuration change. Many users have the misconception that ASM periodically wakes up to perform rebalance. This simply is not true.

■   If you are using similarly sized disks and you still see disk group imbalance, either a previous rebalance operation failed to complete (or was cancelled) or the administrator set the rebalance power to 0 via a rebalance command. A manual rebalance should fix these cases.

■   If a server goes down while you're executing a rebalance, the rebalance will be automatically restarted after ASM instance/crash recovery. A persistently stored record indicates the need for a rebalance. The node that does the recovery sees the record indicating that a rebalance is in progress and that the rebalance was running on the instance that died. It will then start a new rebalance. The recovering node may be different from the node that initiated the rebalance.

■   Many factors determine the speed of rebalance. Most importantly, it depends on the underlying I/O subsystem. To calculate the lower bound of the time required for the rebalance to complete, determine the following:

1.   Calculate amount of data that has to be moved. ASM relocates data proportional to the amount of space being added. If you are doubling the size of the disk group, then 50 percent of the data will be moved; if you are adding 10 percent more storage, then at least 10 percent of the data will be moved; and so on.

2.   Determine how long it will take the I/O subsystem to perform that amount of data movement. As described previously, ASM does relocation I/Os as a synchronous 1 AU read followed by a synchronous 1 AU write. Up to ASM_POWER_LIMIT I/Os can operate in parallel depending on the rebalance power. This calculation is a lower bound, because ASM has additional synchronization overhead.

3. The impact of rebalance should be low because ASM relocates and locks extents one at a time. ASM relocates multiple extents simultaneously only if rebalance is running with higher power. Only the I/Os against the extents being relocated are blocked; ASM does not block I/Os for all files in the ASM disk group. I/Os are not actually blocked per se; reads can proceed from the old location during relocation, whereas some writes need to be temporarily stalled or may need to be reissued if they were in process during the relocation I/O. The writes to these extents can be completed after the extent is moved to its new location. All this activity is transparent to the application. Note that the chance of an I/O being issued during the time that an extent is locked is very small. In the case of the Flash disk group, which contains archive logs or backups, many of the files being relocated will not even be open at the time, so the impact is very minimal.

- When a rebalance is started for newly added disks, ASM immediately begins using the free space on them; however, ASM continues to allocate files evenly across all disks. If a disk group is almost full, and a large disk (or set of disks) is then added, the RDBMS could get out-of-space (ORA-15041) errors even though there is seemingly sufficient space in the disk group. With the WAIT option to the ADD DISK command, control does not return to the user until rebalance is complete. This may provide more intuitive behavior to customers who run near capacity.

- If disks are added very frequently, the same data is relocated many times, causing excessive data movement. It is a best practice to add and drop multiple disks at a time so that ASM can reorganize partnership information within ASM metadata more efficiently. For normal- and high-redundancy disk groups, it is very important to batch the operations for adding and dropping disks rather than doing them in rapid succession. The latter option generates much more overhead because mirroring and failure groups place greater constraints on where data can be placed. In extreme cases, nesting many adds and drops without allowing the intervening rebalance to run to completion can lead to the error ORA-15074.

Summary

Every ASM disk is divided into fixed-size allocation units. The AU is the fundamental unit of allocation within a disk group, and the usable space in an ASM disk is a multiple of this size. The AU size is a disk group attribute specified at disk group creation and defaults to 1MB, but may be set as high as 64MB. An AU should be large enough that accessing it in one I/O operation provides very good throughput—

that is, the time to access an entire AU in one I/O should be dominated by the transfer rate of the disk rather than the time to seek to the beginning of the AU.

ASM spreads the extents of a file evenly across all disks in a disk group. Each extent comprises an integral number of AUs. Most files use coarse striping. With coarse striping, in each set of extents, the file is striped across the set at 1 AU granularity. Thus, each stripe of data in a file is on a different disk than the previous stripe of the file. A file may have fine-grained striping rather than coarse-grained. The difference is that the fine-grained striping granularity is 128K rather than 1 AU.

Rebalancing a disk group moves file extents between disks in the disk group to ensure that every file is evenly distributed across all the disks in the disk group. When all files are evenly distributed, all disks are evenly filled to the same percentage. This ensures load balancing. Rebalancing does not relocate data based on I/O statistics, nor is it started as a result of statistics. ASM automatically invokes rebalance only when a storage configuration change is made to an ASM disk group.

CHAPTER
9

ASM Operations

Τhis chapter describes the flow of the critical operations for ASM disk groups and files. It also describes the key interactions between the ASM and relational database management system (RDBMS) instances.

Note that many of these ASM operations have been optimized in Engineered Systems (Exadata and ODA) and thus have significantly different behavior. Chapter 12 covers these optimizations. This chapter describes ASM operations in non–Engineered Systems.

ASM Instance Discovery

The first time an RDBMS instance tries to access an ASM file, it needs to establish its connection to the local ASM instance. Rather than requiring a static configuration file to locate the ASM instance, the RDBMS contacts the Cluster Synchronization Services (CSS) daemon where the ASM instance has registered. CSS provides the necessary connect string for the RDBMS to spawn a Bequeath connection to the ASM instance. The RDBMS authenticates itself to the ASM instance via operating system (OS) authentication by connecting as SYSDBA. This initial connection between the ASM instance and the RDBMS instance is known as the *umbilicus,* and it remains active as long as the RDBMS instance has any ASM files open. The RDBMS side of this connection is the ASMB process. (See the "File Open" section for an explanation of why ASMB can appear in an ASM instance.) The ASM side of the connection is a foreground process called the *umbilicus foreground (UFG).* RDBMS and ASM instances exchange critical messages over the umbilicus. Failure of the umbilicus is fatal to the RDBMS instance because the connection is critical to maintaining the integrity of the disk group. Some of the umbilicus messages are described later in the "Relocation" section of this chapter.

RDBMS Operations on ASM Files

This section describes the interaction between the RDBMS and ASM instances for the following operations on ASM files:

- File Create
- File Open
- File I/O
- File Close
- File Delete

File Create

ASM filenames in the RDBMS are distinguished by the fact that they start with a plus sign (+). ASM file creation consists of three phases:

- File allocation in the ASM instance
- File initialization in the RDBMS instance
- File creation committed in the RDBMS and ASM instance

When an RDBMS instance wants to create an ASM file, it sends a request to create the ASM file. The RDBMS instance has a pool of processes (the o0nn processes) that have connections to the foreground process in the ASM instance is called the Network Foreground (NFG), and are used for tasks such as file creations. The file-creation request sent over the appropriate connection includes the following information:

- Disk group name
- File type
- File block size
- File size
- File tag

The request may optionally include the following additional information:

- Template name
- Alias name

ASM uses this information to allocate the file (the topic of file allocation is described in greater detail in the "ASM File Allocation" section). ASM determines the appropriate striping and redundancy for the file based on the template. If the template is not explicitly specified in the request, the default template is used based on the file type. ASM uses the file type and tag information to create the system-generated filename. The system-generated filename is formed as follows:

```
+diskgroup name/db unique name/file type/file tag.file #.incarnation#
```

After allocating the file, ASM sends extent map information to the RDBMS instance. ASM creates a Continuing Operations Directory (COD) entry to track the pending file creation. The RDBMS instance subsequently issues the appropriate I/O to initialize the file. When initialization is complete, the RDBMS instance messages ASM to commit the creation of the file.

When ASM receives the commit message, ASM's LGWR flushes the Active Change Directory (ACD) change record with the file-creation information. ASM's DBWR subsequently asynchronously writes the appropriate allocation table, file directory, and alias directory entries to disk. Thus, the high-level tasks for DBWR and LGWR are similar in the ASM instance as they are in the RDBMS instance.

If the RDBMS instance explicitly or implicitly aborts the file creation without committing the creation, ASM uses the COD to roll back the file creation. Rollback marks the allocation table entries as free, releases the file directory entry, and removes the appropriate alias directory entries. Note that rollbacks in ASM do not use the same infrastructure (undo segments) or semantics that the RDBMS instance uses.

File Open

When an RDBMS instance needs to open an ASM file, it sends to the ASM instance a File Open request, with the filename, via one of the o0nn processes. ASM consults the file directory to get the extent map for the file. ASM sends the extent map to the RDBMS instance. The extent maps of the files are sent in batches to the database instance. ASM sends the first 60 extents of the extent map to the RDBMS instance at file-open time; the remaining extents are paged in on demand by the database instance. This delayed shipping of extent maps greatly improves the time it takes to open the database.

Opening the spfile at RDBMS instance startup is a special code path. This open operation cannot follow the typical open path, because the RDBMS instance System Global Area (SGA) does not yet exist to hold the extent map. The SGA sizing information is contained in the spfile. In this specific case, the RDBMS does proxy I/O through the ASM instance. When the ASM instance reads user data, it does a loop-back connection to itself. This results in ASM having an ASMB process during RDBMS instance startup. After the RDBMS has gotten the initial contents of the spfile, it allocates the SGA, closes the proxy open of the spfile, and opens the spfile again via the normal method used for all other files.

ASM tracks all the files an RDBMS instance has open. This allows ASM to prevent the deletion of open files. ASM also needs to know what files an RDBMS instance has open so that it can coordinate extent relocation, as described later in this chapter.

File I/O

RDBMS instances perform ASM file I/O directly to the ASM disks; in other words, the I/O is performed unbuffered and directly to the disk without involving ASM. Keep in mind that each RDBMS instance uses the extent maps it obtains during file open to determine where on the ASM disks to direct its reads and writes; thus, the RDBMS instance has all the information it needs to perform the I/O to the database file.

MYTH

RDBMS instances proxy all I/O to ASM files through an ASM instance.

File Close

When an RDBMS instance closes a file, it sends a message to the ASM instance. ASM cleans up its internal state when the file is closed. Closed files do not require messaging to RDBMS instances when their extents are relocated via rebalance.

ASM administrators can issue the following command to delete closed files manually:

```
ALTER DISKGROUP … DROP FILE …
```

The DROP FILE command fails for open files (generating an ORA-15028 error message "ASM file *filename* not dropped; currently being accessed"). Generally, manual deletion of files is not required if the ASM files are Oracle Managed Files (OMFs), which are automatically deleted when they are no longer needed. For instance, when the RDBMS drops a tablespace, it will also delete the underlying data files if they are OMFs.

File Delete

When an RDBMS instance deletes a file, it sends a request to the ASM instance. The ASM instance creates a COD entry to record the intent to delete the file. ASM then marks the appropriate allocation table entries as free, releases the file directory entry, and removes the appropriate alias directory entries. If the instance fails during file deletion, COD recovery completes the deletion. The delete request from the RDBMS instance is not complete until ASM completes freeing all of the allocated space.

ASM File Allocation

This section describes how ASM allocates files within an external redundancy disk group. For simplicity, this section explains ASM striping and variable-sized extents for ASM files in the absence of ASM redundancy. The concepts in striping and variable-sized extents also apply to files with ASM redundancy. A later section explains allocation of files with ASM redundancy.

External Redundancy Disk Groups

ASM allocates files so that they are evenly spread across all disks in a disk group. ASM uses the same algorithm for choosing disks for file allocation and for file rebalance. In the case of rebalance, if multiple disks are equally desirable for extent placement, ASM chooses the disk where the extent is already allocated if that is one of the choices.

MYTH
ASM chooses disks for allocation based on I/O statistics.

MYTH
ASM places the same number of megabytes from a file on each disk regardless of disk size.

ASM chooses the disk for the first extent of a file to optimize for space usage in the disk group. It strives to fill each disk evenly (proportional to disk size if the disks are not the same size). Subsequently, ASM tries to spread the extents of the file evenly across all disks. As described in the file directory persistent structure, ASM extent placement is not bound by strict modulo arithmetic; however, extent placement tends to follow an approximately round-robin pattern across the disks in a disk group. ASM allocation on a disk begins at the lower-numbered AUs (typically the outer tracks of disks). Keeping allocations concentrated in the lower-numbered AUs tends to reduce seek time and takes advantage of the highest-performing tracks of the disk. Note that the assumption about the mapping of lower-numbered AUs to higher-performing tracks is generally true for physical disks, but may not hold true for LUNs presented by storage arrays. ASM is not aware of the underlying physical layout of the ASM disks.

A potentially nonintuitive side effect of ASM's allocation algorithm is that ASM may report out-of-space errors even when it shows adequate aggregate free space for the disk group. This side effect can occur if the disk group is out of balance. For external redundancy disk groups, the primary reason for disk group imbalance is an incomplete rebalance operation. This can occur if a user stops a rebalance operation by specifying rebalance power 0, or if rebalance was cancelled/terminated. Also, if a disk group is almost full when new disks are added, allocation may fail on the existing disks until rebalance has freed sufficient space. It is a best practice to leave at minimum 20 percent free uniformly across all disks.

Variable-Sized Extents

In disk groups with COMPATIBLE.RDBMS lower than 11.1, all extents are a fixed size of one allocation unit (AU). If COMPATIBLE.RDBMS is 11.1 or higher, extent sizes increase for data files as the file size grows. A multi-AU extent consists of multiple contiguous allocation units on the same disk. The first 20,000 extents in a file are one AU. The next 20,000 extents are four AUs. All extents beyond 40,000 are 16 AUs. This allows ASM to address larger files more efficiently. For the first

20,000 extents, allocation occurs exactly as with fixed-extent-size files. For multi-AU extents, ASM must find contiguous extents on a disk. ASM's allocation pattern tends to concentrate allocations in the lower-numbered AUs and leave free space in the higher-numbered AUs. File shrinking or deletion can lead to free space fragmentation. ASM attempts to maintain defragmented disks during disk group rebalance. If during file allocation ASM is unable to find sufficient contiguous space on a disk for a multi-AU extent, it consolidates the free space until enough contiguous space is available for the allocation. Defragmentation uses the relocation locking mechanism described later in this chapter.

ASM Striping

ASM offers two types of striping for files. Coarse striping is done at the AU level. Fine-grained striping is done at 128K granularity. Coarse striping provides better throughput, whereas fine-grained striping provides better latency. The file template indicates which type of striping is performed for the file. If a template is not specified during file creation, ASM uses the default template for the file type.

ASM striping is performed logically at the client level. In other words, RDBMS instances interpret extent maps differently based on the type of striping for the file. Striping is opaque to ASM operations such as extent relocation; however, ASM takes striping into account during file allocation.

Coarse Striping

With single AU extents, each extent contains a contiguous logical chunk of the file. Because ASM distributes files evenly across all disks at the extent level, such files are effectively striped at AU-sized boundaries.

With multi-AU extents, the ASM file is logically striped at the AU level across a stripe set of eight disks. For instance, with 1MB AUs, the first MB of the file is written to the first disk, the second MB is written to the second disk, the third MB is written to the third disk, and so on. The file allocation dictates the set of eight disks involved in the stripe set and the order in which they appear in the stripe set. If fewer than eight disks exist in the disk group, then disks may be repeated within a stripe set.

Figure 9-1 shows a file with coarse striping and 1MB fixed extents. The logical database file is 6.5MB. In the figure, each letter represents 128K, so uppercase *A* through *Z* followed by lowercase *a* through *z* cover 6.5MB. Each extent is 1MB (represented by eight letters, or 8 × 128K) and holds the contiguous logical content of the database file. ASM must allocate seven extents to hold a 6.5MB file with coarse striping.

Figure 9-2 represents a file with variable-sized extents and coarse striping. In order for the figure to fit on one page, it represents a disk group with eight disks. The

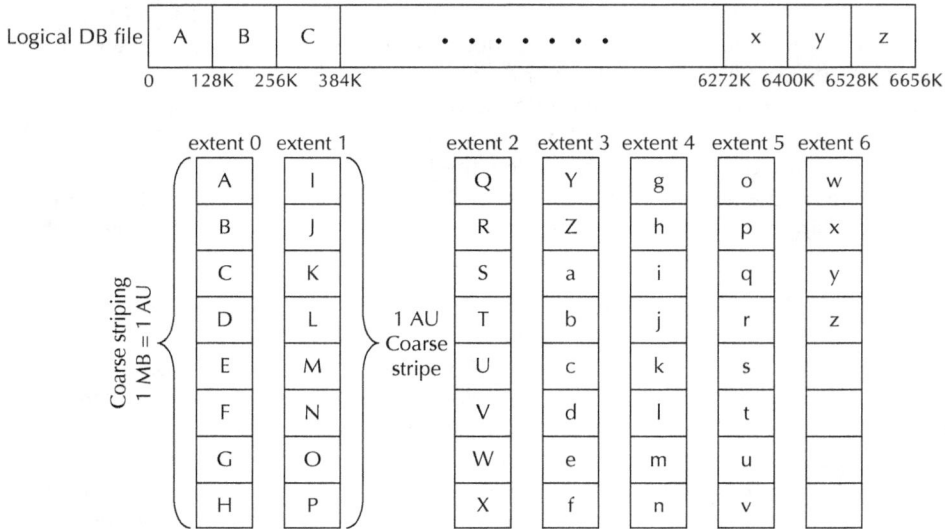

FIGURE 9-1. *Coarse striping*

file represented is 20,024MB. In the figure, each capital letter represents 1MB in the database file. The file has 20,008 extents. The first 20,000 are one AU, whereas the next eight are eight AU extents. Notice that the eight AU extents are allocated in sets of eight so that ASM can continue to stripe at the AU level. This file uses 20,064MB of space in the disk group.

Fine-Grained Striping

Fine-grained striped ASM files are logically striped at 128K. For each set of eight extents, the file data is logically striped in a round-robin fashion: bytes 0K through 127K go on the first disk, 128K through 255K on the second disk, 256K through 383K on the third disk, and so on. The file allocation determines the set of eight disks involved in the stripe set and the order in which they appear in the stripe set. If fewer than eight disks exist in the disk group, then disks may be repeated within a stripe set.

Disk 0
extent# (value)

0	0(A)
1	8(I)
2	16(G)

2500	20000(A)
2501	20000(I)
2502	20000(Q)
2503	20000
2504	20000
2505	20000
2506	20000
2507	20000

Disk 1
extent# (value)

0	1(B)
1	9(J)
2	17(R)

2506	20001(B)
2501	20001(I)
2502	20001(Q)
2503	20001
2504	20001
2505	20001
2506	20001
2507	20001

Disk 7
extent# (value)

0	7(H)
1	15(P)
2	23(X)

2506	20007(H)
2501	20007(P)
2502	20007(X)
2503	20007
2504	20007
2505	20007
2506	20007
2507	20007

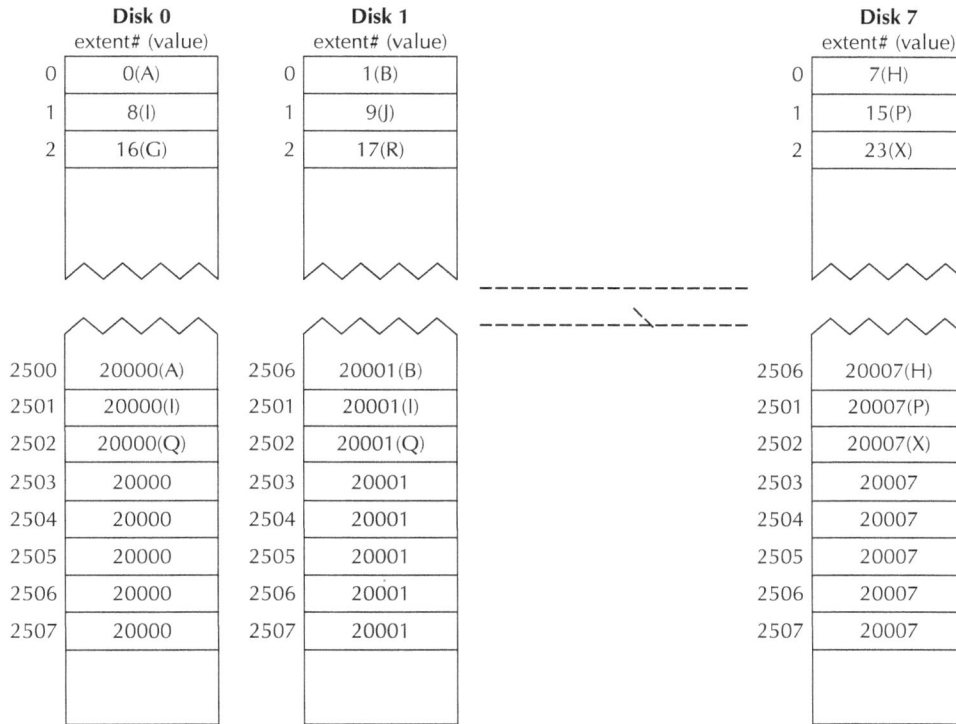

FIGURE 9-2. *Coarse striping variable-sized extents*

MYTH
*Fine-grained striped ASM files have smaller extent
sizes than files with coarse striping.*

Figure 9-3 shows a file with fine-grained striping and 1MB fixed extents. The logical database file is 6.5MB (and is the same as the file shown in Figure 9-1). In the figure, each letter represents 128K, so uppercase A through Z followed by lowercase a through z cover 6.5MB. Each extent is 1MB (representing eight letters or 8 × 128K). ASM must allocate eight extents to hold a 6.5MB file with fine-grained striping. As described previously, the logical contents of the database file are striped across the eight extents in 128K stripes.

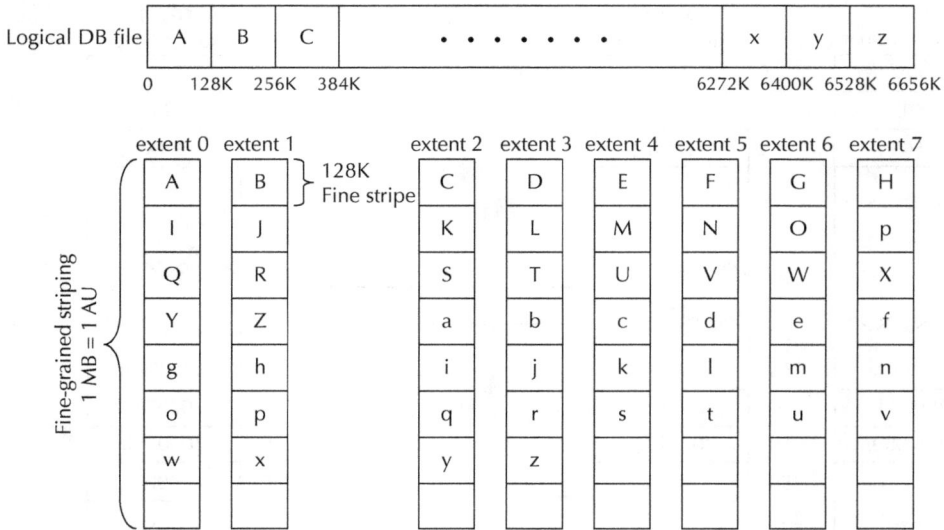

FIGURE 9-3. *Fine-grained striping*

ASM Redundancy

Unlike traditional volume managers, ASM mirrors extents rather than mirroring disks. ASM's extent-based mirroring provides load balancing and hardware utilization advantages over traditional redundancy methods.

In traditional RAID 1 mirroring, the disk that mirrors a failed disk suddenly must serve all the reads that were intended for the failed drive, and it also serves all the reads needed to populate the hot spare disk that replaces the failed drive. When an ASM disk fails, the load of the I/Os that would have gone to that disk is distributed among the disks that contain the mirror copies of extents on the failed disk.

MYTH

ASM mirroring makes two disks look identical.

RAID 5 and RAID 1 redundancy schemes have a rigid formula that dictates the placement of the data relative to the mirror or parity copies. As a result, these schemes require hot spare disks to replace drives when they fail. "Hot spare" is a euphemism for "usually idle." During normal activity, applications cannot take advantage of the I/O capacity of a hot spare disk. ASM, on the other hand, does not require any hot spare disks; it requires only spare capacity. During normal operation, all disks are actively serving I/O for the disk group. When a disk fails, ASM's flexible extent pointers allow extents from a failed disk to be reconstructed from the mirror copies distributed across the disk partners of the failed disk. The reconstructed extents can be placed on the remaining disks in the disk group. See Chapter 12 for the specialized layout and configurations on Engineered Systems.

Failure Groups

Because of the physical realities of disk connectivity, disks do not necessarily fail independently. Certain disks share common single points of failure, such as a power supply, a host bus adapter (HBA), or a controller. Different users have different ideas about which component failures they want to be able to tolerate. Users can specify the shared components whose failures they want to tolerate by specifying failure groups. By default, each disk is in its own failure group; in other words, if the failgroup specification is omitted, ASM automatically places each disk into its own failgroup. The only exceptions are Exadata and ODA. In Exadata, all disks from the same storage cell are automatically placed in the same failgroup. In ODA, disks from specific slots in the array are automatically put into a specific failgroup.

   ASM allocates mirror extents such that they are always in a different failure group than the primary extent. In the case of high-redundancy files, each extent copy in an extent set is in a different failure group. By placing mirror copies in different failure groups, ASM guarantees that even with the loss of all disks in a failure group, a disk group will still have at least one copy of every extent available. The way failure groups are managed and extents are distributed has been specialized and specifically designed to take advantage of the Engineered Systems. See Chapter 12 for the details on disk, failure group, and recovery management on Engineered Systems.

Disk Partners

ASM disks store the mirror copies of their extents on their disk partners. A disk partnership is a symmetric relationship between two disks in the same disk group but different failure groups. ASM selects partners for a disk from failure groups other than the failure group to which the disk belongs, but an ASM disk may have multiple partners that are in the same failure group. Limiting the number of partners for each disk minimizes the number of disks whose overlapping failures could lead to loss of data in a disk group. Consider a disk group with 100 disks. If an extent could be mirrored between any two disks, the failure of any two of the 100 disks could lead to data loss. If a disk mirrors its extents on only up to 10 disks, then when one disk fails, its 10 partners must remain online until the lost disk's contents are reconstructed by rebalance, but a failure of any of the other 89 disks could be tolerated without loss of data.

ASM stores the partnership information in the Partnership Status Table (PST). Users do not specify disk partners; ASM chooses disk partners automatically based on the disk group's failure group definitions. A disk never has any partners in its own failure group. Disk partnerships may change when the disk group configuration changes. Disks have a maximum of 10 active partnerships, but typically it is eight active partnerships. When disk group reconfigurations cause disks to drop existing partnerships and form new partnerships, the PST tracks the former partnerships until rebalance completes to ensure that former partners no longer mirror any extent between them. PST space restrictions limit each disk to a total of 20 total and former partners. For this reason, it is more efficient to perform disk reconfiguration (that is, to add or drop a disk) in batches. Too many nested disk group reconfigurations can exhaust the PST space and result in an "ORA-15074: diskgroup requires rebalance completion" error message.

Allocation with ASM Redundancy

File allocation in normal- and high-redundancy disk groups is similar to allocation in external redundancy disk groups. ASM uses the same algorithm for allocating the primary extent for each extent set. ASM then balances mirror extent allocation among the partners of the disk that contains the primary extent.

Because mirror extent placement is dictated by disk partnerships, which are influenced by failure group definitions, it is important that failure groups in a disk group be of similar sizes. If some failure groups are smaller than others, ASM may return out-of-space errors during file allocation if the smaller failure group fills up sooner than the other failure groups.

I/O to ASM Mirrored Files

When all disks in an ASM disk group are online, ASM writes in parallel to all copies of an extent and reads from the primary extent. Writes to all extent copies are necessary for correctness. Reads from the primary extent provide the best balance of I/O across disks in a disk group.

MYTH
ASM needs to read from all mirror sides to balance I/O across disks.

Most traditional volume managers distribute reads evenly among the mirror sides in order to balance I/O load among the disks that mirror each other. Because each ASM disk contains a combination of primary and mirror extents, I/O to primary extents of ASM files spreads the load evenly across all disks. Although the placement of mirror extents is constrained by failure group definitions, ASM can allocate primary extents on any disk to optimize for even distribution of primary extents.

Read Errors

When an RDBMS instance encounters an I/O error trying to read a primary extent, it will try to read the mirror extent. If the read from the mirror extent is successful, the RDBMS can satisfy the read request, and upper-layer processing continues as usual. For a high-redundancy file, the RDBMS tries to read the second mirror extent if the first mirror extent returns an I/O error. If reads fail to all extent copies, the I/O error propagates to the upper layers, which take the appropriate action (such as taking a tablespace offline). A read error in an RDBMS instance never causes a disk to go offline.

The ASM instance handles read errors in a similar fashion. If ASM is unable to read any copy of a virtual metadata extent, it forces the dismounting of the disk group. If ASM is unable to read physical metadata for a disk, it takes the disk offline, because physical metadata is not mirrored.

Read errors can be due to the loss of access to the entire disk or due to bad sectors on an otherwise healthy disk. ASM tries to recover from bad sectors on a disk. Read errors in the RDBMS or ASM instance trigger the ASM instance to attempt bad block remapping. ASM reads a good copy of the extent and copies it to the disk that had the read error. If the write to the same location succeeds, the underlying allocation unit is deemed healthy (because the underlying disk likely did its own bad block relocation). If the write fails, ASM attempts to write the extent to a new allocation unit of the same disk. If that write succeeds, the original allocation unit is marked as unusable. If the write to the new allocation unit fails, the disk is taken offline. The process of relocating a bad allocation unit uses the same locking logic discussed later in this chapter for rebalance.

One unique benefit on ASM-based mirroring is that the RDBMS instance is aware of the mirroring. For many types of logical file corruptions, if the RDBMS instance reads unexpected data (such as a bad checksum or incorrect System Change Number [SCN]) from the primary extent, the RDBMS proceeds through the mirror sides looking for valid content. If the RDBMS can find valid data on an alternate mirror, it can proceed without errors (although it will log the problem in the alert log). If the process in the RDBMS that encountered the read is in a position to obtain the appropriate locks to ensure data consistency, it writes the correct data to all mirror sides.

Write Errors

When an RDBMS instance encounters a write error, it sends to the ASM instance a disk offline message indicating which disk had the write error. If the RDBMS can successfully complete a write to at least one extent copy and receive acknowledgment of the offline disk from the ASM instance, the write is considered successful for the purposes of the upper layers of the RDBMS. If writes to all mirror sides fail, the RDBMS takes the appropriate actions in response to a write error (such as taking a tablespace offline).

When the ASM instance receives a write error message from an RDBMS instance (or when an ASM instance encounters a write error itself), ASM attempts to take the disk offline. ASM consults the PST to see whether any of the disk's partners are offline. If too many partners are already offline, ASM forces the dismounting of the disk group on that node. Otherwise, ASM takes the disk offline. ASM also tries to read the disk header for all the other disks in the same failure group as the disk that had the write error. If the disk header read fails for any of those disks, they are also taken offline. This optimization allows ASM to handle potential disk group reconfigurations more efficiently.

Disk offline is a global operation. The ASM instance that initiates the offline sends a message to all other ASM instances in the cluster. The ASM instances all relay the offline status to their client RDBMS instances. If COMPATIBLE.RDBMS is less than 11.1, ASM immediately force-drops disks that have gone offline. If COMPATIBLE.RDBMS is 11.1 or higher, disks stay offline until the administrator issues an online command or until the timer specified by the DISK_REPAIR_TIME attribute expires. If the timer expires, ASM force-drops the disk. The "Resync" section later in this chapter describes how ASM handles I/O to offline disks.

Mirror Resilvering

Because the RDBMS writes in parallel to multiple copies of extents, in the case of a process or node failure, it is possible that a write has completed to one extent copy but not another. Mirror resilvering ensures that two mirror sides (that may be read) are consistent.

MYTH
ASM needs a Dirty Region Log to keep mirrors in sync after process or node failure.

Most traditional volume managers handle mirror resilvering by maintaining a Dirty Region Log (DRL). The DRL is a bitmap with 1 bit per chunk (typically 512K) of the volume. Before a mirrored write can be issued, the DRL bit for the chunk must be set on disk. This results in a performance penalty if an additional write to the DRL is required before the mirrored write can be initiated. A write is unnecessary if the DRL bit is already set because of a prior write. The volume manager lazily clears DRL bits as part of other DRL accesses. Following a node failure, for each region marked in the DRL, the volume manager copies one mirror side to the other as part of recovery before the volume is made available to the application. The lazy clearing of bits in the DRL and coarse granularity inevitably result in more data than necessary being copied during traditional volume manager resilvering.

Because the RDBMS must recover from process and node failure anyway, RDBMS recovery also addresses potential ASM mirror inconsistencies if necessary. Some files, such as archived logs, are simply re-created if there was a failure while they were being written, so no resilvering is required. This is possible because an archive log's creation is not committed until all of its contents are written. For some operations, such as writing intermediate sort data, the failure means that the data will never be read, so the mirror sides need not be consistent and no recovery is required. If the redo log indicates that a data file needs a change applied, the RDBMS reads the appropriate blocks from the data file and checks the SCN. If the SCN in the block indicates that the change must be applied, the RDBMS writes the change to both mirror sides (just as with all other writes). If the SCN in the block indicates that the change is already present, the RDBMS writes the block back to the data file in case an unread mirror side does not contain the change. The resilvering of the redo log itself is handled by reading all the mirror sides of the redo log and picking the valid version during recovery.

The ASM resilvering algorithm also provides better data integrity guarantees. For example, a crash could damage a block that was in the midst of being written. Traditional volume manager resilvering has a 50-percent chance of copying the damaged block over the good block as part of applying the Dirty Region Log (DRL). When RDBMS recovery reads a block, it verifies that the block is not corrupt. If the block is corrupt and mirrored by ASM, each mirrored copy is examined to find a valid version. Thus, a valid version is always used for ASM resilvering.

ASM's mirror resilvering is more efficient and more effective than traditional volume managers, both during normal I/O operation and during recovery.

Preferred Read

Some customers deploy extended clusters for high availability. Extended clusters consist of servers and storage that reside in separate data centers at sites that are usually several kilometers apart. In these configurations, ASM normal-redundancy disk groups have two failure groups: one for each site. From a given server in an extended cluster, the I/O latency is greater for the disks at the remote site than for the disks in the local site. When COMPATIBLE.RDBMS is set to 11.1 or higher, users can set the PREFERRED_READ_FAILURE_GROUPS initialization parameter for each ASM instance to specify the local failure group in each disk group for that instance. When this parameter is set, reads are preferentially directed to the disk in the specified failure group rather than always going to the primary extent first. In the case of I/O errors, reads can still be satisfied from the nonpreferred failure group.

To ensure that all mirrors have the correct data, writes must still go to all copies of an extent.

Rebalance

Whenever the disk group configuration changes—whenever a disk is added, dropped, or resized—ASM rebalances the disk group to ensure that all the files are evenly spread across the disks in the disk group. ASM creates a COD entry to indicate that a rebalance is in progress. If the instance terminates abnormally, a surviving instance restarts the rebalance. If no other ASM instances are running, when the instance restarts, it restarts the rebalance.

MYTH
An ASM rebalance places data on disks based on I/O statistics.

MYTH
ASM rebalances dynamically in response to hot spots on disks.

ASM spreads every file evenly across all the disks in the disk group. Because of the access patterns of the database, including the caching that occurs in the database's buffer cache, ASM's even distribution of files across the disks in a disk group usually leads to an even I/O load on each of the disks as long as the disks share similar size and performance characteristics.

Because ASM maintains pointers to each extent of a file, rebalance can minimize the number of extents that it moves during configuration changes. For instance, adding a fifth disk to an ASM disk group with four disks results in moving 20 percent of the extents. If modulo arithmetic were used—changing placement to every fifth extent of a file on each disk from every fourth extent of a file on each disk—then almost 100 percent of the extents would have needed to move. Figures 9-4 and 9-5 show the differences in data movement required when adding a one disk to a four-disk disk group using ASM rebalance and traditional modulo arithmetic.

The RBAL process on the ASM instance that initiates the rebalance coordinates rebalance activity. For each file in the disk group—starting with the metadata files and continuing in ascending file number order—RBAL creates a plan for even

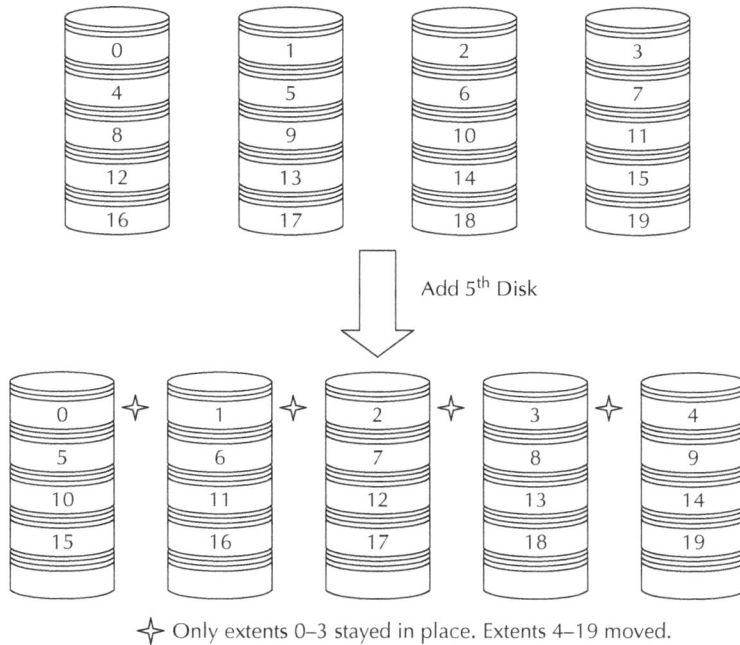

FIGURE 9-4. *Data movement using traditional module arithmetic*

placement of the file across the disks in the disk group. RBAL dispatches the rebalance plans to the ARB*n* processes in the instance. The number of ARBs is dictated by the power of the rebalance. Each ARB*n* relocates the appropriate extents according to its plan. Coordination of extent relocation among the ASM instances and RDBMS instances is described in the next section. In 11.2.0.2 and above (with compatible.asm set to 11.2.0.2), the same workflow occurs, except there is only one ARB0 process that performs all the relocations. The rebalance power dictates the number of outstanding async I/Os that will be issued or in flight. See the "Relocation" section for details on relocation mechanisms.

ASM displays the progress of the rebalance in V$ASM_OPERATION. ASM estimates the number of extents that need to be moved and the time required to complete the task. As rebalance progresses, ASM reports the number of extents moved and updates the estimates.

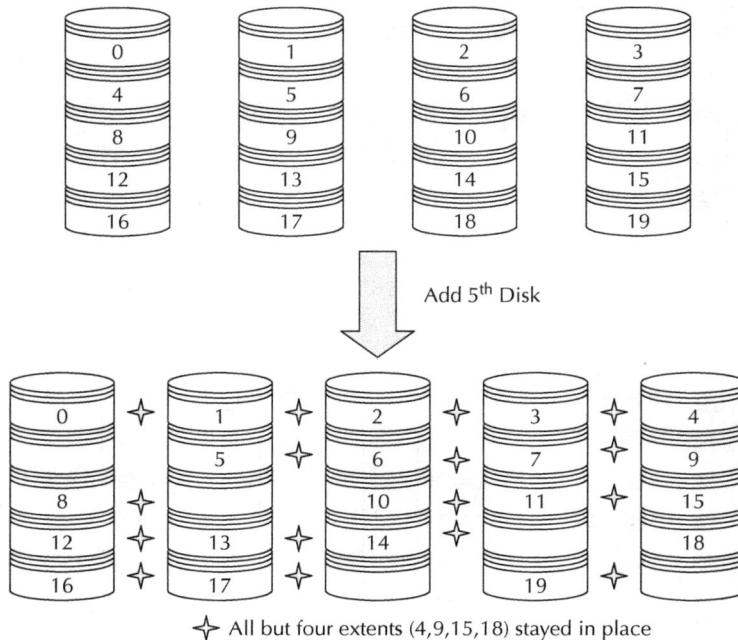

Add 5th Disk

All but four extents (4,9,15,18) stayed in place

FIGURE 9-5. *Data movement using ASM rebalance*

Resync

Resync is the operation that restores the updated contents of disks that are brought online from an offline state. Bringing online a disk that has had a transient failure is more efficient than adding the disk back to the disk group. When you add a disk, all the contents of the disk must be restored via a rebalance. Resync restores only the extents that would have been written while the disk was offline.

When a disk goes offline, ASM distributes an initialized slot of the Staleness Registry (SR) to each RDBMS and ASM instance that has mounted the disk group with the offline disk. Each SR slot has a bit per allocation unit in the offline disk. Any instance that needs to perform a write to an extent on the offline disk persistently sets the corresponding bit in its SR slot and performs the writes to the extent set members on other disks.

When a disk is being brought online, the disk is enabled for writes, so the RDBMS and ASM instances stop setting bits in their SR slots for that disk. Then ASM reconstructs the allocation table (AT) and free space table for the disk. Initially, all the AUs (except for the physical metadata and AUs marked as unreadable by block remapping) are marked as free. At this point, deallocation is allowed on the disk. ASM then examines all the file extent maps and updates the AT to reflect the extents that are allocated to the disk being brought online. The disk is enabled for new allocations. To determine which AUs are stale, ASM performs a bitwise OR of all the SR slots for the disk. Those AUs with set bits are restored using the relocation logic described in the following section. After all the necessary AUs have been restored, ASM enables the disk for reads. When the online is complete, ASM clears the SR slots.

Relocation

Relocation is the act of moving an extent from one place to another in an ASM disk group. Relocation takes place most commonly during rebalance, but also occurs during resync and during bad block remapping. The relocation logic guarantees that the active RDBMS clients always read the correct data and that no writes are lost during the relocation process.

Relocation operates on a per-extent basis. For a given extent, ASM first checks whether the file is open by any instance. If the file is closed, ASM can relocate the file without messaging any of the client instances. Recovery Manager (RMAN) backup pieces and archive logs often account for a large volume of the space used in ASM disk groups, especially if the disk group is used for the Fastback Recovery Area (FRA), but these files are usually not open. For closed files, ASM reads the extent contents from the source disk and writes them to the specified location on the target disk. ASM keeps track of the relocations that are ongoing for closed files so that if a client opens a file which is in the middle of relocation, the appropriate relocation messages are sent to the client as part of the file open.

If the file being relocated is open, the instance performing the relocation sends to all other ASM instances in the cluster a message stating its intent to relocate an extent. All ASM instances send a message, which indicates the intent to relocate the extent over the umbilicus to any RDBMS clients that have the file open. At this point, the RDBMS instances delay any new writes until the new extent location is available. Because only one extent is relocated at a time, the chances are very small of an RDBMS instance writing to the extent being relocated at its time of relocation. Each RDBMS instance acknowledges receipt of this message to its ASM instance. The ASM instances in turn acknowledge receipt to the coordinating ASM instance. After all acknowledgments arrive, the coordinating ASM instance reads the extent contents from the source disk and writes them to the target disk. After this is complete, the same messaging sequence occurs, this time to indicate the new location of the extent set. At this time, in-flight reads from the old location are still valid. Subsequent reads are issued to the new location. Writes that were in flight must be reissued to the new location. Writes that were delayed based on the first relocation message can now be issued to the new location. After all in-flight writes issued before the first relocation message are complete, the RDBMS instances use the same message-return sequence to notify the coordinating ASM instance that they are no longer referencing the old extent location. At this point, ASM can return the allocation unit(s) from the old extent to the free pool. Note that the normal RDBMS synchronization mechanisms remain in effect in addition to the relocation logic.

ASM Instance Recovery and Crash Recovery

When ASM instances exit unexpectedly due to a shutdown abort or an ASM instance crash, ASM performs recovery. As with the RDBMS, ASM can perform crash recovery or instance recovery. ASM performs instance recovery when an ASM instance mounts a disk group following abnormal instance termination. In a clustered configuration, surviving ASM instances perform crash recovery following the abnormal termination of another ASM instance in the cluster. ASM recovery is similar to the recovery performed by the RDBMS. For ASM recovery, the ACD is analogous to the redo logs in the RDBMS instance. The ASM COD is similar to the undo tablespaces in the RDBMS. With ASM, recovery is performed on a disk group basis. In a cluster, different ASM instances can perform recovery on different disk groups.

CSS plays a critical role in RAC database recovery. With RAC databases, CSS ensures that all I/O-capable processes from a crashed RDBMS instance have exited before a surviving RDBMS instance performs recovery. The OS guarantees that terminated processes do not have any pending I/O requests. This effectively fences off the crashed RDBMS instance. The surviving RDBMS instances can then proceed with recovery with the assurance that the crashed RDBMS instances cannot corrupt the database.

CSS plays a similar role in ASM recovery. Even a single-node ASM deployment involves multiple Oracle instances. When an ASM instance mounts a disk group, it registers with CSS. Each RDBMS instance that accesses ASM storage registers with CSS, which associates the RDBMS instance with the disk group that it accesses and with its local ASM instance. Each RDBMS instance has an umbilicus connection between its ASMB process and the UFG in the local ASM instance. Because ASMB is a fatal background process in the RDBMS, and the failure of a UFG kills ASMB, the failure of an ASM instance promptly terminates all its client RDBMS instances. CSS tracks the health of all the I/O-capable processes in RDBMS and ASM instances. If an RDBMS client terminates, CSS notifies the local ASM instance when all the I/O-capable processes have exited. At this point, ASM can clean up any resource held on behalf of the terminated RDBMS instances. When an ASM instance exits abnormally, its client RDBMS instances terminate shortly thereafter because of the severed umbilicus connection. CSS notifies the surviving ASM instances after all the I/O-capable processes from the terminated ASM instance and its associated RDBMS instances have exited. At this point, the surviving ASM instances can perform recovery knowing that the terminated instance can no longer perform any I/Os.

During ASM disk group recovery, an ASM instance first applies the ACD thread associated with the terminated ASM instance. Applying the ACD records ensures that the ASM cache is in a consistent state. The surviving ASM instance will eventually flush its cache to ensure that the changes are recorded in the other persistent disk group data structures. After ACD recovery is complete, ASM performs COD recovery. COD recovery performs the appropriate actions to handle long-running operations that were in progress on the terminated ASM instance. For example, COD recovery restarts a rebalance operation that was in progress on a terminated instance. It rolls back file creations that were in progress on terminated instances. File creations are rolled back because the RDBMS instance could not have committed a file creation that was not yet complete. The "Mirror Resilvering" section earlier in this chapter describes how ASM ensures mirror consistency during recovery.

ASM recovery is based on the same technology that the Oracle Database has used successfully for years.

Disk Discovery

Disk discovery is the process of examining disks that are available to an ASM instance. ASM performs disk discovery in several scenarios, including the following:

- Mount disk group
- Create disk group
- Add disk
- Online disk
- Select from V$ASM_DISKGROUP or V$ASM_DISK

The set of disks that ASM examines is called the *discovery set* and is constrained by the ASM_DISKSTRING initialization parameter and the disks to which ASM has read/write permission. The default value for ASM_DISKSTRING varies by platform, but usually matches the most common location for devices on the platform. For instance, on Linux, the default is /dev/sd*. On Solaris, the default is /dev/rdsk/*. The ASM_DISKSTRING value should be broad enough to match all the disks that will be used by ASM. Making ASM_DISKSTRING more restrictive than the default can make disk discovery more efficient.

The basic role of disk discovery is to allow ASM to operate on disks based on their content rather than the path to them. This allows the paths to disks to vary between reboots of a node and across nodes of a cluster. It also means that ASM disk groups are self-describing: All the information required to mount a disk group is found on the disk headers. Users need not enumerate the paths to each disk in a disk group to mount it. This makes ASM disk groups easily transportable from one node to another.

Mount Disk Group

When mounting a disk group, ASM scans all the disks in the discovery set to find each disk whose header indicates that it is a member of the specified disk group. ASM also inspects the PSTs to ensure that the disk group has a quorum of PSTs and that it has a sufficient number of disks to mount the disk group. If discovery finds each of the disks listed in the PST (and does not find any duplicate disks), the mount completes and the mount timestamp is updated in each disk header.

If some disks are missing, the behavior depends on the version of ASM and the redundancy of the disk group. For external-redundancy disk groups, the mount fails if any disk is missing. For normal-redundancy disk groups, the mount can succeed as long as none of the missing disks are partners of each other. The mount succeeds if the instance is the first in the cluster to mount the disk group. If the disk group is already mounted by other instances, the mount will fail. The rationale for this behavior is that if the missing disk had truly failed, the instances with the disk group mounted would have already taken the disk offline. As a result, the missing disk on the node trying to mount is likely to be the result of local problems, such as incorrect permissions, an incorrect discovery string, or a local connection problem. Rather than continuing the schizophrenic mount behavior in Oracle Database 11*g*, ASM introduced a FORCE option to mount. If you do not specify FORCE (which is equivalent to specifying NOFORCE), the mount fails if any disks are missing. If you specify FORCE to the mount command, ASM takes the missing disks offline (if it finds a sufficient number of disks) and completes the mount. A mount with the FORCE option fails if no disks need to be taken offline as part of the mount. This is to prevent the gratuitous use of FORCE during a mount.

If multiple disks have the same name in the disk header, ASM does its best to pick the right one for the mount. If another ASM instance already has the disk group mounted, the mounting ASM instance chooses the disk with the mount timestamp that matches the mount timestamp cached in the instance that already has the disk group mounted. If no other instance has the disk group mounted or if multiple disks have the same ASM disk name and mount timestamp, the mount fails. With multipathing, the ASM_DISKSTRING or disk permissions should be set such that the discovery set contains only the path to the multipathing pseudo-device. The discovery set should not contain each individual path to each disk.

Create Disk Group

When creating a disk group, ASM writes a disk header to each of the disks specified in the CREATE DISKGROUP SQL statement. ASM recognizes disks that are formatted as ASM disks. Such disks have a MEMBER in the HEADER_STATUS field of V$ASM_DISK. Other patterns, such as those of database files, the Oracle Clusterware voting disk, or the Oracle Cluster Registry (OCR), appear as FOREIGN, if stored on raw devices outside of ASM, in the HEADER_STATUS of V$ASM_DISK. By default, ASM disallows the use of disks that have a header status of FOREIGN or MEMBER. Specifying the FORCE option to a disk specification allows the use of disks with these header statuses. ASM does not allow reuse of any disk that is a member of a mounted disk group. ASM then verifies that it is able to find exactly one copy of each specified disk by reading the headers in the discovery set. If any disk is not found during this discovery, the disk group creation fails. If any disk is found more than once, the disk group creation also fails.

Add Disk

When adding a disk to a disk group, ASM writes a disk header to each of the disks specified in the ADD DISK SQL statement. ASM verifies that it can discover exactly one copy of the specified disk in the discovery set. In clusters, the ASM instance adding the disk sends a message to all peers that have the disk group mounted to verify that they can also discover the new disk. If any peer ASM instance with the disk group mounted fails to discover the new disk, the ADD DISK operation fails. In this case, ASM marks the header as FORMER. ADD DISK follows the same rules for FORCE option usage as CREATE DISKGROUP.

Online Disk

The online operation specifies an ASM disk name, not a path. The ASM instance searches for the disk with the specified name in its discovery set. In a cluster, ASM sends a message to all peer instances that have the disk group mounted to verify that they can discover the specified disk. If any instance fails to discover the specified disk, ASM returns the disk to the OFFLINE state.

Select from V$ASM_DISK and V$ASM_DISKGROUP

Select from V$ASM_DISK or V$ASM_DISKGROUP reads all the disk headers in the discovery set to populate the tables. V$ASM_DISK_STAT and V$ASM_DISKGROUP_STAT return the same information as V$ASM_DISK and V$ASM_DISKGROUP, but the _STAT views do not perform discovery. If any disks were added since the last discovery, they will not be displayed in the _STAT views.

Summary

ASM is a sophisticated storage product that performs complex internal operations to provide simplified storage management to the user. Most of the operations described in this chapter are transparent to the user, but understanding what happens behind the curtains can be useful for planning and monitoring an ASM deployment.

CHAPTER
10

ACFS Design
and Deployment

There is a big movement in the industry toward consolidation and cloud computing. At the core of all this is centralized-clustered storage, which requires a centralized file store such as a file system.

In Oracle Grid Infrastructure 11*g* Release 2, Oracle extends the capability of ASM by introducing the ASM Cluster File System, or ACFS. ACFS is a feature-rich, scalable, POSIX-compliant file system that is built from the traditional ASM disk groups. In Oracle Clusterware 11*g*R2 11.2.0.3, Oracle introduced a packaging suite called the Oracle Cluster File System, Cloud Edition, which provides a clustered file system for cloud storage applications, built on Automatic Storage Management, and includes advanced data management and security features. Oracle Cluster File System, Cloud Edition includes the following core components:

- Automatic Storage Management (ASM)
- ASM Dynamic Volume Manager (AVDM)
- ASM Cluster File System (ACFS)

In addition, it provides the following services:

- ACFS file tagging for aggregate operations
- ACFS read-only snapshots
- ACFS continuous replication
- ACFS encryption
- ACFS realm-based security

This chapter focuses on ACFS, its underlying architecture, and the associated data services.

ASM Cluster File System Overview

ACFS is a fully POSIX-compliant file system that can be accessed through native OS file system tools and APIs. Additionally, ACFS can be exported and accessed by remote clients via standard NAS file access protocols such as NFS and CIFS. In addition to ACFS, Oracle introduces ASM Dynamic Volume Manager (ADVM) to provide scalable volume management capabilities to support ACFS. Despite its name, ACFS can be utilized as a local file system as well as a cluster file system.

ACFS provides shared, cluster-wide access to various file types, including database binaries, trace files, Oracle BFILEs, user application data and reports, and other non-database application data. Storing these file types in ACFS inherently provides consistent global namespace support, which is the key to enabling uniform, cluster-wide file access and file pathing of all file system data. In the past, to get consistent namespace across cluster nodes meant implementing third-party cluster file system solutions or NFS.

ACFS is built on top of the standard vnode/VFS file system interface ubiquitous in the Unix/Linux world, and it uses Microsoft standard interfaces on Windows. ACFS supports Windows APIs, command-line interfaces (CLIs) and tools (including Windows Explorer). ACFS uses standard file-related system calls like other file systems in the market. However, most file systems on the market are platform specific; this is especially true of cluster file systems. ACFS is a multiplatform cluster file system for Linux, Unix, and Windows, with the same features across all OS and platforms.

ACFS provides benefits in the following key areas:

- **Performance**   ACFS is an extent-based clustered file system that provides metadata caching and fast directory lookups, thus enabling fast file access. Because ACFS leverages ASM functionality in the back end, it inherits a wide breadth of feature functionality already provided by ASM, such as maximized performance via ASM's even extent distribution across all disks in the disk group.

- **Manageability**   A key aspect of any file system container is that it needs to be able to grow as the data requirements change, and this needs to be performed with minimized downtime. ACFS provides the capability to resize the file system while the file system is online and active. In addition, ACFS supports other storage management services, such as file system snapshots. ACFS (as well as its underlying volumes) can be easily managed using various command-line interfaces or graphical tools such as ASM Configuration Assistant (ASMCA) and Oracle Enterprise Manager (EM). This wide variety of tools and utilities allows ACFS to be easily managed and caters to both system administrators and DBAs. Finally, ACFS management is integrated with Oracle Clusterware, which allows automatic startup of ACFS drivers and mounting of ACFS file systems based on dependencies set by the administrator.

- **Availability**   ACFS, via journaling and checksums, provides the capability to quickly recover from file system outages and inconsistencies. ACFS checksums cover ACFS metadata. Any metadata inconsistency will be detected by checksum and can be remedied by performing fsck.

ACFS also leverages ASM mirroring for improved storage reliability. Additionally, because ACFS is tightly integrated with Oracle Clusterware, all cluster node membership and group membership services are inherently leveraged. Table 10-1 provides a summary of the features introduced in each of the 11gR2 patch set releases.

11gR2 Release	ACFS New Supported OS Platforms and Data Services
11.2.0.3.1 (11.2.0.3 GI PSU #1)	UEK 2.6.32-200
11.2.0.3	OEL5/RHEL5 Update 3 and later (2.6.18-based kernels)
	UEK 2.6.32-100.34.1 and later updates to "-100" kernels
	SLES10 SP3 and later, and SLES11 SP1*
	Windows 2003 R1 (64-bit)
	Windows 2003 R2 (64-bit)
	Windows 2008 R1 (64-bit)
	Windows 2008 R2 (64-bit)
	Solaris 10 Update 6 and later
	ACFS is not supported on Solaris Containers, only on the global container/zone
	AIX 6.1 TL4 SP1 and later, AIX 7.1
	Replication, tagging (Linux, Windows)
	Enhanced security and encryption (Linux, Windows)
	Read-write snapshots
11.2.0.2	OEL5/RHEL5 Update 3 and later (2.6.18-based kernels)
	SLES10 SP3 and later
	Windows 2003 R1 (64-bit)
	Windows 2003 R2 (64-bit)
	Windows 2008 R1 (64-bit)
	Windows 2008 R2 (64-bit)
	Solaris 10 Update 6 and later
	AIX 6.1 TL4 SP1 and later
	Replication, tagging (Linux only)
	Enhanced security and encryption (Linux only)
11.2.0.1 (initial release of ACFS)	OEL5 and RHEL5
	Windows 2003 R1 (64-bit)
	Windows 2003 R2 (64-bit)
	Read-only snapshots (Linux)

TABLE 10-1. *Features Introduced in Each of the 11gR2 Patch Set Releases*

NOTE
ACFS is supported on Oracle Virtual Machine (OVM) in both Paravirtualized and Hardware Virtualized guests.

ACFS File System Design

This section illustrates the inner workings of the ACFS file system design—from the file I/O to space management.

ACFS File I/O

All ACFS I/O goes through ADVM, which maps these I/O requests to the actual physical devices based on the ASM extent maps it maintains in kernel memory. ACFS, therefore, inherits all the benefits of ASM's data management capability.

ACFS supports POSIX read/write semantics for the cluster environment. This essentially means that writes from multiple applications to the same file concurrently will result in no interlaced writes. In 11.2.0.4, ACFS introduces support flock/fcntl for cluster-wide serialization, thus, if whole file exclusive locks are taken out across multiple nodes of a cluster, they do not block each other.

ACFS shares the same cluster interconnect as Oracle RAC DB, Clusterware, and ASM; however, no ACFS I/Os travel across the interconnect. In other words, all ACFS I/Os are issued directly to the ASM storage devices. ACFS maintains a coherent distributed ACFS file cache (using the ACFS distributed lock manager) that provides a POSIX-compliant shared read cache as well as exclusive write caching to deliver "single-system POSIX file access semantics cluster-wide." Note that this is cache coherency for POSIX file access semantics. ACFS delivers POSIX read-after-write semantics for a cluster environment. When an application requests to write a file on a particular node, ACFS will request an exclusive DLM lock. This, in turn, requires other cluster nodes to release any shared read or exclusive write locks for the file and to flush, if required, and invalidate any cached pages. However, it is important to contrast this with POSIX application file locking—cluster cache coherency provides POSIX access coherency (single-node coherency) semantics. POSIX file locking provides for application file access serialization, which is required if multiple users/applications are sharing a given file for reading and writing. ACFS does not provide cluster-wide POSIX file locking presently. However, it does support node local POSIX file locking.

Starting in 11.2.0.3, ACFS supports direct I/O—the ability to transfer data between user buffers and storage without additional buffering done by the operating system. ACFS supports the native file data caching mechanisms provided by different operating systems. Any caching directives settable via the open(2) system call are also honored. ACFS supports enabling direct I/O on a file-by-file basis using OS-provided mechanism; for example, using the O_DIRECT flag to open(2) on Linux and the FILE_FLAG_NO_BUFFERING flag to CreateFile on Windows. A file may be open in direct I/O mode and cached mode (the default) at the same time. ACFS ensures that the cache coherency guarantees mentioned earlier are always met even in such a mixed-usage scenario.

ACFS Space Allocation

ACFS file allocation is very similar to other POSIX-compliant file systems: The minimum file size is an ACFS block (4KB), with metadata sized 512 bytes to 4KB. ACFS also does file preallocation of storage as a means to efficiently manage file growth. This applies to regular files as well as directories. This preallocation amount is based on currently allocated storage.

The following is the basic algorithm for regular files:

```
if (current_storage_allocation < 128k)
    preallocate the current size of the file
else
    preallocate MIN(1/4 current storage allocation, 5MB)
```

The following are three use-case examples of ACFS file preallocation to illustrate this algorithm:

- If a file is currently 64KB in size and the user writes 4KB to the file, ACFS will allocate 64KB of storage, bringing the file to a total of 128KB.

- If a file is 4MB in size and the user writes 4KB, ACFS will allocate 1MB of storage, bringing the file to a total of 5MB.

- If a file has zero bytes of storage—which may be the case if the file is brand new or was truncated to zero bytes—then at `write()` time no preallocation will be done.

The scenario is slightly different for directories. For directories, the algorithm is as follows:

```
Preallocate MIN (the current size of the directory, 64k)
```

Thus, if a directory is 16KB and needs to be extended, ACFS allocates another 16KB, bringing the directory to a total of 32KB. If the directory needs to be extended again, ACFS will allocate another 32KB, bringing it to a total of 64KB. Because the directory is now 64KB, all future extensions will be 64KB.

In addition to the preceding scenarios, if the desired storage cannot be contiguously allocated, ACFS will search for noncontiguous chunks of storage to satisfy the request. In such cases, ACFS will disable all preallocation on this node for a period of time, which is triggered when or until some thread on this node frees up some storage or a certain amount of time passes, with the hope that another node may have freed up some storage.

The salient aspects of ACFS file space management are:

■ ACFS tries to allocate contiguous space for a file when possible, which gives better performance for sequential reads and writes.

■ To improve performance of large file allocation, ACFS will preallocate the space when writing data.

■ This storage is not returned when the file is closed, but it is returned when the file is deleted.

■ ACFS allocates local metadata files as nodes mount the file system for the first time. This metadata space is allocated contiguously per node, with the maximum being 20MB.

■ ACFS maintains local bitmaps to reduce contention on the global storage bitmap. This local bitmap becomes very important during the search for local free space. Note that because of local space reservation (bitmap), when disk space is running low, allocations may be successful on one cluster node and fail on another. This is because no space is left in the latter's local bitmap or the global bitmap.

It is important to note that this metadata space allocation may cause minor space discrepancies when used space is displayed by a command such as Unix/Linux df (for example, the disk space reported by the df command as "in use," even though some of it may not actually be allocated as of yet). This local storage pool can be as large as 128MB per node and can allow space allocations to succeed, even though commands such as df report less space available than what is being allocated.

Distributed Lock Manager (DLM)

DLM provides a means for cluster-wide exclusive and shared locks. These DLM locks are taken whenever cluster-wide consistency and cache coherency must be guaranteed, such as for metadata updates and file reads and writes. ACFS uses the DLM services provided by Oracle Kernel Services (OKS). At a high level, a SHARED lock is requested when the cluster node is going only to read the protected entity. This SHARED lock is compatible with other SHARED locks and is incompatible with other EXCLUSIVE locks. An EXCLUSIVE lock is taken if the protected entity needs to be modified. Locks are cached on that node until some other node requests them in a conflicting mode. Therefore, a subsequent request for the same lock from the same node can be serviced without sending any internode messages, and the lock grant is quick.

When a node requests a lock that it does not hold or if the lock is not cached on that node, a blocking asynchronous system trap (BAST) is sent to the nodes that are holding the block. If one or more nodes are currently holding the lock in a conflicting mode, the request is queued and is granted when the lock is released on that node (if there is no other request ahead in the queue). ACFS has eight threads (called "BAST handlers") per node to service BAST requests. These threads are started at ACFS kernel module load time and service all file systems mounted on the node. For example:

```
# ps -ef | grep bast
root     15319     1  0 02:36 ?        00:00:00 [acfs_bast0]
root     15320     1  0 02:36 ?        00:00:00 [acfs_bast1]
root     15321     1  0 02:36 ?        00:00:00 [acfs_bast2]
root     15322     1  0 02:36 ?        00:00:00 [acfs_bast3]
root     15323     1  0 02:36 ?        00:00:00 [acfs_bast4]
root     15324     1  0 02:36 ?        00:00:00 [acfs_bast5]
root     15325     1  0 02:36 ?        00:00:00 [acfs_bast6]
root     15326     1  0 02:36 ?        00:00:00 [acfs_bast7]
```

The following syslog entry shows a BAST request being handled:

```
F2 5226945.686/130601173229 acfs_bast6[18674] ofs_delete_inode: BAST inprogress
```

Metadata Buffer Cache

ACFS caches metadata for performance reasons. Some examples of metadata are inodes, data extent headers, and directory blocks. Access to metadata is arbitrated using DLM locks, as described earlier. All operations (such as file deletes and renames) involving metadata updates are done within a transaction, and modified metadata buffers are marked dirty in the buffer cache. In case of any errors, the transaction is aborted and the metadata changes are reverted. For all successfully completed transactions, dirty metadata buffers are written to disk in a special location called the Volume Log. Periodically, a kernel thread reads the Volume Log and applies these metadata changes to the actual metadata locations on disk. Once written into the Volume Log, a transaction can be recovered even if the node performing that transaction crashes before the transaction is applied to actual metadata locations.

Recovery

This section describes how the ACFS and ADVM layers handle various recovery scenarios.

ACFS and ADVM Recovery

All ACFS file systems must be cleanly dismounted before ASM or the GI stack is stopped. Typically this is internally managed by CRS; however, there are cases when emergency shutdown of the stack is necessary. A forced shutdown of ASM via SHUTDOWN ABORT should be avoided when there are mounted ACFS file systems; rather, a clean ACFS dismount followed by a graceful shutdown of ASM should be used.

When there is a component or node failure, a recovery of the component and its underlying dependent resource is necessary. For example, if an ACFS file system is forcibly dismounted because of a node failure, then recovery is necessary for ASM, the ASM Dynamic volume, as well as ACFS. This recovery process is implicitly performed as part of the component restart process. For example, if an ASM instance crashes due to node failure, then upon restart, ASM will perform crash recovery, or in the case of RAC, a surviving instance will perform instance recovery on the failed instance's behalf. The ASM Dynamic volume is implicitly recovered as part of ASM recovery, and ACFS will be recovered using the ACFS Metadata Transaction Log.

The ADVM driver also supports cluster I/O fencing schemes to maintain cluster integrity and a consistent view of cluster membership. Furthermore, ASM Dynamic volume mirror recovery operations are coordinated cluster-wide such that the death of a cluster node or ASM instance does not result in mirror inconsistency or any other form of data corruption. If ACFS detects inconsistent file metadata returned from a read operation, based on the checksum, ACFS takes the appropriate action to isolate the affected file system components and generate a notification that fsck should be run as soon as possible. Each time the file system is mounted, a notification is generated with a system event logger message until fsck is performed. Note that fsck only repairs ACFS metadata structures. If fsck runs cleanly but the user still perceives the user data files to be corrupted, the user should restore those files from a backup, but the file system itself does not need to be re-created.

Unlike other file systems, when an ACFS metadata write operation fails, the ACFS drivers do not interrupt or notify the operating system environment; instead, ACFS isolates errors by placing the file system in an offline error state. For these cases, a umount of the "offlined" file system is required for that node. If a node fails, then another node will recover the failed node's transaction log, assuming it can write the metadata out to the storage.

To recover from this scenario, the affected underlying ADVM volumes must be closed and reopened by dismounting any affected file systems. After the instance is restarted, the corresponding disk group must be mounted with the volume enabled, followed by a remount of the file system.

However, it might not be possible for an administrator to dismount a file system while it is in the offline error state if there are processes referencing the file system, such as a directory of the file system being the current working directory for a process. In these cases, to dismount the file system you need to identify all processes on the node that have file system references to files and directories. The Linux fuser and lsof commands will list processes with open files.

ADVM and Dirty Region Logging

If ASM Dynamic volumes are created in ASM redundancy disk groups (normal or high), dirty region logging (DRL) is enabled via an ASM DRL volume file.

The ADVM driver will ensure ASM Dynamic volume mirror consistency and the recovery of only the dirty regions in cases of node and ASM instance failures. This is accomplished using DRL, which is an industry-common optimization for mirror consistency and the recovery of mirrored extents.

ADVM Design

Most file systems are created from an OS disk device, which is generally a logical volume device, created by a logical volume manager (LVM). For example, a Linux ext3 file system is generally created over a Linux LVM2 device with an underlying logical volume driver (LVD). ACFS is similar in this regard; however, it is created over an ADVM volume device file and all volume I/O is processed through the ADVM driver.

In Oracle ASM 11g Release 2, ASM introduces a new ASM file type, called asmvol, that is associated with ADVM Dynamic volumes. These volume files are similar to other ASM file types (such as archive logs, database data files, and so on) in that once they are created their extents are evenly distributed across all disks in the specified disk group. An ASM Dynamic volume file must be wholly contained in a single disk group, but there can be many volume files in one disk group.

As of 11.2.0.3, the default ADVM volume is now allocated with 8MB extents across four columns and a fine-grained stripe width of 128KB. ADVM writes data as 128KB stripe chunks in round-robin fashion to each of the four columns and fills a stripe set of four 8MB extents with 250 stripe chunks before moving to a second stripe set of four 8MB extents. Although the ADVM Dynamic volume extent size and the stripe columns can be optionally specified at volume creation, this is not a recommended practice.

If the ASM disk group AU size is 8MB or less, the ADVM extent size is 8MB. If the ASM disk group AU size is configured larger than 8MB, ADVM extent size is the same as the AU size.

Note that setting the number of columns on an ADVM dynamic volume to 1 effectively turns off fine-grained striping for the ADVM volume, but maintains the coarse-grained striping of the ASM file extent distribution. Consecutive stripe columns map to consecutive ASM extents. For example, if in a normal ASM file, four ASM extents map to two LUNs in alternating order, then the stripe-column-to-LUN mapping works the same way.

This section covers how to create an ADVM volume, which will subsequently be used to create an ACFS file system. Note that these steps are not needed if you're deploying an ACFS file system using ASM Configuration Assistant (ASMCA). If you are not using ASMCA, you will need to do this manually.

To create a volume in a previously created disk group, use the following command:

```
asmcmd> volcreate -G DATA etldata 25G
```

The -G flag specifies the disk group where this volume will be created. This will create an ADVM volume file that is 25GB. All the extents of this volume file are distributed across all disks in the DATA disk group. Note that the volume name is limited to 11 characters on Linux and 23 characters on AIX.

Once the ASM Dynamic volume file is created inside ASM, an ADVM volume device (OS device node) will be automatically built in the /dev/asm directory. On Linux, udev functionality must be enabled for this device node to be generated. A udev rules file in /etc/udev/rules.d/udev_rules/55-usm.rules contains the rule for /dev/asm/* and sets the group permission to asmadmin.

For clarity, we refer to the logical volume inside ASM as the ASM Dynamic volume, and the OS device in /dev/asm as the ADVM volume device. There is a direct one-for-one mapping between an ASM Dynamic volume and its associated ADVM volume device:

```
[grid@node1]$ ls -l /dev/asm/
brwxrwx--- 1 root dba 252, 58881 Feb 3 08:35 etldata-173
```

Notice that the volume name is included as part of the ADVM volume device name. The three-digit (suffix) number is the ADVM persistent cluster-wide disk group number. It is recommended that you provide a meaningful name such that it is easily identifiable from the OS device.

The ADVM volume device filenames are unique and persistent across all cluster nodes. The ADVM volume devices are created when the ASM instance is active with the required disk group mounted and dynamic volumes enabled.

Note that the on-disk format for ASM and ACFS is consistent between 32-bit and 64-bit Linux. Therefore, customers wanting to migrate their file system from 32-bit to 64-bit should not have to convert their ASM- and ACFS-based metadata.

ACFS Configuration and Deployment

Generally space, volume, and file system management are performed with a typical workflow process. The following describes how a traditional file system is created:

- The SAN administrator carves out the LUNs based on performance and availability criteria. These LUNs are zoned and presented to the OS as disk devices.

- The system administrator encapsulates these disks into a storage pool or volume group. From this pool, logical volumes are created. Finally, file systems are created over the logical volumes.

So how does this change in the context of ACFS/ADVM/ASM? Not much. The following is the process flow for deploying ACFS/ADVM/ASM:

- The SAN administrator carves out LUNs based on the defined application performance and availability SLA and using the ASM best practices, which state that all disks in an ASM disk group should be of the same size and have similar performance characteristics. This best practice and guideline makes LUN management and provisioning easier to build. Finally, the provisioned LUNs are zoned and presented to the OS as disk devices.

■ The system administrator or DBA creates or expands an ASM disk group using these disks. From the disk group, ASM (logical) volumes are created. If using SQL*Plus or ASMCMD, the user needs to be connected as SYASM for ADVM or ACFS configuration. Alternatively, ASMCA or EM can be used. Finally, file systems are created over these volume devices.

Note that although Oracle Grid Infrastructure 11*g* Release 2 supports RH/EL 4, 5, and 6, ACFS/ADVM requires a minimum of RH/EL 5.x. If you try to deploy ACFS on unsupported platforms, an error message similar to the following will be displayed:

```
$ ./acfsload start -s
ADVM/ACFS is not supported on centos-release-5-3.el5.centos.1
```

Configuring the Environment for ACFS

In this section, we discuss ACFS and ADVM concepts as well as cover the workflow in building the ACFS infrastructure.

Although you can configure/manage ACFS in several ways, this chapter primarily illustrates ASMCMD and ASMCA. Note that every ASMCMD command shown in this chapter can also be performed in ASMCA, Enterprise Manager, or SQL*Plus. However, using ASMCA, Enterprise Manager, or ASMCMD is the recommended method for administrators managing ASM/ACFS.

The first task in setting up ACFS is to ensure the underlying disk group is created and mounted. Creating disk groups is described in Chapter 4.

Before the first volume in an ASM disk group is created, any dismounted disk groups must be mounted across all ASM instances in the cluster. This ensures uniqueness of all volume devices names. The ADVM driver cannot verify that all disk groups are mounted; this must be ensured by the ASM administrator before adding the first volume in a disk group.

Also, compatible.asm and compatible.advm must be minimally set to 11.2.0.0 if this disk group is going to hold ADVM Dynamic volumes. The compatible.rdbms can be set to any valid value.

As part of the ASM best practices, we recommend having two ASM disk groups. It is recommended that you place the ADVM volumes in either the DATA or RECO disk group, depending on the file system content. For example, the DATA disk group can be used to store ACFS file systems that contain database-related data or general-purpose data. The RECO disk group can be used to store ACFS file systems that store database-recovery-related files, such as archived log files, RMAN backups, Datapump dump sets, and even database ORACLE_HOME backups (possibly zipped backups).

It is very typical to use ACFS file systems for GoldenGate. More specifically, for storing trail files. In these scenarios, a separate disk group is configured for holding GolenGate trail files. This also requires ACFS patch 11825850. Storing archived log files, RMAN backups, and Datapump dump sets is only supported in ACFS 11.2.0.3 and above. However, ACFS does not currently support snapshots of file systems housing these files.

ACFS Deployment

The two types of ACFS file systems are CRS Managed ACFS file systems and the Registry Managed ACFS file systems. Both of these ACFS solutions have similar benefits with respect to startup/recovery and leveraging CRS dependency modeling, such as unmounting and remounting offline file systems, mounting (pulling up) a disk group if not mounted, and enabling volumes if not enabled.

CRS Managed ACFS file systems have associated Oracle Clusterware resources and generally have defined interdependencies with other Oracle Clusterware resources (database, ASM disk group, and so on). CRS Managed ACFS is specifically designed for ORACLE_HOME file systems. Registry Managed ACFS file systems are general-use file systems that are completely transparent to Oracle Clusterware and its resources. There are no structural differences between the CRS Managed ACFS and Registry Managed ACFS file systems. The differences are strictly around Oracle Clusterware integration. Once an ACFS file system is created, all standard Linux/Unix file system commands can be used, such as the df, tar, cp, and rm commands. In 11gR2, storing any files that can be natively stored in ASM is not supported; in other words, you cannot store Oracle Database files (control files, data files, archived logs, online redo logs, and so on) in ACFS. Also, the Grid Infrastructure Home cannot be installed in ACFS; it must be installed in a separate file system, such as in ext3.

CRS Managed ACFS File Systems

As stated previously, the primary use for CRS Managed ACFS is storing the database Oracle Home. Figures 10-1 through 10-3 show how to create a CRS Managed ACFS file system. It is recommended that ACFS file systems used to house your database ORACLE_HOME have an OFA-compliant directory structure (for example, $ORACLE_BASE/product/11.2/dbhomex, where x represents the database home). Using ASMCA is the recommended method for creating a CRS Managed ACFS file system. ASMCA creates the volume and file system and establishes the required Oracle Clusterware resources.

Figure 10-1 displays the ASMCA screen used to launch the Create the CRS Managed ACFS File System Wizard. Right-click the Create Diskgroup task on a specific disk group and then select the Create ACFS for Database Home option.

Figure 10-2 displays the Create ACFS Hosted Database Home screen, which will prompt for the volume name, file system mount point, and file system owner. The ADVM volume device name is taken from the volume name, which is specified during volume creation.

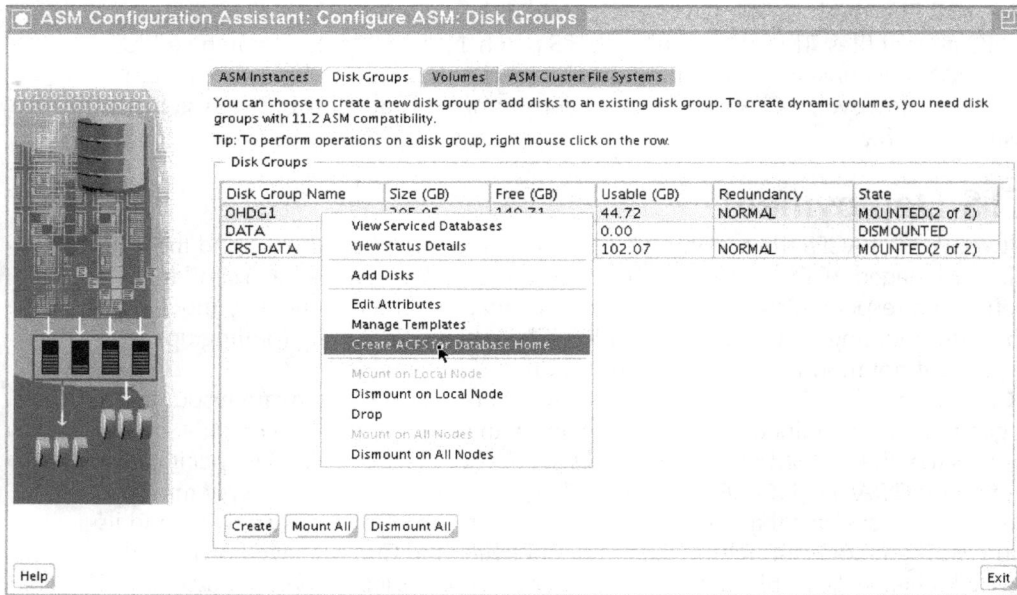

FIGURE 10-1. *ASMCA screen for file system management*

Figure 10-3 displays the Run ACFS Script window.

This script, which needs to run as root, is used to add the necessary Oracle Clusterware resources for the file system as well as mount the file system. Here's what the script contains:

```
[grid@rst-2850-05 scripts]$ cat acfs_script.sh
#!/bin/sh

/u01/app/11.2.0/grid/bin/srvctl add filesystem -d /dev/asm/dataoh_db2-32
-g DATAOH -v dataoh_db1 -m /u01/app/11.2.0/db3 -u oracle
if [ $? = "0" -o $? = "2" ]; then
    /u01/app/11.2.0/grid/bin/srvctl start filesystem -d /dev/asm/dataoh_db1-32
  if [ $? = "0" ]; then
      chown oracle:oinstall /u01/app/11.2.0/db3
      chmod 775 /u01/app/11.2.0/db3
      exit 0
  fi
fi
```

Once this script is run, the file system will be mounted on all nodes of the cluster.

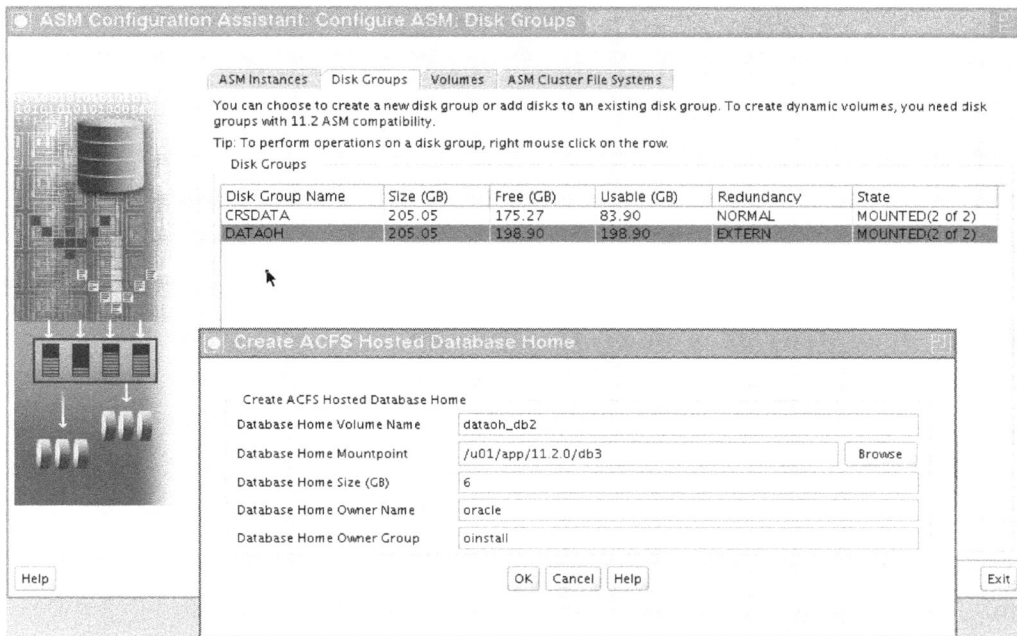

FIGURE 10-2. *File system creation screen*

Registry Managed ACFS

Besides storing the database software binaries on ACFS, ACFS can be used to store other database-related content. The following are some use-case scenarios for a Registry Managed ACFS file system:

- **Automatic Diagnostic Repository (ADR)** A file system for a diagnostics logging area. Having a distinct file system for diagnostic logs provides a more easily managed container rather than placing this within ORACLE_ BASE or ORACLE_HOME locations. Plus, a node's logs are available even if that node is down for some reason.

- **External database data** This includes Oracle external file types, such as BFILEs and ETL data/external tables.

- **Database exports** Create a file system for storing the old database exports as well as Datapump exports. This is only supported in Grid Infrastructure stack 11.2.0.3 and above.

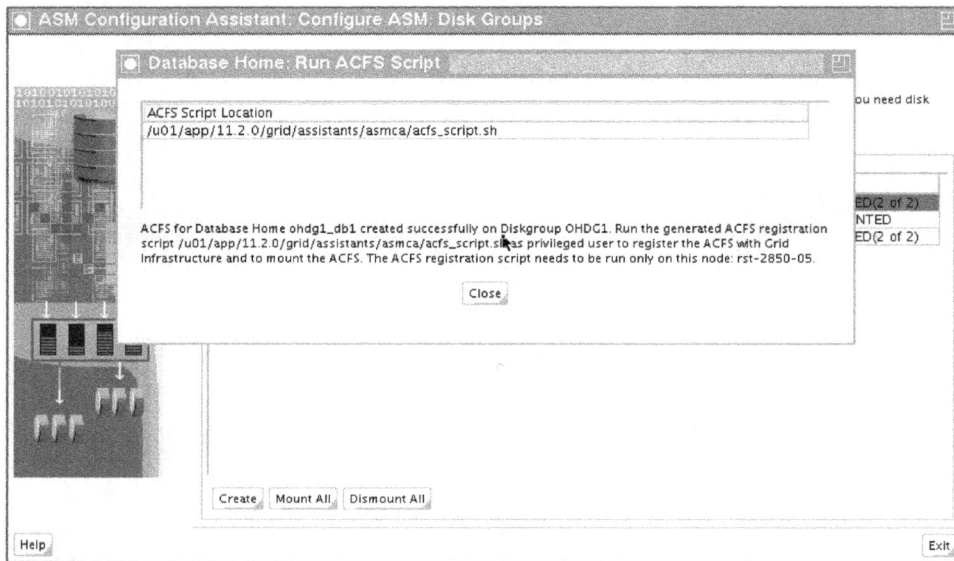

FIGURE 10-3. *Complete file system creation*

■ **Utility log file repository**   For customers who want a common log file repository for utilities such as RMAN, SQL*Loader, and Datapump, an ACFS file system can be created to store these log files.

■ **Directory for UTL_FILE_DIR and Extproc**   In a RAC environment, a shared file system plays an important role for customers who use UTL_FILE_DIR (PL/SQL file I/O), a shared file repository for CREATE DIRECTORY locations, and external procedures via Extproc calls.

■ **Middle-tier shared file system for Oracle applications**   For example, E-Business Suite as well as Siebel Server have a shared file system requirement for logs, shared documents, reports output, and so on.

In order to use the ACFS file system that is created in the database tier, one can export the ACFS file system as an NFS file system and NFS mount on the middle-tier nodes. This allows for customers to consolidate their storage and have integrated storage management across tiers.

Creating Registry Managed ACFS File Systems

This section describes Registry Managed ACFS file system creation. In this case, a node-local file system will be created for a given RAC node. To create a Registry Managed ACFS file system, you must create an ADVM volume first. Note that root access is not required to create an ACFS file system, but mounting and creating the CRS resource will require root access. Here are the steps:

1. Create the volume:

   ```
   [oracle@node1]$ asmcmd volcreate -G data bfile_data -s 6G
   ```

2. Once the ASM Dynamic volume is created and enabled, the file system can be created over the ADVM volume device. Create the file system:

   ```
   [oracle@node1]$/sbin/mkfs.acfs /dev/asm/bfile_data-115
   ```

> **NOTE**
> *When a volume is created, it is automatically enabled.*

3. Mount the file system:

   ```
   [root@node1]# mount /dev/asm/bfile_data-115
   /u01/app/11.2.0/acfsdata/bfile_data
   ```

4. Verify that the volume was created and mounted:

   ```
   [grid@node1]$ asmcmd volinfo -G data bfile_data
   Diskgroup Name: DATA

           Volume Name: BFILE_DATA
           Volume Device: /dev/asm/bfile_data-115
           State: ENABLED
           Size (MB): 4096
           Resize Unit (MB): 256
           Redundancy: MIRROR
           Stripe Columns: 4
           Stripe Width (K): 128
           Usage: ACFS
           Mountpath: /u01/app/acfsdata/bfile_data
   ```

Setting Up Registry Managed ACFS

An ACFS Mount Registry is used to provide a persistent entry for each Registry Managed ACFS file system that needs to be mounted after a reboot. This ACFS Mount

Registry is very similar to /etc/fstab on Linux. However, in cluster configurations, file systems registered in the ACFS Mount Registry are automatically mounted globally, similar to a cluster-wide mount table. This is the added benefit Oracle ACFS Mount Registry has over Unix fstab. The ACFS Mount Registry can be probed, using the acfsutil command, to obtain file system, mount, and file information.

When a general-purpose ACFS file system is created, it should be registered with the ACFS Mount Registry to ensure that the file system gets mounted on cluster/node startup. Users should not create ACFS Mount Registry entries for CRS Managed ACFS file systems.

Continuing from the previous example, where an ADVM volume and a corresponding file system were created, we will now register those file systems in the ACFS Mount Registry on their respective nodes so they can be mounted on node startup. When ACFS is in a cluster configuration, the acfsutil registry command can be run from any node in the cluster:

```
# /sbin/acfsutil registry -a -f -n node1 /dev/asm/bfile_data-115 \
/u01/app/11.2.0/acfsdata/bfile_data
```

The following shows some examples of the acfsutil registry command. Note that the acfsutil command can be run using either the root or oracle user. To check the ACFS Mount Registry, use the following query:

```
[grid@node1]$ /sbin/acfsutil registry
Mount Object:
  Device: /dev/asm/bfile_data-115
  Mount Point: /u01/app/11.2.0/acfsdata/bfile_data
  Disk Group: DATA
  Volume: bfile_data
  Options: none
  Nodes: node1
```

To get more detailed information on a currently mounted file system, use the acfsutil info fs command:

```
[grid@node1]$ /sbin/acfsutil info fs  /u01/app/11.2.0/acfsdata/bfile_data
    ACFS Version: 11.2.0.0.2.0
    flags:          MountPoint,Available
    mount time:     Mon Mar  2 19:19:19 2009
    volumes:        1
    total size:     4294967296
    total free:     317132800
    primary volume: /dev/asm/bfile_data-115
        label:
        flags:                   Primary,Available,ADVM
        on-disk version:         38.0
        allocation unit:         4096
        major, minor:            252, 88577
```

```
        size:                  4294967296
        free:                  317132800
        ADVM diskgroup         DATA
        ADVM resize increment: 268435456
        ADVM redundancy:       2
        ADVM stripe columns:   4
        ADVM stripe width:     131072
   number of snapshots:  0
 snapshot space usage: 0
```

Note that because these file systems will be used to store database-related content, they will need to have CRS resources against them. The following example illustrates how to create these resources:

```
[root@node1]# srvctl add filesystem -d /dev/asm/bfile_data-115 \
 -m /u01/app/11.2.0/acfsdata/bfile_data  -g data -u grid
```

NOTE
You cannot have ACFS registry entries and CRS resources defined for the same file system.

The same operation can be performed using ACMCA or Enterprise Manager.

Managing ACFS and ADVM

This section describes how to manage typical tasks related to ACFS and ADVM as well as illustrates the relationships among ACFS, ADVM, ASM, and Oracle Clusterware.

ACFS File System Resize

An ACFS file system can be dynamically grown and shrunk while it is online and with no impact to the user. The ACFS file system size and attributes are managed using the /sbin/acfsutil command. The ACFS extend and shrink operations are performed at the file system layer, which implicitly grows the underlying ADVM volume in multiples of the volume allocation unit.

The following example shows the acfsutil size command:

```
[grid@node1]$ /acfsutil size +200G -d /dev/asm/bfile_data-115
/u01/oracle/acfs-test-area/
acfsutil size: new file system size: 322122547200 (307200MB)
```

Currently, the limit on the number of times an ACFS file system can be resized is four.

ACFS starts with one extent and can grow out to four more extents, for a total of five global bitmaps extents. To determine the number of times the file system has been resized, use the acfsdbg utility to list the internal file system storage bitmap:

```
# acfsdbg -r /dev/asm/bfile_data-115
# acfsdbg> fenum 5
```

Look at the Extent[*] fields for nonzero Length fields. The number of remaining zero-length extents is an indication of the minimum number of times you can grow the file system. If the number of times the file system is resized exceeds five times, the users need to take the mount point offline globally (across all nodes) and then run fsck -a to consolidate the internal storage bitmap for resize:

```
/sbin/fsck -a -v -y -t acfs /dev/asm/bfile_data-115
```

Unmounting File Systems

Unmounting file systems involves a typical OS umount command. Before unmounting the file system, ensure that it is not in use. This may involve stopping dependent databases, jobs, and so on. In-use file systems cannot be unmounted. You can use various methods to show open file references of a file system:

■ **Linux/Unix lsof command**   Shows open file descriptors for the file system

■ **Unix/Linux fuser command**   Displays the PIDs of processes using the specified file systems

Any users or processes listed should be logged off or killed (kill –9).

Next we'll look at the steps required to unmount an ACFS file system. The steps to unmount a CRS Managed ACFS file system and a Registry Managed ACFS file system are slightly differ.

To unmount a general-purpose ACFS file system, unmount the file system. This command needs to be run on all nodes where the file system is currently mounted:

```
umount /u01/app/11.2.0/acfsdata/bfile_data
```

The steps are different to unmount a CRS Managed ACFS file system. Because CRS Managed ACFS file systems have associated CRS resources, the following steps need to be performed to stop the Oracle Clusterware resource and unmount the file system:

1. Once the application has stopped using the file system, you can stop the Oracle Clusterware file system resource. The following command will also unmount the file system. Here, we unmount the file system across all nodes.

```
srvctl stop filesystem -d /dev/asm/dataoh_db2-32
```

NOTE
If srvctl stop does not include a node or node list, it will be unmounted on all nodes.

2. To unmount only a specific node, specify the node name in the –n flag:

```
srvctl stop filesystem -d /dev/asm/dataoh_db2-32 -n node1
```

3. Verify the file system resource is unmounted:

```
srvctl status filesystem -d /dev/asm/dataoh_db2-32
ACFS file system is not running
```

As stated, it is highly recommended that you unmount any ACFS file systems first before the ASM instance is shut down. A forced shutdown or failure of an ASM instance with a mounted ACFS file system will result in I/O failures and dangling file handles; in other words, the ACFS file system user data and metadata that was written at the time of the termination may not be flushed to storage before ASM storage is fenced off. Thus, a forced shutdown of ASM will result in the ACFS file system having an offline error state. In the event that a file system enters into an offline error state, the ACFS Mount Registry and CRS Managed Resource action routines attempt to recover the file system and return it to an online state by unmounting and remounting the file system.

Deleting File Systems

Similar to unmounting ACFS file systems, the steps to delete an ACFS file system slightly differ between CRS Managed ACFS and Registry Managed ACFS.

To unmount and delete a Registry Managed ACFS file system, execute the following, which needs to be run on all nodes where the file system is currently mounted:

```
umount /u01/app/11.2.0/bfile_data
acfsutil rmfs /u01/app/11.2.0/bfile_data
asmcmd voldelete -G data bfile_data
```

Next, delete the acfsutil registry entry for the file system:

```
acfsutil registry -d /u01/app/11.2.0/bfile_data
```

CRS Managed ACFS file systems have Oracle Clusterware resources that need to be removed. To do this, follow these steps:

1. Run the following command, which unmounts the file system and stops the Oracle Clusterware resources. (Although this command can be executed from any node in the cluster, it will have to be rerun for each node.)

   ```
   srvctl stop filesystem -d /dev/asm/dataoh_db2-32 -n node1
   ```

   NOTE
   The format for stop filesystem is srvctl stop filesystem -d <device name> -n <nodelist where fs is mounted>.

2. Repeat this for each node.

3. Verify the file system resource is unmounted:

   ```
   srvctl status filesystem -d /dev/asm/dataoh_db2-32
   ACFS file system is not running
   ```

4. Once this file system is stopped and unmounted on all nodes where it was started, the Clusterware resource definitions need to be removed (this should only be run once from any node) and then the volume can be deleted:

   ```
   srvctl remove filesystem -d /dev/asm/dataoh_db2-32
   asmcmd voldelete -G ohdg ohdg_vol2
   ```

ADVM Management

Generally it is not necessary to perform ADVM management; however, in rare cases, volumes may need to be manually disabled or dropped. The /sbin/advmutil and ASMCMD commands should be used for these tasks. For details on command usage and various command options, review the *Oracle Storage Administrator's Guide*.

You can get volume information using the advmutil volinfo command:

```
[Grid@node1]$ /sbin/advmutil volinfo /dev/asm/etldata-173
Interface Version: 1
Size (MB): 4096
Resize Increment (MB): 256
Redundancy: mirror
Stripe Columns: 4
Stripe Width (KB): 128
Disk Group: DATA
Volume: ETLDATA
```

The same information can be displayed by the asmcmd volinfo command; however, the asmcmd uses the ASM Dynamic volume name, whereas the advmutil uses the ADVM volume device name:

```
[grid@node1]$ asmcmd volinfo -G data etldata
Diskgroup Name: OHDG1

        Volume Name: ETLDATA
        Volume Device: /dev/asm/etldata-173
        State: ENABLED
        Size (MB): 4096
        Resize Unit (MB): 256
        Redundancy: MIRROR
        Stripe Columns: 4
        Stripe Width (K): 128
        Usage: ACFS
        Mountpath: /u01/app/acfsdata/etl_data
```

To enable or disable the ASM Dynamic volumes, you can use ASMCMD. Enabling the volume instantiates (creates) the volume device in the /dev/asm/ directory. Here's the command to enable the volume:

```
[grid@node1]$ asmcmd volenable -G data etl_data
```

And the following command can be used to disable volume:

```
[grid@node1]asmcmd voldisable -G data etl_data
```

The disable command only disables the volume and removes the ADVM volume device node entry from the OS (or more specifically from the /dev/asm directory); it does not delete the ASM Dynamic volumes or reclaim space from the ASM disk group. To delete (drop) the ASM Dynamic volume, use the drop command:

```
asmcmd voldelete -G data etl_data
```

NOTE
You cannot delete or disable a volume or file system that is currently in use.

ACFS Management
Like any other file system, ACFS consists of background processes and drivers. This section describes the background processes and their roles, reviews the ACFS kernel drivers, and discusses the integration of ACFS and Oracle Clusterware.

ASM/ACFS-Related Background Processes

Several new ASM instance background processes were added in Oracle 11*g*R2 to support the ACFS infrastructure. The following processes will be started upon the first use of an ADVM volume on the node:

- **VDBG** The Volume Driver Background process is very similar to the Umbilicus Foreground (UFG) process, which is used by the database to communicate with ASM. The VDBG will forward ASM requests to the ADVM driver. This communication occurs in the following cases:

  - When an extent is locked/unlocked during ASM rebalance operations (ASM disk offline, add/drop disk, force dismount disk group, and so on).

  - During volume management activities such as a volume resize.

- **VBGx** The Volume Background processes are a pool of worker processes used to manage requests from the ADVM driver and coordinate with the ASM instance. A typical case for this coordination is the opening/closing of an ADVM volume file (for example, when a file system mount or unmount request occurs).

- **VMBx** The VMB is used to implement an I/O barrier and I/O fencing mechanism. This ensures that ASM instance recovery is not performed until all ADVM I/Os have completed.

- **ACFSx** The ACFS Background process coordinates cluster membership and group membership with the ASM instance. The ACFS process communicates this information to the ACFS driver, which in turn communicates with both the OKS and ADVM drivers. When a membership state/transition change is detected, an ioctl call is sent down to the kernel, which then begins the process of adding/removing a node from the cluster.

The following shows the new background processes highlighted in bold:

```
[grid@node1]$ ps -ef|grep asm
grid      4687      1  0  2008 ?        00:00:04 asm_pmon_+ASM1
grid      4691      1  0  2008 ?        00:00:00 asm_vktm_+ASM1
grid      4695      1  0  2008 ?        00:00:00 asm_diag_+ASM1
grid      4697      1  0  2008 ?        00:00:00 asm_ping_+ASM1
grid      4699      1  0  2008 ?        00:00:00 asm_psp0_+ASM1
grid      4701      1  0  2008 ?        00:00:09 asm_dia0_+ASM1
grid      4703      1  0  2008 ?        00:00:26 asm_lmon_+ASM1
grid      4706      1  0  2008 ?        00:00:00 asm_lmd0_+ASM1
grid      4708      1  0  2008 ?        00:00:00 asm_lms0_+ASM1
grid      4715      1  0  2008 ?        00:00:00 asm_mman_+ASM1
grid      4717      1  0  2008 ?        00:00:00 asm_dbw0_+ASM1
grid      4719      1  0  2008 ?        00:00:00 asm_lgwr_+ASM1
```

```
grid      4721   1   0   2008  ?         00:00:00 asm_ckpt_+ASM1
grid      4723   1   0   2008  ?         00:00:00 asm_smon_+ASM1
grid      4725   1   0   2008  ?         00:00:00 asm_rbal_+ASM1
grid      4727   1   0   2008  ?         00:00:00 asm_gmon_+ASM1
grid      4729   1   0   2008  ?         00:00:00 asm_mmon_+ASM1
grid      4731   1   0   2008  ?         00:00:00 asm_mmnl_+ASM1
grid      4736   1   0   2008  ?         00:00:00 asm_lck0_+ASM1
grid     16636   1   0   2008  ?         00:00:00 asm_vbg0_+ASM1
grid     16638   1   0   2008  ?         00:00:00 asm_acfs_+ASM1
grid     17290   1   0   2008  ?         00:00:00 asm_vbg1_+ASM1
grid     17292   1   0   2008  ?         00:00:00 asm_vbg2_+ASM1
grid     17294   1   0   2008  ?         00:00:00 asm_vdbg_+ASM1
grid     17296   1   0   2008  ?         00:00:00 asm_vmb0_+ASM1
```

The following are ACFS kernel threads dedicated to the management of ACFS and ADVM volumes devices:

```
[grid@node1 admin]$ ps -ef|egrep -i 'acfs|oks'
root      6257   1   0   Oct01  ?         00:00:00 [acfsvol17]
root      6259   1   0   Oct01  ?         00:00:00 [acfsds17]
root      6260   1   0   Oct01  ?         00:00:00 [acfssnap17]
root     11160   1   0   Oct01  ?         00:00:00 [acfsioerrlog]
root     11945   1   0   Oct01  ?         00:00:00 [oks_wkq]
grid     12396   1   0   Oct01  ?         00:00:00 [oks_rbld]
grid     12399   1   0   Oct01  ?         00:00:00 [oks_conn]
grid     24325   1   0   Oct01  ?         00:00:01 [oks_comm]
```

The user mode processes, discussed earlier, are used to perform extent map services in support of the ADVM driver. For example, ASM file extents map the ADVM volume file to logical blocks located on specific physical devices. These ASM extent pointers are passed to the ADVM driver via the user space processes. When the driver receives I/O requests on the ADVM volume device, the driver redirects the I/O to the supporting physical devices as mapped by the target ADVM volume file's extents. Because of this mapping, user I/O requests issued against ACFS file systems are sent directly to the block device (that is, ASM is not in the I/O path).

ACFS/ADVM Drivers

The installation of the Grid Infrastructure (GI) stack will also install the ACFS/ADVM drivers and utilities. Three drivers support ACFS and ADVM. They are dynamically loaded (in top-down order) by the OHASD process during Oracle Clusterware startup, and they will be installed whether the ACFS is to be used or not:

- **oracleoks.ko**   This is the kernel services driver, providing memory management support for ADVM/ACFS as well as lock and cluster synchronization primitives.

- **oracleadvm.ko** The ADVM driver maps I/O requests against an ADVM volume device to blocks in a corresponding on-disk ASM file location. This ADVM driver provides volume management driver capabilities that directly interface with the file system.

- **oracleacfs.ko** This is the ACFS driver, which supports all ACFS file system file operations.

During install, kernel modules are placed in /lib/modules/2.6.18-8.el5/extra/usm. These loaded drivers can be seen (on Linux) via the lsmod command:

```
# /sbin/lsmod |grep oracle
Module              Size    Used by
oracleacfs          781476  5
oracleadvm          212736  9
        oracleoks           224864   2 oracleacfs,oracleadvm
```

Linux OS vendors now support a "white list" of kernel APIs (kABI compatible or weak modules), which are defined not to change in the event of OS kernel updates or patches. The ACFS kernel APIs were added to this white list, which enables ACFS drivers to continue operation across certain OS upgrades and avoids the need for new drivers with every OS kernel upgrade.

Integration with Oracle Clusterware

When a CRS Managed ACFS file system is created, Oracle Clusterware will manage the resources for ACFS. In Oracle Clusterware 11g Release 2, the Oracle High Availability Services daemon (OHASd) component is called from the Unix/Linux init daemon to start up and initialize the Clusterware framework. OHASd's main functions are as follows:

- Start/restart/stop the Clusterware infrastructure processes.

- Verify the existence of critical resources.

- Load the three ACFS drivers (listed previously).

The correct ordering of the startup and shutdown of critical resources is also maintained and managed by OHASd; for example, OHASd will ensure that ASM starts after ACFS drivers are loaded.

- Several key Oracle Clusterware resources are created when Grid Infrastructure for Cluster is installed or when the ADVM volume is created. Each of these

CRS resources is node local and will have a corresponding start, stop, check, and clean action, which is executed by the appropriate Clusterware agents. These resources include the following:

- **ACFS Driver resource** This resource is created when Grid Infrastructure for Cluster is installed. This resource is created as ora.drivers.acfs and managed by the orarootagent. The ASM instance has a weak dependency against the ACFS driver resource. The Clusterware start action will start the ACFS driver resource when the ASM instance is started, and will implicitly load the ACFS/ADVM kernel drivers. These drivers will remain loaded until the GI stack is shut down.

- **ASM resource** This resource, ora.asm, is created as part of Grid Infrastructure for Cluster installation. This resource is started as part of the standard bootstrap of the GI stack and managed by the oraagent agent.

- **ACFS Registry resource** The Registry resource is created as part of the Grid Infrastructure for Cluster installation and managed by orarootagent. The activation of this resource will also mount all file systems listed in the ACFS Registry. This Registry resource also does file system recovery, via check action script, when file systems in an offline state are detected.

- **ACFS file system resource** This resource is created as ora.<diskgroup>.<volume>.acfs when the ASM Configuration Assistant (ASMCA) is used to create a DB Home file system. When the Database Configuration Assistant (DBCA) is used to create a database using the DB Home file system, an explicit dependency between the database, the ACFS file system hosting the DB Home, and ASM is created. Thus, a startup of ASM will pull up the appropriate ACFS file system along with the database.

ACFS/Clusterware Resource

Once the Oracle database software is installed in the CRS Managed ACFS file system and the database is created in ASM, Oracle Clusterware will implicitly create the resource dependencies between the database, the CRS Managed ACFS file system, and the ASM disk group. These dependencies are shown via the start/stop actions for a database using the following command:

```
crsctl stat res <database resource name> -p
```

The output has been condensed to focus on the start/stop dependencies items:

```
[grid@node1]$ crsctl stat res ora.yoda.db -p
NAME=ora.yoda.db
TYPE=ora.database.type
ACL=owner:grid:rwx,pgrp:oinstall:rwx,other::r--
```

```
AGENT_FILENAME=%CRS_HOME%/bin/oraagent%CRS_EXE_SUFFIX%
CLUSTER_DATABASE=true
DB_UNIQUE_NAME=yoda
DEFAULT_TEMPLATE=PROPERTY(RESOURCE_CLASS=database) PROPERTY(DB_UNIQUE_NAME=
CONCAT(PARSE(%NAME%, ., 2), %USR_ORA_DOMAIN%, .)) ELEMENT(INSTANCE_NAME=
%GEN_USR_ORA_INST_NAME%)
DEGREE=1
DESCRIPTION=Oracle Database resource
SERVER_POOLS=ora.yoda
SPFILE=+CRSDATA/yoda/spfileyoda.ora
START_DEPENDENCIES=hard(ora.CRSDATA.dg,ora.crsdata.crsdata_db1.acfs)
weak(type:ora.listener.type,global:type:ora.scan_listener.type,
uniform:ora.ons,uniform:ora.eons) pullup(ora.CRSDATA.dg)
START_TIMEOUT=600
STOP_DEPENDENCIES=hard(intermediate:ora.asm,shutdown:ora.CRSDATA.dg,
intermediate:ora.crsdata.crsdata_db1.acfs)
STOP_TIMEOUT=600
```

ACFS Startup Sequence

The start action, which is the same for CRS Managed and general-purpose file system resources, is to mount the file system. The CRS resource action includes confirming that the ACFS drivers are loaded, the required disk group is mounted, the volume is enabled, and the mount point is created, if necessary. If the file system is successfully mounted, then the state of the resource is set to online; otherwise, it is set to offline.

When the OS boots up and Oracle Clusterware is started, the following Clusterware operations are performed:

- OHASd will load the ACFS drivers and start ASM.

- As part of the ASM instance startup, all the appropriate disk groups, as listed in the ASM asm_diskgroup parameter, will also be mounted. As part of the disk group mount, all the appropriate ASM Dynamic volumes are enabled.

- The CRS agent will start up and mount the CRS Managed ACFS file systems.

- The appropriate CRS agents will start their respective resources. For example, oraagent will start up the database. Note that just before this step, all the resources necessary for the database to start are enabled, such as the ASM instance, disk group, volume, and CRS Managed ACFS file systems.

- The ACFS Mount Registry agent will mount any ACFS file systems that are listed in the ACFS Mount Registry.

ACFS Shutdown Sequence

Shutdown includes stopping of the Oracle Grid Infrastructure stack via the crsctl stop cluster command or node shutdown. The following describes how this shutdown impacts the ACFS stack:

- As part of the infrastructure shutdown of CRS, the Oracle Clusterware orarootagent will perform unmounts for file systems contained on ADVM volume devices. If any file systems could not be unmounted because they are in use (open file references), then an internal grace period is set for the processes with the open file references. At the end of the grace period, if these processes have not exited, they are terminated and the file systems are unmounted, resulting in the closing of the associated dynamic volumes.

- The ASM Dynamic volumes are then disabled; ASM and its related resources are stopped.

All ACFS and ADVM logs for startup/shutdown and errors will be logged in the following places:

- Oracle Clusterware home (for example, $ORACLE_HOME/log/<hostname>/ alert.log)

- ASM alert.log

- $ORACLE_HOME/log/<hostname>/agent/ohasd/rootagent

ACFS Startup on Grid Infrastructure for Standalone

Grid Infrastructure for Standalone, Oracle Restart, does not support managing root-based ACFS start actions. Thus, the following operations are not automatically performed:

- Loading Oracle ACFS drivers

- Mounting ACFS file systems listed in the Oracle ACFS Mount Registry

- Mounting resource-based Oracle ACFS database home file systems

The following steps outline how to automate the load of the drivers and mount the file system (note that the root user needs to perform this setup):

1. Create an initialization script called /etc/init.d/acfsload. This script contains the runlevel configuration and the acfsload command:

```
#!/bin/sh

# chkconfig: 2345 30 21
```

```
# description: Auto load ACFS/ADVM driver

ORACLE_HOME=/u01/app/product/11.2.0/grid
export ORACLE_HOME

$ORACLE_HOME/bin/acfsload start -s
```

2. Modify the permissions on the /etc/init.d/acfsload script to allow it to be executed by root:

```
[root@racnode1 ~]# chmod 755 /etc/init.d/acfsload
```

3. Use the chkconfig command to build the appropriate symbolic links for the rc2.d, rc3.d, rc4.d, and rc5.d runlevel directories:

```
[root@racnode1 ~]# chkconfig --add acfsload
```

4. Verify that the chkconfig runlevel is set up correctly:

```
[root@racnode1 ~]# chkconfig --list | grep acfsload
acfsload   0:off   1:off   2:on   3:on   4:on   5:on
6:off
```

Finally, these file systems can be listed in Unix/Linux /etc/fstab and a similar rc initialization script can be used to mount them:

```
# /bin/mount  -t acfs -o all none none
```

Exporting ACFS for NFS Access

Many customers want to replace their existing NFS appliances that are used for middle-tier apps with low-cost solutions. For example, Siebel architectures require a common file system (the Siebel file system) between nodes on the mid-tier to store data and physical files used by Siebel clients and the Siebel Enterprise Server. A similar common file system is required for E-Business Suite and PeopleSoft, as well as other packaged applications.

An NAS file access protocol is used to communicate file requests between an NAS client system and an NAS file server. NAS file servers provide the actual storage. ACFS can be configured as an NAS file server and, as such, can support remote file access from NAS clients that are configured with either NFS or CIFS file access protocols. Because ACFS is a cluster file system, it can support a common file system namespace cluster-wide; thus, each cluster node has access to the file system. If a node fails, the Grid Infrastructure stack transitions the state of the cluster, and the remaining cluster nodes continue to have access to ACFS file system data. Note that SCAN names cannot be used as NFS node service names; NFS mounting the ACFS exported file system using "hard" mount options is not supported.

In the current version, there is no failover of the NFS mount. The file system will need to be remounted on another node in the cluster.

When exporting ACFS file systems through NFS on Linux, you must specify the file system identification handle via the fsid exports option. The fsid value can be any 32-bit number. The use of the file system identification handle is necessary because the ADVM block device major numbers are not guaranteed to be the same across reboots of the same node or across different nodes in the cluster. The fsid exports option forces the file system identification portion of the file handle, which is used to communicate with NFS clients, to be the specified number instead of a number derived from the major and minor number of the block device on which the file system is mounted. If the fsid is not explicitly set, a reboot of the server (housing the ACFS file system) will cause NFS clients to see inconsistent file system data or detect "Stale NFS file handle" errors.

The following guidelines must be followed with respect to the fsid:

■ The value must be unique among all the exported file systems on the system.

■ The value must be unique among members of the cluster and must be the same number on each member of the cluster for a given file system.

Summary

The ASM Cluster File System (ACFS) extends Automatic Storage Management (ASM) by providing a robust, modern, general-purpose, extent-based, journaling file system for files beyond the Oracle database files and thus becomes a complete storage management solution. ACFS provides support for files such as Oracle binaries, report files, trace files, alert logs, and other application data files. ACFS scales from small files to very large files (exabytes) and supports large numbers of nodes in a cluster.

In Oracle Grid Infrastructure 11*g* Release 2, ASM simplifies, automates, and reduces cost and overhead by providing a unified and integrated solution stack for all your file management needs, thus eliminating the need for third-party volume managers, file systems, and Clusterware platforms.

With the advent of ACFS, Oracle ASM 11*g* Release 2 has the capability to manage all data, including Oracle database files, Oracle Clusterware files, and nonstructured general-purpose data such as log files and text files.

CHAPTER
11

ACFS Data Services

As mentioned in the previous chapter, the Oracle Cloud File System simplifies storage management across file systems, middleware, and applications in private clouds with a unified namespace. The Oracle Cloud File System offers rapid elasticity and increased availability of pooled storage resources as well as an innovative architecture for balanced I/O and highest performance without tedious and complex storage administration.

One of the key aspects of the Oracle Cloud File System (ACFS) is support for advanced data services such as point-in-time snapshots, replication, file tagging, and file system security and encryption features. This chapter covers the inner workings and implementation of the ACFS data services.

ACFS Snapshots

Snapshots are immutable views of the source file system as it appeared at a specific point in time. Think of it as a way to go into the past to see what files or directories looked like at some point in time (when the snapshot was taken).

ACFS provides snapshot capability for the respective file system. The snapshot starts out with a set of duplicate pointers to the extents in the primary file system. When an update is to be made, there is no need to copy extents to the snapshot because it already points to the existing blocks. New storage is allocated for the updates in the primary file system.

This snapshot uses the first copy-on-write (FCOW or COW) methodology to enable a consistent, version-based, online view of the source file system. Snapshots are initially a sparse file system, and as the source file system's files change, the before-image extent of those files is copied into the snapshot directory. The before-image granularity is an ACFS extent, so if any byte in an extent is modified, the extent is COW'ed and any subsequent changes in that extent require no action for the snapshot.

ACFS supports read-only and read-write snapshot services. Note that ACFS snapshots cannot be used on file systems that house RMAN backups, archived logs, and Datapump dump sets; this restriction is removed in the Oracle 12g release.

When snapshots are created, they are automatically available and always online while the file system is mounted. Snapshots are created as a hidden subdirectory inside the source file system called .ACFS/snaps/, so no separate mount operation is needed and no separate file store needs to be maintained for the snapshots.

ACFS supports a total of 63 read-only, read-write, or combination of read-only and read-write snapshot views for each file system.

ACFS Read-Only Snapshots

Because ACFS read-only snapshots are a point-in-time view of a file system, they can be used as the source of a file system logical backup. An ACFS snapshot can support the online recovery of files inadvertently modified or deleted from a file system.

ACFS Read-Write Snapshots

ACFS read-write snapshots enable fast creation of a snapshot image that can be both read and written without impacting the state of the ACFS file system hosting the snapshot images. To use ACFS read-write snapshots, the disk group compatibility attribute for ADVM must be set to 11.2.0.3.0 or higher. If you create a read-write snapshot on an existing ACFS file system from a version earlier than 11.2.0.3.0, the file system is updated to the 11.2.0.3.0 format. After a file system has been updated to a higher version, it cannot be returned to an earlier version.

The read-write snapshots can be used for the following purposes:

■ Testing new versions of application software on production file data reflected in the read-write snapshot image without modifying the original production file system.

■ Running test scenarios on a real data set without modifying the original production file system.

■ Testing ACFS features such as encryption or tagging. Data in snapshots can be encrypted and workloads can be run to assess the performance impact of the encryption before the live data is encrypted.

ACFS Snapshot by Example

The following shows how to create ACFS snapshots. In this example, a snapshot of the database ORACLE_HOME is created:

```
# /sbin/acfsutil snap create oh_db_snap /u01/app/11.2.0/db3
acfsutil snap create: Snapshot operation is complete.

[root@node1] /u01/app/11.2.0/db3/.ACFS/snaps]# ls -l

drwxrwxr-x 69 oracle oinstall 8192 May 15 21:33 oh_db_snap
```

The following acfsutil command can be used to obtain information about ACFS snapshots and the file system:

```
[root@node1] /bin/acfsutil info fs /u01/app/11.2.0/db3
ACFS Version: 11.2.0.3.0.0
     flags:          MountPoint,Available
     mount time:     Thu May 15 21:33:12 2012
     volumes:        1
     total size:     6442450944
     total free:     1733464064
     primary volume: /dev/asm/dataoh_db2-32
        label:
        flags:                   Primary,Available,ADVM
        on-disk version:         39.0
```

```
allocation unit:       4096
major, minor:          252, 178689
size:                  6442450944
free:                  1733464064
ADVM diskgroup         DATA
ADVM resize increment: 268435456
ADVM redundancy:       mirror
ADVM stripe columns:   4
ADVM stripe width:     131072
```
number of snapshots: 1
snapshot space usage: 129355776

To list all snapshots available in the cluster, execute the following query:

```
SQL> SELECT SUBSTR(fs_name,1,34) FILESYSTEM,
SUBSTR(snap_name,1,28) SNAPSHOT, CREATE_TIME TIME FROM V$ASM_ACFSSNAPSHOTS;

FILESYSTEM                    SNAPSHOT        TIME
--------------------          ---------       ---------
/u01/app/acfsdata/etldata etldata1_snap   26-JUN-12

/u01/app/acfsdata/bfiles  bfiles_snap1    26-JUN-12

/u01/app/11.2.0/db3        db3_snap        26-JUN-12
```

Accessing the snapshot will always provide a point-in-time view of a file; thus, ACFS snapshots can be very useful for file-based recovery or for file system logical backups. If file-level recovery is needed (for the base file system), it can be performed using standard file copy or replace commands.

A possible use-case scenario for snapshots could be to create a consistent recovery point set between the database ORACLE_HOME and the database. This is useful, for example, when a recovery point needs to be established before applying a database patch set. Here are the steps to follow for this scenario:

1. Create an ORACLE_HOME snapshot:

    ```
    # /sbin/acfsutil snap create prepatch_snap
    /u01/oracle/11.2.0/db3
    ```

2. Create a guaranteed restore point (GRP) in the database;

    ```
    SQL>CREATE RESTORE POINT before_upgrade
    GUARANTEE FLASHBACK DATABASE;
    ```

3. Apply the patch set.

4. If the patch set application fails, take one of the following actions:

    ■ Restore the database to the GRP.

    ■ Recover the file system by leveraging the snapshot.

ACFS Tagging

ACFS tagging enables associating tag names with files, logically grouping files that may be present in any location (directory) in a file system. ACFS replication can then select files with a unique tag name for replication to a different remote cluster site. The tagging option avoids having to replicate an entire Oracle ACFS file system. Tags can be set or unset, and tag information for files can be displayed using the command acfsutil tag.

At creation time, files and directories inherit any tags from the parent directory. When a new tag is added to a directory, existing files in the directory do not get tagged with the same tag unless the –r option is specified with the acfsutil tag set command. Any files created in the future, however, do inherit the tag, regardless of whether or not the –r option was specified with the acfsutil tag set command.

ACFS implements tagging using extended attributes. Some editing tools and backup utilities do not retain the extended attributes of the original file by default, unless a specific switch is supplied. The following list describes the necessary requirements and switch settings for some common utilities to ensure ACFS tag names are preserved on the original file:

■ Install the coreutils library (version coreutils-5.97-23.el5_4.1.src.rpm or coreutils-5.97-23.el5_4.2.x86_64.rpm or later) on Linux to install a version of the cp command that supports extended attribute preservation with the --preserve=xattr switch and a version of the mv command that supports extended attribute preservation without any switches.

■ The vi editor requires the set bkc=yes option in the .vimrc (Linux) or _vimrc (Windows) file to make a backup copy of a file and overwrite the original. This preserves tag names on the original file.

■ emacs requires that the backup-by-copying option is set to a non-nil value to preserve tag names on the original filename rather than a backup copy. This option must be added to the .emacs file.

■ The rsync file-transfer utility requires the -X flag option to preserve tag names. In addition, you must set the -l and -X flags to preserve the tag names assigned to symbolic link files themselves.

■ The tar backup utility on Linux requires the --xattrs flag to be set on the command line to preserve tag names on a file. However, tar does not retain the tag names assigned to symbolic link files, even with the --xattrs flag.

■ The tar backup utility on Windows currently provides no support for retaining tag names because no switch exists to save extended attributes.

As of 11.2.0.3, the ACFS tagging feature is available only on Linux and Windows. To use the ACFS tagging functionality on Linux, the disk group compatibility attributes for ASM and ADVM must be set to 11.2.0.2 or higher. To use ACFS tagging functionality on Windows, the disk group compatibility attributes for ASM and ADVM must be set to 11.2.0.3.

This can be done with SQL*Plus, as illustrated here (notice that SQL*Plus is executed from user Oracle on node1):

```
[oracle@node1 ~]$ sqlplus / as sysasm
SQL> alter diskgroup data set attribute 'compatible.asm' = '11.2.0.2.0';
Diskgroup altered.
SQL> alter diskgroup data set attribute 'compatible.advm' = '11.2.0.2.0';
Diskgroup altered.
```

ACFS Replication Overview

In Oracle Release 11.2.0.2, the ACFS file system replication feature was introduced on the Linux platform. This feature enables replication of an ACFS file system across a network to a remote site. This capability is useful for providing disaster recovery capability. Similarly to Data Guard, which replicates databases by capturing database redo operations, ACFS replication captures ACFS file system changes on a primary file system and transmits these changes to a standby file system.

ACFS replication leverages OracleNet and the NETWORK_FILE_TRANSFER PL/SQL package for transferring replicated data from a primary node to the standby file system node. ACFS replication is only supported on Grid Infrastructure for Cluster, as selected on the Oracle Installer. ACFS replication is not supported on Grid Infrastructure for a Standalone Server. However, you can install Grid Infrastructure for a Cluster on a single node by supplying the necessary information for a single node during installation.

The combination of Oracle Real Application Clusters, Data Guard, and ACFS Replication provides comprehensive site and disaster recovery policies for all files inside and outside the database.

Primary File System

The source ACFS file system is referred to as a primary file system and the target ACFS file system as a standby file system. For every primary file system there can be only be one standby file system. ACFS replication captures, in real time, file system changes on the primary file system and saves them in files called *replication logs (rlogs)*. These rlogs are stored in the .ACFS/repl directory of the file system that is being replicated. If the primary node is part of a multinode cluster, all rlogs (one rlog per node) created at a specific instance are collectively called a *cord*. Rlogs combined into a cord are then transmitted to the standby node. The cord is then used to update the standby file system.

Keep in mind that data written to files is first buffered in a file system cache (unless direct IO is used); then at a later point in time it is committed to disk. ACFS guarantees that when data is committed to disk it will also be written to the standby file system.

Current Restrictions (11.2.0.3)

The following are consideration points when implementing ACFS file system replication in an Oracle Clusterware 11.2.0.3 system.

■ The minimum file system size that can be replicated is 4GB.

■ ACFS currently supports a maximum of eight node clusters for the primary file system.

■ The primary and standby file systems must be the same OS, architecture, and endianness.

■ ACFS cannot currently use encryption or security for replicated file systems.

■ Cascading standbys are not supported.

■ The ACFS standby file system must be empty before replication is initiated.

Standby File System

Replication logs are asynchronously transported to the node hosting the standby file system, at which point, replication logs are then read and applied to the standby file system. When the replication logs have been successfully applied to the standby file system, they are deleted on both the primary and standby file systems. Because the standby file system is a read-only file system, it can be the source of consistent file system backups after all the outstanding logs are applied.

NOTE
If needed, a read-write snapshot can be taken of the standby file system.

Planning for ACFS Replication

This section describes how to enable ACFS replication. The examples assume that the Grid Infrastructure software has been installed on nodes hosting the ACFS file system and that the ADVM volumes are enabled and the ACFS file systems are mounted.

Note that the primary and standby sites can have differing configurations. In other words, the primary can be a multinode cluster and the standby can be a single-node cluster. If a standby node is used for disaster recovery purposes, it is recommended that the standby node have a configuration similar to the cluster configuration.

There are no rigid primary and standby node roles; that is, a primary node can provide the role of primary for one file system and also provide the role of standby for another file system. However, for simplicity, this chapter will use the term *primary node* to indicate the node hosting the primary file system and the term *standby node* for the node hosting the standby file system.

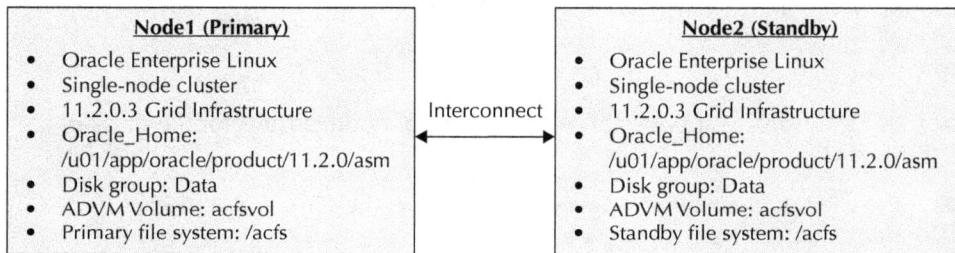

Node1 (Primary)	Node2 (Standby)

• Oracle Enterprise Linux
• Single-node cluster
• 11.2.0.3 Grid Infrastructure
• Oracle_Home:
  /u01/app/oracle/product/11.2.0/asm
• Disk group: Data
• ADVM Volume: acfsvol
• Primary file system: /acfs
	• Oracle Enterprise Linux
	• Single-node cluster
	• 11.2.0.3 Grid Infrastructure
	• Oracle_Home:
	  /u01/app/oracle/product/11.2.0/asm
	• Disk group: Data
	• ADVM Volume: acfsvol
	• Standby file system: /acfs

Interconnect ◄──────►

This configuration represents the system used in the following examples. With respect to replication, some commands, such as acfsutil, must be executed with root privileges. Other commands, such as sqlplus, are issued from the oracle user ID. In the examples, the user ID is shown with the command prompt.

Tagging Considerations

ACFS tagging can be a key aspect of to ACFS replication, as it allows users to assign a common naming attribute to a group of files. This is done by leveraging OS-specific extended attributes and implementing generic tagging CLIs. ACFS replication can use these tags to select files with a unique tag name for replication to a different remote cluster site. Thus, rather than an entire file system being replicated, ACFS tagging enables a user to select specific tagged files and directories for replication, by assigning a common naming attribute to a group of files. ACFS replication uses this tag to filter files with unique tag names for remote file system replication. Tagging enables data- or attribute-based replication.

The following example illustrates recursively tagging all files of the /acfs directory with the "reptag" tag:

```
[root@node1 ~]#  /sbin/acfsutil tag set -r Boston /acfs
```

Using tagging with ACFS replication requires that a replication tag be specified when replication is first initiated on the primary node. Tagging with replication cannot be implemented after replication has been initiated. To begin tagging after replication has been initiated requires that replication first be terminated and then restarted with a tag name.

Before you implement ACFS replication, it is important to determine how and what will be replicated; for example, will all file system data be replicated, certain directories, or only specific ACFS tagged files? This choice will impact file system sizing.

Keep in mind that the tags specified on the init command line need not be applied to files at the time of the initialization. For example, you can replicate files with the tags Chicago and Boston, when at the time of replication only files with the Chicago tag exist (that is, no files with the Boston tag exist). Any subsequent files tagged with Boston will also begin to be replicated.

Setting Up Replication

Before initializing ACFS replication, ensure that the primary file system has a minimum of 4GB of free space multiplied by the number of nodes mounting the file system. This should be done prior to executing the acfsutil repl init command; otherwise, this command will fail.

ACFS replication also requires that the compatible.asm and compatible.advm attributes for the disk group containing the ACFS file system are set to a minimum of 11.2.0.2.0 for Linux (or 11.2.0.3 on Windows) on both the primary and standby nodes. If this was not done in the earlier steps (for enabling tagging or other features), then it can be done now with the sqlplus command, as illustrated here:

```
[oracle@node1 ~]$ sqlplus / as sysasm
SQL> alter diskgroup data set attribute 'compatible.asm' = '11.2.0.3.0';
Diskgroup altered.

SQL> alter diskgroup data set attribute 'compatible.advm' = '11.2.0.3.0';
Diskgroup altered.
```

Admin User Setup

In most cases, the SYS user in an ASM instance can be used as the ACFS replication administrator, in which case the SYS user will need to be granted the SYSDBA privilege (on the ASM instance). If there is a need to have separate roles for replication management (replication admin) and daily ASM management, then a separate ASM user can be set up. This user must be granted SYSASM and SYSDBA privileges. The following example shows how to set up a replication admin user with a user ID of *admin* and a password of *admin1*.

If an ASM password file does not exist, you should create the password file for ASM on all nodes (primary/standby and secondary nodes with multinode clusters), as follows:

```
[oracle@node1 ~]$ orapwd file=$ORACLE_HOME/dbs/orapw+ASM
password=oracle123 entries=5
```

NOTE
Please use a password appropriate for your installation.

Next, create the ASM user on the primary node and assign the appropriate roles:

```
[oracle@node1 ~]$ sqlplus / as sysasm
SQL> create user admin identified by admin1;
SQL> grant sysasm to admin;
SQL> grant sysdba to admin;
```

Then create the ASM user on the standby node and assign the appropriate roles:

```
[oracle@node2 ~]$ sqlplus / as sysasm
SQL> create user admin identified by admin1;
SQL> grant sysasm to admin;
SQL> grant sysdba to admin;
```

Finally, review changes to the password file by querying v$pwfile_users:

```
SQL> select * from v$pwfile_users;
USERNAME                           SYSDBA SYSOP SYSASM
------------------------------     ------ ----- -------
SYS                                TRUE   TRUE  FALSE
ADMIN                              TRUE   FALSE TRUE
```

Hereafter, the ACFS administrator role "admin" will refer to the role that manages ACFS file system replication.

File System Setup

Before initiating replication, the ACFS admin must ensure that the primary file system is mounted and the standby file system is only mounted on one node (in cluster configurations).

It is recommended that users have the same file system name for the standby and primary file systems. Also, ensure that if you're replicating the entire file system (that is, not using ACFS tagging) that the standby file system is created with a size that is equal to or larger than the primary file system.

Also, you should ensure that sufficient disk space is available on both the primary and the standby file systems for storing the replication logs. The "Pause and Resume Replication" section later in this chapter covers file system sizing details when replication is used. It is recommended that ACFS administrators monitor and prevent both the primary file system and the standby file system from running out of space. Enterprise Manager (EM) can be used for this monitoring and for sending alerts when the file system approaches more than 70-percent full.

In 11.2.0.3, the auto-terminate safeguard functionality was introduced to prevent the primary file system from running out of space. If 2GB or less of free space is available, ACFS will terminate replication on the node. Auto-terminate prevents further consumption of disk space for replication operations and frees disk space consumed by any replication logs that remain. Before reaching the 2GB limit, ACFS writes warnings about the free space problem in the Oracle Grid Infrastructure home alert log. Note, using the Auto-terminate feature exposes the administrator to lose the ability to use the standby if the primary fails when it is running near full capacity. We advice that this feature should be used with extreme caution.

If the primary file system runs out of space, the applications using that file system may fail because ACFS cannot create a new replication log. If the standby file system runs out of space, it cannot accept new replication logs from the primary node; therefore, changes cannot be applied to the standby file system, which causes replication logs to accumulate on the primary file system as well. In cases where the ACFS file system space becomes depleted, ACFS administrators can expand the file system, remove unneeded ACFS snapshots, or remove files to reclaim space (although the latter option is not recommended). If the primary file system runs out of space and the ACFS administrator intends to remove files to free up space, then only files that are not currently being replicated (such as when ACFS tagging is used) should be removed because the removal of a file that is replicated will itself be captured in a replication log.

Network Setup

Two steps are needed to configure the network for ACFS replication:

1. Generate the appropriate Oracle Network files. These files provide communication between the ASM instances and ACFS replication.

2. Set the appropriate network parameters for network transmission. Because ACFS replication is heavily tied to network bandwidth, the appropriate settings need to be configured.

Generating the Oracle Network Files

ACFS replication utilizes Oracle Net Services for transmitting replication logs between primary and standby nodes. The principal OracleNet configuration is a file called tnsnames.ora, and it resides at $ORACLE_HOME/network/admin/tnsnames.ora. This file can be edited manually or through a configuration assistant called netca in the Grid Home. The tnsnames.ora file must be updated on each of the nodes participating in ACFS replication. The purpose of a tnsnames.ora file is to provide the Oracle environment the definition of a remote endpoint used during replication. For example, there are tnsnames.ora files for both primary and standby nodes.

Once the file systems are created, use $ORACLE_HOME/bin/netca (from Grid Home) to create connect strings and network aliases for the primary/standby sites. Figures 11-1 and 11-2 illustrate the usage of NETCA to create Net Services for ACFS Replication.

On netca exit, the following message should be displayed if the services were set up correctly:

```
Oracle Net Services Configuration:
Oracle Net Configuration Assistant is launched from Grid Infrastructure
home.
Network configuration will be clusterwide.
Default local naming configuration complete.
    Created net service name: PRIMARY_DATA
Default local naming configuration complete.
    Created net service name: STANDBY_DATA
Oracle Net Services configuration successful. The exit code is 0
```

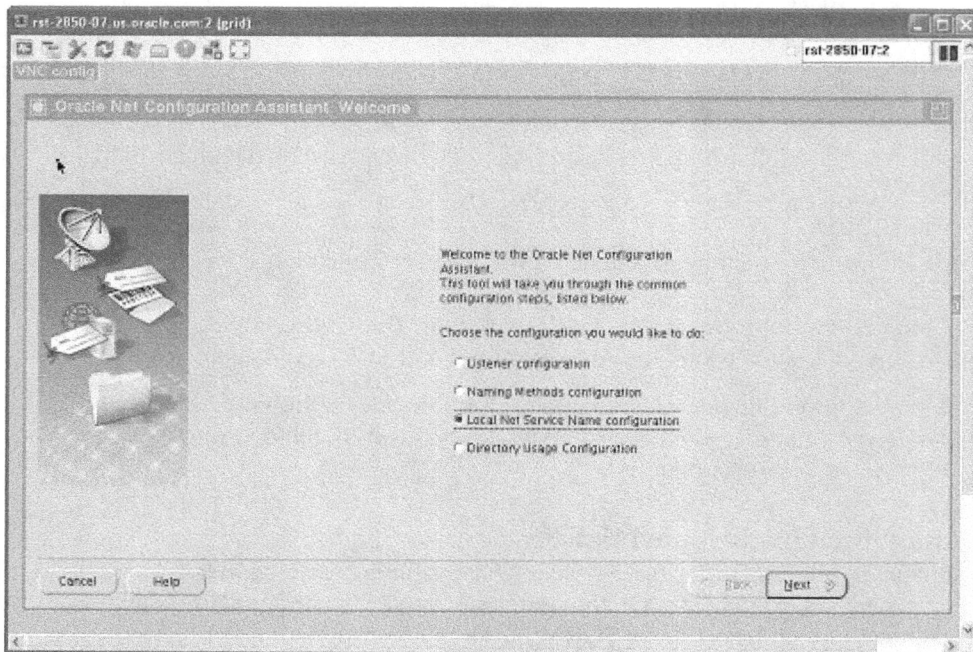

FIGURE 11-1. *NETCA configuration step 1*

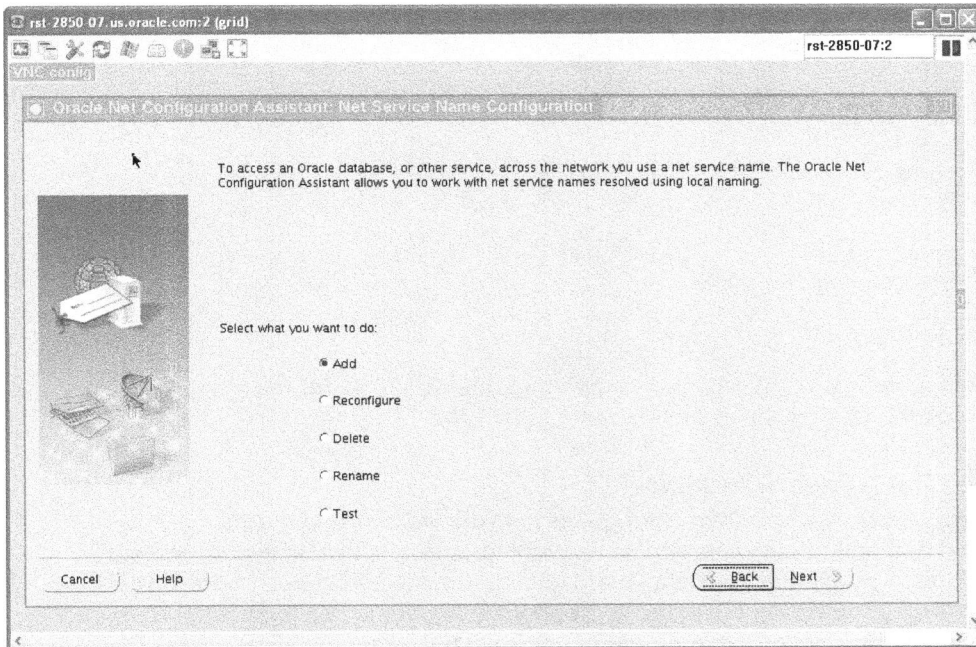

FIGURE 11-2. *NETCA Add Service configuration*

In our example, we created a PRIMARY_DATA service and STANDBY_DATA service for the primary file system and standby file system, respectively. In this example, the tnsnames.ora file used for the primary node is

```
[oracle@node1 ~]$ cat $ORACLE_HOME/network/admin/tnsnames.ora
STANDBY =
  (DESCRIPTION =
    (ADDRESS_LIST =
      (ADDRESS = (PROTOCOL = TCP)(HOST = node2)(PORT = 1521))
    )
    (CONNECT_DATA =
      (SERVICE_NAME = acfs_fs)
    )
  )
```

The important elements are the alias name (STANDBY), the hostname (node2), the default port (1521), and the service name (acfs_fs). This tnsnames.ora defines the remote endpoint for replication (in this case, standby to node1, which is the primary node). The standby node requires a tnsnames.ora file that defines the primary endpoint. It contains the following:

```
[oracle@node2 ~]$ cat $ORACLE_HOME/network/admin/tnsnames.ora
PRIMARY =
  (DESCRIPTION =
    (ADDRESS_LIST =
      (ADDRESS = (PROTOCOL = TCP)(HOST = node1)(PORT = 1521))
    )
    (CONNECT_DATA =
      (SERVICE_NAME = acfs_fs)
    )
  )
```

Notice the symmetry between the two tnsnames.ora files. For the sake of simplicity, the service names are the same.

Setting the Network Tunables

Successful replication deployment requires network efficiency and sufficient bandwidth; therefore, the appropriate network tuning must be performed. For ACFS replication, first determine if Data Guard (DG) is already configured on the hosts. If DG is set up appropriately with the appropriate network tunable parameters, then ACFS replication can leverage the same settings. If DG is not enabled, use the Data Guard best practices guide for network setup. The following document describes these best practices (see the "Redo Transport Best Practices" section of this paper):

http://www.oracle.com/technetwork/database/features/availability/maa-wp-10gr2-dataguardnetworkbestpr-134557.pdf\

Validating Network Configuration

Use the tnsping utility and SQL*Plus to test and ensure that the tnsnames.ora files are set up correctly and basic connectivity exists between both sites.

Execute the following to test connectivity from the primary node:

```
[oracle@node1 ~]$ tnsping standby
TNS Ping Utility for Linux: Version 11.2.0.3.0 - Production on 01-DEC-2010
12:58:13
Copyright (c) 1997, 2010, Oracle.  All rights reserved.
Used parameter files:
/u01/app/oracle/product/11.2.0/asm/network/admin/sqlnet.ora
Used TNSNAMES adapter to resolve the alias
Attempting to contact (DESCRIPTION = (ADDRESS_LIST = (ADDRESS = (PROTOCOL =
TCP)(HOST = node2)(PORT = 1521))) (CONNECT_DATA = (SERVICE_NAME = acfs_fs)))
OK (0 msec)
```

```
[oracle@node1 ~]$ sqlplus admin/admin1 as sysasm@primary
SQL*Plus: Release 11.2.0.3.0 Production on Wed Dec 1 12:58:39 2010
Copyright (c) 1982, 2010, Oracle.  All rights reserved.
Connected to:
Oracle Database 11g Enterprise Edition Release 11.2.0.3.0 - 64bit Production
With the Real Application Clusters and Automatic Storage Management options
SQL>
```

Execute the following to test connectivity from the standby node:

```
[oracle@node2 ~]$ tnsping primary
TNS Ping Utility for Linux: Version 11.2.0.3.0 - Production on 01-DEC-2010
13:01:26
Copyright (c) 1997, 2010, Oracle.  All rights reserved.
Used parameter files:
/u01/app/oracle/product/11.2.0/asm/network/admin/sqlnet.ora
Used TNSNAMES adapter to resolve the alias
Attempting to contact (DESCRIPTION = (ADDRESS_LIST = (ADDRESS = (PROTOCOL =
TCP)(HOST = node1)(PORT = 1521))) (CONNECT_DATA = (SERVICE_NAME = acfs_fs)))
OK (0 msec)

[oracle@node2 ~]$ sqlplus admin/admin1 as sysasm@primary
SQL*Plus: Release 11.2.0.3.0 Production on Wed Dec 1 13:01:46 2010
Copyright (c) 1982, 2010, Oracle.  All rights reserved.
Connected to:
Oracle Database 11g Enterprise Edition Release 11.2.0.3.0 - 64bit Production
With the Real Application Clusters and Automatic Storage Management options
```

Replication Configuration and Initiation

For good measure, the following ensures that file systems are mounted on each node.
Execute the following to initiate replication from the primary node:

```
[oracle@node1 ~]$ df -h
File system              Size  Used Avail Use% Mounted on
/dev/mapper/VolGroup00-LogVol00
                         25G   11G   13G  45% /
/dev/sda1                99M   16M   78M  17% /boot
tmpfs                   1.5G  192M  1.3G  13% /dev/shm
.host:/                 923G  295G  628G  32% /mnt/hgfs
/dev/asm/acfsvol-269    5.0G  1.2G  3.9G  23% /acfs
```

Execute the following to validate replication from the standby node:

```
[oracle@node2 ~]$ df -h
File system              Size  Used Avail Use% Mounted on
/dev/mapper/VolGroup00-LogVol00
                         25G   11G   13G  46% /
/dev/sda1                99M   16M   78M  17% /boot
tmpfs                   1.5G  192M  1.3G  13% /dev/shm
.host:/                 923G  295G  628G  32% /mnt/hgfs
/dev/asm/acfsvol-343    5.0G  101M  5.0G   2% /acfs
```

Initializing the Standby File System

Replication is first initiated on the standby node, followed by initiation on the primary. Replication on the standby is initiated using the /sbin/acfsutil command by the root user, like so:

```
[root@node2 ~]# /sbin/acfsutil repl init standby -p \
    admin/admin1@primary /acfs
```

NOTE
If this command is interrupted for any reason, the user must re-create the standby file system, mount it only on one node of the site hosting the standby file system, and then rerun the command.

This command uses the following configuration information:

- The –p option indicates the username connection to the primary file system site as well as the service name to be used to connect as ASMADMIN on the primary file system node.

- The file system listed is the standby file system (/acfs).

- If the standby site is using a different service name than the primary file system site, the command –c *service_name* is required. (Note that this is optional and not shown in the example.)

Now you need to verify that the standby file system is initiated:

```
[root@node2 ~]# /sbin/acfsutil repl info -c /acfs
Site:                              Standby
Standby status:                    Online
Standby mount point:               /acfs
Standby Oracle Net service name:   acfs_fs
Primary mount point:
Primary Oracle Net service name:   acfs_fs
Primary Oracle Net alias:          admin/****@primary
Replicated tags:
Log compression:                   Off
Debug log level:                   0
```

Initializing the Primary File System

Once the standby node has been enabled, the ACFS admin can initialize replication on the primary file system by running the acfsutil repl init primary command:

```
[root@node1 ~]# /sbin/acfsutil repl init primary \
    -s admin/admin1@standby /acfs
remote connection has been established
waiting for the standby replication site to initialize
waiting for the standby replication site to initialize
The standby replication site is initialized. ACFS replication will begin.
```

This command allows for the following configuration information:

- The –s option, followed by the connect string used to connect as ASMADMIN on the standby node.

- The ACFS file system that is to be replicated.

- The mount point on the standby node (-m *mountp*). This is optional and not shown in the example. If not specified, it is assumed that this mount point path is the same on the standby node as it is on the primary file system node.

- The –c option, which is used to indicate the primary service name. Again, this is optional and not shown in the example.

If tagging was enabled for this directory, then the tag name "reptag" can be added in the initialization command, as follows:

```
[root@node1 ~]# /sbin/acfsutil repl init primary \
    -s admin/admin1@standby reptag /acfs
validating the remote connection
remote connection has been established
waiting for the standby replication site to initialize
The standby replication site is initialized. ACFS replication will begin.
```

Next, you need to verify that the primary file system is initiated:

```
[root@node1 ~]# /sbin/acfsutil repl info -c /acfs
Site:                             Primary
Primary status:                   Online
Primary mount point:              /acfs
Primary Oracle Net service name:  acfs_fs
Standby mount point:              /acfs
Standby Oracle Net service name:  acfs_fs
Standby Oracle Net alias:         admin/****@standby
Replicated tags:                  reptag
Log compression:                  Off
Debug log level:                  2
```

Once the acfsutil repl init primary command completes successfully, replication will begin transferring copies of all specified files to the standby file system.

The replication happens in two phases: The initial phase copies just the directory tree structure, and the second phase copies the individual files. During this second phase, all updates or truncates to replicated files are blocked. Once a file is completely copied to the standby file system, replication logging for that particular file is enabled. All changes to copied files are logged, transported, and applied to the standby file system.

Next, you need to validate replication instantiation:

```
[root@node1 ~]# /sbin/acfsutil repl info /acfs
Time: Wed Dec  1 13:24:58 2010
Event: Replication Synchronized
Sync Time: Wed Dec  1 13:24:58 2010
Logs were applied
Time: Wed Dec  1 13:24:53 2010
Event: Initialization Files Complete
Cord Number: 1
```

The rate of data change on the primary file system can be monitored using the command

```
acfsutil info fs -s
```

where the –s flag indicates the sample rate. The amount of change includes all user and metadata modifications to the file system. The following example illustrates its usage:

```
[root@node1 ~]# /sbin/acfsutil info fs -s 10 /acfs
/acfs
    amount of change since mount:        0.28 MB
    amount of change: 128.36 MB   rate of change: 13144 KB/s
    amount of change: 93.50 MB   rate of change: 9574 KB/s
```

This "amount" value approximates the size of replication logs generated when capturing changes to the file system. This command is useful for approximating the extra space required for storing replication logs in cases of planned or unplanned outages.

Pause and Resume Replication

The acfsutil repl pause command is used in instances when replication needs to be temporarily halted, such as for planned downtime on either the primary or standby site. The ACFS pause command can be issued on either the primary or a standby file system node. However, there is a difference in behavior between the two scenarios.

A pause command issued on the standby node will continue to generate and propagate replication logs from the primary to the standby file system, but these rlogs will not be applied to the standby file system; in other words, it does not suspend transfer of rlogs from the primary node, only the application is deferred. Consequently, rlogs will continue to accumulate at the node hosting the standby file system. As noted earlier, replication logs are deleted on the primary and standby sites only after they are successfully applied to the file system on the standby node; therefore, care should be taken to ensure that this does not cause the primary and standby file systems to run out of space.

A pause command issued on the primary node will generate replication logs but not propagate them to standby; in other words, it will generate rlogs but suspend their propagation. In this scenario, rlogs will continue to accumulate at the primary file system. This may cause the primary file system to run out of space. Thus, when paused on the standby, it is possible to run out of space on both primary and standby, while pausing on primary has the potential to just cause issue for the primary. This would be relevant when a standby system is destination for multiple file systems.

In both cases, ACFS administrators should run the acfsutil repl resume command at the earliest point possible, before the accumulated replication logs fill the file system. Note that the resume command should be executed at the same location where replication was paused.

In cases where there is a planned outage and the standby and primary file systems have to be unmounted, it is best to ensure that all the changes are propagated and applied on the standby file system. The acfsutil repl sync command is used for this purpose. It is used to synchronize the state of the primary and standby file systems, and it implicitly causes all outstanding replication data to be transferred to the standby file system. The acfsutil repl sync command returns success when this transfer is complete or when all these changes have been successfully applied to the standby file system, if the apply parameter is supplied. This command can only be run on the node hosting the primary file system.

For unplanned outages, if the cluster (or node) hosting the primary file system fails, the administrator of the standby file system should decide whether or not the situation is a disaster. If it is not a disaster, then when the primary site recovers, replication will automatically restart. If it is a disaster, you should issue an acfsutil terminate command on the standby file system to convert it into a primary. If replication needs to reinstantiated, then once the original primary is restarted, replication initialization will need to be performed again.

If the node hosting the standby file system fails, a major concern is the amount of update activity that occurs on the primary file system relative to the amount of free space allocated to address standby file system outages. If the free space in the primary file system is exceeded because of the inability to transfer updates to the standby file system, a "file system out of space" condition will occur and space will need to be made available—for example, by removing items no longer needed (particularly snapshots), performing a file system resize to add space, and so on. However, assuming the standby comes back, then as soon as primary file system space is available, replication will continue. During this interval, where no space is available, the file system will return errors in response to update requests. If the standby file system is going to be down for a long period of time, it is recommended that the primary file system be unmounted to avoid update activity on the file system that could result in an out-of-space condition. When the standby file system becomes available, the primary file system could be remounted and replication will restart automatically. Alternatively, the primary file system admin could elect to terminate and reinstantiate once the site hosting the standby file system is recovered.

Sizing ACFS File Systems

To size the primary and standby file systems appropriately for these planned and unplanned outages, you can use the acfsutil fs info command, described earlier, as a guide to determine the rate of replication log creation. First, determine the approximate time interval when the primary file system is unable to send replication logs to the standby file system at its usual rate or when standby file systems are inaccessible while undergoing maintenance. Although it is not easy to determine how long an unplanned will last, this exercise helps in determining the overall impact when an unplanned outage occurs.

As an aid, run acfsutil info fs -s 1200 on the primary file system to collect the average rate of change over a 24-hour period with a 20-minute interval:

```
[root@node1 ~]# /sbin/acfsutil info fs -s 1200 /acfs
```

The output from this command helps determine the average rate of change, the peak rate of change, and how long the peaks last. Note that this command only collects data on the node it is executed on. For clustered configurations, run the command and collect data for all nodes in the cluster.

In the following scenario, assume that t = 60 minutes is the time interval that would adequately account for network problems or maintenance on the site hosting the standby file system. The following formula approximates the extra storage capacity needed for an outage of 60 minutes:

- ■ N = Number of cluster nodes in the primary site generating rlogs

- ■ p_t = Peak amount of change generated across all nodes for time t

- ■ t = 60 minutes

Therefore, the extra storage capacity needed to hold the replication logs is $(N * 1GB) + p_t$.

In this use-case example, assume a four-node cluster on the primary where all four are generating replication logs. Also, during peak workload intervals, the total amount of change reported for 60 minutes is approximately 6GB for all nodes. Using the preceding storage capacity formula, 10GB of excess storage capacity on the site hosting the primary file system is required for the replication logs, or (4 * 1GB) + 6GB = 10GB.

ACFS Compare Command

In certain situations, users may want to compare the contents of the primary and standby file systems. The acfsutil repl compare command can be used to compare the entire ACFS file system or a subset of files (such as tagged files).

The acfsutil repl compare command requires that the standby file system be mounted locally for comparison. This can be accomplished by NFS mounting the standby file system onto the primary. As with any compare operation, it is recommend that the primary has limited or no file changes occurring.

The acfsutil repl compare command with the -a option can be used to compare the entire contents of the primary file system against those on the standby file system. The -a option also tests for extra files on the standby file system that do not currently exist on the primary.

The -a option is typically used when no tag names were specified during the acfsutil repl init operation. When only tagged files need to be compared, the -t option can be used. Users can even compare multiple sets of tagged files by listing comma-separated tag names. This option first locates all filenames on the primary file system with the specified tag names and compares them to the corresponding files on the standby. The -t option also tests for extra files on the standby file system that do not have an associated tag name specified during the acfsutil repl init operation. The acfsutil repl info -c option can be used to determine what tags were specified during the acfsutil repl init operation. If neither the -a nor -t option is provided, a primary-to-standby file comparison is done without testing tag names or extended attributes.

The following shows a sample execution of acfsutil repl compare:

```
# date; ./acfsutil repl compare /primary /nfs_standby; date
Tue May 15 14:05:10 EDT 2012
Comparing primary mount point (<<<) to standby mount point (>>>):
Testing for extra files on standby.
Standby mount point (<<<) to primary mount point (>>>):
Results for file comparison of primary to standby mount points:
 Files successfully compared = 31986
 Files which failed comparison = 0
Results for extra files on standby test:
 Total files checked = 31986
 Extra files found = 0
Tue May 15 14:06:40 EDT 2012
# date; ./acfsutil repl compare /primary /nfs_standby; date
Tue May 16 15:53:14 EDT 2012
```

```
Comparing primary mount point (<<<) to standby mount point (>>>):
<<< /primary/test/d281/f3
>>> >>> File missing!
<<< file size or file contents comparison failed, file:
/primary/test/d825/f1
>>> >>> file size or file contents comparison failed, file:
/nfs_standby/test/d825/f1
<<< file attribute comparison failed: permissions=rw-r--r--,
links=1, uid=0, gid=0, bytes=102400, file: /primary/test/d825/f1
>>> >>> file attribute comparison failed: permissions=rw-r--r--,
links=1, uid=0, gid=0, bytes=102401, file: /nfs_standby/test/d825/f1
<<< file size or file contents comparison failed, file:
/primary/test/d825/f8
>>> >>> file size or file contents comparison failed, file:
/nfs_standby/test/d825/f8
<<< file attribute comparison failed: permissions=rwxr-xr-x,
links=2, uid=0, gid=0, bytes=4096, file: /primary/test/d1719
>>> >>> file attribute comparison failed: permissions=rwxrwxrwx,
links=2, uid=0, gid=0, bytes=4096, file: /nfs_standby/test/d1719
Testing for extra files on standby.
Standby mount point (<<<) to primary mount point (>>>):
<<< /nfs_standby/test/d1/ishan
>>> >>> File missing!
Results for file comparison of primary to standby mount points:
 Files successfully compared = 31982
 Files which failed comparison = 4
Results for extra files on standby test:
 Total files checked = 31986
 Extra files found = 1
Tue May 16 16:05:12 EDT 2012
```

Termination of Replication

The acfsutil repl terminate command is used to abort the ongoing replication. The terminate command operates on a specific file system. A graceful termination can be achieved by terminating the replication first on the primary followed by the standby node. A graceful termination allows for the standby to apply all outstanding logs.

The following command terminates replication on primary node:

```
[root@node1 ~]# /sbin/acfsutil repl terminate primary /acfs
```

Next to terminate replication on standby node:

```
STANDBY NODE
```

After the standby is terminated, the file system is automatically converted to writable mode:

```
[root@node2 ~]# /sbin/acfsutil repl terminate standby /acfs
acfsutil repl terminate: ACFS-05060: waiting for ACFS replication
to terminate
```

Once file system replication termination has completed for a specific file system, no replication infrastructure exists between that primary and standby file systems. The termination of replication is a permanent operation and requires a full reinitialization to instantiate again. To restart replication, use the acfsutil repl init command, as previously illustrated.

ACFS Security and Encryption

As discussed in Chapter 10, ACFS provides standard POSIX file system support; however, ACFS also provides other file system services, such as security, encryption, tagging, snapshots, and replication. In this section we cover ACFS Security and ACFS Encryption. ACFS Security and Encryption—along with Oracle Database Vault and Oracle Advanced Security Option (ASO) —provide a comprehensive security solution for unstructured data residing outside the database and database-resident structured data, respectively. Note that ACFS Security and Encryption are not part of the ASO license; they must be licensed separately via the Cloud Edition.

There are two aspects of security on a file system. One is the restriction of logical access to the data, such as obtaining file information or file location. The other is preventing physical access to the data, such as opening, reading, or writing to data (files). The former is handled by ACFS Security and the latter by ACFS Encryption.

Databases and Security

Databases generally have peripheral data (data that lives outside the database, but has direct ties to the data within the database), such as medical reports and images, text files, contracts, metadata, and other unstructured data. This data needs to be kept secured and must meet regulatory compliancy (for example, SOX, HIPAA, PCI, or PII).

ACFS supports the Unix "user, group, others" model and supports Access Control Lists (ACLs) on Windows. These constructs are based on the Discretionary Access Control (DAC) model. In the DAC model, controls are discretionary in the sense that a subject with certain access permission is capable of passing that permission (perhaps indirectly) on to any other subject. In the case of a file system, the owner of a file can pass the privileges to anybody.

Besides some of the issues in DAC, such as transfer of ownership, a major concern is that the root user or administrator will bypass all user security and have the privileges to access or modify anything on the file system. For databases where the DBA (database administrator) has more privileges than required to perform his duties, Oracle addresses this problem with a security product called Oracle Database Vault, which helps users address such security problems as protecting against insider threats, meeting regulatory compliance requirements, and enforcing separation of duty. It provides a number of flexible features that can be used to apply fine-grained access control to the customer's sensitive data. It enforces industry-standard best practices in terms of separating duties from traditionally powerful users. It protects data from privileged users but still allows them to maintain Oracle databases.

The goal of Oracle Database Vault, however, is limited to Oracle databases. Today, customers need the same kind of fine-grained access control to data outside the database (such as Oracle binaries, archive logs, redo logs, and application files such as Oracle Apps). ACFS Security fills this gap with a similar paradigm, in which realms, rules, rule sets, and command rules (described later) provide fine-grained access to data.

ACFS Security

ACFS Security provides finer-grained access policy definition and enforcement than allowed by an OS-provided access control mechanism alone. Another goal of ACFS Security is to provide a means to restrict users' ability to pass privileges of the files they own to other users if they are not consistent with the global policies set within an organization. Lastly, ACFS Security follows the principle of least privilege in the facilities it provides for the definition and administration of security policies.

ACFS Security uses realms, rules, rule sets, and command rules for the definition and enforcement of security policies:

- **Realm** An ACFS realm is a functional grouping of file system objects that must be secured for access by a user or a group of users. File system objects can be files or directories. By having these objects grouped in the form of a realm, ACFS Security can provide fine-grained access control to the data stored in ACFS. For realm protection to take effect, objects must be added to a realm. Objects can be added to more than one realm. The definition of a realm also includes a list of users and groups. Only those users who are part of the realm directly or indirectly via the groups are allowed access to the realm. Only those users who are part of the realm can access the objects within the realm if the rules are satisfied.

- **Rule** A rule is a Boolean expression that evaluates to TRUE or FALSE based on some system parameter on which the rule is based. An option of ALLOW or DENY can be associated with each rule. Rules can be shared among multiple rule sets. For example, a "5–9PM" rule evaluates to TRUE if the system time is between 5 P.M. and 9 P.M. when the rule is evaluated. ACFS Security supports four types of rules:

- **Time**   Evaluates to TRUE or FALSE based on whether the current system time falls between the start time and end time specified as part of rule definition.

- **User**   Evaluates to TRUE or FALSE based on the user executing the operation.

- **Application**   Evaluates to TRUE or FALSE based on the application that is accessing the file system object.

- **Hostname**   Evaluates to TRUE or FALSE based on the hostname accessing the file system object. The hostname specified must be a cluster member and not a client host accessing an ACFS file system via NFS, for example.

- **Rule set**   A rule set is a collection of rules that evaluates to "allow" or "deny" based on the assessment of its constituent rules. Rule sets can be configured to evaluate to "allow" if all constituent rules evaluate to TRUE with the option "allow" or if at least one rule evaluates to TRUE with the option "allow" depending on the rule set options.

- **Command rule**   Oracle ACFS command rules are associations of the file system operation with a rule set. For example, the association of a file system create, delete, or rename operation with a rule set makes a command rule. Command rules are associated with a realm.

ACFS Security Administrator

In accordance with the principle of least privilege, ACFS Security mandates that security policy definition and management be the duty of a user with a well-defined security administrator role and not a user with the system administrator role. To this end, as part of initializing ACFS Security, the system administrator is required to designate an OS user as an ACFS *security administrator*. A temporary password is set for this security administrator, and it should be changed immediately to keep the security administrator's role secure. This security administrator can then designate additional users as security administrators using the acfsutil sec admin add command. Only a security administrator can designate or remove another user as a security administrator. There is always at least one security administrator once ACFS Security has been initialized, and the last security administrator cannot be removed using the acfsutil sec admin remove command.

The security administrator creates and manages security policies using realms, rules, rule sets, and command rules. For any administrative tasks, the security administrator must authenticate himself using a password that is different from his OS account password. Each security administrator has a unique password, which can be changed only by that security administrator. These passwords are managed by ACFS Security infrastructure and are kept in a secure Oracle Wallet stored in the Oracle Cluster Repository (OCR). Security administrators are allowed to *browse* any part of the file system tree. This allows them to list and choose files and directories to be realm-secured. No security administrator, however, is allowed to *read* the contents of any files without appropriate OS and realm permissions.

Enabling and Disabling ACFS Security

ACFS Security can be enabled or disabled on a file system by running the acfsutil sec enable and acfsutil sec disable commands, respectively. Disabling ACFS Security on a file system preserves all the security policies defined for that file system, but disables their enforcement, which implies access to files and directories on that file system is arbitrated only through only the OS mechanism. To enable enforcement, the ACFS security administrator can run the acfsutil sec enable command. Security can be enabled and disabled at the file system or realm level. By default, ACFS Security is enabled on a file system when it is prepared for security. A newly created realm can have it enabled or disabled based via a command-line option (the default is enabled). Disabling ACFS Security at the file system level disables enforcement via all realms defined for that file system. Enable and disable capability can be useful when security policies are not completely defined and the security administrator wishes to experiment with some policies before finalizing them.

Configuring ACFS Security

ACFS Security is supported only for ASM 11*g* Release 2, and the disk group compatibility attributes for ASM and ADVM must be set to 11.2.0.*x*, where *x* represents the version of the ASM installed.

ACFS file systems can be configured to use ACFS Security via the acfsutil sec commands or the ASMCA utility. ACFS Security must be *initialized* before any file systems can be configured to use it. This is done using the acfsutil sec init command, which needs to be run only once for the entire cluster. As part of the acfsutil sec init command, an OS user is designated to be the first security administrator. It is recommended that this OS user be distinct from the DBA user. This user must also be in an existing OS group designated as the Security Administrator group. Additional users can be designated as security administrators. All security administrators, however, must be members of the designated security OS group. Moreover, initializing ACFS Security also creates the storage necessary to house the security administrator's security credentials.

Once ACFS Security has been initialized for the cluster, the security administrator can *prepare* a file system to use it by running the acfsutil sec prepare command.

This step is a prerequisite for defining security policies for the file system. The acfs sec prepare command performs the following actions:

- It initializes ACFS Security metadata for the file system.

- It enables ACFS Security on the file system.

- It creates the following directories in the file system that is being prepared:

  - .Security

  - .Security/backup

  - .Security/logs

- It builds the following system security realms:

  - **SYSTEM_Logs** Protects ACFS Security log files in the .Security/realm/logs/ directory.

  - **SYSTEM_SecurityMetadata** Protects the ACFS Security metadata XML file in the .Security/backup/ directory.

- On the Windows platform, the SYSTEM_Antivirus realm is created to provide installed antivirus software programs access to run against the ACFS file system. The SYSTEM_Antivirus realm can only perform the OPEN, READ, READDIR, and setting time attribute operations on a file or directory. Generally, antivirus software programs inoculate and delete infected files. For the antivirus software programs to perform these actions successfully, the ACFS security will need to be disabled. For every realm-protected file or directory, the SYSTEM_Antivirus realm is evaluated when authorization checks are performed to determine if the SYSTEM_Antivirus realm allows access to the file or directory. To allow the antivirus process to access realm-protected files or directories, you must add the LocalSystem or SYSTEM group to the realm with the acfsutil sec realm add command. If antivirus processes are running as administrator, then the user administrator must be added to the SYSTEM_Antivirus realm to allow access to realm-protected files and directories. If no antivirus products have been installed, do not add any users or groups to the SYSTEM_Antivirus realm. Because users or groups added to the SYSTEM_Antivirus realm have READ and READDIR access, you should limit the users or groups added to this realm. ACFS administrators can restrict the time window when the users or groups of this realm can access the realm-protected files or directories with time-based rules. Additionally, ACFS administrators can also have application-based rules if they can identify the process name for the antivirus installation that scans the files.

Once a file system has been prepared for security, the security administrator can start defining security policies for the data in the file system by considering the following:

- What data needs to be protected? Files to be protected must to be added to one or more realms.

- Who has access to data? Users intended to be allowed access to files in the realm must be added to the realm.

- What actions are the users allowed or not allowed to take on data? Command rules (in conjunction with rule sets) define these actions.

- Under what conditions can the data be accessed? Rules and rule sets define these criteria.

Access to files in a realm of an ACFS file system must be authorized by both the realm and the underlying OS permissions (that is, the standard "owner, group, other" permissions on typical Unix/Linux platforms or Access Control Lists (ACLs) on Windows). Accessing a file that has security enabled involves tiered validation. First, access is checked against all realms that the file is a part of. If even a single realm denies access, overall operation is not allowed. If realm authorization allows access, then OS permissions are checked. Also, if authorized by the latter, the overall operation is allowed.

ACFS Security and Encryption Logging

Auditing is a key aspect of any security configuration, and ACFS Security is no exception. Auditing and diagnostic data are logged for ACFS Security and Encryption. These log files include information such as the execution of acfsutil commands, use of security or system administrator privileges, run-time realm-check authorization failures, setting of encryption parameters, rekey operations, and so on. Logs are written to the following log files:

- **$GRID_HOME/.Security/realm/logs/sec-host_name.log**   This file is created during the acfsutil sec prepare command and is itself protected by ACFS Security using the SYSTEM_Logs realm.

- **$GRID_HOME/log/host_name/acfssec/acfssec.log**   This file contains messages for commands that are not associated with a specific file system, such as acfsutil sec init. The directory is created during installation and is owned by the root user.

When an active log file grows to a predefined maximum size (10MB), the file is automatically moved to *log_file_name*.bak, the administrator is notified, and logging continues to the regular log file name. When the administrator is notified, he must archive and remove the *log_file_name*.bak file. If an active log file grows to the maximum size and the *log_file_name*.bak file exists, logging stops until the backup file is removed. After the backup log file is removed, logging restarts automatically.

Databases and Encryption

Although mechanisms natively built into the Oracle Database and those provided by Oracle Database Vault can control access to data stored in the database, this data is not protected from direct access via physical storage. A number of third-party tools can be used to provide read and write access to data stored on secondary storage, thus circumventing protection provided by the database and the OS. Furthermore, these database and OS protections mechanisms do not protect against data loss or theft. For example, storage can be re-attached on a completely different system from the one it was intended for. Features in Oracle Database's Advanced Security Option (ASO) provide protection against such scenarios. Transparent Data Encryption (TDE) provides the capability for encrypting data at the column and tablespace levels, service data protection, and compliance needs of customers.

ACFS and File Encryption

The same threats as those mentioned previously for database data exist for file system data too. ACFS Encryption protects from these threats by encrypting data stored on a secondary device, or *data at rest*. It should be noted that ACFS Encryption protects *user data and not file system metadata*. Keeping data at rest encrypted renders the data useless without encryption keys in case of theft of the physical storage on which the data resides.

Encryption can be applied to individual files, directories, or an entire ACFS file system. Furthermore, both encrypted and nonencrypted files can exist in the same ACFS file system. Applications need no modification to continue to work seamlessly with encrypted files. Data is automatically encrypted when it is written to disk and automatically decrypted when accessed by the application. It should be noted that encryption is used for protecting stored data. It does not provide access control or protection against malicious access, both of which fall under the purview of ACFS Security and OS-level access control mechanisms. Thus, a user authorized to read a file would always get plain-text data.

Figure 11-3 shows the application and internal view of ACFS Encryption.

ACFS Encryption imposes no penalty on cached reads and writes because the data in the OS page cache is in plain text. Data is encrypted when it is flushed to disk and decrypted when read from disk into the OS page cache for the first time.

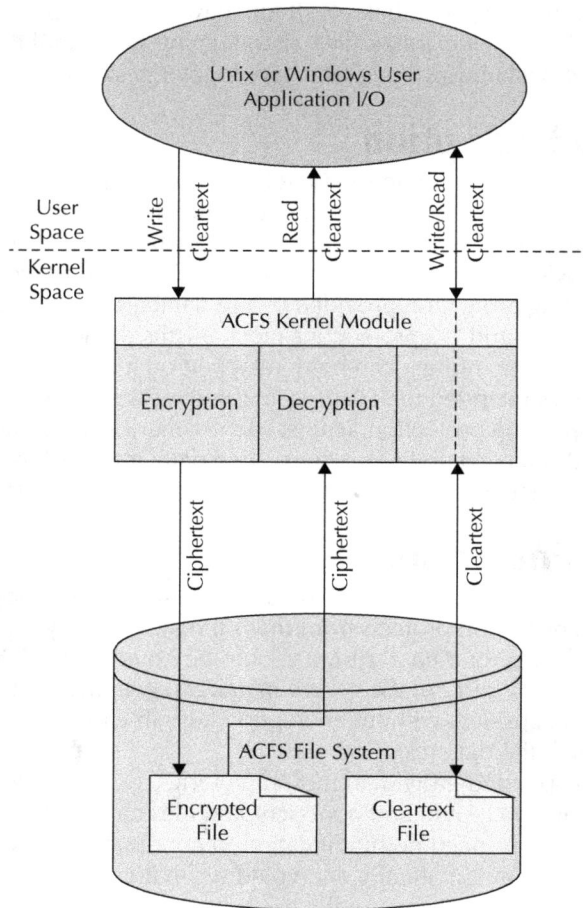

FIGURE 11-3. *ACFS Encryption hierarchy*

ACFS Encryption Key Management

ACFS Encryption requires minimal key management tasks to be performed by the administrator. Keys are transparently created and securely stored with minimal user intervention. ACFS Encryption uses two-level keys to minimize the amount of data that is encrypted with a single key. A file encryption key (FEK) is a per-file unique key. A file's data is encrypted using the FEK. A volume encryption key (VEK), a per-file

Volume encryption keys (VEKs) are stored on separate storage from that used for file systems.

Oracle Wallet (Secret Store)

File System 1

VEK1

File System 2

VEK2

Per-file-system volume encryption keys (VEKs) is used to encrypt FEKs for that file system. VEKs are stored in Oracle Wallet and are accessible from all cluster nodes.

File System 1

Encrypted File 1

FEK1

Encrypted File 2

FEK2

File System 2

Encrypted File 1

FEK1

Encrypted File 1

FEK2

File encryption keys (FEKs) are stored in encrypted format on disk. The key used for encrypting FEKs is the file system's VEK.

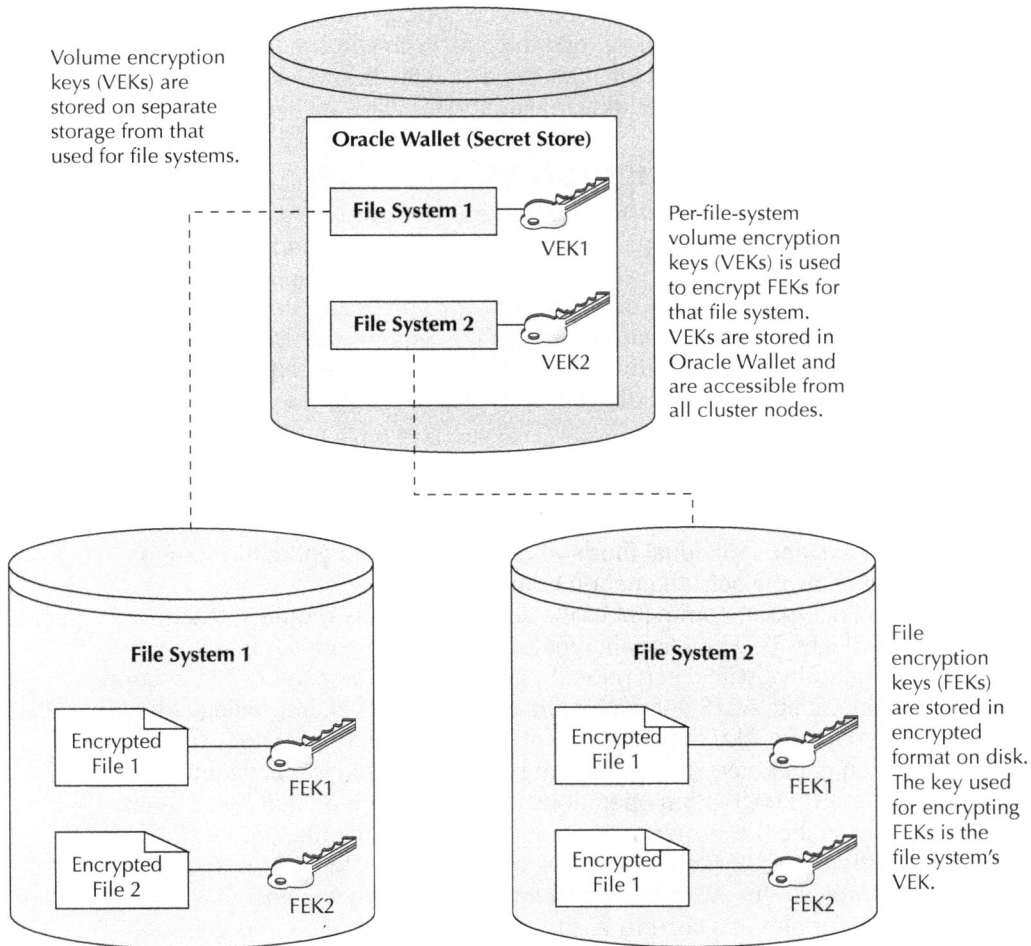

FIGURE 11-4.   *A file encryption key (FEK) and volume encryption key (VEK) relationship*

system key, serves as a *wrapping key,* and each FEK is stored on disk encrypted using the VEK. Figure 11-4 shows the relationship between the two types of keys.

The encryption keys are never stored on disk or in memory in plain text. The keys are either obfuscated or encrypted using a user-supplied password. ACFS Encryption supports the Advanced Encryption Standard (AES), which is a symmetric cipher algorithm, defined in Federal Information Processing (FIPS) Standard 197.

AES provides three approved key lengths: 256, 192, and 128 bits. The key length can be specified when you are configuring ACFS Encryption for a file system.

ACFS Encryption supports the "rekey" operation for both VEKs and FEKs. The rekey operation generates a new key and reencrypts the data with this new key. For FEKs, the data to encrypt is the user data residing in files and for VEKs the data is the FEKs.

ACFS Encryption Configuration and Use

Before using ACFS Encryption, the system administrator needs to create storage for encryption keys using the acfsutil encr init command. This command needs to be run once per cluster, and it must be run before any other encryption commands. ACFS Encryption provides an option to create password-protected storage for encryption keys. Creating password-protected storage requires that the password be supplied whenever an operation is going to read or modify the encryption key store. The three operations that read or modify the encryption key store are acfsutil encr set, acfsutil encr rekey –v, and mount.

Once ACFS Encryption has been initialized, a file system can be configured to use it via the acfsutil encr set command. This command sets or changes encryption parameters, algorithm, and key length for a file system. Once this command has been run on a file system, individual files and directories or the entire file system can be encrypted using the acfsutil encr on command.

Certain ACFS Encryption command usage and functionality requires system administrator privileges. This functionality includes the commands for initiating, setting, and reconfiguring ACFS Encryption. System administrators and ACFS security administrators can initiate ACFS encryption operations; however, unprivileged users can initiate encryption for files they own. An ACFS security administrator can manage encryption parameters on a per-realm basis. After a file is placed under realm security, file-level encryption operations are not allowed on that file. Even if ACFS Security allows the file owner or the root user to open the file, file-level encryption operations are blocked. Encryption of realm-protected files is managed exclusively or entirely by the ACFS security administrator, who can enable and disable encryption for files at a security realm level. After a directory has been added to a security realm, all files created in the directory inherit the realm-level encryption parameters. When a file is removed from its last security realm, the file is encrypted or decrypted to match the file system-level encryption status. The file is not re-encrypted to match file system-level parameters if it was already encrypted with security realm parameters.

A system administrator cannot rekey realm-secured files at the file system or file level. To ensure all realm-secured files are encrypted with the most recent VEK, you must first remove encryption from all realms, and then re-enable encryption. This action re-encrypts all files with the most recent VEK.

Encryption information for Oracle ACFS file systems is displayed in the (G) V$ASM_ACFS_ENCRYPTION_INFO view or using acfsutil sec info or acfsutil encr info command sets.

ACFS Snapshots, Security, and Encryption

Users cannot modify security or encryption metadata in read-only snapshots. That is, security policies cannot be modified or created and files cannot be encrypted, decrypted, or rekeyed in a read-only snapshot. Files in a snapshot, however, preserve their security and encryption statuses, as they existed, at the time of snapshot creation. Changing the encryption or security status of a file in the live file system does not change its status in the snapshot, whether read-only or read-write. Therefore, if a file was not secured by a realm in the snapshot, it cannot be realm-secured by adding the corresponding file in the active file system to a security realm. If a file was not encrypted in the snapshot, that file cannot be encrypted by encrypting the corresponding file in the active file system. Therefore, unprotected files in snapshots present another potential source of data for malicious users. When applying security and encryption policies, an administrator should be aware of these potential backdoors to unprotected data. To that end, when certain encryption operations such as enabling of file system–level encryption and rekey are attempted, a warning is printed to let the administrator know that these will not affect the files in the snapshot(s). To ensure no unprotected copies of data are available for misuse, administrators should confirm that no snapshots exist when security and encryption policies are applied.

Because read-write snapshots allow changes to files in the snapshot, the encryption status of files can also be changed. They can be encrypted, decrypted, or rekeyed by specifying as the target a path in a read-write snapshot. An encryption, decryption, or rekey operation specified at the file system level, however, does not process files and directories of snapshots, read-only or read-write, in the .ACFS/snaps directory. For the purpose of these operations, the file system boundary includes only the live file system and not its snapshots. To do these operations on read-write snapshot files, the administrator can specify as the target a path in the read-write snapshot.

In the 11.2.0.3 release, changing or creating security policies in a read-write snapshot is not yet supported. Furthermore, files in a read-write snapshot cannot be added to or removed from realms. A new file created in a realm-secured directory in a read-write snapshot, however, inherits the realm security attributes of the parent directory. If the realm protecting the new file has encryption turned on, the file is encrypted with the encryption parameters set in the realm. If the realm protecting the new file has encryption turned off, the file is decrypted. Files and directories in a read-write snapshot cannot be added to or removed from any security realm.

ACFS Security and Encryption Implementation

This section describes the steps to implement ACFS Security and Encryption. These steps can be performed by using the command line or the ASMCA utility. A mixture of both will be shown for simplicity.

Here's the use-case scenario: Company ABC provides escrow services to buyers and sellers. As part of the value-add services, ABC provides access to an information library. This library, which is managed and maintained by ABC, stores historical content such as preliminary reports, pro forma, and escrow final reports. ABC loads all these reports from the front-end servers to the ACFS file system that runs on a RAC cluster, with one directory per escrow. ABC now wants to encrypt and secure all the escrow content.

In this example, it is assumed that the RAC cluster is built, the ACFS file system is created with the appropriate directories, and the content is loaded. Here are the steps to follow:

1. Create or identity the OS user who will be the ACFS security administrator for the cluster. In our use case, we will create a user named orasec in the orasec group.

2. Launch ASMCA to initialize ACFS Security and Encryption (see Figure 11-5).

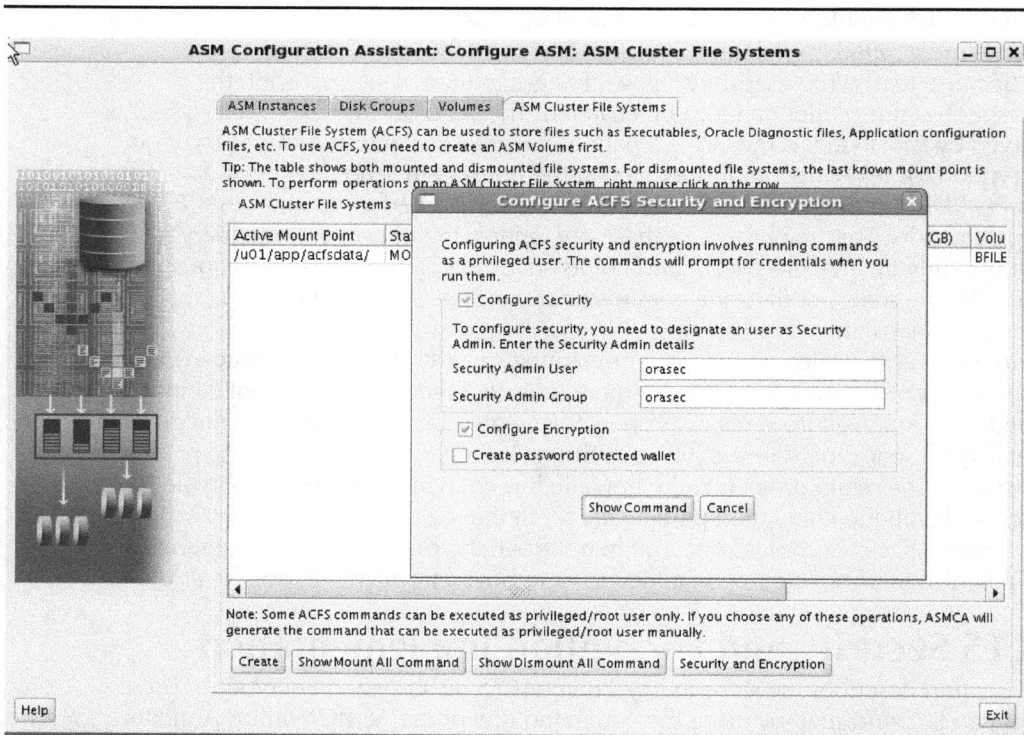

FIGURE 11-5. *Configure ACFS cluster file system security using ASMCA*

Because enabling ACFS Security can only be done by a privileged user, the
Show Command button will display the command to be issued, by root.
The user will be prompted to enter a new password for the ACFS security
administrator, which must be eight characters long. Note that this password is
not the login password for the OS user but rather the password for the ACFS
security administrator. Here's the command to configure ACFS Security:

```
[root@racpk11gr2 ~]# /sbin/acfsutil sec init -u orasec -g orasec
Password for new ACFS Security administrator:
Re-enter password for new ACFS Security administrator:
acfsutil sec init: Security wallet created.
```

And here's the command to configure ACFS Encryption:

```
[root@racpk11gr2 ~]# /sbin/acfsutil encr init
Creating SSO key store for encryption...
acfsutil encr init: Encryption key store created.
```

3. Verify that orasec has the appropriate authorization to display ACFS Security
   information. Execute the acfsutil sec info commands using only the chosen
   user ID:

```
[oracle@racpk11gr2 ~]$ /sbin/acfsutil sec info -m /u01/app/acfsdata
acfsutil sec info: ACFS-10606: User 'oracle' is not a
security administrator.
[orasec@racpk11gr2 ~]$ /sbin/acfsutil sec admin info
ACFS Security administrator password:
The following users have security administrative privileges:
        orasec
```

4. Configure the ASM disk group compatibility attributes for ADVM and ASM.
   ASM has several disk group attributes, but in the context of ACFS Security
   and Encryption the relevant ones are the following:

```
ASMCMD [+] > lsattr -l -G DATA
Name                       Value
access_control.enabled     FALSE
access_control.umask       066
au_size                    1048576
cell.smart_scan_capable    FALSE
compatible.advm            11.2.0.0.0
compatible.asm             11.2.0.0.0
compatible.rdbms           10.1.0.0.0
disk_repair_time           3.6h
sector_size                512
Set the diskgroup attributes to 11.2.0.3 for both compatible.advm
and compatible.asm
ASMCMD [+] > setattr -G DATA compatible.asm 11.2.0.3
ASMCMD [+] > setattr -G DATA compatible.advm 11.2.0.3
```

5. Create or identify the ACFS file system that will be secured. Once this is identified, prepare the file system for ACFS Security. In our case, we want to enable ACFS Security on the /u01/app/acfsdata/bfile_data file system:

```
[orasec@racpk11gr2 ~]$ /sbin/acfsutil sec prepare
-m /u01/app/acfsdata/bfile_data
ACFS Security administrator password:
System realm 'SYSTEM_SecurityMetadata' created.
System realm 'SYSTEM_Logs' created.
System realm 'SYSTEM_BackupOperators' created.
```

6. Verify that security is enabled:

```
[orasec@racpk11gr2 ~]$ /sbin/acfsutil sec info
-m /u01/app/acfsdata
ACFS Security administrator password:
File system: /u01/app/acfsdata
    Security status: ENABLED
```

7. As stated earlier, ACFS Security can be used in conjunction with ACFS Encryption. For these cases, encryption must be initialized and set before encryption is enabled on a security realm. Keep in mind that in our example we initialized ACFS Security and Encryption in one command (see step 2). However, if this was not done in step 2, the following needs to executed as root:

```
#/sbin/acfsutil encr init
Creating SSO key store for encryption...
acfsutil encr init: Encryption key store created.
```

On the other hand, if it was performed in step 2, then run the following as root:

```
#/sbin/acfsutil encr set -m /u01/app/acfsdata
acfsutil encr set: ACFS-10412: Encryption parameters were not
provided, using default algorithm (AES) and key length (192)
FS-level encryption parameters have been set to:
Algorithm (AES 192-bit), Key length (24 bytes)
```

Note that we did not specify an AES encryption algorithm or key length for which ACFS picked up the defaults. To set a different key length (AES is the only supported algorithm), use the –k option. For example, to set AES encryption of 256 bits, execute the following:

```
#/sbin/acfsutil encr set -m /u01/app/acfsdata -a AES -k 256
FS-level encryption parameters have been set to:
Algorithm (AES 256-bit), Key length (32 bytes)
```

The acfsutil encr set command transparently generates a volume encryption key that is kept in the key store that was previously configured with the acfsutil encr init command.

Here's the command to verify that encryption has been set:

```
# acfsutil encr info -m /u01/app/acfsdata
File system: /u01/app/acfsdata
        Encryption status: OFF
        Algorithm: AES 256-bits
        Key length: 32 bytes
```

Note that "Encryption status" here is set to OFF. This is because the acfsutil encr set command does not encryption any data on the file system, but only creates a volume encryption key (VEK) and sets the encryption parameters for the file system.

8. Enable encryption at the file system level with the following command:

```
# /sbin/acfsutil encr on -m /u01/app/acfsdata
Encryption has been enabled on (/u01/app/acfsdata)
Encrypting (/u01/app/acfsdata/.Security)...
done.
Encrypting (/u01/app/acfsdata/.Security/encryption)...
done.
Encrypting (/u01/app/acfsdata/.Security/encryption/logs)...
done.
Encrypting (/u01/app/acfsdata/.Security/encryption/logs/
encr-racpk11gr2.log)...
done.
```

9. Create the ACFS Security rule sets and then the rules:

```
$ /sbin/acfsutil sec ruleset create EscrowSecurityRuleset
-m /u01/app/acfsdata/bfile_data -o ANY_TRUE
```

This example specifies a rule type and a rule value. The rule type can be application, hostname, time, or username. The rule value depends on the type of rule. A rule can be added to a rule set, and that rule set can be added to a realm. However, you can create singleton rules without having the hierarchy of the rule set and realms.

10. Add new rules to the rule set:

```
$ /sbin/acfsutil sec rule create NishaC21EscrowTime -m
/u01/app/acfsdata/bfile_data -t time 08:00:00,16:00:00 -o ALLOW
$ /sbin/acfsutil sec rule create NishaC21EscrowUser -m
/u01/app/acfsdata/bfile_data -t username nisha -o ALLOW
```

```
$ /sbin/acfsutil sec ruleset edit EscrowSecurityRuleset -m
/u01/app/acfsdata/bfile_data -a NishaC21EscrowTime,
NishaC21EscrowUser
```

All these definitions could be listed in a file executed in batch using the acfsutil sec batch command.

Summary

ACFS Data Services such as Replication, Tagging, Snapshots, Security, and Encryption complement Oracle's Database Availability and Security technologies, such as Data Guard, Database Vault, and Transparent Data Encryption. In addition, ACFS Data Services provides rich file support for unstructured data.

CHAPTER
12

ASM Optimizations in Oracle Engineered Solutions

When implementing a private cloud solution, a common question is, "Should I build or buy?" In the "build" option, the IT personnel would create a cloud pool by purchasing all the essential components, such as servers, HBAs, storage arrays, and fabric switches. Additionally, all software components—RAC, ASM, Grid Infrastructure, and Database—would have to be installed and validated. Although this approach allows IT the flexibility to pick and choose the appropriate components, it does increase mean time to deploy as well as the chances of misconfiguration.

With the "buy" approach, users can deploy Engineered Solutions or integrated solutions, which are pretested, prevalidated, and preconfigured. Both provide fast deployment and simplified management. Examples of integrated solutions include HP CloudSystem and vCloud by VCE. Engineered Solutions, such as Oracle's Exadata, are not just integrated solutions, but the application software (the Oracle database, in this case) and the hardware are tightly and intelligently woven together.

Oracle Exadata Database Machine, Oracle Database Appliance, and Oracle SPARC SuperCluster are solutions designed to be optimal platforms for Oracle Database and therefore ideal platforms for Private Database Cloud computing. This chapter focuses on the ASM optimizations developed specifically for Oracle Exadata and Oracle Database Appliance. This chapter is not meant to be an exhaustive look at Exadata or ODA; many papers are available on Oracle Technology Network (OTN) that cover this topic.

Overview of Exadata

Oracle Exadata Database Machine includes all the hardware and software required for private cloud deployments. Exadata combines servers, storage, and networks into one engineered package, eliminating the difficult integration problems typically faced when building your own private cloud. Rather than going through the entire rationalization and standardization process, IT departments can simply implement Oracle Exadata Database Machine for database consolidation onto a private cloud.

Exadata Components

This section covers the important components of the Exadata system.

Compute Servers

Compute servers are the database servers that run the Grid Infrastructure stack (Clusterware and ASM) along with the Oracle Real Application Clusters stack. The compute servers behave like standard database servers, except that in Exadata they are linked with the libcell library, which allows the databases to communicate with the cellserv interface in the Exadata Storage Server.

Exadata Storage Server

In the Exadata X2 configuration, the Exadata Storage cells (Exadata Cells) are servers preconfigured with 2×6-core Intel Xeon L5640 processors, 24GB memory, 384GB of Exadata Smart Flash Cache, 12 disks connected to a storage controller with 512MB battery-backed cache, and dual-port InfiniBand connectivity. Oracle Enterprise Linux operating system (OS) is the base OS for Exadata Cells as well as for the compute nodes. All Exadata software comes preinstalled when delivered. The 12 disks can be either High Performance (HP) Serial Attached SCSI (SAS) disks that are 600GB 15,000 rpm or High Capacity (HC) SAS disks that are 3TB 7,200 rpm.

Each of the 12 disks represents a Cell Disk residing within an Exadata Storage cell. The Cell Disk is created automatically by the Exadata software when the physical disk is discovered. Cell Disks are logically partitioned into one or more Grid Disks. Grid Disks are the logical disk devices assigned to ASM as ASM disks. Figure 12-1 illustrates the relationship of Cell Disks to Grid Disks in a more comprehensive Exadata Storage grid.

Once the Cell Disks and Grid Disks are configured, ASM disk groups are defined across the Exadata configuration. When the data is loaded into the database, ASM will evenly distribute the data and I/O within disk groups. ASM mirroring is enabled for these disk groups to protect against disk failures.

Cellsrv (Cell Services), a primary component of the Exadata software, provides the majority of Exadata storage services and communicates with database instances on the

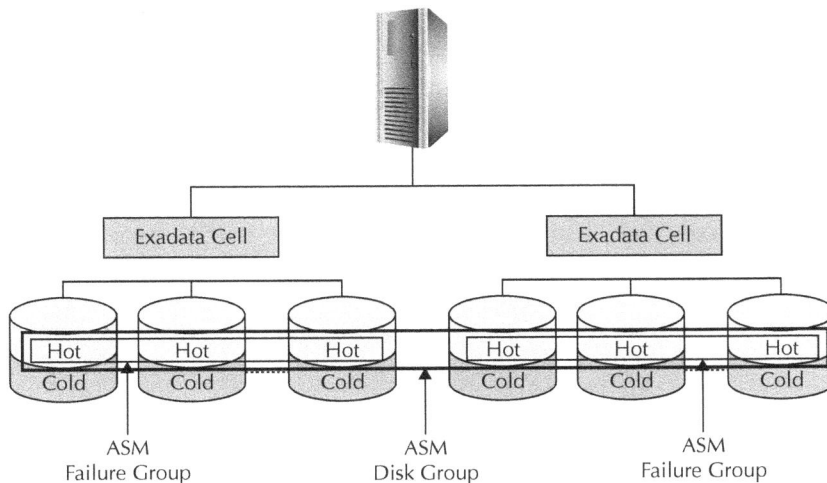

FIGURE 12-1. *Grid layout*

database server using the iDB protocol. Cellsrv provides the advanced SQL offload capabilities, serves Oracle blocks when SQL offload processing is not possible, and implements the DBRM I/O resource management functionality to meter out I/O bandwidth to the various databases and consumer groups issuing I/O. Cellsrv maintains a file called griddisk.owners.dat, which has details such as the following:

- ASM disk name
- ASM disk group name
- ASM failgroup name
- Cluster identifier

When IORM is used, the IORM (I/O Resource Manager) manages the Exadata cell I/O resources on a per-cell basis. Whenever the I/O requests reach the cell's disks threshold, IORM schedules I/O requests according to the configured resource plan. When the cell is operating below capacity, IORM does not queue I/O requests. IORM schedules I/Os by immediately queuing requests and issuing other I/O requests. IORM selects these I/Os to issue based on the resource plan's allocations; databases and consumer groups with higher allocations are scheduled more frequently than those with lower allocations.

When IORM is enabled, it automatically manages background I/Os. Critical background I/Os such as log file syncs and control file reads and writes are prioritized. Databases with higher resource allocations are able to issue disk I/Os more rapidly. Resource allocation for workloads within a database is specified through the database resource plan. If no database resource plan is enabled, all user I/O requests from the database are treated equally. Background I/Os, however, are still prioritized automatically.

Two other components of Oracle software running in the cell are the Management Server (MS) and Restart Server (RS). The MS is the primary interface to administer, manage, and query the status of the Exadata cell. MS manageability, which is performed using the Exadata cell command-line interface (CLI) or EM Exadata plug-in, provides standalone Exadata cell management and configuration. For example, from the cell, CLI commands are issued to configure storage, query I/O statistics, and restart the cell. The distributed CLI can also be used to issue commands to multiple cells, which eases management across cells. Restart Server (RS) ensures ongoing functioning of the Exadata software and services. RS also ensures storage services are started and running, or services are restarted when required.

InfiniBand infrastructure

The Database Machine includes an InfiniBand interconnect between the compute nodes and Exadata Storage Server. The InfiniBand network was chosen to ensure sufficient network is in place to support the low-latency and high-bandwidth requirements. Each database server and Exadata cell has dual-port Quad Data Rate (QDR) InfiniBand connectivity for high availability. The same InfiniBand network also provides a high-performance cluster interconnect for the Oracle Database Real Application Clusters (RAC) nodes.

iDB Protocol

The database servers and Exadata Storage Server software communicate using the Intelligent Database protocol (iDB), which is implemented in the database kernel. iDB runs over InfiniBand and leverages ZDP (Zero-loss Zero-copy Datagram Protocol), a zero-copy implementation of the industry-standard Reliable Datagram Sockets (RDSv3) protocol. ZDP is used to minimize the number of data copies required to service I/O operations. The iDB protocol implements a function shipping architecture in addition to the traditional data block shipping provided by the database; for example, iDB is used to ship SQL operations down to the Exadata cells for execution and to return query result sets to the database kernel. This allows Exadata cells to return only the rows and columns that satisfy the SQL query, instead of returning the entire database blocks as in typical storage arrays. Exadata Storage Server operates like a traditional storage array when offload processing is not possible. But when feasible, the intelligence in the database kernel enables table scans to be passed down to execute on the Exadata Storage Server so only requested data is returned to the database server.

11gR2 Database Optimizations for Exadata

Oracle Database 11g Release 2 has been significantly enhanced to take advantage of Exadata storage. One of the unique things the Exadata storage does compared to traditional storage is return only the rows and columns that satisfy the database query rather than the entire table being queried. Exadata pushes SQL processing as close to the data (or disks) as possible and gets all the disks operating in parallel. This reduces CPU consumption on the database server, consumes much less bandwidth moving data between database servers and storage servers, and returns a query result set rather than entire tables. Eliminating data transfers and database server workload can greatly benefit data warehousing queries that traditionally become bandwidth and CPU constrained. Eliminating data transfers can also have a significant benefit on online transaction processing (OLTP) systems that often include large batch and report processing operations.

Exadata Storage Servers also run more complex operations in storage:

- Join filtering
- Incremental backup filtering

- I/O prioritization

- Storage indexing

- Database-level security

- Offloaded scans on encrypted data

- Data mining model scoring

- Smart file creation

The application is transparent to the database using Exadata. In fact, the exact same Oracle Database 11*g* Release 2 that runs on traditional systems runs on the Database Machine. Existing SQL statements, whether ad hoc or in packaged or custom applications, are unaffected and do not require any modification when Exadata storage is used. The offload processing and bandwidth advantages of the solution are delivered without any modification to the application.

ASM Optimizations for Exadata

ASM provides the same functionality in standard RAC clusters as in Exadata configurations. In Exadata, ASM redundancy (ASM mirroring) is used, where each Exadata cell is defined as a failure group. ASM automatically stripes the database data across Exadata cells and disks to ensure a balanced I/O load and optimum performance. The ASM mirroring in Exadata can be either normal or high redundancy, but Maximum Availability Architecture (MAA) best practices recommend high redundancy for higher resiliency.

ASM in Exadata automatically discovers grid disks presented by the Exadata Storage Server. The pathname for discovered Grid Disks has the format of *o/cell-ip-address/griddisk-name*.

The following is a sample listing of an Exadata Grid Disk discovered by ASM:

```
SQL> select name, path, state, mount_status, header_status,
mode_status from v$asm_disk_stat
  where group_number=(select group_number from v$asm_diskgroup where
name='RECO_EXAD')
  order by path


NAME                           PATH
STATE     MOUNT_S HEADER_STATU MODE_ST
------------------------------ --------------------------------------------
-- -------- ------- ------------ -------
RECO_EXAD_CD_00_EXADCEL01      o/192.168.10.3/RECO_EXAD_CD_00_exadcel01
NORMAL    CACHED  MEMBER       ONLINE
RECO_EXAD_CD_01_EXADCEL01      o/192.168.10.3/RECO_EXAD_CD_01_exadcel01
NORMAL    CACHED  MEMBER       ONLINE
```

```
RECO_EXAD_CD_02_EXADCEL01      o/192.168.10.3/RECO_EXAD_CD_02_exadcel01
NORMAL    CACHED    MEMBER      ONLINE
RECO_EXAD_CD_03_EXADCEL01      o/192.168.10.3/RECO_EXAD_CD_03_exadcel01
NORMAL    CACHED    MEMBER      ONLINE
RECO_EXAD_CD_04_EXADCEL01      o/192.168.10.3/RECO_EXAD_CD_04_exadcel01
NORMAL    CACHED    MEMBER      ONLINE
RECO_EXAD_CD_05_EXADCEL01      o/192.168.10.3/RECO_EXAD_CD_05_exadcel01
NORMAL    CACHED    MEMBER      ONLINE
RECO_EXAD_CD_06_EXADCEL01      o/192.168.10.3/RECO_EXAD_CD_06_exadcel01
NORMAL    CACHED    MEMBER      ONLINE
RECO_EXAD_CD_07_EXADCEL01      o/192.168.10.3/RECO_EXAD_CD_07_exadcel01
NORMAL    CACHED    MEMBER      ONLINE
RECO_EXAD_CD_08_EXADCEL01      o/192.168.10.3/RECO_EXAD_CD_08_exadcel01
NORMAL    CACHED    MEMBER      ONLINE
RECO_EXAD_CD_09_EXADCEL01      o/192.168.10.3/RECO_EXAD_CD_09_exadcel01
NORMAL    CACHED    MEMBER      ONLINE
RECO_EXAD_CD_10_EXADCEL01      o/192.168.10.3/RECO_EXAD_CD_10_exadcel01
NORMAL    CACHED    MEMBER      ONLINE
RECO_EXAD_CD_11_EXADCEL01      o/192.168.10.3/RECO_EXAD_CD_11_exadcel01
NORMAL    CACHED    MEMBER      ONLINE
RECO_EXAD_CD_00_EXADCEL02      o/192.168.10.4/RECO_EXAD_CD_00_exadcel02
NORMAL    CACHED    MEMBER      ONLINE
RECO_EXAD_CD_01_EXADCEL02      o/192.168.10.4/RECO_EXAD_CD_01_exadcel02
NORMAL    CACHED    MEMBER      ONLINE
```

The *o* in the Grid Disk pathname indicates that it's presented via libcell. Keep in mind that these disks are not standard block devices; therefore, they cannot be listed or manipulated with typical Linux commands such as fdisk and multipath.

The IP address in the pathname is the address of the cell on the InfiniBand storage network. The Grid Disk name is defined when the Grid Disk was provisioned in Exadata Storage. Alternatively, the name may be system generated, by concatenating an administrator-specified prefix to the name of the Cell Disk on which the Grid Disk resides. Note that all Grid Disks from the same cell use the same IP address in their pathname.

Disk Management Automation in Exadata

In Exadata, many of the manual ASM operations have been internally automated and several disk-partnering capabilities have been enhanced. ASM dynamic add and drop capability enables non-intrusive cell and disk allocation, deallocation, and reallocation.

The XDMG is a new background process in the ASM instance that monitors the cell storage for any state change. XDMG also handles requests from the cells to online, offline, or drop/add a disk based on an user event or a failure. For example, if a cell becomes inaccessible from a transient failure, or if a Grid Disk or Cell Disk in the cell is inactivated, then XDMG will automatically initiate an OFFLINE operation in the ASM instance.

The XDMG process works with the XDWK process, which also runs within the ASM instance. The XDWK process executes the ONLINE or DROP/ADD operation as requested by XDMG. The new processes in the ASM instance automatically handles storage reconfiguration after disk replacement, after cell reboots, or after cellsrv crashes.

Exadata Storage Server has the capability to proactively drop a disk if needed, and is effective for both true disk failures and predictive failures. When a disk fails, all I/Os to that disk will fail. The proactive disk drop feature will then automatically interrupt the existing drop operation (triggered by the prior disk predictive failure) and turn it into a disk drop force. This is to ensure that redundancy gets restored immediately without having to wait for the disk repair timer to kick in.

The following output displays the action taken by the XDWK process to drop a disk:

```
Tue May 15 15:20:35 2012
  XDWK started with pid=33, OS id=19744
  SQL> /* Exadata Auto Mgmt: Proactive DROP ASM Disk */
  alter diskgroup DATA drop
    disk DATA_CD_08_ RECO_EXAD_CD_02_EXADCEL01
```

To list the condition of Exadata disks, the following cellcli commands can be run on the Exadata Storage Server:

```
For Failed Disks:

CellCLI> LIST PHYSICALDISK WHERE diskType=HardDisk AND status=critical DETAIL

For Failing Disks (potential to fail)

    CellCLI> LIST PHYSICALDISK WHERE diskType=HardDisk AND status= \
"predictive failure" DETAIL

AND

    CellCLI> LIST PHYSICALDISK WHERE diskType=HardDisk AND status= \
"poor performance" DETAIL
```

In addition to the new ASM processes just mentioned, there is one master diskmon process and one slave diskmon process (dskm) for every Oracle database and ASM instance. The diskmon is responsible for the following:

- Handling of storage cell failures and I/O fencing

- Monitoring of Exadata Server state on all storage cells in the cluster (heartbeat)

- Broadcasting intra-database IORM (I/O Resource Manager) plans from databases to storage cells

- Monitoring of the control messages from the database and ASM instances to storage cells

- Communicating with other diskmons in the cluster

The following output shows the diskmon and the dskm processes from the database and ASM instances:

```
# ps -ef | egrep "diskmon|dskm" | grep -v grep
oracle    3205    1  0 Mar16 ?      00:01:18 ora_dskm_yoda2
oracle    10755   1  0 Mar16 ?      00:32:19 /u01/app/11.2.0.3/grid/
bin/diskmon.bin -d -f
oracle    17292   1  0 Mar16 ?      00:01:17 asm_dskm_+ASM2
oracle    24388   1  0 Mar28 ?      00:00:21 ora_dskm_obiwan2
oracle    27962   1  0 Mar27 ?      00:00:24 ora_dskm_yada2
```

Exadata ASM Specific Attributes

The CONTENT.TYPE attribute identifies the disk group type, which can be DATA, RECOVERY, or SYSTEM. The type value determines the *distance* to the nearest partner disk/failgroup. The default value is DATA, which specifies a distance of 1. The value of RECOVERY specifies a distance of 3, and the value of SYSTEM specifies a distance of 5. The primary objective of this attribute is to ensure that failure at a given Exadata Storage Server does take out all the disk groups configured on that RACK. By having different partners based on the content type, a failure of a disk/cell does not affect the same set of disk partners in all the disk group.

NOTE
For CONTENT.TYPE to be effective one needs to have a full RACK of the DB machine.

The CONTENT.TYPE attribute can be specified when you're creating or altering a disk group. If this attribute is set or changed using ALTER DISKGROUP, then the new configuration does not take effect until a disk group rebalance is explicitly run.

The CONTENT.TYPE attribute is only valid for disk groups that are set to NORMAL or HIGH redundancy. The COMPATIBLE.ASM attribute must be set to 11.2.0.3 or higher to enable the CONTENT.TYPE attribute for the disk group.

ODA Overview

The Oracle Database Appliance (ODA) is a fully integrated system of software, servers, storage, and networking in a single chassis. Like Exadata, Oracle Database Appliance is not just preconfigured; it is prebuilt, preconfigured, pretested, and pretuned. This configuration is an ideal choice for a pay-as-you-grow Private Database Cloud. Customers can continually consolidate and enable CPU capacity as needed.

An appliance like ODA reduces the time in procuring individual components and completely minimizes the effort required to set up an optimal configuration. The OS, network components, SAN, storage redundancy, multipathing, and more, all become configured as part the ODA system enablement.

ODA Components

Oracle Database Appliance is made up of building blocks similar to Exadata. These can be broken down into two buckets: hardware and software. Each component is built and tested together to provide maximum availability and performance.

Software Stack

ODA comes with preinstalled Oracle Unbreakable Linux and Oracle Appliance Manager (OAK) software. The OAK software provides one-button automation for the entire database stack, which simplifies and automates the manual tasks typically associated with installing, patching, managing, and supporting Oracle database environments.

Hardware

The Oracle Database Appliance is a four-rack unit (RU) server appliance that consists of two server nodes and twenty-four 3.5 SAS/SSD disk slots.

Each Oracle Database Appliance system contains two redundant 2U form factor server nodes (system controllers SC0 and SC1).

Each server node plugs into the Oracle Database Appliance chassis and operates independently of the other. A failure on one server node does not impact the other node. The surviving node uses cluster failover event management (via Oracle Clusterware) to prevent complete service interruption. To support a redundant cluster, each server node module contains a dual-port Ethernet controller internally connected between the two server node modules through the disk midplane. This internal connection eliminates the need for external cables, thus making ODA a self-contained database appliance.

Each server contains two CPU sockets for the Intel Xeon Processer X5675 CPUs, providing up to 12 enabled-on-demand processor cores and 96GB of memory. On each ODA node are two dual-ported LSI SAS controllers. They are each connected to an SAS expander that is located on the system board. Each of these SAS expanders connects to 12 of the hard disks on the front of the ODA. Figure 12-2 shows the detailed layout of disk to expander relationship. The disks are dual-ported SAS, so that each disk is connected to an expander on each of the system controllers (SCs). The Oracle Database Appliance contains twenty 600GB SAS hard disk drives that are shared between the two nodes.

ASM and Storage   Notice that expander-to-disk connectivity is arranged such that Expander-0 from both nodes connects to disks in columns 1 and 2, whereas Expander-1 from both nodes connects to disks in columns 3 and 4.

ASM high redundancy is used to provide triple-mirroring across these devices for highly available shared storage. This appliance also contains four 73GB SAS solid state drives for redo logs, triple mirrored to protect the Oracle database in case of instance failure. Each disk is partitioned into two slices: p1 and p2. The Oracle Linux Device Mapper utility is used to provide multipathing for all disks in the appliance.

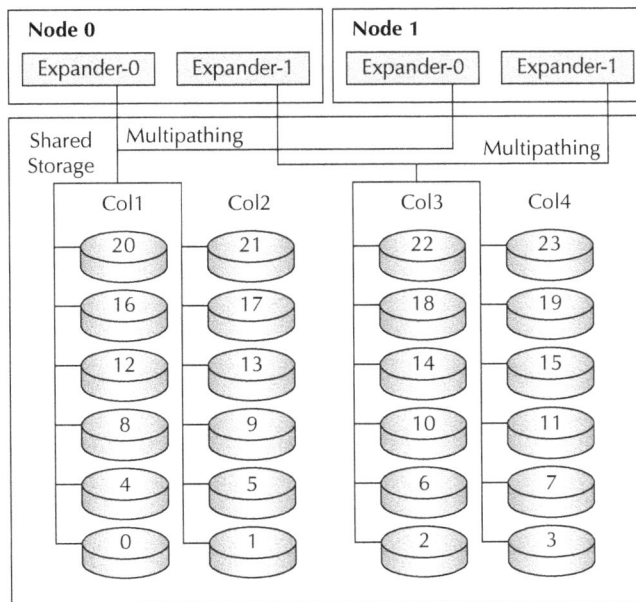

FIGURE 12-2.   *ODA disk and expander layout*

Brief Overview on Storage Layout (Slots/Columns)   The ASM storage layout includes the following:

- ASM Diskgroup +DATA size 1.6TB (high redundancy)

- ASM Diskgroup +RECO size 2.4TB (high redundancy) or size 0.8TB (high redundancy with external storage for backups)

- ASM Diskgroup +REDO size 97.3GB (high redundancy)

The following output displays the disk naming and mapping to the ASM disk group. Note that the output has been shortened for brevity. ODA uses a specific naming convention to identify the disks. For example, disk HDD_E0_S05_971436927p2 indicates that it resides inside Expander 0 (E0) and slot 5 (S05).

```
SELECT dg.name AS DG, a.path, a.failgroup, a.os_mb AS "Size(MB)"
FROM V$ASM_DISKGROUP dg, V$ASM_DISK a
WHERE dg.group_number = a.group_number
ORDER BY dg, a.path;;
DG    Disk                                   Fail Group              Size  (MB)
----  -----------------------------------    ----------------------  ---------
DATA  /dev/mapper/HDD_E0_S00_977448283p1    HDD_E0_S00_977448283P1  491,520
DATA  /dev/mapper/HDD_E0_S01_977561747p1    HDD_E0_S01_977561747P1  491,520
DATA  /dev/mapper/HDD_E0_S04_975085971p1    HDD_E0_S04_975085971P1  491,520
...........
RECO  /dev/mapper/HDD_E0_S00_977448283p2    HDD_E0_S00_977448283P2   80,800
RECO  /dev/mapper/HDD_E0_S01_977561747p2    HDD_E0_S01_977561747P2   80,800
RECO  /dev/mapper/HDD_E0_S04_975085971p2    HDD_E0_S04_975085971P2   80,800
...........
REDO  /dev/mapper/SSD_E0_S20_805650385p1    SSD_E0_S20_805650385P1   70,004
REDO  /dev/mapper/SSD_E0_S21_805650582p1    SSD_E0_S21_805650582P1   70,004
REDO  /dev/mapper/SSD_E1_S22_805650581p1    SSD_E1_S22_805650581P1   70,004
```

ASM Optimizations for ODA

The Oracle Appliance Manager (OAK), in conjunction with ASM, automatically configures, manages, and monitors disks for performance and availability. Additionally, OAK provides alerts on performance and availability events as well as automatically configures replacement drives in case of a hard disk failure.

The Storage Management Module feature has the following capabilities:

- It takes corrective action on appropriate events.

- It interacts with ASM for complete automation.

  - Oracle Applicance Manager daemon (OAKd) monitors the physical state of disks.

  - Monitors disk status in ASM.

- Based on events interacts with ASM for corrective actions.

- ASM takes actions as directed by OAKd.

OAK tracks the configuration and layout of all storage devices in the system. If a storage device fails, it detects the failure and sends an alert by e-mail. When an alert is received, users have the option to remove the failed disk and replace it. When OAK detects a disk has been replaced, it verifies the disk size and other characteristics, such the firmware level. OAK then rebuilds the partition table on the new disk to match the table on the failed disk. Because ODA disks map the disk slot exactly to an expander group and failgroup, the disk is added back to the appropriate ASM disk group without intervention from the user. This mitigates incorrect ASM disk adds.

The oakcli command can be used to display the status of all disks in the engineered package. This is shown here using the oakcli show disk command:

```
[root@odacn1 ~]# /opt/oracle/oak/bin/oakcli show disk
    NAME            PATH            TYPE        STATE       STATE_DETAILS
    pd_00           /dev/sdam       HDD         ONLINE      Good
    pd_01           /dev/sdaw       HDD         ONLINE      Good
    pd_02           /dev/sdaa       HDD         ONLINE      Good
    pd_03           /dev/sdak       HDD         ONLINE      Good
    pd_04           /dev/sdan       HDD         ONLINE      Good
    pd_05           /dev/sdax       HDD         ONLINE      Good
    pd_06           /dev/sdab       HDD         ONLINE      Good
    pd_07           /dev/sdal       HDD         ONLINE      Good
    pd_08           /dev/sdao       HDD         ONLINE      Good
    pd_09           /dev/sdau       HDD         ONLINE      Good
    pd_10           /dev/sdac       HDD         ONLINE      Good
    pd_11           /dev/sdai       HDD         ONLINE      Good
    pd_12           /dev/sdap       HDD         ONLINE      Good
    pd_13           /dev/sdav       HDD         ONLINE      Good
    pd_14           /dev/sdad       HDD         ONLINE      Good
    pd_15           /dev/sdaj       HDD         ONLINE      Good
    pd_16           /dev/sdaq       HDD         ONLINE      Good
    pd_17           /dev/sdas       HDD         ONLINE      Good
    pd_18           /dev/sdae       HDD         ONLINE      Good
    pd_19           /dev/sdag       HDD         ONLINE      Good
    pd_20           /dev/sdar       SSD         ONLINE      Good
    pd_21           /dev/sdat       SSD         ONLINE      Good
    pd_22           /dev/sdaf       SSD         ONLINE      Good
    pd_23           /dev/sdah       SSD         ONLINE      Good
```

The oakcli command can also be used to display the status of a specific disk. This is shown here using the oakcli show disk <disk_name> command:

```
[root@odacn1 ~]# /opt/oracle/oak/bin/oakcli show disk pd_23
Disk: pd_23
        ActionTimeout   :       600
        ActivePath      :       /dev/sdah
        AsmDiskList     :       |redo_23|
```

```
           AutoDiscovery    :       1
           AutoDiscoveryHi  :       |data:43:HDD||reco:57:HDD||redo:100
           CheckInterval    :       100
           ColNum           :       3
           DiskId           :       35000a720300497f4
           DiskType         :       SSD
           Enabled          :       0
           ExpNum           :       1
           IState           :       0
           Initialized      :       0
           MonitorFlag      :       0
           MultiPathList    :       |/dev/sdah||/dev/sdv|
           Name             :       pd_23
           NewPartAddr      :       0
           PrevState        :       0
           PrevUsrDevName   :
           SectorSize       :       4096
           SerialNum        :       STM00013F9D5
           Size             :       73407865344
           SlotNum          :       23
           State            :       Online
           StateChangeTs    :       1338401584
           StateDetails     :       Good
           TotalSectors     :       17921842
           TypeName         :       0
           UsrDevName       :       SSD_E1_S23_805607412
           gid              :       0
           mode             :       660
           uid              :       0


[root@odacn1 ~]# /opt/oracle/oak/bin/oakcli show disk pd_23 -all
           scsi-disk-capacity = 73407865344:73gb
           scsi-naa-logical-unit = 0x5000a720300497f4
           scsi-naa-scsi-target = 0x5000a720300497f4
           scsi-naa-target-port = 0x5000a72a300497f4
           scsi-product-id = ZeusIOPs G3
           scsi-product-revision = E125
           scsi-relative-target-port = 1
           scsi-serial-number = STM00013F9D5
           scsi-vendor-id = STEC



ASMCMD [+] > lsattr -G data -l
Name                        Value
access_control.enabled      FALSE
access_control.umask        066
au_size                     4194304
cell.smart_scan_capable     FALSE
compatible.asm              11.2.0.2.0
compatible.rdbms            11.2.0.2.0
disk_repair_time            3.6h
idp.boundary                auto
idp.type                    dynamic
sector_size                 512
```

```
SQL> select DISK, NUMBER_KFDPARTNER, NAME, FAILGROUP from V$ASM_DISK A,
X$KFDPARTNER B
where DISK = 23 and B.NUMBER_KFDPARTNER = A.DISK_NUMBER

DISK NUMBER_KFDPARTNER NAME                   FAILGROUP
---- ---------------- --------------------- ------------------------------
  23               22 SSD_E1_S22_805607499P1  SSD_E1_S22_805607499P1

  23               21 SSD_E0_S21_805607442P1  SSD_E0_S21_805607442P1

  23               20 SSD_E0_S20_805607396P1  SSD_E0_S20_805607396P1
```

ODA and NFS

Optionally, customers can use NFS storage as Tier 3 external storage and can be connected using one of the 10GB cards inside ODA. This NFS storage can be used to offload read-mostly or archived datasets. Oracle recommends using ZFS Storage Appliance ZFSSSA storage or other NFS appliance hardware. If the NFS appliance contains read-only datasets, its recommended to convert these data files to read-only using

```
alter database set tablespace <..> read only
```

and then set the init.ora parameter to READ_ONLY_OPEN_DELAYED=TRUE. This will improve database availability in case the NFS appliance becomes unavailable. Note that having NFS-based files presented to ASM as disks is neither recommended nor supported.

Summary

Oracle Exadata Database Machine, Oracle Database Appliance, and Oracle SPARC SuperCluster are excellent Private Cloud Database consolidation platforms. These solutions provide preintegrated configurations of hardware and software components engineered to work together and optimized for different types of database workloads. They also eliminate the complexity of deploying a high-performance database system. Engineered systems such as ODA and Exadata are tested in the factory and delivered ready to run. Because all database machines are the same, their characteristics and operations are well known and understood by Oracle field engineers and support. Each customer will not need to diagnose and resolve unique issues that only occur on their configuration. Performance tuning and stress testing performed at Oracle are done on the exact same configuration that the customer has, thus ensuring better performance and higher quality. Further, the fact that the hardware and software configuration and deployment, maintenance, troubleshooting, and diagnostics processes are prevalidated greatly simplifies the operation of the system, significantly reduces the risks, and lowers the overall cost while producing a highly reliable, predictable database environment. The ease and completeness of the predictive, proactive, and reactive management processes possible on Oracle Database Appliance are simply nonexistent in other environments.

Applications do not need to be certified against engineered systems. Applications that are certified with Oracle Database 11.2 RAC will run against the engineered systems. Choosing the best platform for your organization will be one of the key milestones in your roadmap to realizing the benefits of cloud computing for your private databases.

CHAPTER

ASM Tools and Utilities

M any tools can be used to manage ASM, such as SQL*Plus, ASMCMD, and Enterprise Manager (EM). In Oracle Clusterware 11*g*R2, these tools were enhanced and several new tools were introduced to manage ASM and its storage. These tools and utilities can be broken down into two categories: fully functional ASM management and standalone utilities.

Fully functional ASM management:

■ ASMCA

■ ASMCMD

■ Enterprise Manager

■ SQL*Plus

Standalone utilities:

■ Renamedg

■ ASRU

■ KFOD

■ AMDU

This chapter focuses on ASMCA, ASMCMD, and the standalone utilities.

ASMCA

ASMCA is a multipurpose utility and configuration assistant like DBCA or NETCA. ASMCA is integrated and invoked within the Oracle Universal Installer (OUI). It can be used as a tool to upgrade ASM or run as a standalone configuration tool to manage ASM instances, ASM disk groups, and ACFS.

ASMCA is invoked by running $GI_HOME/asmca. Prior to running asmca, ensure that the ORACLE_SID for ASM is set appropriately.

The following example illustrates ASMCA usage:

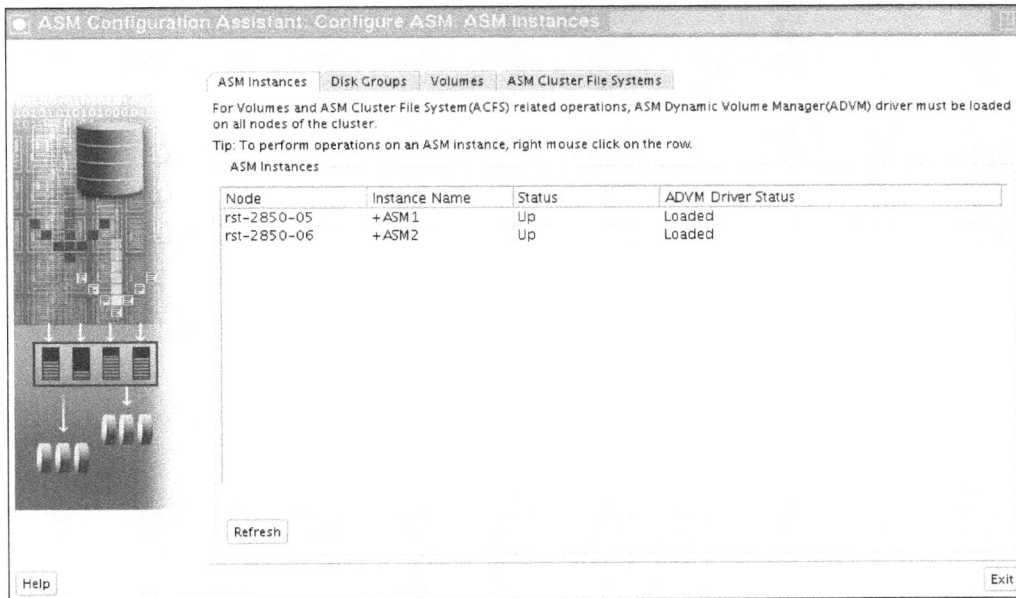

This illustration shows the ASM Instances tab, where ASM instances can be started, stopped, and upgraded. ASMCA uses a combination of SQL*Plus and Clusterware commands to configure the ASM instance. By default, the ASM server parameter file (SPFILE) is always stored in the disk group, allowing the instance to bootstrap on its own.

The Disk Groups tab of ASMCA, as shown in Figure 13-1, allows the user to configure ASM disk groups based on the availability requirements of the deployment. The Disk Groups tab allows the user to modify disk group attributes.

If the user wants to create a new disk groups then ASMCA allows disk group creations as shown in Figure 13-2. The default discovery string used to populate the candidate disks is either obtained by what the server uses or the OS specific default is used. As part of the disk group creation the user get to choose the redundancy of the disk group.

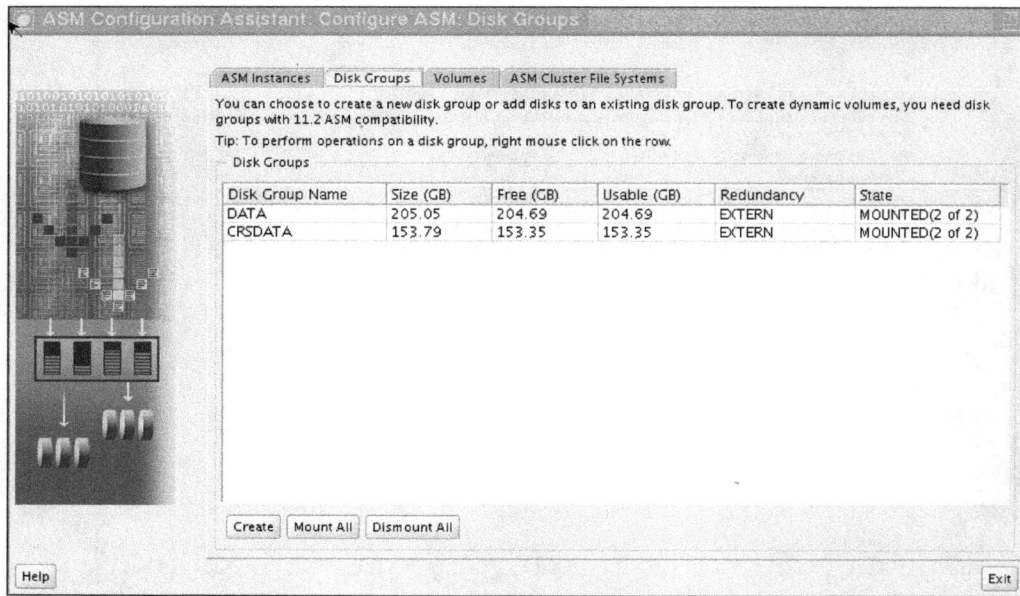

FIGURE 13-1. *The Disk Groups tab*

Finally Figure 13-3 shows the list of disk groups that were created and are available for users to either create database or ACFS file systems on.

To leverage additional configuration menu options, users can right-click any of the listed disk groups. The menu options enable you to perform the following actions:

- Add disks to the disk group

- Edit the disk group attributes

- Manage templates for the disk group

- Create an ACFS-based database home on the selected disk group

- Dismount and mount the disk group, either locally or globally on all nodes of the cluster

- Drop the disk group

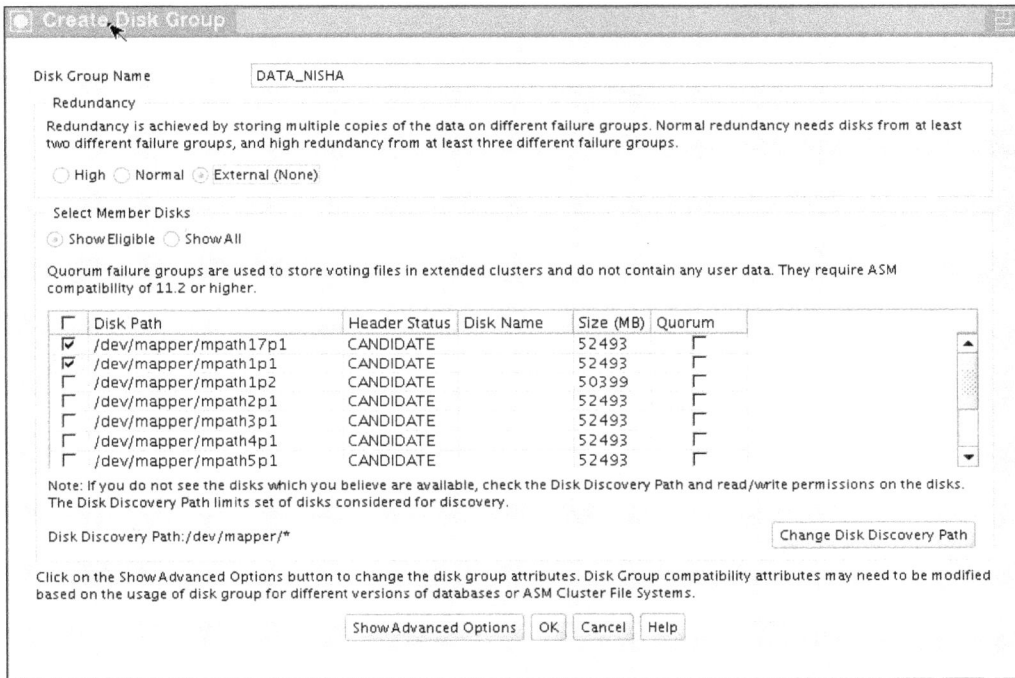

FIGURE 13-2.   *How to create disk groups using ASMCA*

Using ASMCA to manage and configure ACFS and ADVM is covered in Chapter 11.
Although we showed ASMCA usage via GUI access, ASMCA can also be used in
command-line mode as well. The command line provides opportunities to script
ASM configuration. The following example illustrates ASMCA command-line usage
by creating an ASM disk group:

```
asmca  -silent -configureASM -sysAsmPassword nishan2012 -asmsnmpPassword
nishan2012  -diskstring 'ORCL:*'   -diskGroupName CRSDATA   -disk 'ORCL:*'
-au_size 64  -compatible.asm '11.2.0.0.0' -compatible.rdbms '11.2.0.0.0'
-compatible.advm '11.2.0.0.0'  -redundancy External
```

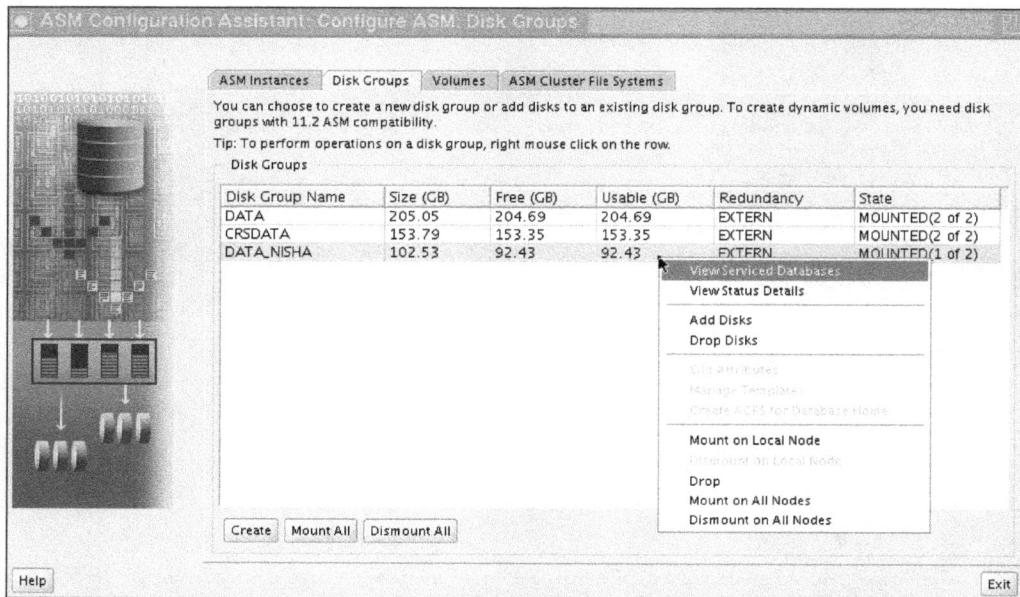

FIGURE 13-3. *A list of the disk groups created*

ASMCMD

ASMCMD was first introduced in 10gR2 with a basic command set for managing ASM files; however, in 11gR2 the asmcmd command has been expanded to fully manage ASM. In previous versions, fully managing ASM was only possible via EM and SQL*Plus. This section only focuses on the key new commands introduced in 11gR2. For the complete reference of the ASMCMD command set, refer to the *Oracle Storage Administrator's Guide.*

ASMCMD, like ASMCA, needs to have the ORACLE_SID set to the ASM instance SID. In Oracle Clusterware 11gR2, the "asmcmd -a" flag has been deprecated; in its place, the ASM privilege must be set. ASMCMD can be used in interactive mode or noninteractive (batch) mode.

The new capabilities found in 11.2 ASMCMD include ASM instance management, disk group and disk management, ASM file management, and ACFS/ADVM management. ASMCMD is profiled throughout this book, please refer to the specific chapter for appropriate ASMCMD command usage.

ASM instance management includes the following capabilities:

- Starting and stopping ASM instances
- Modifying and listing ASM disk strings
- Creating/modifying/removing ASM users and groups
- Backing up and restoring the SP file
- Adding/removing/modifying/listing users from the password file
- Backing up and restoring the metadata of disk groups
- Displaying connected clients

Disk group and disk management includes the following capabilities:

- Showing directory space utilization using the Linux/Unix-like command du
- Mounting/dismounting/creating/altering/dropping disk groups
- Rebalancing the disk groups
- Displaying disk group attribute
- Onlining or offlining the disks/failure groups
- Repairing physical blocks
- Displaying disk I/O statistic

ASM file management includes the following capabilities:

- Managing ASM directories, templates, and aliases
- Copying the files between the disk groups and OS
- Adding/removing/modifying/listing the templates
- Managing and modifying the ASM file ACLs

Finally, ACFS/ADVM management includes the capability to create, delete, enable, and list the ADVM volumes.

Renamedg

In many cases, users may need to rename disk groups. This could include cloned disk groups that will used be on different hosts for test environments or snapshots of disk groups that are to be mounted on the same host. Oracle Clusterware 11gR2 introduces a command that provides this capability: the renamedg command. The renamedg command can be executed using a single phase or two phases. Phase one generates a configuration file to be used in phase two, and phase two uses the configuration file to perform the renaming of the disk group.

The following example shows the steps in renaming a disk group:

1. Before the disk group can be renamed, it must first be dismounted. If databases or ACFS file systems are using this disk group, they must be unmounted before the renamedg is executed. Note that this must be done on all nodes on a RAC configuration. For RAC configurations, it's best to use ASMCA to globally dismount the disk group. Additionally, if the ASM spfile exists in this disk group, it must be moved to another location or disk group. The asmcmd lsof command can be used to determine whether any open files exist in the disk group before a dismount is attempted.

   For example: Use asmcmd to dismount the diskgroup:

   ```
   [grid@node1]$ asmcmd umount data_nisha
   ```

2. Verify that the desired disk group was dismounted:

   ```
   # asmcmd lsdg

   State   Type   Rebal  Sector  Block  AU   Total_MB   Free_MB   Req_
   mir_free_MB Usable_file_MB  Offline_disks  Voting_files  Name
   MOUNTED  EXTERN  N    512   4096  4194304   157476    157028
   0        157028             0            Y  CRSDATA/
   MOUNTED  EXTERN  N         512  4096  1048576   209972
   209602          0          209602            0
   N  DATA_NISHA/
   ```

3. Rename the disk group:

   ```
   renamedg phase=both dgname=data_nisha
   newdgname=data_ishan01 verbose=true
   asm_diskstring='/dev/mapper/*'
   ```

   The renamedg command can also be run in dry-run mode. This may be useful to verify the execution. This check mode verifies all the disks can be discovered and that the disk group can be successfully renamed. The following example shows the check option of the renamedg command:

```
renamedg phase=both dgname=data_nisha
newdgname=data_ishan01 verbose=true
check=true asm_diskstring='/dev/mapper/*'
```

Once the check has verified appropriate behavior, we can run the actual renamedg command:

```
[grid@node1]$ renamedg phase=both dgname=data_nisha
newdgname=data_ishan01
verbose=true  asm_diskstring='/dev/mapper/*'
Parsing parameters..
Parameters in effect:
        Old DG name        : DATA_NISHA
        New DG name          : DATA_ISHAN01
        Phases             :
                Phase 1
                Phase 2
        Discovery str      : /dev/mapper/*
        Clean            : TRUE
        Raw only         : TRUE
renamedg operation: phase=both dgname=data_nisha
newdgname=data_ishan01
verbose=true asm_diskstring=/dev/mapper/*
Executing phase 1
Discovering the group
Performing discovery with string:/dev/mapper/*
Identified disk UFS:/dev/mapper/mpath17p1 with
disk number:0 and timestamp
(32956931 -2110368768)
Identified disk UFS:/dev/mapper/mpath1p1 with
disk number:1 and timestamp
(32956931 -2110368768)
Checking for heartbeat...
Re-discovering the group
Performing discovery with string:/dev/mapper/*
Identified disk UFS:/dev/mapper/mpath17p1 with
disk number:0 and timestamp
(32956931 -2110368768)
Identified disk UFS:/dev/mapper/mpath1p1 with
disk number:1 and timestamp
(32956931 -2110368768)
Checking if the diskgroup is mounted or used by CSS
Checking disk number:0
Checking disk number:1
```

```
Generating configuration file..
Completed phase 1
Executing phase 2
Looking for /dev/mapper/mpath17p1
Modifying the header
Looking for /dev/mapper/mpath1p1
Modifying the header
Completed phase 2
Terminating kgfd context 0xb7e62050
```

4. Once the renamedg command completes, we can remount the disk group. Mounting the disk group inherently validates the disk group header:

```
# asmcmd mount DATA_ISHAN01

# asmcmd lsdg

[grid@rst-2850-05 trace]$ asmcmd lsdg
State     Type     Rebal  Sector  Block        AU  Total_MB  Free_MB
Req_mir_free_MB  Usable_file_MB  Offline_disks  Voting_files  Name
MOUNTED   EXTERN   N       512    4096   4194304    157476    157028
0              157028                  0              Y   CRSDATA/
MOUNTED   EXTERN   N       512    4096   1048576    209972    209602
0              209602                  0              N   DATA/
MOUNTED   EXTERN   N       512    4096   1048576    104986     94646
0               94646                  0              N   DATA_ISHAN01/
```

This disk group name change is also reflected in the CRS resource status automatically:

```
[grid@node1]$ crsctl stat res | more
....
NAME=ora.DATA_ISHAN01.dg
TYPE=ora.diskgroup.type
TARGET=ONLINE                 , ONLINE
STATE=ONLINE on rst-2850-05, ONLINE on rst-2850-06
```

Although the renamedg command updates the CRS resource with the new disk group name, the old CRS disk group resource still exists within CRS. In our example the DATA_NISHA disk group is still listed as a CRS resource, although it is in the offline state:

```
crsctl stat res | more
....
NAME=ora.DATA_ISHAN01.dg
TYPE=ora.diskgroup.type
TARGET=ONLINE                 , ONLINE
```

```
STATE=ONLINE on rst-2850-05, ONLINE on rst-2850-06
....

NAME=ora.DATA_NISHA.dg
TYPE=ora.diskgroup.type
TARGET=OFFLINE, OFFLINE
STATE=OFFLINE, OFFLINE
```

To remove this defunct CRS resource, users should run the srvctl remove –g <diskgroup> command (note that users should not use the crsctl delete resource ora.<diskgroup>.dg command because it is unsupported):

```
[grid@node1]$ srvctl remove diskgroup -g DATA_NISHA
```

The renamedg command currently does not rename the disks that belong to the disk group. In our example, the original disk group was named DATA_NISHA, so all underlying member disk names started with DATA_NISHA by default. After the renamedg command is run, the disk group is renamed to DATA_ISHAN01; however, the disks are still named DATA_NISHA. This should not have any operational impact. As reported in the example below:

```
ASMCMD> lsdsk -k
Total_MB  Free_MB  OS_MB  Name  Failgroup  Failgroup_Type  Library  Label
UDID  Product  Redund  Path
52493    47322    52493  DATA_NISHA_0000  DATA_NISHA_0000  REGULAR System
UNKNOWN  /dev/mapper/mpath17p1
   52493    47324  52493  DATA_NISHA_0001  DATA_NISHA_0001  REGULAR System
UNKNOWN  /dev/mapper/mpath1p1
```

The renamedg command does not rename the pathname references for the data files that exist within that disk group. To rename the data files appropriately and have this reflected in the database control file, we can use the following database SQL to generate a data file rename script:

```
DB_SQL> spool /tmp/rename_datafiles.sql
DB_SQL> select 'alter database rename file '''||name||''' to
''+DATA_ISHAN01'||substr(name,instr(name,'/',1,1))||''';' from V$DATAFILE;

DB_SQL> select 'alter database rename file '''||member||''' to ''
+ DATA_ISHAN01'||substr(member,instr(member,'/',1,1))||''';' from
V$logfile;
```

Renaming disk groups that contain the Clusterware files requires more careful planning. The following steps illustrate this procedure. (Note that the Clusterware files must be relocated to another disk group.)

1. Back up the OCR manually using either of the following commands:

   ```
   # ocrconfig -manualbackup
   ```

or

```
# ocrconfig -add ...
```

2. Create a temporary disk group, like so:

```
SQL> create diskgroup <temp_dg>;
```

We can use a shared file system instead of a temporary disk group.

3. Confirm that Grid Infrastructure on all nodes is active:

```
$ crsctl check crs
$ crsctl stat res -t
```

4. Move the OCR, the voting files, and the ASM spfile to a temporary disk group:

```
OCR
# ocrconfig -add +<temp_dg>
# ocrconfig -delete +<current_dg>

Voting files
# crsctl replace votedisk +<temp_dg>

ASM spfile
ASMCMD> spcopy -u <current location of ASM SPFILE>
<temporary location>
```

We can use a shared file system instead of a temporary disk group as the destination for clusterware files as well as ASM spfile.

5. Restart the Grid Infrastructure on all nodes and confirm that it is active on all nodes:

```
$ crsctl check crs
$ crsctl stat res -t
```

6. Rename the disk group, like so:

```
$ srvctl stop diskgroup -g <current_dg>
$ crsctl stat res -t
$ renamedg phase=both dgname=<current_db>
newdgname=<new_name_dg> verbose=true
```

7. Mount the disk group:

```
$ asmcmd mount <new_name_dg>
```

The diskgroup (.dg) resource is registered automatically.

```
$ srvctl start diskgroup -g <new_name_dg>
$ crsctl stat res -t
```

8. Remove the old disk group (.dg) resource:

```
$ srvctl remove diskgroup -g <current_dg>
```

9. Move the OCR, the voting files, and the ASM spfile to <new_name_dg>:

```
OCR
# ocrconfig -add +<new_name_dg>
# ocrconfig -delete +<temp_dg>

Voting files
# crsctl replace votedisk +<new_name_dg>

ASM spfile
ASMCMD> spcopy -u <temporary location of ASM SPFILE>
<new location in new_name_dg>
```

10. Restart the Grid Infrastructure on all nodes and confirm that it is active on all nodes:

```
$ crsctl check crs
crsctl stat res -t
```

Although the renamedg command was introduced as part of Oracle Clusterware 11gR2, in many cases a disk group in a 10g or 11.1 environment needs to be renamed. You can use this tool to rename your 10g or 11gR1 ASM disk group.

In these cases, the 11gR2 stack, or more specifically Oracle Restart (Oracle Grid Infrastructure for Single Instance), needs to be installed on the server(s) where the disk group operation will be performed. It is not necessary to install 11gR2 RAC for this. Also, it is not necessary to start the Oracle Restart stack (you simply need the dormant software installation for the renamedg command). Here are the steps to follow:

1. Install 11.2.0.x Oracle Restart (Oracle Grid Infrastructure for Single Instance).

2. Unmount the disk group that will be renamed.

3. Run renamedg from the Oracle Restart home.

4. Use the renamedg tool to rename the 10g or 11gR1 disk group.

5. Optionally, uninstall the Oracle Restart software stack. If frequent disk group renames will be needed, this step is not recommended.

6. Mount the disk group.

NOTE
The disk group cannot be renamed when it contains offline disks.

ASM Storage Reclamation Utility (ASRU)

Storage costs—both in administrative overhead and capital expenses—are growing concerns for most enterprises. Storage vendors have introduced many features to reduce the acquisition cost side of storage. One such feature is *thin provisioning,* which is a feature common to many storage arrays. Thin provisioning enables on-demand allocation rather than up-front allocation of physical storage. This storage feature reduces unused space and improves storage utilization. Deploying Oracle databases with cost-effective thin provisioned storage is an ideal way to achieve high storage efficiency and dramatic storage capacity savings. By boosting storage utilization, thin provisioning drives savings in purchased capacity, associated power, and cooling costs. Although ASRU can be used against storage vendor providing thin provisioning, this section illustrates the ASRU feature usage against 3Par's storage to provide context.

The Oracle ASRU feature offers the ability to improve storage efficiency for Oracle Database 10*g* and 11*g* environments by reclaiming unused (but allocated) ASM disk space in thin provisioned environments.

Overview of ASRU Operation

Two key features allow thin provision storage reclamation:

■ Oracle ASRU compacts the ASM disks, writes zeros to the free space, and resizes the ASM disks to the original size with a single command, online and without disruption.

■ 3Par Thin Persistence software detects zero writes and eliminates the capacity associated with free space in thin provisioned volumes—simply, quickly, and without disruption. 3Par Thin Persistence leverages the unique, built-in, zero-detection capabilities.

Oracle ASM Storage Reclamation Utility (ASRU) is a standalone utility used to reclaim storage in an ASM disk group that was previously allocated but is no longer in use. ASRU accepts the name of the disk group for which space should be reclaimed. When executed, it writes blocks of zeros to regions on ASM disks where space is currently unallocated. The storage array, using the zero-detect capability of the array, will detect these zero blocks and reclaim any corresponding physical storage.

The ASM administrator invokes the ASRU utility, which operates in three phases:

■ **Compaction phase** In this phase, ASRU logically resizes the disks downward such that the amount of space in the disk group is at the allocated amount of file space in the disk group, plus a reserve capacity. The default value for the reserve amount is 25 percent; however, the reserve value is a tunable option in the utility. The resize operation of the disks is logical to ASM and has no effect on the physical disks. The effect of the resize operation is that file data in the ASM disk group is compressed near the beginning of the disks, which is accomplished by an ASM rebalance of the disk group. The utility uses the appropriate ASM V$ views to determine the current allocated size of the disk group. The next phase does not begin until the ASM rebalance for the disk group has completed and has been verified as complete.

- **Deallocation phase**   During this phase, ASRU writes zeros above the region where the ASM disks have been resized. The ASRU utility invokes another script called zerofill that does the writing of zeros. It is during this deallocation phase that the zero-detect algorithm within the 3Par Thin Engine will return the freed storage blocks to the free storage pool.

- **Expansion phase**   In the final phase, all the ASM disks will be resized to their original size as determined when ASRU was started. This resize operation is a logical resize of the disks with respect to ASM and does not result in a reorganization of file data in the disk group.

When to Use ASRU to Reclaim Storage

Storage reclamation should be considered for the following database storage events:

- Dropping one or more databases in an ASM disk group.

- Dropping one or more tablespaces.

- Adding new LUNs to an ASM disk group to replace old LUNs. This triggers an ASM rebalance to move a subset of the data from the old LUNs to the new LUNs. The storage released from the old volumes is a candidate for reclamation.

To determine whether storage reclamation will be beneficial after one of these operations, it is important to consider the effect of the reserve maintained by ASRU when the utility reduces the size of the disk group during the compaction phase. The temporarily reduced size is equal to the allocated space plus a reserve, which allows active databases to grow during the reclamation process; the default reserve is

25 percent of the allocated storage. Storage reclamation is likely to be beneficial if the amount of allocated physical storage significantly exceeds the amount of storage allocated within ASM plus the reserve.

The amount of physical storage allocated on a 3Par InServ array can be determined using the 3Par InForm operating system's showvv command, available from the InForm command-line interface (CLI), to show information about the virtual volumes (VVs) used by ASM. Here is the standard way of using this command to obtain information related to the effectiveness of thin provisioning for a group of volumes matching oel5.*:

```
cli% showvv -s oel5.*
```

The –s option produces voluminous output. Therefore, to make the output easier to understand, we will use more complex options that show just the data columns that are directly relevant to thin provisioning:

```
cli% showvv - showcols \
Name,Usr_Rsvd_MB,Usr_Used_MB,Usr_Used_Perc,Tot_Rsvd_MB,VSize_MB oel5.*
Name       Usr_Rsvd_MB Usr_Used_MB Usr_Used_Perc Tot_Rsvd_MB VSize_MB
oel5.1_asm     208896      206433         80.6      209152   256000
oel5.2_asm     208896      206499         80.6      209152   256000
oel5.3_asm     208896      206445         80.6      209152   256000
oel5.4_asm     208896      206443         80.6      209152   256000
-------------------------------------------------------------------
total          835584      825770                  914944  1024000
```

The Usr_Used_MB column indicates how many megabytes are actually allocated to user data. In this example, 825,770MB of storage within ASM's volumes has been written.

ASM's view of how much storage is in use can be determined with a SQL query:

```
SQL> select name, state, type, total_mb, free_mb from v$asm_diskgroup where
name = 'LDATA';

NAME                            STATE       TYPE    TOTAL_MB    FREE_MB
------------------------------- ----------- ------- ----------- ----------
LDATA                           MOUNTED     EXTERN  1023984     197986
```

This example shows 197,986MB of free storage out of 1,023,984MB available, or about 19.3 percent. The difference between these quantities—825,998MB—is how much storage within ASM is in use (that is, has actual written data).

Using ASRU to Reclaim Storage on 3Par: Use Cases

To illustrate storage reclamation using Oracle ASRU and the 3Par InServ Storage Server, a 1TB ASM disk group was created using four 250GB thin provisioned virtual volumes (TPVVs) on the 3Par InServ array. Zero detection is enabled for the volumes from the InForm CLI, as detailed in the following use cases.

Use Case #1

This use case involves reclaiming storage space after dropping a database/data file. The steps involve creating a DB named "yoda," creating a 15GB data file tablespace and filling it with data, and then dropping the data file and reclaiming the space via ASRU.

1. Create an ASM disk group and create a database using DBCA. Now use the showvv command to view space consumed:

```
South-T400 cli% showvv -showcols \Name,Usr_Rsvd_MB,Usr_Used_MB,Usr_Used_
Perc,Tot_Rsvd_MB,VSize_MB oraDBtest*
Name                Usr_Rsvd_MB Usr_Used_MB Usr_Used_Perc Tot_Rsvd_MB VSize_MB
oraDBtest_1950-02_inst1     4608        4284        41.8         4736      10240
oraDBtest_1950-02_inst2     4608        4283        41.8         5376      10240
oraDBtest_1950-02_inst3     4608        4283        41.8         5376      10240
oraDBtest_1950-02_inst4     4608        4283        41.8         5376      10240
--------------------------------------------------------------------------
total                      18432       17133                   20864      40960
```

2. Create a 15GB tablespace (data file) called par3_test. Create table BH in the par3_test tablespace and fill it with test data:

```
South-T400 cli% showvv -showcols \Name,Usr_Rsvd_MB,Usr_Used_MB,Usr_Used_
Perc,Tot_Rsvd
_MB,VSize_MB oraDBtest*
Name                Usr_Rsvd_MB Usr_Used_MB Usr_Used_Perc Tot_Rsvd_MB VSize_MB
oraDBtest_1950-02_inst1     5120        4694        45.8         5248      10240
oraDBtest_1950-02_inst2     5120        4697        45.9         8448      10240
oraDBtest_1950-02_inst3     5120        4691        45.8         8448      10240
oraDBtest_1950-02_inst4     5120        4694        45.8         8448      10240
--------------------------------------------------------------------------
total                      20480       18776                   30592      40960
```

3. Drop tablespace par3_test and then reclaim the space using ASRU:

```
[oracle@pe-1950-02 ~]$ /usr/local/bin/ASRU/ASRU data
Checking the system ...done
Calculating the new sizes of the disks ...done
Writing the data to a file ...done
Resizing the disks...done
/u01/app/oracle/product/11.2.0/grid/perl/bin/perl -I
/u01/app/oracle/product/11.2.0/grid/perl/lib/5.10.0 /usr/local/bin/ASRU/
zerofill 1
```

```
/dev/mapper/mpath4 5283 10240 /dev/mapper/mpath2 5283 10240 /dev/mapper/mpath3
5284 10240

/dev/mapper/mpath5 5284 10240
........................
........................
Calculating the new sizes of the disks ...done
Resizing the disks...done
Dropping the file ...done
```

4. **Recheck space usage in 3Par:**

```
South-T400 cli% showvv -showcols \Name,Usr_Rsvd_MB,Usr_Used_MB,Usr_Used_
Perc,Tot_Rsvd
_MB,VSize_MB oraDBtest*
Name                Usr_Rsvd_MB Usr_Used_MB Usr_Used_Perc Tot_Rsvd_MB VSize_MB
oraDBtest_1950-02_inst1    5120         773          7.5       5376      10240
oraDBtest_1950-02_inst2    5120         522          5.1      10496      10240
oraDBtest_1950-02_inst3    5120         771          7.5      10496      10240
oraDBtest_1950-02_inst4    5120         774          7.6      10496      10240
-----------------------------------------------------------------------------
total                     20480        2840                  36864      40960


=============================================
```

Use Case #2

In this use case, a new database is created along with a (single) new tablespace (15GB). Data is then seeded in it. Then the table is truncated and a check is done to determine whether ASRU can reclaim space from this space transaction.

1. **Create the table:**

```
SQL> create tables bh tablespace par3_test as select * from x$bh;
```

2. **Load the data:**

```
SQL> insert into bh  select * from bh;  /* repeated to loaded 13.5GB of 15GB
   SQL> select name, BYTES/(1024*1024), CREATE_BYTES/(1024*1024) from
v$datafile;
        NAME              BYTES/(1024*1024) CREATE_BYTES/(1024*1024)
   ---------------- -------------------------- -----------------------
     +DATA/obiwan/datafile/par3_test.260.718715789    15360          15360
```

3. **Truncate the table:**

```
SQL> truncate table bh;
Table truncated.
```

4. Recheck space usage in 3Par:

```
[oracle@pe-1950-02 ~]$ /usr/local/bin/ASRU/ASRU data
Checking the system ...done
Calculating the new sizes of the disks ...done
Writing the data to a file ...done
Resizing the disks...done
/u01/app/oracle/product/11.2.0/grid/perl/bin/perl -I
/u01/app/oracle/product/11.2.0/grid/perl/lib/5.10.0 /usr/local/bin/ASRU/
zerofill 1

/dev/mapper/mpath4 5283 10240 /dev/mapper/mpath2 5283 10240 /dev/mapper/mpath3
5284 10240

/dev/mapper/mpath5 5284 10240
........................

........................
Calculating the new sizes of the disks ...done
Resizing the disks...done
Dropping the file ...done
South-T400 cli% showvv -showcols \Name,Usr_Rsvd_MB,Usr_Used_MB,Usr_Used_
Perc,Tot_Rsvd
_MB,VSize_MB oraDBtest*
Name            Usr_Rsvd_MB Usr_Used_MB Usr_Used_Perc Tot_Rsvd_MB VSize_MB
oraDBtest_1950-02_inst1     5120        4280          41.8         5376    10240
oraDBtest_1950-02_inst2     5120        4249          41.5        10496    10240
oraDBtest_1950-02_inst3     5120        4283          41.8        10496    10240
oraDBtest_1950-02_inst4     5120        4280          41.8        10496    10240
---------------------------------------------------------------------------
total                      20480       17092                     36864    40960
```

5. No space was reclaimed, as expected.

NOTE
Typically DBAs will drop database segments (tables, indexes, and so on) or truncate tables in order to reclaim space. Although this operation does reclaim space back to the tablespace (and to the overall database), it does not release physical space back to the storage array. In order to reclaim physical space back to the storage array, a physical data file (or files) must be dropped or shrunk.

6. Now shrink the data file (since space HWM was already done via truncate):

```
[oracle@pe-1950-02 ~]$ sqlplus "/ as sysdba"
SQL> alter database datafile '+DATA/obiwan/datafile/par3_test.260.718715789'
resize 100M;
SQL> select name, bytes/(1024*1024) from v$datafile;
NAME                                             BYTES/(1024*1024)
------------------------------------------------ -----------------
+DATA/obiwan/datafile/par3_test.260.718715789                  100
```

7. Recheck space usage in 3Par:

```
[oracle@pe-1950-02 ~]$ /usr/local/bin/ASRU/ASRU data
Checking the system ...done
Calculating the new sizes of the disks ...done
Writing the data to a file ...done
Resizing the disks...done
/u01/app/oracle/product/11.2.0/grid/perl/bin/perl -I
/u01/app/oracle/product/11.2.0/grid/perl/lib/5.10.0 /usr/local/bin/ASRU/
zerofill 1

/dev/mapper/mpath4 514 10240 /dev/mapper/mpath2 514 10240 /dev/mapper/mpath3
516 10240

/dev/mapper/mpath5 514 10240

.............................

.............................
Calculating the new sizes of the disks ...done
Resizing the disks...done
Dropping the file ...done


South-T400 cli% showvv -showcols \Name,Usr_Rsvd_MB,Usr_Used_MB,Usr_Used_
Perc,Tot_Rsvd
_MB,VSize_MB oraDBtest*
Name                 Usr_Rsvd_MB Usr_Used_MB Usr_Used_Perc Tot_Rsvd_MB VSize_MB
oraDBtest_1950-02_inst1    5120         742         7.2          5376    10240
oraDBtest_1950-02_inst2    5120         775         7.6         10496    10240
oraDBtest_1950-02_inst3    5120         777         7.6         10496    10240
oraDBtest_1950-02_inst4    5120         775         7.6         10496    10240
----------------------------------------------------------------------------
total                     20480        3069                     36864    40960
```

KFOD

This section describes the purpose and function of the KFOD utility. KFOD is used to probe the system for disks that can be used for ASM. Note that KFOD does not perform any unique discovery; in other words, it uses the same discovery mechanism invoked by the ASM instance. KFOD is also invoked within the Oracle Universal Installer (OUI) for Grid Infrastructure stack installation. This section is not intended to be an exhaustive command reference; you can find that information in the *Oracle Storage Administrator's Guide*. Instead, we will cover the most important and relevant features and commands.

Recall from Chapter 4 that ASM stamps every disk that it adds to a disk group with a disk header. Therefore, when KFOD lists candidate disks, these are all disks that do not include the disk header. KFOD can list "true" candidate disks if the keyword status=TRUE is specified. True candidate disks are ones identified with the header status of CANDIDATE, FOREIGN, or FORMER. Note that disks with a header status of CANDIDATE include true candidate disks as well as FORMER disks (that is, disks that were previously part of an ASM diskgroup). KFOD does not distinguish between the two.

KFOD can display MEMBER disks if disks=all or disks=asm is specified. KFOD will include the disk group name if dscvgroup=TRUE is specified. KFOD will also discover and list Exadata grid disks.

You can specify the name of the disk group to be discovered by KFOD. KFOD lists all disks that are part of this disk group. At most one disk group name can be specified at a time. This command is valid only if an ASM instance is active.

For disk discovery, KFOD can use the default parameters, command-line options, or read options from a pfile. Specifying a pfile allows users to determine what disks would be available to an ASM instance using a configured pfile. If parameters and a pfile are specified, the pfile is not read; otherwise, if a pfile is specified, the parameters are taken from it.

As of 11*g*, KFOD supports a clustered environment. This means that KFOD is aware of all ASM instances currently running in the cluster and is able to get information about disk groups and ASM clients pertaining to all instances in the cluster. The "hostlist" parameter can be used to filter the output for the specified node in the cluster. 11*g*R2 ASM also introduces a display format, which is invoked using the cluster=true keyword. The default is to run in noncluster mode for backward compatibility. The next set of examples shows KFOD usage.

Here's how to list all active ASM instances in the ASM cluster:

```
[oracle@racovm1 ~]$ kfod op=insts
--------------------------------------------------------------------
------
ORACLE_SID ORACLE_HOME
====================================================================
======
     +ASM2 /u01/app/11.2.0/grid
     +ASM1 /u01/app/11.2.0/grid
```

Here's how to display the client databases accessing the local ASM instance:

```
[oracle@racovm1 ~]$ kfod op=clients
------------------------------------------------------------------
ORACLE_SID VERSION
==================================================================
     +ASM1 11.2.0.3.0
     ORCL1 11.2.0.3.0
     +ASM2 11.2.0.3.0
     ORCL2 11.2.0.3.0


[oracle@racovm1 ~]$ kfod disks=asm status=true dscvgroup=true
------------------------------------------------------------------
 Disk     Size Header    Path                  Disk Group   User    Group
==================================================================
    1:    3813 Mb MEMBER   /dev/xvdc1             DATA        oracle  dba
    2:    3813 Mb MEMBER   /dev/xvdd1             DATA        oracle  dba
    3:    3813 Mb MEMBER   /dev/xvde1             DATA        oracle  dba
    4:    3813 Mb MEMBER   /dev/xvdf1             DATA        oracle  dba
    5:    3813 Mb MEMBER   /dev/xvdg1             DATA        oracle  dba
------------------------------------------------------------------
ORACLE_SID ORACLE_HOME
==================================================================
     +ASM2 /u01/app/11.2.0/grid
     +ASM1 /u01/app/11.2.0/grid
```

KFOD can be used to display the total megabytes of metadata required for a disk group, which it calculates using numbers of disks, clients, nodes, and so on, provided on the command line or by default. The metadata parameters can be overridden to perform what-if scenarios.

Here's how to display the total megabytes of metadata required for a disk group with specified parameters:

```
kfod op=metadata metadata_ausize=4 metadata_clients=2 metadata_disks=36
metadata_nodes=4 metadata_redundancy=3
Approximate Metadata Size:   3159
```

AMDU

The ASM Metadata Dump Utility (AMDU) is part of the Oracle Grid Infrastructure distribution. AMDU is used to extract the available metadata from one or more ASM disks and generate formatted output of individual blocks.

AMDU also has the ability to extract one or more files from an unmounted disk group and write them to the OS file system. This dump output can be shipped to Oracle Support for analysis. Oracle Support can use the dump output to generate formatted block printouts. AMDU does not require the disk group to be mounted or the ASM instance to be active.

AMDU performs three basic functions. A given execution of AMDU may perform one, two, or all three of these functions:

- Dump metadata from ASM disks to the OS file system for later analysis.

- Extract the contents of an ASM file and write it to an OS file system even if the disk group is not mounted.

- Print metadata blocks.

The AMDU input data may be the contents of the ASM disks or ingested from a directory created by a previous run of AMDU:

```
$ amdu -diskstring="ORCL:*" -extract DATA.276
-output nisha_file.276 -noreport -nodir
AMDU-00204: Disk N0001 is in currently mounted diskgroup DATA
AMDU-00201: Disk N0001: 'ORCL:DISK1'

$ ls -l nisha_file.276
-rw-r--r-- 1 grid oinstall 9748480 Sep 22 22:42 nisha_file.276
```

AMDU produces four types of output files:

- **Extracted files**   One extracted file is created for every file listed under the -extract option on the command line.

- **Image files**   Image files contain block images from the ASM disks. This is the raw data that is copied from the disks.

- **Map files**   Map files are ASCII files that describe the data in the image files for a particular disk group.

- **Report file**   One report file is generated for every run of the utility without the -directory option (except if -noreport is specified).

In this first example, we will use AMDU to extract a database control file. The disk group is still mounted and we'll extract one of the control files for a database named ISHAN.

1. Determine the ASM disk string:

```
ASMCMD> dsget
parameter:/dev/xvd[c-g]1
profile:/dev/xvd[c-g]1
```

2. Determine the location of all the control files:

```
$ ASMCMD> find --type CONTROLFILE +data *
+data/ORCL/CONTROLFILE/Current.260.776324441
```

In this example, we have a single copy of the control file in the disk group DATA.

3. Determine the disks for the DATA disk group:

```
ASMCMD> lsdsk -G DATA
Path
/dev/xvdc1
/dev/xvdd1
/dev/xvde1
/dev/xvdf1
/dev/xvdg1
```

4. Extract the control file out of the disk group DATA onto the file system. Here are the options used:

- **-diskstring**   This is either the full path to disk devices or the value of the ASM_DISKSTRING parameter.

- **-extract**   The disk group name, followed by a period, followed by the ASM file number.

- **-output**   The output file name (in the current directory).

- **-noreport**   Indicates not to generate the AMDU run report.

- **-nodir**   Indicates not to create the dump directory.

```
amdu -diskstring="/dev/xvd[c-g]1" -extract DATA.260
-output control.260 -noreport -nodir
[oracle@racovm1 ~]$ ls -l control.260
-rw-r--r-- 1 oracle oinstall 18497536 Apr 12 19:38 control.260
```

In this second example, we extract a data file when the disk group is not mounted using AMDU. The objective is to extract a single data file, named something like USERS, from the disk group DATA, which is dismounted. This will require us to dump all metadata for the disk group DATA.

```
$ cd /tmp
$ amdu -dump DATA -noimage
amdu_2011_09_22_22_57_05/
$ cd amdu_2011_09_22_22_57_05
$ ls -l
total 28
-rw-r--r-- 1 grid oinstall  5600 Sep 22 22:57 DATA.map
-rw-r--r-- 1 grid oinstall 10462 Sep 22 22:57 report.txt
```

Report.txt contains information about the server, the amdu command, the options used, a list of disks that are members of the disk group DATA, and information about the allocation units (AUs) on those disks. Let's review the contents of the report file:

```
$ more report.txt
-*-amdu-*-
****************************** AMDU Settings ******************************
ORACLE_HOME = /u01/app/11.2.0/grid
System name:    Linux
Node name:      racovm1
Release:        2.6.18-274.0.0.0.1.el5xen
Version:        #1 SMP Mon Jul 25 15:05:20 EDT 2011
Machine:        x86_64
amdu run:       18-APR-12 19:07:43
Endianess:      1


----------------------------- Operations ----------------------------
     -dump DATA
---------------------------- Disk Selection --------------------------
 -diskstring '/dev/xvd[c-g]1'
--------------------------- Reading Control --------------------------
--------------------------- Output Control ---------------------------        -noimage
****************************** DISCOVERY ******************************
--------------------------- DISK REPORT N0001 ------------------------
                 Disk Path: /dev/xvdc1
            Unique Disk ID:
                Disk Label:
       Physical Sector Size: 512 bytes
                 Disk Size: 3813 megabytes
                Group Name: DATA
                 Disk Name: DATA_0000
        Failure Group Name: DATA_0000
               Disk Number: 0
             Header Status: 3
        Disk Creation Time: 2012/02/27 05:26:35.570000
          Last Mount Time: 2012/04/15 18:06:19.547000
     Compatibility Version: 0x0b200000(11020000)
          Disk Sector Size: 512 bytes
          Disk size in AUs: 3813 AUs
          Group Redundancy: 1
       Metadata Block Size: 4096 bytes
                   AU Size: 1048576 bytes
                    Stride: 113792 AUs
        Group Creation Time: 2012/02/27 05:26:33.394000
    File 1 Block 1 location: AU 2
               OCR Present: YES
This repeated for each in the diskgroup...
*********************** SCANNING DISKGROUP DATA***********************
            Creation Time: 2012/02/27 05:26:33.394000
         Disks Discovered: 5
                Redundancy: 1
                   AU Size: 1048576 bytes
```

```
        Metadata Block Size: 4096 bytes
       Physical Sector Size: 512 bytes
           Metadata Stride: 113792 AU
    Duplicate Disk Numbers: 0
------------------------- SCANNING DISK N0001 -------------------------
Disk N0001: '/dev/xvdc1'
AMDU-00204: Disk N0001 is in currently mounted diskgroup DATA
AMDU-00201: Disk N0001: '/dev/xvdc1'
** HEARTBEAT DETECTED **
             Allocated AU's: 784
                  Free AU's: 3029
       AU's read for dump: 26
       Block images saved: 5126
       Map lines written: 26
           Heartbeats seen: 1
   Corrupt metadata blocks: 0
         Corrupt AT blocks: 0
This repeated for each disk in the diskgroup
------------------------ SUMMARY FOR DISKGROUP DATA --------------
             Allocated AU's: 3778
                  Free AU's: 15287
       AU's read for dump: 117
       Block images saved: 25870
       Map lines written: 117
           Heartbeats seen: 1
   Corrupt metadata blocks: 0
         Corrupt AT blocks: 0
******************************END OF REPORT ***********************
```

The file DATA.map contains the data map. The following shows a sampling of DATA.map that was generated:

```
$ more DATA.map
N0001 D0000 R00 A00000000 F00000000 I0 E00000000 U00 C00256 S0000 B0000000000
N0001 D0000 R00 A00000001 F00000000 I0 E00000000 U00 C00256 S0000 B0000000000
N0001 D0000 R00 A00000002 F00000001 I0 E00000000 U00 C00256 S0000 B0000000000
N0001 D0000 R00 A00000003 F00000003 I0 E00000001 U00 C00256 S0000 B0000000000
N0001 D0000 R00 A00000004 F00000003 I0 E00000011 U00 C00256 S0000 B0000000000
...
N0002 D0001 R00 A00000421 F00000259 I1 E00000000 U00 C00002 S0000 B0000000000
......
```

Of immediate interest are fields starting with A and F. The field A0000421, for example, indicates that this line is for allocation unit (AU) 421, and the field F00000259 indicates that this line is about ASM file 259.

ASM metadata file 6 is the alias directory, so that is the first place to look. From DATA.map, we can work out AUs for ASM file 6:

```
$ grep F00000006 DATA.map
N0003 D0002 R00 A00000010 F00000006 I0 E00000000 U00 C00256 S0000
B0000000000
```

This single line in the map indicates that all the file aliases fit in a single AU; in other words, there are not many files in this disk group. If the output listed multiple lines from the grep command, this would reflect that many ASM files exists in this disk group.

From the preceding grep output, the alias directory seems to be in allocation unit 10 (A00000010) on disk 2 (D0002). From report.txt, we know that disk 2 is /dev/xvde1 and that the AU size is 1MB. Let's have a look at the alias directory. You can use kfed for this:

```
[oracle@racovm1 amdu_2012_04_18_19_07_43]$ kfed read /dev/xvde1 aun=10 | more
kfbh.endian:                      1 ; 0x000: 0x01
kfbh.hard:                      130 ; 0x001: 0x82
kfbh.type:                       11 ; 0x002: KFBTYP_ALIASDIR
kfbh.datfmt:                      1 ; 0x003: 0x01
kfbh.block.blk:                   0 ; 0x004: blk=0
kfbh.block.obj:                   6 ; 0x008: file=6
kfbh.check:               2813538233 ; 0x00c: 0xa7b32fb9
```

KFBTYP_ALIASDIR indicates that this is the alias directory. Now look for a data file named USERS:

```
for (( i=0; i<256; i++ ))
do
   kfed read /dev/oracleasm/disks/DISK2 aun=8 blkn=$i | grep -1 USERS
done
```

This gives us the following output:

```
[oracle@racovm1 amdu_2012_04_18_19_07_43]$ /tmp/usersdbf.sh
kfade[3].entry.refer.incarn:      0 ; 0x114: A=0 NUMM=0x0
kfade[3].name:                USERS ; 0x118: length=5
kfade[3].fnum:                  259 ; 0x148: 0x00000103
```

The USERS tablespace is ASM file 259. Now extract the file:

```
$ amdu -diskstring="/dev/xvd*" -extract DATA.259 -output FDATA.259
  -noreport -nodir
$ [oracle@racovm1 tmp]$ ll FDATA.259
-rw-r--r-- 1 oracle oinstall 994844672 Apr 18 19:59 FDATA.259

To verify that this file is indeed a datafile, use DBV utility:
[oracle@racovm1 tmp]$ dbv file=FDATA.259
DBVERIFY: Release 11.2.0.3.0 - Production on Wed Apr 18 20:04:39 2012
Copyright (c) 1982, 2011, Oracle and/or its affiliates.  All rights reserved.
DBVERIFY - Verification starting : FILE = /tmp/FDATA.259
DBVERIFY - Verification complete
Total Pages Examined        : 121440
Total Pages Processed (Data) : 113097
Total Pages Failing    (Data) : 0
```

```
Total Pages Processed (Index): 2
Total Pages Failing   (Index): 0
Total Pages Processed (Other): 908
Total Pages Processed (Seg)  : 0
Total Pages Failing   (Seg)  : 0
Total Pages Empty            : 7433
Total Pages Marked Corrupt   : 0
Total Pages Influx           : 0
Total Pages Encrypted        : 0
Highest block SCN            : 4153530 (0.4153530)
```

These steps can be repeated for the System and Sysaux data files as well as the control files. Then these can used to open the database, or then plug the extracted files into another database and recover.

It is important to note that although the amdu command will extract the file, the file itself may be corrupt or damaged in some way. After all, there is a reason for the disk group not mounting—chances are the ASM metadata is corrupt or missing, but that can be the case with the data file as well. The point is that there's no substitute for a backup, so keep that in mind.

Summary

Various tools can be used to manage ASM. These tools and utilities handle a range of tasks—from managing daily ASM activities, to assisting in the recovery of ASM files and renaming ASM disk groups. As a best practice, the ASMCMD utility or Enterprise Manager should be used to manage ASM.

CHAPTER
14

Oracle 12c ASM:
A New Frontier

Whorken Automatic Storage Management (ASM) was introduced in 10gR1, it was simply marketed as the volume manager for the Oracle database. ASM was designed as a purpose-built host-based volume management and file system that is integrated with the Oracle database. These simple ideas delivered a powerful solution that eliminates many headaches DBAs and storage administrators once had with managing storage in an Oracle environment.

However, ASM has now become an integral part of the enterprise stack. ASM is not only a significant part of the Oracle Clusterware stack, but is also a core component of Engineered Systems such as Exadata and ODA. Oracle 12c was announced in 2013, and along with this 12c release came significant changes for ASM. This chapter covers some of the key management and high availability features introduced in 12c ASM. You will get a glimpse of these advancements, the history behind the new features, and why these features are a necessary part of the future of ASM.

The main theme of 12c ASM is extreme scalability and management of real-world data types. In addition, it removes many of the limitations of previous ASM generations. This chapter previews some of the key features of ASM and cloud storage in Oracle 12c. Note that this chapter does not provide an exhaustive overview of the new features, just the key features and optimizations. This chapter was written using the Beta2 version, so the examples and command syntax may be different from the production 12c version.

Password Files in ASM

In releases prior to Oracle 12c, most of the Oracle database and ASM-related files could be stored in ASM disk groups. The key exception was the oracle password file—neither the ASM and database password files could be stored in a disk group. These password files, created by orapwd utility, resided in the $ORACLE_HOME/dbs directory by default and therefore were local to the node and instance. This required manual synchronization of the password file. If the password file became out of sync between instances, it could cause inconsistent login behavior. Although Oracle 11gR2 provided the capability for cross-instance calls (CIC) to synchronize the password file, if an instance or node was inactive, synchronization was not possible, thus still leaving the password file inconsistent. Inconsistent ASM password file is more problematic for ASM instances because ASM does not have a data dictionary to fall back on when the file system–based password file was inconsistent.

In Oracle 12c (for new installations), the default location of the password file is in an ASM disk group. The location of the password file becomes a CRS resource attribute of the ASM and database instance. The ASM instance and the disk group that is storing the password file needs to be available before password file authentication is possible. The SYSASM or SYDBA privilege can be used for the password file in ASM.

For the ASM instance, operating system authentication is performed to bootstrap the startup of the ASM instance. This is transparently handled as part of the Grid Infrastructure startup sequence. As in previous releases, the SYSASM privilege is required to create the ASM password file.

Note that the compatible.asm disk group attribute must be set to 12.1 or later to enable storage of shared password files in an ASM disk group.

The following illustrates how to set up a password in ASM:

Database password file:

1. Create a password file:

```
$ orapwd file='+CRSDATA'  dbuniqueue='yoda' password='oracle1'
```

2. Move the existing password into ASM:

```
$ pwmove dbuniqueue='yoda' $ORACLE_HOME/dbs/orapwyoda +DATA
```

or

```
Asmcmd> pwcreate  --dbuniqueue yoda -G DATA oracle1
```

ASM password file:

Create an ASM password file. Note the asm=y option to distinguish this creation from regular password file creation.

```
$  orapwd asm=y file='+CRSDATA'  password='asmoracle1'
```

or

```
Asmcmd> pwcreate  --asm -G DATA asmoracle1
```

Disk Management and Rebalance New Features

In 12*c* there are several new features that improve disk management functions—specifically improved availability from transient disk or failgroup failures. This section covers these key disk management features.

Fast Disk Resync and Checkpoints

The 11*g* disk online feature provides the capability to online and resync disks that have incurred transient failures. Note that this feature is applicable only to ASM disk groups that use ASM redundancy.

The resync operation updates the ASM extents that were modified while the disk or disks were offline. However, prior to Oracle 12*c*, this feature was single threaded; i.e., using a single online process thread to bring the disk(s) completely online. For disks that have been offline for a prolonged period of time, combined with a large number of extent changes, could make the disk resync operation very long. In Oracle 12c, the online and resync operation becomes a multi-threaded operation very similar to the ASM rebalance operation.

Thus the disk online can leverage a power level from 1 to 1024, with 1 being the default. This power level controls how many outstanding IOs will be issued to the IO subsystem, and thus has a direct impact on the performance of the system. Keep in mind that you are still bounded by the server's IO subsystem layer, thus setting a very large power level does not necessarily improve resync time. This is because a server where the resync operation is submitted can only process a certain number of IO. A power level between 8 and 16 has proven beneficial for resyncing a single disk, whereas a power level of 8–32 has proven useful for bringing a failure group (with multiple disks) online.

In versions prior to Oracle 12c, the resync operation sets and clears flags (in Staleness Registry) at the beginning and end of the resync operation; an interrupted resync operation would need to be started from the beginning since the stale extent bit flags are cleared at the end of the resync operation. In 12c ASM, resync operations now support checkpoints. These checkpoints are now set after a batch of extents are updated and their stale extent flags cleared, thus making auto-restart begin at the last checkpoint. If the resync operation fails or gets interrupted, it is automatically restarted from the last resync phase and uses internally generated resync checkpoints.

The following illustrates the command usage for performing an ASM fast disk resync:

```
--Fast Resync for single disk
SQL> alter diskgroup data online disk data_0001 power 32;
--Fast Resync for multiple disks in diskgroup
SQL> alter diskgroup data online all power 64;
Or
asmcmd> online -G data -d data_0001  --power 32
```

Fast Disk Replacement

In versions 11gR2 and prior, a failed disk is taken offline or dropped, a new disk put in its place (generally in the same tray slot), and then this disk is added back into the ASM disk group. This procedure required a complete disk group rebalance. In Oracle 12c, the Fast Disk Replacement feature allows a failed disk (or disks) to be replaced without requiring a complete disk group rebalance operation. With the Fast Disk Replacement feature, the disk is replaced in the disk tray slot and then added back into the ASM disk group as a *replacement disk*. Initially this disk is in an offline state and resynced (populated) with copies of ASM extents from mirror extents from its partners. Note that because this is a replacement disk, it inherits the same disk name and is automatically placed back into the same failure group. The key benefit of the Fast Disk Replacement feature is that it allows ASM administrators to replace a disk using a fast, efficient, atomic operation with minimal system impact because no disk group reorganization is necessary.

The main difference between Fast Disk Resync and Fast Disk Replacement is that the disk has failed and is implicitly dropped in Fast Disk Replacement, whereas in Fast Disk Resync the disk is temporarily offline due to a transient path or component failure. If the disk repair timer expires before the replacement disk can be put in place, then users would have to use the regular disk add command to add the replacement disk to the disk group.

The following illustrates the command for performing ASM Fast Disk Replacement:

```
--Fast Disk Replace for single disk
SQL> alter diskgroup data replace disk data_0001 with /dev/sdd1;
```

Failure Group Repair Timer

When an individual disk fails, the failure is often terminal and the disk must be replaced. When all the disks in a failure group fail simultaneously, it is unlikely that all the disks individually failed at the same time. Rather, it is more likely that some transient issue caused the failure. For example, a failure group could fail because of a storage network outage. Because failure group outages are more likely to be transient in nature, and because replacing all the disks in a failure group is a far more expensive operation than replacing a single disk, it makes sense for failure groups to have a larger repair time to ensure that all the disks don't get dropped automatically in the event of a failure group outage. Administrators can now specify a failure group repair time similar to the 11*g* disk repair timer. This includes a new disk group attribute called failgroup_repair_time. The default setting is 24 hours.

```
SQL> alter diskgroup reco set attribute 'failgroup_repair_time = 36h';
```

Rebalance Time Estimations

In Oracle 12*c*, the different phases of the ASM rebalance operation are itemized with time estimations. In versions prior to Oracle Database 12, the rebalance work estimates were highly variable.

With Oracle Database 12*c*, a more detailed and accurate work plan is created at the beginning of each rebalance operation. Additionally, administrators can produce a work plan estimate before actually performing a rebalance operation, allowing administrators to better plan storage changes and predict impact.

In Oracle Database 12*c*, administrators can now use the new ESTIMATE WORK command to generate the work plan. This work estimate populates the V$ASM_ESTIMATE view, and the EST_WORK column can be used to estimate the number of ASM extents units that will be moved by the operation.

It is important to note that the unit in the V$ASM_ESTIMATE view is ASM extents, and this does not provide an explicit time estimate, such as the one provided in V$ASM_OPERATION.

The time estimate in V$ASM_OPERATION is based on the current work rate observed during execution of the operation. Because the current work rate can vary considerably, due to variations in the overall system workload, administrators should use knowledge of their environment and workload patterns to convert the data in V$ASM_ESTIMATE into a time estimate if required.

The first step is generating a work estimate for the disk group rebalance operation:

```
SQL> explain work set statement_id='DROP_ORCL:RECO_0004' for
        alter diskgroup reco drop disk ORCL:RECO_004;
```

Now, the work plan estimate that's generated can be viewed:

```
SQL> select est_work from v$asm_estimate where  statement_id='DROP_
ORCL:RECO_0004';
```

File Priority Rebalance

When a disk fails and no replacement is available, the rebalance operation redistributes the data across the remaining available disks in order to quickly restore redundancy.

With Oracle Database 12c, ASM implements file priority ordered rebalance, which provides priority-based restoration of the redundancy of critical files, such as control files and online redo log files, to ensure that they are protected if a secondary failure occurs soon afterward.

Flex ASM

In releases prior to 12c, an ASM instance ran on every node in a cluster, and the databases communicated via this local ASM instance for storage access. Furthermore, the ASM instances communicated with each other and presented shared disk groups to the database clients running in that cluster. This collection of ASM instances form what is known as an *ASM cluster domain*.

Although this ASM architecture has been the standard since the inception of ASM, it does have some drawbacks:

- Database instances are dependent on a node-specific ASM instance. Thus, if an ASM instance fails, all the database instances on that server fail as well. Additionally, as the ASM cluster size grows, the number of ASM instances grows and the communication overhead associated with managing the storage increases.

- ASM overhead scales with the size of the cluster, and cluster reconfiguration events increase with the number of servers in a cluster. From an ASM perspective, larger clusters mean more frequent reconfiguration events. A reconfiguration event is when a server enters or departs a cluster configuration. From a cluster management perspective, reconfiguration is a relatively expensive event.

- With Private Database Cloud and database consolidation, as the number of database instances increases on a server, the importance and dependence on the ASM instance increases.

The new feature Flex ASM, in Oracle Release 12*c*, changes this architecture with regard to ASM cluster organization and communication. The Flex ASM feature includes two key sub-features or architectures: Flex ASM Clustering and Remote ASM Access.

Flex ASM Clustering

In Oracle Release 12*c*, a smaller number of ASM instances run on a subset of servers in the cluster. The number of ASM instances is called the *ASM cardinality*. The default ASM cardinality is three, but that can be changed using the srvctl modify asm command. 12*c* database instance connectivity is connection time load balanced across the set of ASM instances. If a server running an ASM instance fails, Oracle Clusterware will start a new ASM instance on a different server to maintain the cardinality. If a 12*c* database instance is using a particular ASM instance, and that instance is lost because of a server crash or ASM instance failure, then the Oracle 12*c* database instance will reconnect to an ASM instance on another node. The key benefits of the Flex ASM Clustering feature include the following:

- It eliminates the requirement for an ASM instance on every cluster server.

- Database instances connect to any ASM instance in the cluster.

- Database instances can fail over to a secondary ASM instance.

- Administrators specify the cardinality of ASM instances (the default is three).

- Clusterware ensures ASM cardinality is maintained.

The Flex ASM feature can be implemented in three different ways:

- **Pure 12*c* mode**   In this mode, the Grid Infrastructure and database are both running the 12*c* version. In this model, the database fully leverages all the new 12*c* features.

- **Mixed mode**   This mode includes two sub-modes: Standard mode and Flex Cluster mode.

With Standard mode, 12c Clusterware and ASM are hard-wired to each node, similar to the pre-12c deployment style. This model allows pre-12c and 12c databases to coexist. However, in the event of a node or ASM failure, only 12c databases can leverage the failover to an existing ASM instance (on another node).

In Flex Cluster mode, ASM instances only run on specific nodes (as noted by cardinality). Pre-12c databases connect locally where ASM is running, and 12c database can be running on any node in the cluster and connect to ASM remotely.

Flex ASM Listeners

In order to support the Flex ASM feature, the ASM listener was introduced. The ASM Listener, which is functionally similar to the SCAN Listener, is a new global CRS resource with the following key characteristics:

- Three ASM listeners in Flex ASM and runs where ASM Instance is running.

- ASM instances register with all ASM listeners.

- Connectivity is load balanced across ASM instances.

Clients (DB instances) connect to ASM using ASM listener endpoints. These clients connect using connect data credentials defined by the Cluster Synchronization Services (CSS) Group Membership Services (GMS) layer. The clients seek the best connection by using the ASM Listener if it's running on the same local node; if no local-node ASM, then the clients connect to (any) remote ASM instance in the cluster.

Flex ASM Network

In versions prior to 12c, Oracle Clusterware required a public network for client application access and a private network for internode communication within the cluster; this included ASM traffic. The Flex ASM Network feature also provides the capability to isolate ASM's internal network traffic to its own dedicated private network. The Oracle Universal Installer (OUI) presents the DBA with a choice as to whether a dedicated network is to be used for ASM. The ASM network is the communication path in which all the traffic between database instances and ASM instances commence. This traffic is mostly metadata, such as a particular file's extent map. If the customer chooses, the ASM private network can be dedicated for ASM traffic or shared with CSS, and a dedicated network is not required.

Remote ASM Access

In previous versions, ASM clients use OS authentication to connect to ASM. This was a simplistic model because ASM clients and servers are always on the same server. With Oracle Database 12*c*, ASM clients and ASM servers can be on different servers (as part of the Flex ASM Network configuration). A default configuration is created when the ASM cluster is formed, which is based on the password specified for the ASM administrator at installation time. Also, by default, the password file for ASM is now stored in an ASM disk group. Having a common global password file addresses many issues related to synchronizing separate password files on many servers in a cluster. Additionally, the storing of password files in a disk group is also extended to Oracle 12 databases as well. For database instances, the DBCA utility executes commands to create an ASM user for the operating system user creating the database. This is done automatically without user intervention. Following this process, the database user can remotely log into ASM and access ASM disk groups.

ASM Optimizations on Engineered Systems

In Chapter 12, we described some of the ASM optimizations that were made specifically for Engineered Systems such as Exadata and the Oracle Database Appliance (ODA). There are several other important features in Oracle 12*c* ASM that support Engineered Systems. This section describes further ASM optimizations and features added in Oracle 12*c* for supporting Engineered Systems:

- Oracle Database 12*c* allows administrators to control the amount of resources dedicated to disk resync operations. The ASM power limit can now be set for disk resync operations, when disks are brought back online. This feature is conceptually similar to the power limit setting for disk group rebalance, with the range being 1 (least system resources) to 1024 (most system resources).

- If a resync operation is interrupted and restarted, the previously completed phases of the resync are skipped and processing recommences at the beginning of the first remaining incomplete phase. Additionally, these disk resync operations now have checkpoints enabled, such that an interrupted resync operation is automatically restarted.

With Oracle Database 12*c*, extent relocations performed by a rebalance operation can be offloaded to Exadata Storage Server. Using this capability, a single offload request can replace multiple read and write I/O requests. Offloading relocations avoids sending data to the ASM host, thus improving rebalance performance.

- For NORMAL and HIGH redundancy ASM disk groups, the algorithm that determines the placement of secondary extents uses an adjacency measure to determine the placement. In prior versions of ASM, the same algorithm and adjacency measure were used for all disk groups. Oracle Database 12c ASM provides administrators with the option to specify the content type associated with each ASM disk group. Three possible settings are allowed: data, recovery, and system. Each content type setting modifies the adjacency measure used by the secondary extent placement algorithm. The result is that the contents of disk groups with different content type settings are distributed across the available disks differently. This decreases the likelihood that a double-failure will result in data loss across NORMAL redundancy disk groups with different content type settings. Likewise, a triple-failure is less likely to result in data loss for HIGH redundancy disk groups with different content type settings.

Administrators can specify the content type to reach disk group using the disk group attribute CONTENT.TYPE. Possible values for the content type are data, recovery, or system. Specifying different content types decreases the likelihood of a single disk failure from impacting multiple disk groups in the same way.

Error Checking and Scrubbing

In previous Oracle Database versions, when data was read, a series of checks was performed on data to validate its logical consistency. If a logical corruption was detected, ASM could automatically recover by reading the mirror copies on NORMAL and HIGH redundancy disk groups. One problem with this approach is that corruption to seldom-accessed data could go unnoticed in the system for a long time between reads. Also, the possibility of multiple corruptions affecting all the mirror copies of data increases over time, so seldom-accessed data may simply be unavailable when it is required. Additionally, in releases prior to Oracle 12c, when an ASM extent was moved during a rebalance operation, it was read and written without any additional content or consistency checks.

ASM in Oracle 12c introduces proactive scrubbing capabilities, which is the process of checking content consistency in flight (as it's accessed). Scrubbing provides the capability to perform early corruption detection. Early detection of corruption is vital because undetected corruption can compromise redundancy and increases the likelihood of data loss.

Scrubbing is performed by a new background process, SCRB, that performs various checks for logical data corruptions. When a corruption is detected, the scrubbing process first tries to use available mirrors to resolve the situation. If all the mirror copies of data are corrupt or unavailable, the scrubbing process gives up and the user can recover the corrupted blocks from an RMAN backup if one is available.

■ Scrubbing can be implicitly invoked during rebalance operations or areas can be scrubbed on-demand at a disk group level, on specific areas, by an administrator. To perform on-demand scrubbing, the following command can be executed:

```
SQL> alter diskgroup data scrub repair;

SQL> alter diskgroup data scrub disk data_0004 norepair;
```

■ When scrubbing occurs during a rebalance, extents that are read during the rebalance undergo a series of internal checks to ensure their logical integrity. Scrubbing in the rebalance operation requires a new attribute to be set for the disk group.

```
SQL> alter diskgroup data set attribute 'content.check' = 'TRUE'
```

The content checking includes hardware assisted resilient data (HARD), which includes checks on user data, validation of file types from the file directory against the block contents and file directory information, and mirror side comparisons.

Other Miscellaneous Flex ASM Features

Other features that are part of Flex ASM that are notable include:

■ The maximum number of ASM disk groups is increased from 63 to 511.

■ ASM instances in an ASM cluster validate the patch level of each other. However, this is disabled for the purposes of rolling upgrades. At the end of rolling upgrades the patch level consistency is validated.

■ ASM physical metadata such as disk headers and allocation tables are now replicated. Previously, only virtual metadata had been replicated when ASM mirroring was used.

Summary

Since its inception, ASM has grown from being a purpose-built volume manager for the database to a feature-rich storage manager that supports all database-related files and includes a POSIX-complaint cluster file system. In addition, ASM has become the centerpiece of the Oracle Engineered Systems. The 12*c* ASM addresses extreme scalability and the management of real-world data types. In addition, it removes many of the limitations of previous generations of ASM. ASM also has evolved cloud computing demands of consolidation, high utilization, and high availability.

APPENDIX

Best Practices for Database Consolidation in Private Clouds

This book would not be complete if we did not touch on the overall deployment best practices for a Private Database Cloud and consolidation. Consolidation is one of the major strategies that organizations are pursuing to achieve greater efficiencies in their operations. Consolidation allows organizations to increase the utilization of IT resources, which lowers costs because fewer resources are required to achieve the same outcome. Operational costs are also reduced because fewer components and objects need to be monitored, managed, and maintained.

In this appendix, we describe how Oracle Database 11*g* can be successfully consolidated onto a private cloud through two deployment models which are based on RAC and ASM. The two models include: Provision Native Databases and Provision a schema onto a shared database. We also describe the system resources that require special sizing considerations, define workloads that should be consolidated, and address tenant isolation.

Private Database Cloud Consolidation: The Business Drivers

Three key business drivers typically motivate database consolidation onto a private cloud:

- **Reduced cost** It is well known that IT budgets are under constant scrutiny to reduce both capital expense and operating expense without compromising key business requirements. Shared resources via consolidation replace underutilized infrastructures that are typically siloed. Using shared resource pools lowers the overall costs and increases resource utilization. Capital expenditure can be reduced beyond simply shrinking server footprint by creating a higher density of databases per server through multitenancy configurations. Operational expenditure can be reduced by improving efficiency through automation, improving management productivity, and having fewer elements to manage.

- **Reduced complexity** By reducing the number of supported configurations through rationalization, standardization, and consolidation, IT departments can simplify their environments. By standardizing on a common set of building blocks, IT departments can easily deploy predefined configurations. This reduction in complexity makes it easier to manage.

- **Improved agility** Increasingly, businesses are looking to develop more agile and flexible configurations that will enable quicker mean time to market and allow rapid responses to changing business needs. Improving agility requires a simplification of the deployment stack. With improved agility, business units can enjoy faster deployment cycles, rapid provisioning, and resource elasticity.

By reducing overall complexity, creating standardized building blocks, and striving for greater consolidation, customers can benefit from not only reduced capital and operating expenses, but also quicker time to market.

Initial Server Pool Sizing

The first step in the deployment of Private Database Clouds is a move toward a standardized infrastructure. This includes the type and size of hardware stack.

To begin building the Private Database Cloud, you will need to size the cloud (or server) pool appropriately. The initial cluster size of the Private Database Cloud will depend on the number and type of applications housed as well as their capacity requirements. It is very typical to build midsize four-node server pools.

Server pools should be built and aligned with the following requirements:

- Business

    - Build separate server pools for lines of business (LOB) or departments

    - Create separate server pools for different application service levels or governance compliance

- Functional

    - Build a server pool for similar functioning applications (for example, internal-facing vs. external-facing applications)

- Technical

    - Separate server pools based on OS type, database version, or isolation requirements

    - Server pools for applications with complementary workloads

    - Server pools built around specific high-availability goals

Server pools are built for specific configurations and support specific business requirements. For example, customers can build server pools for their 11gR1 databases, one based on their regulatory data requirements (PCI, PII, HIPAA, and so on) and another for their business-critical 11gR2 applications. It is a best practice for applications with similar SLA requirements to coexist in a consolidated environment; in other words, do not mix mission-critical applications with noncritical applications in the same server pool.

The number of applications that can be consolidated will depend on size, resource consumption, and the SLAs of the applications that will be consolidated. Furthermore, a predefined threshold of the system resource usage will also dictate how much can be consolidated.

Standardized modular building blocks should be used. For example, you could standardize on a four-node cluster consisting of dual sockets, with 10 cores per socket. It is recommended to have a minimum of three servers in a server pool, as this will tolerate the failure of one or two servers and protect from server failure during planned outages, such as rolling upgrades scenarios. However, careful consideration should be given to CPU, memory, and storage configurations. Each of these resources is covered in this appendix.

Sizing applications that will be placed in the private cloud depends on if these are new or existing applications. For new applications, initial sizing of the pool is the same as any current capacity planning exercise; this includes leveraging tools such as AWR reports, vmstat, and iostat to determine consumption. EM 12c Consolidation Planner provides a streamlined approach for gathering this dataset.

The next section describes considerations when configuring physical resources for the private cloud.

CPU

Initial sizing for the CPU should include understanding what applications will be housed and the scope for this base. Then you should include 10-percent overhead for operational tasks, such as backups, ASM rebalance jobs, and so on, and 15-percent overhead to account for failover of the workload. This generally leaves the CPU capacity at 75 percent. It is recommended that you operate the server pool nodes at 75-percent CPU capacity to allow for a good balance between system usage and headroom.

A database that gets provisioned in the server pool should get a default minimum of two CPUs. This can be enforced using the CPU_COUNT init.ora parameter or using the Instance Caging feature (for which you also set the CPU_COUNT). Here is the difference between implementing Instance Caging and setting CPU_COUNT:

■ The CPU_COUNT init.ora parameter setting simply limits the number of CPUs that the database "sees" and implicitly establishes internal SGA memory structures as well as database background process settings. Additionally, many exposed and internal init.ora parameters are derived from this CPU_COUNT setting (for example, dbwr_processes and library_cache_latches). Note that CPU_COUNT does not enforce any resource limits.

■ Instance Caging employs the Database Resource Manager (DBRM) feature as well as leverages CPU_COUNT to enforce resource usage limits. For example, if a database instance is using Instance Caging with CPU_COUNT set to 4, then no more than four active user processes will consume CPU at the same time. Instance Caging does not enforce resource limits on background processes (DBWR, LGWR, PMON, and so on). It is highly recommended that you implement Instance Caging in consolidated configurations.

Partitioning vs. Overprovisioning

Instance Caging is a means of reducing contention for CPU resources between multiple database instances sharing the same server. This is done by setting a maximum on the number of CPUs on which the processes associated with a given instance are scheduled. There are two approaches to defining the number of CPUs available to an instance: partitioning and overprovisioning.

Partitioned CPU Approach

The partitioned CPU approach ensures that the aggregate CPU_COUNT setting across all database instances on a given node does not exceed the number of CPUs. The partitioned approach is therefore recommended for mission-critical databases.

With this configuration, there should be no contention for CPU resources between database instances. However, if the database instances do not consistently use their CPU resources, these resources cannot be utilized by the other database instances, making it inefficient from a utilization perspective.

The following recommendation can be used in the partitioned CPU approach for an instance. This recommendation ensures that CPU resources are available for other critical Clusterware resources and processes, such as ASM, CSS, and CRS agents:

```
Sum (CPU_COUNT) < 75% x Total CPUs
```

Oversubscription Approach

As the name states, the oversubscription approach employs an oversubscription of CPUs on a given node (that is, the sum of the CPU_COUNT across all instances on a node can exceed the number of CPUs). The advantage of the overprovisioning approach is better resource utilization; however, there can be potential CPU contention if all databases are heavily loaded at the same time, which will degrade database performance and can affect availability. This approach should be deployed for test/development databases, noncritical databases, or any databases that do not have stringent SLA requirements. Furthermore, databases that consume heavy I/O resources or are highly transactional should not be consolidated into an overprovisioned server pool.

For this model, use the following recommendation, which limits the sum of CPU_COUNTs to two times the number of CPUs:

```
Sum (CPU_COUNT) <= up to 2 x Total CPUs
```

This calculation is based on hyper-threading of two CPU-threads per core, typical in x86 systems. Care should be taken when overprovisioning CPUs on SMT or CMT systems, because the CPU-thread ratio can be quite high. It is important to note that Oracle determines the number of CPUs on the system based on the value returned back from the OS. In cases where the server has enabled hyper-threading (HT), the value returned could be threads and not actual cores. Threads are not real CPUs and thus overprovisioning CPUs based on thread count may result in inefficient and unpredictable results when workloads peak at the same time.

> **NOTE**
> *In overprovisioned systems under heavy load there is very little or no room left for the critical clusterware resources, potentially leading to clusterwide failures due to single node failure.*

Memory

Configuring memory can be more straightforward in the server pool than CPU sizing. Note that unlike for CPU configuration, it is highly discouraged that you overcommit memory resources.

For existing databases that will be consolidated, you determine SGA and PGA memory using AWR reports, V$SGASTAT/V$PGASTAT, or EM Automatic Memory Advisor. For new applications, set conservative values for memory_target and aggressive values for memory_max_target, after the basic sizing exercise is performed.

The following are general guidelines for the memory footprints. Once the SGA/PGA information is obtained, evaluate the following before each migration or placement into the private cloud.

OLTP applications:

```
SUM of databases (SGA_TARGET + PGA_AGGREGATE_TARGET) < 80%
Physical Memory per Database Node
```

DW/BI applications:

```
SUM of databases (SGA_TARGET + 3 * PGA_AGGREGATE_TARGET) < 80%
Physical Memory per Database Node
```

Storage

It is recommended that you review existing applications' storage usage before consolidation. Databases in siloed configuration are typically provisioned with more storage than they will use, so one of the key items to review is how much of the allocated storage is actually in use (that is, how much is free and how much contains data). Be watchful of systems that use thin provisioned storage, as this can be misleading with respect to provisioned storage. Gross overallocation of storage allows for a good opportunity to consolidate storage space. Before migrating applications into the Private Database Cloud, application owners should ensure that obsolete or unneeded data is cleansed or archived. This not only improves storage efficiency, but also improves overall migration time.

Storage IOPS is probably the most overlooked area in database consolidation. After all, consolidating databases is essentially the aggregation of IOPS. DBAs should look at average and peak IOPS for each database to be consolidated as part of the consolidation planning exercise.

Use AWR reports to collect the following I/O metrics:

```
IOPS = "physical reads total I/O requests" + "physical writes total I/O requests"
MBytes/s = "physical reads total bytes" + "physical writes total bytes"
```

These metrics will aid in determining the storage throughput needed to support the application. Aggregate the IOPS or MBytes/s for all nodes if the existing application is running on RAC. Keep in mind that each layer in the I/O stack should be able to sustain this I/O load as well as future consolidated loads.

Complementary Workloads

One of the key aspects of a successful Private Database Cloud deployment is to ensure that only complementary workloads are housed. Mixing noncomplementary workloads leads to missed SLAs, outages, and a poor consolidation deployment. When consolidating workloads, ensure that the consolidated workloads' peak CPU usage does not overwhelmingly exceed the average CPU usage; in other words, the gap between peak and average CPU usage should be minimal. Satisfying this goal means that the CPUs are being utilized as fully as possible. Here are some points to keep in mind:

- When complementary workloads are combined, the average overall load increases more than the peak.

- When optimally complementary workloads are combined, only the average increases; the peak remains unchanged.

- In antagonistic workloads, the peak increases more than the average; that is, during low-usage periods, CPUs are underutilized but must be kept available for the peak loads.

Isolation

Isolation requirements can influence the method or degree of consolidation possible. Whether you consolidate multiple application schemas in a single database, host multiple databases on a single platform, or some combination of both approaches, depends on the level of isolation the system demands. The two basic deployments are database consolidation and schema consolidation.

Database Consolidation

Before building out a database consolidation environment, it is important to define what applications will be hosted in the server pool—production, noncritical production, or test/dev. Applications of differing criticality or SLA should not be consolidated together.

Schema Consolidation

In this deployment model, the consolidated database essentially consists of one or more application schemas running across one or more servers in a server pool. Customers with whom we have worked in deploying this model typically consolidate 15–20 applications (schemas). In the schema consolidation model, the tenancy granularity is the schema. Therefore, the schema needs to have proper isolation.

Although schema consolidation provides the highest level of consolidation, careful consideration and planning must be done to ensure that the consolidated applications can coexist. For example, check for schema namespace collisions and confirm certification of packaged applications to run in these consolidation configurations. The implementation schema consolidation has become very streamlined with the 12c pluggable databases feature. However, you'll need to be implementing 12c databases to take advantage of this feature. In the meantime, you can follow our best practices in this section.

Isolation can be categorized into four areas: fault, resource, security, and operational. Each cloud model deals with isolation slightly differently, using OS and/ or Database built-in capabilities, often in combination with advanced features or products to provide a more complete solution, commensurate with the risk.

The following sections focus on considerations for tenant isolation in the Private Database Cloud, showing the differences for each model.

Fault Isolation in Database Consolidation

In the database consolidation model, the multitenancy granularity is the database, so each database (and each database instance) is isolated from the other databases in the server pool. Although all the databases may run from the same Oracle Home installation, database faults are generally isolated to a failing instance; that is, fault isolation is maintained by fencing off the offending instance. For example, if a database instance becomes unresponsive, then one of the neighboring node's LMS process will request CSS to perform a "member kill" operation against the offending instance. In rare cases, where the unresponsive instance cannot be killed, an invasive operation such as a node reboot is invoked; in these rare cases, other database instances will be affected. However, proper application design and implementation of documented best practices can limit the impact of instance or node failure. For example, the use of RAC features such as Fast Application Notification (FAN) and Fast Connection Failover provide a faster mechanism for event notification (node or database instance down events) to the application. This allows the application to reconnect more quickly, minimizing the overall impact of the outage.

Fault Isolation in Schema Consolidation

In this model, an application fault in one schema will not cause other applications to fail. However, login storms or improperly configured application/mid-tiers can impact other consolidated applications. To minimize the impact of login storms, configure mid-tier connection pools appropriately. In some cases, login-rate limiters can be defined for the Oracle Listener. Poorly written database resident code, such as PL/SQL, can also affect other unrelated applications. A thorough testing of the application as well as code review is necessary to prevent application faults.

Operational Isolation in Database Consolidation

Operational isolation ensures that any management or maintenance performed on a database or its operating environment does not affect other running databases in the pool, including startup/shutdown of instances, patching, and backup/recovery.

Startup/Shutdown   In most consolidation configurations, the number of Oracle Homes is kept to a minimum, and typically one Oracle Home is used for all the consolidated databases. To provide operational isolation, create named users for each Cloud DBA for the database, and add those users to the password file (needs REMOTE_LOGIN_PASSWORDFILE set to EXCLUSIVE). Then grant SYSDBA privileges to those named users. By having different password files for each database, users can gain SYSDBA privileges only to their database. To perform operational functions, such as startup or shutdown, the Cloud DBA should connect to the appropriate database user with the SYSDBA privilege. Typically this is performed via EM; therefore, the necessary database credentials need to be established in EM.

Patching   Patching databases in a consolidated environment involves two tasks: planning for the patch application (logistics) and the actual patch execution itself. When you're building Private Cloud environments, downtime SLAs and expectations should be set for scheduled as well as unscheduled patching. The request for one-off patching (or frequent patching) is not efficient and should be discouraged, as the patching may affect many databases. A schedule for patch application should be predefined and acknowledged by all participating tenants. For example, a schedule for Oracle Patch Set Updates (PSUs) should be well defined. One-off patches should be evaluated for priority and relevance with respect to the entire database consolidated community. When patches need to be applied, the most efficient method is to stage the patch, which involves cloning the Oracle Home, applying the patch to the cloned home, and finally switching the Oracle Home. Rolling patch application should be leveraged where possible.

If the patch management logistics across databases is not practical or if sharing of SYSDBA across databases is not desired, then a separate Oracle Home for a group of databases can be an alternative. For these cases, each Oracle Home should use a distinct username and OSDBA. However, running database instances from different Oracle Homes does increase complexity and will affect overall efficiency.

Operational Isolation in Schema Consolidation

Operational isolation for this model includes minimizing the impact of the recovery/ restore of lost data or patch management. Here are some key points:

- For the most efficient data restore possible, a careful design of the backup policy is needed. The backup method should include the restore granularity appropriate for the application. Typically for schema consolidation, nightly backups as well as Datapump exports of the schema are needed. If data is lost or deleted, then features such as Flashback Table, Flashback Query, and Flashback Transaction should be used to provide the least invasive approach for restore.

- The patching issues in schema consolidation are similar to those in database consolidation.

Resource Isolation in Database Consolidation

Resource isolation deals with the allocation and segregation of system resources. In database consolidation, the competing resources include CPU, memory, and I/O (storage capacity as well as IOPs):

- **Memory**   Appropriate memory_target and memory_ max_target values need to be set on a per-instance basis for each node, and must be maintained consistently across all instances of the same database. Note that memory_ target does not enforce a hard ceiling for PGA values.

- **CPU**   Like memory settings, the CPU values should be set appropriately. As discussed in the previous section, this can be done by setting CPU_COUNT to a specific value or enabling the 11gR2 Instance Caging feature. The latter is recommended because it also enforces a Database Resource Manager (DBRM) resource plan providing better control of CPU consumption. Follow the best practices outlined in the "CPU" section.

- **I/O**   Providing I/O isolation would involve either creating different Diskgroups for each of the databases or using I/O Resource Manager (available only in Exadata environment) to control the IOPS.

Resource Isolation in Schema Consolidation

With multiple applications contending for the same database and systems resources, resource management is a necessity for schema consolidation. Oracle Database resource profile limits provide basic "knobs" to control consumption and can be supplemented with Oracle Database Resource Manager along with Oracle QoS. Applications can be put into consumer groups with an appropriate resource plan directive mapping with a resource plan. This will specify how CPU, I/O, and parallel server resources are to be allocated to the consumer group.

The key challenge in these environments is storage capacity management. Cloud DBAs can cap the storage consumed by applications using tablespace quota. There should be close monitoring of the tablespace space usage by each schema so that growth patterns and thresholds can be managed.

Security Isolation in Database Consolidation

In any consolidated environment, a security implementation should use the "least privileges" approach to hardening the environment. In most cases, a single Oracle Home will be used by all database instances on a given node. If several databases are sharing the same Oracle Home, then any user who is part of the OSDBA group for that Oracle Home will have SYSDBA access to all database instances running from that home. This is a good approach to reduce manageability overhead; however, it does open security issues.

It is recommended that you implement the following best practices for this type of configuration:

- Minimize access to the database server (that is, SQL*Net Pipe-only access).

- Use named user accounts for DBAs with sudo access for privileged commands.

- Implement and enable Database Vault to provide role separation to control user data access:

  - To protect application and schema data from unauthorized access employ Database Vault using Realms. The security administrator should enable Realms for each application upon provisioning the database.

  - For E-Business Suite, Siebel, and PeopleSoft users, deploy the redefined Data Vault Realms.

  - Encrypt data where necessary.

Security Isolation in Schema Consolidation

Security isolation between schemas is one of the most important aspects of cloud management. Out-of-the-box security for Oracle database profiles can be used to limit access to data. However, many times, deeper security measures and policies must be put in place. This may include protecting data at rest, granular access control, as well as security auditing. For these cases, encryption should be implemented where necessary, via Advanced Security, realm-based access control, Database Vault, and Audit Vault for run-time audit management. The following are also security best practices for schema consolidation:

- Only Cloud DBA should have SYSDBA, SYSOPER, and SYSASM access.

- Guest DBAs only have schema-level access and V$ view access.

- Ensure use of private synonyms.

- Use strong database user passwords.

- Set appropriate values for PASSWORD_LOCK_TIME and FAILED_LOGIN_ ATTEMPTS.

Summary

Deploying databases with private clouds is a proven model for the delivery of database services. Consolidation onto shared resources in a private cloud enables IT departments to improve quality of service levels—as measured in terms of database performance, availability, and data security—and reduce capital and operating costs. Private clouds consolidate servers, storage, operating systems, databases, and mixed workloads (schemas) onto a shared hardware and software infrastructure. The higher the consolidation density achieved, the greater the return on investment. Oracle's complete technology stack of hardware and software, showcased in Oracle's Engineered Systems, offers unique capabilities for all levels of consolidation.

This appendix described the best practices for consolidating Oracle Databases in the database consolidation and schema consolidation private cloud deployment models. Server pool sizing, selection of workloads to consolidate, resource management, and tenant isolation were discussed in detail, preparing you for an efficient and effective consolidation plan.

Index

Symbols and Numbers

+ (plus) sign, in ASM filenames, 217
3Par InServ Storage Server
  thin provisioning and, 338
  using ASRU with, 340–344

A

ABORT clause, in ASM instance shutdown, 33
ACCESS_CONTROL.ENABLED attribute
  for ACL, 188
  function of, 99
ACCESS_CONTROL.UMASK attribute
  for ACL, 188
  function of, 99
ACD (Active Change Directory), 218
ACFS. *See* ASM Cluster File System (ACFS)
ACFS Encryption
  configuration/utilization of, 302
  features of, 299
  hierarchy, 300
  implementation of, 303–308
  key management for, 300–302
ACFS replication
  admin user setup for, 279–280
  compare command in, 291–292
  creating Net Services for, 281–284
  file system setup for, 280–281
  initiation of, 285–288
  network setup for, 281
  overview of, 276
  pause and resume in, 288–290
  planning for, 277–278
  primary file systems in, 276–277
  restrictions/standby file systems in, 277
  setting network tunable parameters for, 284
  sizing file systems in, 290–291
  tagging with, 278–279
  termination of, 292–293
  validating network configuration for, 284–285
ACFS Security
  configuration of, 296–298
  enabling/disabling, 296
  encryption logging and, 298–299
  features of, 294–295
  implementation of, 303–308
  security administrator in, 295–296
ACFS snapshots
  creating, 273–274
  read-only, 272
  read-write, 273
  security/encryption in, 303
ACFS tagging
  with ACFS replication, 278–279
  overview of, 275–276
ACFSx volume background process, 262
ACL. *See* File Access Control (ACL)
Active Change Directory (ACD), in file creation, 218
ADD command, storage array migration and, 210
ADD DISK SQL statement, 237
admin user setup, for ACFS replication, 279–280
ADR (Automatic Diagnostic Repository), 253
Advanced Encryption Standard (AES), for ACFS
  Encryption keys, 301–302
ADVM. *See* ASM Dynamic Volume Manager (ADVM)
agility improvement, with database consolidation, 366–367
AIX operating system, configuring ASM disks for, 61–63
alert log file, monitoring, 129–132

aliases, creating, 184–185
allocation
file, 217, 219–224
space. *See* space allocation
allocation units (AUs)
extents consisting of, 197
multiple contiguous, 220–221
placing lower-numbered, 220
restoring stale, 232–233
setting larger sizes for, 199–200
in space allocation, 196–197
in striping, 198–199
ALTER DISKGROUP command
modifying templates, 186
for rebalance power management,
204–205
ALTER DISKGROUP DISK ONLINE command, in
disk resynchronization, 88
ALTER DISKGROUP MOUNT RESTRICT
command, in fast rebalance operations, 207
AMDU. *See* ASM Metadata Dump Utility
(AMDU)
AMM (Automatic Memory Management), 44, 46
application rules, in ACFS Security, 295
ARB*x* background processes, 42, 201
archive log files
running out of space, 137–139
transferring between ASM instances,
146–149
ASM. *See* Automatic Storage Management (ASM)
ASM cluster domains, 31, 358–359
ASM Cluster File System (ACFS)
ADVM management in, 260–261
ADVM volume device files for, 248–249
allocated space utilization by, 196–200
background processes supporting,
262–263
combined with ADVM, 5
components of, 240
configuration of, 249–251
CRS Managed file systems in, 251–254
deleting file systems in, 259–260
deployment of, 251
as disk-to-disk backup destination,
145–146
driver resource, 265
drivers supporting, 263–264
exporting for NFS access, 268–269
features of, 240–242
file I/O, 243–244
function of, 2
integration with Oracle Clusterware,
264–265
Mount Registry, 255–257, 266
primary file system, 276–277
recovery, 246–247

Registry Managed file systems, 251,
253–257
Registry resource, 265
resizing file systems in, 257–258
resource dependencies in, 265–266
shutdown sequence for, 267
space allocation, 244–245
startup on GI for standalone server,
267–268
startup sequence for, 266
unmounting file systems in, 258–259
utilizing DLM, 245–246
ASM Configuration Assistant (ASMCA)
ASM Instances tab of, 327
creating CRS Managed ACFS file system,
251–254
Disk Groups tab of, 327–329, 330
implementing ACFS Security/Encryption,
303–304
overview of, 326
ASM Dynamic Volume Manager (ADVM)
COMPATIBLE.ADVM attribute and, 98
dismounting ACFS file systems on, 33
drivers supporting, 263–264
enabling DRL, 247–248
features of, 5
IDP for, 82
management of, 260–261
nonsupport of NFS, 59
recovery, 246–247
volume device files, 248–249
+ASM instance, 36
ASM instance(s)
adding disks to disk groups, 237
ASMCA with, 327
ASMCMD capabilities for, 331
background processes supporting ACFS,
262–263
connecting to RDBMS instances, 216
copying files from one to another,
145–149
creating files and, 217–218
encountering read errors, 227
encountering write errors, 228
examining disks available to, 235–236
forced shutdown of, 247, 259
forming cluster domains, 358–359
managing, 31
metadata and, 30
modes of connecting to, 33
monitoring of, 129–132
mounting disk groups, 236–237
one operating system group for, 34
OS/password file authentication for, 38
parameters used in, 43–46
rebalance operations by, 207, 230–232

recovery, 234–235
relocation and, 233–234
separate OS groups for, 34–35, 36
starting up, 31–32
stopping, 32–33
SYSASM privileges for, 35–38
SYSDBA privileges for, 37
system privileges for, 33–34
ASM Metadata Dump Utility (AMDU)
examples of utilizing, 347–352
functions of, 346–347
ASM password files, 355
ASM Storage Reclamation Utility (ASRU)
with 3Par InServ Storage Server, 340–344
determining when to use, 339–340
features/phases of, 338–339
thin provisioning and, 338
ASMCA. See ASM Configuration Assistant
(ASMCA)
ASMCMD command set
for ADVM management, 260–261
capabilities of, 330–331
ASMCMD cp command
for copying control files, 139
for copying files between ASM instances,
146–149
for processing backup SPFILEs, 41
ASMCMD mkdg command, in creating disk
groups, 97, 111
ASM_DISKSTRING initialization parameter, in
disk discovery, 52–55, 235
ASMLIB tool
components of, 162
configuring, 165–166
creating disks with, 166–168
device discovery with, 160
device management with, 160–161
device mapper and, 172
discovering disks with, 168–169
I/O processing function of, 161–162
installation of, 162–164
migrating to, 169–170
multipathing utilities and, 170–171
renaming disks with, 168
troubleshooting, 173–176
upgrading, 164–165
ASM_POWER_LIMIT parameter
for power management, 204
in rebalance operations, 201, 208
ASM_PREFERRED_READ_FAILURE_GROUPS
initialization parameter, 85–87
+ASMx instance, 31
ASRU. See ASM Storage Reclamation
Utility (ASRU)
ASSM (Automatic Segment Space
Management), 106

attributes, of ASM
compatibility, 97–98
disk group management, 98
Exadata systems, 98–99
file access control, 99
AUs. See allocation units (AUs)
AU_SIZE attribute
in disk group creation, 100, 200
function of, 98
auto-terminate feature, for ACFS primary file
systems, 281
Automatic Diagnostic Repository (ADR), 253
Automatic Extent Allocation, 198
Automatic Memory Management (AMM),
44, 46
Automatic Segment Space Management
(ASSM), 106
Automatic Storage Management (ASM)
added redundancy in, 21–22
background processes of, 42–43
cloning over, 111–116
cloning process, 107–111
cloud computing and, 8–9
in Clusterware startup, 24–26
compatibility, 101–102
components, SYSDBA managing, 37
database interaction with, 106–107,
117–122
development of, 2–3
disk device discovery, 52–56
disk groups in, 27–28, 71–72
expansion of, 5–6
forced shutdown of, 246–247, 259
function of, 2
implementing IDP in, 80–82
issues DBAs encounter with,
136–141
moving databases to, 149–151
moving SPFILE to, 152
moving temporary tablespaces to,
151–152
multipathing and, 64–65
OCR files stored in, 18
optimizations for Exadata, 314–315
rebalance operations, 230–232
resync operations, 232–233
separate authentication groups for,
34–35, 36
storage device configuration, 51–52
storage provisioning, 50–51
SYSASM privilege for administration of,
35–37
thin provisioning compatibility, 4–5
third-party volume managers and, 57
unique features of, 3–4
voting files in, 18–20

Automatic Storage Management (ASM), 12c
release
error checking/scrubbing in, 362–363
failure group repair timer in, 357
Fast Disk Replacement feature in,
356–357
fast disk resync/checkpoints in, 355–356
file priority rebalance in, 358
Flex ASM feature in, 359–361
optimizations for Engineered Systems,
361–362
overview of, 354
password files in, 354–355
rebalance time estimates in, 357–358
remote access to, 361
availability, of ACFS, 241

B

backup files, setting up ACL and, 191–193
Bequeath connection, to ASM instances, 216
blacklist-exceptions section, in multipath
configuration, 68
blacklist section, in multipath configuration, 68
bootstrap, at Clusterware startup, 26
buffer cache, for metadata, 246

C

CANDIDATE HEADER_STATUS of disks, 56, 73
cardinality, Flex ASM and, 359–360
Cell Disks, Exadata, 55, 311
Cell Services (Celsrv), Exadata, 311–312
CELL.SMART_SCAN_CAPABLE attribute, 99
central processing units (CPUs)
partitioning vs. overprovisioning of,
369–370
for Private Database Cloud consolidation,
368–369
reduced overhead, ASMLIB and, 161–162
resource isolation and, 374
checkpoints, resync operations supporting,
355–356
CKPT background processes, 42
cloning process
of ASM software stack, 107–111
command-line mode in, 111–116
role of DB_UNIQUE_NAME in, 142
cloud computing
build vs. buy approach to, 310
database consolidation and. See Private
Database Cloud consolidation
definition of, 2
enterprise, 7–10

features of, 6
key requirements for, 8
managing databases and, 6–7
cluster agents, 24, 26–27
Cluster Ready Services (CRS)
ASM-related resources, 27–28
in Clusterware startup, 25
functions of, 12
Cluster Ready Services daemon (CRSd), 13, 24
Cluster Synchronization Services (CSS)
in ASM instance recovery, 234–235
in Clusterware startup, 25
services of, 12
cluster volume managers (CVMs), third-party, 57
clusters
access to data between, 10
of ASM instances, 31, 358–359
creating stretch, 23
extended, 84–85, 229–230
large/reconfigured, 8
Clusterware. See Oracle Clusterware
coarse striping, 198, 221–222
COD. See Continuing Operations Directory
(COD)
command-line mode
configuring Exadata storage and, 312
creating databases in, 111–116
command rules, in ACFS Security, 295
compaction phase
of ASRU operation, 338–339
of rebalance operations, 201
compare command, in ACFS replication,
291–292
compatibility attributes
database, 101
disk group, 100
overview of, 97–98
RDBMS, 101
COMPATIBLE.ADVM attribute, 98
COMPATIBLE.ASM attribute
with Exadata, 317
function of, 97
for password file storage, 355
COMPATIBLE.RDBMS attribute, 97–98
complementary workloads, in database
consolidation, 371
complexity reduction, with database
consolidation, 366
compute servers, Exadata, 310
configuration
of ACFS, 249–251
of ACFS Encryption, 302
of ACFS Security, 296–298
of ASMLIB, 165–166
of disks for AIX, 61–63
of disks for Linux, 59–60

of disks on NFS, 57–58
multipath, 68–71
of Oracle Net Services, 281–284
of storage devices, 51–52
CONTENT.TYPE attribute
with Exadata, 317
function of, 98
Continuing Operations Directory (COD)
in file creation, 217–218
in file deletion, 219
in rebalance operations, 201, 230
recovery, 235
control files
aliases and, 184
AMDU extracting, 347–348
database dependency and, 27–28, 123
moving to ASM, 139–141, 151
storage of, 73–74, 123
striping and, 198
cords, replication log, 276–277
cost reduction, with database consolidation, 366
CPU_COUNT init.ora parameter, in database
consolidation, 368
CPUs. See central processing units (CPUs)
crash recovery, 234–235
Create ASM Disk Group screen, 16–17
CREATE DISKGROUP command
setting appropriate AU size, 200
specifying failure group, 82
CREATE DISKGROUP SQL statement, 237
CREATE USER command, for SYSASM
privileges, 37
Credentials screen, for ASM, 121
cross-cluster sharing, in enterprise clouds, 10
CRS. See Cluster Ready Services (CRS)
CRS Managed ACFS file systems
creation of, 251–254
deleting, 260
startup sequence, 266
unmounting, 258–259
crsctl stop crs command, for Clusterware
shutdown, 32, 267
CRSDATA disk groups, 73–74
CSS. See Cluster Synchronization Services (CSS)
CVMs. See cluster volume managers (CVMs),
third-party

D

-d option, in ASMLIB disk creation, 166
daemons
CRS/CSS, 12
GI stack management and, 13–14
multithreaded, 24, 26–27
OHASd. See Oracle High Availability
Services daemon (OHASd)

data at rest, encryption for, 299
DATA disk groups
creating, 17–18, 76
extent distribution in, 197–198
placing ADVM volumes in, 250
placing control files in, 139
placing SPFILE in, 40
data files
AMDU extracting, 348–352
ASM filenames and, 180–183
database dependency and, 27–28, 123
specifying default locations for, 143–144
Data Guard
enabling, for ACFS replication, 284
for moving databases to ASM, 149
restoring backup on, 145
data movement, in rebalance operations,
230–232
database administrator (DBA)
in ACFS configuration, 249–250
ASM issues encountered by, 136–141
database area disk groups, 123
Database Configuration Assistant (DBCA)
creating database with, 118–122
launching, 117
database consolidation model
fault isolation in, 372–373
operational isolation in, 373–374
resource isolation in, 374
security isolation in, 375
database consolidation, onto private cloud.
See Private Database Cloud consolidation
database exports, ACFS storage of, 253
Database File Locations screen, 120
database files
creating in disk groups, 180–183
creating templates for, 186–187
privileges categories of, 188
Database Identification screen, DBCA, 119
database password files, 355
database(s)
backing up to FRA disk group, 142–143
compatibility settings, 101
disk group management and, 122–123
encryption for, 299
interaction between ASM and, 106–107
interaction with ASM, 117–122
moving from file system to ASM, 149–151
patching, 373–374
security for, 293–294
DBA. See database administrator (DBA)
DBCA. See Database Configuration Assistant
(DBCA)
DB_CACHE_SIZE value, ASM SGA
component, 44
DB_CREATE_FILE_DEST parameter, enabling
OMF, 181

DB_CREATE_ONLINE_LOG_DEST initialization parameters, default locations and, 143–145
DBMS_FILE_TRANSFER database package, in creating TTSs, 124–128
DB_RECOVERY_FILE_DEST parameter, enabling OMF, 181
DB_UNIQUE_NAME, impact on ASM directory structure, 141–142
DBWR background processes, 42
deallocation phase, of ASRU operation, 339
default locations, for data files/redo logs, 143–145
defaults section, in multipath configuration, 68
deployment
    of ACFS, 251
    of ASMLIB in RAC, 167
    of extended clusters, 84–85
/dev/asmdisk directory, in disk discovery, 53–54
/dev/oracleasm/disks/, ASMLIB and, 166, 175
device mapper, Linux. See Linux device mapper
device-specific settings, in multipath configuration, 68
Direct Network File System (dNFS), 59
directory(ies)
    ACFS space allocation and, 244
    creating user-defined, 183
    hierarchical format of, 184–185
    structure for ASM, impact of DB_UNIQUE_NAME on, 141–142
Dirty Region Logging (DRL)
    ADVM enabling, 247–248
    features of, 91
    mirror resilvering and, 228–229
disaster recovery data center, 146–149
discovery set
    disk discovery and, 235–236
    in mounting disk groups, 236, 237
discovery, voting, 20
Discretionary Access Control (DAC) model, for database security, 293–294
disk devices
    creating in Solaris, 61
    identification of, 52–56
disk discovery
    KFOD utility for, 344–346
    in mounting disk groups, 236
    role of, 235–236
disk failure
    I/O failures and, 93–96
    issues causing, 92
    recovery from, 88–92
disk group(s). See also specific disk groups
    adding disks to, 237
    ASMCA configuring/creating, 327–329, 330
    ASMCMD management of, 331

compatibility, 101–102
compatibility attributes, 100
conveying changes in, 31
creating, 72–76, 237
creating SPFILE in, 41
DATA. See DATA disk groups
database files in, 71–72, 122–123
extent distribution in, 197–198
extent sets in, 83
external redundancy, 18
features of, 71–72
fragmentation in, 200
imbalanced, 207–210, 220
management, attributes of, 98
monitoring, 133–136
mounting, 76, 236–237
moving control files to, 139–141
moving tablespaces between, 153–155
names for, 76–77
normal/high redundancy, 19
numbers, 77
parameters related to, 43
recovery, 235
renamedg command for, 332–337
resizing, 203
resources, CSR-managed, 26–28
sample setup of ACL on, 189–193
as self-describing, 236
setting up ACL on, 188–189
space allocation in, 196–200
space management and, 3–4
templates associated with, 186–187
types of, 72
disk header(s)
    in creating disk groups, 237
    disk numbers in, 77–78
    validation, 72–73, 76
disk names
    ASMLIB management of, 160–161, 166
    assignment of, 76–77
disk partnerships
    features of, 83–84
    mirror extents and, 225–226
Disk Visibility reactive health checker, 47
diskmon processes, for automated disk management, 316–317
DISK_REPAIR_TIME attribute
    disk failures and, 88–89
    disk I/O errors and, 94
    function of, 98
disk(s). See also logical unit numbers (LUNs)
    adding/dropping, 210, 213
    adding to disk groups, 237
    ASMCMD management of, 331
    automated management of, 315–317
    bringing offline/online, 89–91

configuring for AIX, 61–63
configuring for Linux, 59–60
configuring on NFS, 57–58
converting to/from ASMLIB, 169–170
creating ASMLIB, 166–168
discovering ASMLIB, 168–169
extents evenly distributed in, 196–198
header status of, 56
hot spare, 224–225
management/discovery, 160–161
maximum/minimum size of, 51
numbers, 77–78
ODA naming conventions for, 320
offline status of, 228
online status of, 237
renaming ASMLIB, 168
resizing, 203
unequally sized, 208–210
various meanings of, 50
distributed lock manager (DLM), ACFS utilizing, 245–246
dNFS (Direct Network File System), 59
DRL. *See* Dirty Region Logging (DRL)
DROP command, storage array migration and, 210
DROP FILE command, with closed/open files, 219
DROP TEMPLATE command, 186
DROP USER command, SYSASM privileges and, 37–38

E

Ellison, Larry, 4
encryption
in ACFS snapshots, 303
for database data, 299
for file system data. *See* ACFS Encryption
logging, in ACFS Security, 298–299
endianness systems, 211
enterprise cloud computing
cost-efficiency/policy management of, 9–10
key requirements for, 8
managing databases and, 7
error checking, in 12c ASM, 362–363
ERRORS option, in rebalance operations, 205
/etc/init.d/oracleasm utility, for ASMLIB configuration, 165
Exadata
11gR2 optimizations for, 313–314
ASM optimizations for, 314–315
ASM-specific attributes, 317
automated disk management in, 315–317
compute servers, 310
configuring failure groups in, 82

disk discovery in, 55, 314–315
failure groups in, 225
InfiniBand interconnect with, 312–313
Storage Server, 311–312
systems attributes of, 98–99
utilizing iDB protocol, 313
EXCLUSIVE locks, DLM, 245
expander-to-disk connectivity, ODA and, 319
expansion phase, of ASRU operation, 339
extended clusters
deployment of, 84–85
preferred read and, 229–230
extent maps, sent to RDBMS instances, 218
extent sets, ASM, allocation of, 83
extents
allocation units in, 196–197
coarse striping and, 221–222, 223
distribution issues, 211–213
even distribution of, 197–198
file allocation and, 219–220
fine-grained striping and, 222–224
mirroring based on. *See also* mirror extents, 224–225
rebalancing distribution of, 200–203
rebalancing movement of, 230–232
relocation of, 233–234, 361
resync operations and, 232–233
variable-sized, 198, 220–221
external database data, ACFS storage of, 253
external-redundancy disk groups
added redundancy for, 21–22
ASM disk names for, 77
ASM stripping and, 72
features of, 18
file allocation within, 219–220
mounting, 236
OCR recovery in, 22
extproc calls, ACFS file system for, 254
extracted files, AMDU producing, 347

F

-f option, in alert log monitoring, 132
failover path, in multipath configuration, 69
failure groups
ASM redundancy, 225
choice of, 82–83
definition of, 19
disk partners and, 225–226
Fast Disk Replacement feature in, 356–357
Fast Disk Resync feature and, 88–92
levels of mirroring in, 78–79
quorum, 23–24, 85
recovering, 84
repair timer for, 357

Fast Disk Replacement feature, 356–357
Fast Disk Resync feature
    12c ASM improvements in, 355–356
    comparison to DRL, 91
    for disk failure recovery, 88–92
Fast Rebalance, 206–207
Fast Recovery Area (FRA) disk groups
    database backup to, 142–143
    in disk group creation, 74
    features of, 123
    placing control files in, 139–141
    running out of space, 137–139
fault isolation
    in database consolidation model,
        372–373
    in schema consolidation model, 373
FEKs (file encryption keys), 300–302
File Access Control (ACL)
    attributes of, 99
    overview of, 188–189
    setup example, 189–193
file allocation
    in creating files, 217
    in external redundancy disk groups,
        219–220
    in normal-/high-redundancy disk
        groups, 226
    striping during, 221–224
    with variable-sized extents, 220–221
file-creation request, 217
File Drop reactive health checker, 47
file encryption keys (FEKs), 300–302
file numbers, in ASM filename, 180
File Open request, by RDBMS instances, 218
file systems
    data, encryption for. See also ACFS
        Encryption, 299
    moving databases from, 149–151
    moving tablespaces from, 151–152
    snapshots of, 272–274
file systems, ACFS
    CRS Managed, 251–254
    deleting, 259–260
    replicating. See ACFS replication
    resizing, 257–258
    resource, 265
    sizing, 290–291
    unmounting, 258–259
file tagging, ACFS, 275–276
filenames
    ADVM volume device, 249
    creating, 180–183
    forming system-generated, 217
file(s)
    creating in RDBMS/ASM instances,
        217–218

    RDBMS instance opening ASM, 218
    RDBMS instances closing/
        deleting, 219
fine-grained striping, 198, 222–224
Flex ASM
    additional features of, 363
    clustering feature, 359–360
    listeners/Network feature, 360
Flex Cluster mode, 360
FORCE option
    in creating disk groups, 237
    in mounting disk groups, 236
FOREIGN header status, 73, 237, 345
FORMER HEADER_STATUS of disks
    in disk group creation, 73
    function of, 56
FRA. See Fast Recovery Area (FRA) disk groups
fragmentation, in disk groups, 200
free space usage, calculation of, 96–97
fuser command, in unmounting ACFS file
    systems, 258

G

GI. See Grid Infrastructure (GI)
GMON background processes, 42
GPnP. See Grid Plug and Play (GPnP) profile
Grid Disks, Exadata
    ASM discovery of, 55–56, 314–315
    relationship of Cell Disks to, 311
Grid Infrastructure (GI)
    for ASM bundling, 6
    cloning of, 107–111
    cloning over, 111–116
    for Clusterware installation, 15–18
    emergency shutdown of, 246
    installing ACFS/ADVM drivers,
        263–264
    overview of, 13–14
    privileges for ASM instances in, 35
    shutdown, 267
    for standalone server, 15, 267–268
Grid Plug and Play (GPnP) profile
    in Clusterware startup, 25
    discovering SPFILE, 39
    in locating voting files, 20
$GRID_HOME/log/host_name/acfssec/acfssec.log,
    in ACFS Security, 298
$GRID_HOME/.Security/realm/logs/sec-host_
    name.log, in ACFS Security, 298
group services, provided by CSS, 12
group_by_serial/group_by_prio/group_by_node_
    name configuration parameters, in multipath
    configuration, 69

H

HALT option, in rebalance operations, 205
hardware, for ODA, 318–319
HEADER_STATUS of disks, 56
Health Monitor, errors monitored by, 46–48
hierarchical directory format, aliases in, 184–185
High Availability Services (HAS), in ASM instance
    startup, 31
high-redundancy disk groups
    definition of, 19
    disk failure recovery in, 88–92
    in extended cluster configurations, 84
    failure groups and, 79
    file allocation in, 226
    OCR recovery in, 22
    space management views for, 96
    specifying content type for, 362
host-based global storage management, 9
hostname rules, in ACFS Security, 295
hot spare disks, 224–225

I

I/O. *See* input/output (I/O)
I/O Resource Manager (IORM), for Exadata cell
    I/O resources, 312
iDB (Intelligent Database protocol), Exadata
    utilizing, 313
IDP. *See* Intelligent Data Placement (IDP)
    implementation
idp.type attribute, 99
image files, AMDU producing, 347
imbalanced disk groups
    effects of, 208–210
    out-of-space errors in, 220
    reasons for, 207–208
IMMEDIATE clause, in ASM instance
    shutdown, 33
implementation
    of ACFS Security/Encryption, 303–308
    of ACL, 189–193
    of Intelligent Data Placement, 80–82
incarnation number, in ASM filename, 180–181
InfiniBand network, Exadata and, 312–313
initialization of files in RDBMS instance,
    217–218
initialization parameters
    inadequately sized, 138–139
    for specifying default locations, 143–144
    SPFILE with incorrect, 137
initiation, of ACFS replication, 285–288
input/output (I/O)
    ASMLIB processing function of, 161–162
    direct, ACFS supporting, 243–244

    failures, ASM handling of, 93–96
    IORM managing resources/requests, 312
    mirrored files and, 226–230
    multiple paths, 64–65
    RDBMS instances performing, 218
    resource isolation and, 374
    subsystem, rebalance speed and, 212
installation
    of ACFS/ADVM drivers, 263–264
    of ASMLIB, 162–164
    of Clusterware, 15–18
    of GI for standalone server, 15, 267–268
Instance Caging, in database consolidation,
    368–369
instance(s)
    ASM. *See* ASM instance(s)
    level of software compatibility, 101
    management, parameters relative to, 44
    parameters related to, 43–44
    RDBMS. *See* relational database
        management system (RDBMS)
        instance(s)
INSTANCE_TYPE=ASM parameter, for ASM
    instance startup, 31
insufficient disks, mount failure due to, 47
Intelligent Data Placement (IDP) implementation,
    80–82
Intelligent Database protocol (iDB), Exadata
    utilizing, 313
IORM (I/O Resource Manager), 312
isolation models, in Private Database Cloud
    fault, 372–373
    operational, 373–374
    resource, 374–375
    security, 375–376

J

just a bunch of disks (JBOD) storage, IDP for, 80, 81

K

kernel drivers
    ACFS, 264
    ASMLIB, 163, 164–165
key management, for ACFS Encryption, 300–302
KFOD utility, purpose/function of, 344–346

L

LARGE_POOL value, ASM SGA component, 44
LGWR background processes, 42
libknlopt.a, for ASM instance startup, 31–32

Linux
configuring ASM disks for, 59–60
exporting ACFS through NFS on, 268–269
Linux device mapper
ASMLIB and, 172
multipath configuration with, 68–71, 319
topology of, 65–66
Udev in, 67–68
listeners, Flex ASM, 360
lock services, CSS providing, 12
log files, in ACFS Security, 298–299
logical unit numbers (LUNs). *See also* disk(s)
resizing, 203
storage management of, 50–51
logical volume managers (LVMs)
AIX commands, 62–63
third-party, 57
volume groups of, 71–72
lsof command, in unmounting ACFS file
systems, 258

M

major device numbers, in disk device
discovery, 53
manageability, of ACFS, 241
Management Server (MS), Exadata cell
status and, 312
map files, AMDU producing, 347
mapping table, for multipath device, 66
MARK background processes, 43
media sense errors, in disk drive failure, 92
MEMBER_HEADER STATUS, 56, 237
memory allocation
in Private Database Cloud
consolidation, 370
resource isolation, 374
memory-related parameters, 43–44
MEMORY_MAX_TARGET parameter, of ASM
instances, 44–46
MEMORY_TARGET parameter, of ASM instances,
44–46
metadata
ACFS space allocation of, 244–245
ASM instance management of, 30
buffer cache for, 246
DML arbitrating access to, 245–246
dumping of. *See* ASM Metadata Dump
Utility (AMDU)
storage in SGA/disk header, 75
triple mirroring of, 79
migration, of operating system,
210–211
minor device numbers, in disk device
discovery, 53

mirror extents
balanced I/O load and, 226–230
on disk partners, 225–226
failure groups and, 78–79
read errors and, 227
redundancy and, 224–225
write errors and, 227–228
mirror resilvering
function of, 228–229
during recovery, 235
missing disks, mount failure due to, 46–47
Mixed mode, of Flex ASM, 359–360
mknod command
aliasing devices and, 68
creating special files with, 53
deletion of, 54
MOUNT [NOFORCE] command, in I/O
failure, 93
mounting
disk groups, 236–237, 250
failures, reasons for, 46–47
MS (Management Server), Exadata cell status
and, 312
multi-AU extents
features of, 220–221
striping with, 198, 221–222, 223
multibus path, in multipath configuration, 69
multipathing
ASMLIB and, 170–171
configuration, 68–70
creating devices for, 70–71
device mapper for, 65–66
features/benefits of, 64–65
software for, 65
Udev and, 67–68
multipaths section, in multipath configuration, 68
multitenancy, in enterprise clouds, 7

N

NETCA configuration assistant, for ACFS
replication, 281–284
Network File System (NFS)
configuring ASM disks on, 57–58
exporting ACFS for, 268–269
ODA utilizing, 323
Network Foreground (NFG), for file
creations, 217
node failure
ACFS recovery and, 246–247
mirror resilvering and, 228–229
node services, provided by CSS, 12
nodes
DML locks for, 245–246
mounting middle-tier, 254
primary/standby, 278

non-RAC Grid Infrastructure Home, cloning of, 107–111
no_path_retry configuration parameters, in multipath configuration, 69
NORMAL clause, in ASM instance shutdown, 32
normal-redundancy disk groups
    creation of, 79–80
    in extended cluster configurations, 84
    failure groups and, 79
    features of, 19
    file allocation in, 226
    mounting, 236
    OCR recovery in, 22
    space management views for, 96
    specifying content type for, 362
    transient/permanent disk failure recovery in, 88–92
NULL discovery string, for ASMLIB, 160–161, 174
numbers
    disk, 77–78
    disk group, 77

O

OAK (Oracle Appliance Manager), in ASM optimizations for ODA, 318, 320–321
oakcli command, to display disk status, 321–322
OCR. *See* Oracle Clusterware Registry (OCR)
ODA (Oracle Database Appliance), failure groups in, 225
OFA (Optimal Flexible Architecture) standards, 181
offline state
    renaming disk groups and, 337
    resync to restore contents of, 232–233
    write errors and, 228
OHASd. *See* Oracle High Availability Services daemon (OHASd)
OMF (Oracle Managed File), 181–182
online disks, 237
online log, database dependency and, 27–28
operating system (OS) authentication
    for ASM administration, 35–37
    for ASM instances, 33–34, 38
    creating users with, 37–38
    for managing ASM components, 37
    one group for, 34
    separate groups for, 34–35, 36
operating system (OS) migration, 210–211
operational isolation
    in database consolidation model, 373–374
    in schema consolidation model, 374
OPS (Oracle Parallel Server), 2, 3
Optimal Flexible Architecture (OFA) standards, for filename/file locations, 181
oraagent agent, 26–27, 265

ora.asm resource, 265
Oracle 12c ASM. *See* Automatic Storage Management (ASM), 12c release
Oracle Appliance Manager (OAK), in ASM optimizations for ODA, 318, 320–321
Oracle Clusterware
    ACFS integration with, 264–265
    GI for installation of, 15–18
    main components of, 12
    startup sequence for, 24–26
    storage components for, 5–6
    voting files, 13
Oracle Clusterware Registry (OCR)
    in Clusterware startup, 24–26
    contents of, 12–13
    recovery, 22–23
    storage components for, 5
    storage in ASM, 18, 21–22
Oracle Database Appliance (ODA)
    ASM and storage in, 319
    ASM optimizations for, 320–323
    failure groups in, 225
    hardware for, 318–319
    NFS storage and, 323
    software stack for, 318
    storage layout in, 320
Oracle database, storage management for. *See* Automatic Storage Management (ASM)
Oracle Database Vault, for database security, 294
Oracle Exadata Database Machine. *See* Exadata
Oracle High Availability Services daemon (OHASd)
    in Clusterware integration with ACFS, 264–265
    in Clusterware startup, 24, 25
    in GI for Standalone Server, 15
    as Oracle GI sub-stack, 13–14
Oracle Managed File (OMF)
    benefits of, 181
    enabling, 181–182
Oracle Net Services, for ACFS replication, 281–284
Oracle Parallel Server (OPS), storage management and, 2, 3
Oracle Restart
    in GI for Standalone Server, 15, 267–268
    privileges for ASM instances in, 35
Oracle Storage Manager (OSM), 2
Oracle Universal Installer (OUI)
    for GI install, 14
    Storage Option screen, 16
Oracle Virtual Machine (OVM), 243
oracleacfs.ko ACFS driver, supporting ACFS/ADVM, 264
oracleadvm.ko ADVM driver, supporting ACFS/ADVM, 264
oracleasm listdisks command, 167
oracleasm scandisks command, 167

oracleasm.o driver module, in ASMLIB configuration, 165–166
ORACLEASM_SCANEXCLUDE parameter, in multipathing with ASMLIB, 171
ORACLEASM_SCANORDER parameter, in multipathing with ASMLIB, 171
oracleoks.ko kernel services driver, supporting ACFS/ADVM, 263
ora.<diskgroup>.<volume>.acfs file system resource, 265
orarootagent, function of, 27
ORCL:* discovery string, for ASMLIB, 168, 174
OS. See operating system (OS) entries
OSASM group
      privileges for ASM instances, 35
      SYSASM privileges and, 35–36, 38
OSDBA for ASM group, privileges granted to, 35
OSM (Oracle Storage Manager), 2
OSOPER for ASM group, privileges granted to, 35
OUI (Oracle Universal Installer), 14, 16
out-of-space errors, allocation failure and, 46
output files, AMDU producing, 346–347
overprovisioning of CPUs, 369–370
OVM. See Oracle Virtual Machine (OVM)

P

-p option
      in ASMLIB disk creation, 166
      in initiation of ACFS replication, 286
parameters, utilized in ASM instances, 43–46
partitioned CPU approach, in allotting CPU resources, 369
partition(s)
      alignment, on Linux, 59–60
      in storage device configuration, 51–52
Partnership Status Table (PST)
      disk partners and, 226
      in mounting disk groups, 236
      redundancy disk groups and, 22
      write errors and, 228
password file(s)
      in 12c ASM, 354–355
      authentication, for ASM, 38
patching databases, in consolidated environment, 373
path failure, of disk drive, 92
path_checker configuration parameters, in multipathing, 69
path_grouping_policy configuration parameters, in multipathing, 69
pause command, in ACFS replication, 288–290
performance, of ACFS, 241
physical volume identifiers (PVIDs), assigned to AIX disks, 61–62

platform sharing, large-scale, in enterprise clouds, 8
plus (+) sign, in ASM filenames in RDBMS, 217
PMON background processes, 43
point-in-time snapshots, 272–274
policy management, in cloud computing, 10
Portable Operating System Interface (POSIX), ACFS input/output and, 243
power level of 0, in rebalance operations, 205, 208, 211
power management, for rebalance operations, 204–206
preallocation of storage, with ACFS, 244–245
preferred read feature
      extended clusters and, 229–230
      failure groups and, 85–87
prepare command, for ACFS Security, 296–297
primary data center, sending archive logs from, 146–149
primary file systems, ACFS
      in ACFS replication, 280–281
      initiation of, 286–288
      overview of, 276–277
      pausing/resuming replication on, 288–290
      replication termination in, 291–292
      sizing of, 290–292
prio_callout configuration parameters, in multipath configuration, 69
private cloud computing, 7
Private Database Cloud consolidation
      business drivers motivating, 366–367
      complementary workloads, 371
      configuring memory for, 370
      initial server pool sizing in, 367–368
      partitioning vs. overprovisioning CPUs in, 369–370
      reviewing storage usage in, 370–371
      sizing for CPU in, 368–369
      tenant isolation models for, 372–376
process failure, mirror resilvering and, 228–229
Processes parameters, setting, 45
PROVISIONED HEADER_STATUS of disks
      in disk group creation, 73
      features of, 56
PSP0 background processes, 43
PST (Partnership Status Table), 226, 228
public cloud computing, 7
Pure 12c mode, of Flex ASM, 359
PVIDs (physical volume identifiers), 61–62
PZ9x background processes, 43

Q

quorum failure groups
      creating, 23–24
      when mounting disk groups, 85

R

-r option, in ACFS tagging, 275
RAC. *See* Real Application Clusters (RAC)
 databases
random array of independent drives (RAID),
 striping vs., 196
RBAL background processes
  function of, 43
  initiating rebalance, 230–231
  managing rebalance, 200–201
RDBMS. *See* relational database management
 system (RDBMS)
read errors, RDBMS/ASM instances
 encountering, 227
read failures, ASM handling of, 93–94
read-only snapshots
  overview of, 272
  security/encryption in, 303
read operations
  ACFS, recovery and, 247
  preferred, 229–230
  during relocation, 233–234
read-write snapshots
  functions of, 273–274
  security/encryption in, 303
  of standby file system, 277
Real Application Clusters (RAC)
  Cache Fusion infrastructure, 31
  database recovery, 234
  disk groups in, 122–123
  early years of, 2, 3
  quorum failure groups with, 23–24
  usage of ASM for, 4
Real Application Clusters (RAC) databases
  ASMLIB deployment in, 167
  creating with DBCA, 117–122
realms, in ACFS Security, 294, 297
rebalance operations
  data movement in, 230–232
  fast/improved, 206–207
  file priority-based restoration in, 358
  important points about, 211–213
  incomplete, 220
  power management in, 204–206
  process of, 200–203
  scrubbing process in, 362–363
  speed of, 212
  time estimates for, 357–358
reclaiming storage space. *See* ASM Storage
 Reclamation Utility (ASRU)
RECO disk groups, placing ADVM
 volumes in, 250
reconfigured clustering, in enterprise clouds, 8
recovery
  ACFS and ADVM, 246–247
  ASM instance/crash, 234–235

OCR, 22–23
voting file, 20–21
Recovery Configuration screen, DBCA, 122
Recovery Manager (RMAN) backup, creating,
 191–192
Recovery Manager (RMAN) command
  in database backup, 143
  restoring control files to ASM, 139–141
Recovery Manager (RMAN) image copies, in
 moving databases to ASM, 149–150
redo logs
  creating multiplexed, 155–156
  specifying default locations for, 144–145
redundancy
  designing for, 82–83
  disk partners and, 225–226
  extent-based mirroring and, 224–225
  failure groups and, 78–79, 225
  file allocation and, 226
  space management views for, 96–97
Registry Managed ACFS file systems
  creating, 255
  deleting, 259–260
  overview of, 251
  setting up, 255–257
  unmounting, 258–259
  use-case scenarios for, 253–254
relational database management system (RDBMS)
  allocated space utilization by, 196–200
  Automatic Extent Allocation, 198
  compatibility attributes, 101
  operations on ASM files, 216–219
relational database management system (RDBMS)
 instance(s)
  ASM interaction with, 106–107
  closing/deleting ASM files, 219
  connection to ASM instances, 216
  creating ASM files, 217–218
  encountering read errors, 227
  encountering write errors, 227–228
  function of, 30
  mirror resilvering and, 228–229
  opening ASM files, 218
  performing ASM file I/O, 218
  recovery, 234–235
  relocation and, 233–234
  sending extent maps to, 199–200
  storage array migration and, 210
relocation, of extents, 233–234
renamedg command, for disk groups, 332–337
renamedisk command, in ASMLIB, 168
replacement disks, 356–357
replication logs (rlogs)
  in ACFS file system, 276–277
  generating, 288–290
  transmitting between primary/standby
   nodes, 281–284

report files, AMDU producing, 347
REQUIRED_MB_FREE view, in computing free
    space usage, 96–97
resilvering, mirror, 228–229
resource isolation
    in database consolidation model, 374
    in schema consolidation model, 375
resources
    ACFS/Clusterware, 265–266
    ASM disk group, 27–28
    definition of, 26
    relationships, 26–27
Restart Server (RS), Exadata functioning and, 312
RESTRICTED mode, in fast rebalance
    operations, 207
resume command, in ACFS replication,
    288–290
resync operations
    12c ASM optimizations for, 361
    improvements in, 355–356
    process of, 232–233
REVOKE command, for SYSASM privileges,
    37–38
rlogs. See replication logs (rlogs)
RMAN. See Recovery Manager (RMAN) entries
rollbacks, of file creation in RDBMS instance, 218
Rozwat, Charles, 4
RS (Restart Server), 312
rule sets, in ACFS Security, 295
rules, in ACFS Security, 294–295
RUN option, in rebalance operations, 204

S

-s option, in alert log monitoring, 132
SAN (storage area network) administrator,
    249–250
/sbin/acfsutil command
    initiating ACFS replication, 286–287
    managing ACFS file system size, 257
schema consolidation model
    fault isolation in, 373
    operational isolation in, 374
    for Private Database Cloud, 372
    resource isolation in, 375
    security isolation in, 375–376
scrubbing process, in 12c ASM, 362–363
SCSI_INQUIRY command, in multipathing, 64
SECTOR_SIZE attribute, 98
security. See also ACFS Security
    in ACFS snapshots, 303
    for databases, 293–294
security administrator, ACFS, 295–296
security isolation
    in database consolidation model, 375
    in schema consolidation model, 375–376

server parameter file (SPFILE)
    aliases and, 184
    ASM storage of, 38–40
    database dependency with, 27–28
    with incorrect initialization parameter, 137
    managing, 40–41
    moving to ASM, 152
    opening at RDBMS startup, 218
    startup processing of, 26
server pools, sizing of, 367–368
SGA. See System Global Area (SGA)
SHARED locks, DLM, 245
SHARED_POOL value, ASM SGA component, 44
short stroking, implementing, 80
SHUTDOWN command, for ASM instances, 32–33
size parameters, for ASM disks, 51
small computer system interface (SCSI) address, 77
SMON background processes, 43
snapshots, ACFS
    security/encryption in, 303
    types of, 272–274
software
    multipathing, 65
    ODA, 318
Solaris, creating disk devices in, 61
space allocation
    with ACFS, 244–245
    allocation units in, 196–197
    extents in, 197–198
    striping in, 198–199
    for very large databases, 199–200
space management views, for ASM redundancy,
    96–97
space shortage, allocation failure due to, 46
spcopy command, moving SPFILE with, 41
speed of rebalance, factors determining, 212
SPFILE. See server parameter file (SPFILE)
spmoved command, moving SPFILE with, 41
SQL CREATE SPFILE command, to create SPFILE
    in ASM, 41
SRLs (standby redo logs), 156
srvctl stop command, in unmounting ACFS file
    systems, 259
Staleness Registry (SR) slots, in resync operations,
    232–233
standalone server, installing Grid Infrastructure
    for, 15, 267–268
Standard mode, of Flex ASM, 359–360
standby file systems, ACFS
    in ACFS replication, 280–281
    compare command for, 291–292
    initiation of, 286
    overview of, 277
    pausing/resuming replication on, 288–290
    replication termination in, 291–292
    sizing of, 290–291
standby redo logs (SRLs), 156

startup
    for ACFS, 266
    for Oracle Clusterware, 24–26
    for Registry Managed file systems, 255–257
STARTUP RESTRICT command, in fast rebalance
    operations, 207
storage area network (SAN) administrator, in
    ACFS configuration, 249–250
storage array(s)
    migration of, 210
    striping, 52
storage devices
    configuration of, 51–52
    discovery of, with ASMLIB, 160
storage management. See also Automatic Storage
    Management (ASM)
    for ASM disks, 50–51
    host-based global, 9
    impact of cloud computing on, 6–8
    in Private Database Cloud consolidation,
        370–371
storage reclamation. See ASM Storage
    Reclamation Utility (ASRU)
Storage Server, Exadata, 311–312
storage vendors, migration of, 210
STORAGE.TYPE attribute, 99
stretch clusters. See also extended clusters, 23
Stripe and Mirror Everything concept, in ASM, 3–4
striping
    allocation units and, 196
    coarse, 198, 221–222, 223
    features of, 198–199
    fine-grained, 198, 222–224
SYSASM privileges
    to access ASM instances, 33–34
    for administration of ASM, 35–37
    creating users of, 37–38
SYSDBA privileges
    to access ASM instances, 33–34
    managing ASM components, 37
    in operational isolation, 373
SYSOPER privileges, to access ASM instances,
    33–34
System Global Area (SGA)
    metadata storage in, 75
    parameter sizing and, 43–46
SYSTEM_Antivirus security realm, ACFS, 297
SYSTEM_Logs security realm, ACFS, 297
SYSTEM_SecurityMetadata security realm,
    ACFS, 297

T

tablespaces
    creating/altering, 143–144
    moving between disk groups, 153–155
    temporary, moving to ASM, 151–152
    transportable, 124–129
tag names
    in ACFS replication, 278–279
    ACFS tagging and, 275–276
    in ASM filename, 180
target filename, for transferring archive logs,
    148–149
templates
    creating/modifying, 186–187
    functions of, 185–186
    V$ASM_TEMPLATE view, 187
temporary tablespaces, moving to ASM, 151–152
termination, of ACFS replication, 292–293
thin provisioning storage
    ASRU and. See ASM Storage Reclamation
        Utility (ASRU)
    benefits of, 338
    compatibility with ASM, 4–5
third-party volume managers, ASM and, 57
time estimates, for rebalance operations,
    357–358
time rules, in ACFS Security, 295
tnsnames.ora files
    for ACFS replication, 281–284
    validating configuration of, 284–285
too-many-offline-disks condition, mount failure
    and, 47
tools, for multipathing, 64–65
topology
    device mapper, 65–66
    Udev, 67–68
TRANSACTIONAL clause, in ASM instance
    shutdown, 33
transportable tablespaces (TTSs), creation of,
    124–129
troubleshooting, for ASMLIB, 173–176

U

Udev, multipath implementation with, 67–68
umbilicus foreground (UFG)
    in ASM instance discovery, 216
    in ASM instance recovery, 234–235
umount command, for ACFS file systems,
    258–259
UNBALANCED column, in V$ASM_
    DISKGROUP, 208
Unbreakable Linux Network (ULN), installing
    ASMLIB for, 163–164
USABLE_FILE_MB view, in computing free space
    usage, 97
user-defined directories, creation of, 183
user rules, in ACFS Security, 295
user_friendly_names configuration parameters, in
    multipath configuration, 69

/usr/sbin/oracleasm-discover command, in
    ASMLIB disk discovery, 168–169
utility log file repository, ACFS file system for, 254
UTL_FILE_DIR, ACFS repository for, 254

V

Variable Sized Extents, for space allocation,
    198–199
V$ASM_DISK, selecting from, 237–238
V$ASM_DISKGROUP
        selecting from, 237–238
        UNBALANCED column in, 208
V$ASM_ESTIMATE, for rebalance operations,
        357–358
V$ASM_OPERATIONS
        rebalance estimates reported in, 201,
            205, 358
        rebalance progress displayed in, 231
V$ASM_TEMPLATE view, 187
VBGx volume background processes, 262
very large databases (VLDBs), setting AU sizes
        for, 199–200
v$hm_finding, based on Health Check trigger, 48
virtualization, in enterprise clouds, 7
VMBx volume background processes, 262
volume device files, ADVM, 248–249
Volume Driver Background (VDBG) process, 262
volume encryption keys (VEKs), 300–302

volume groups, of LVMs, 71–72
Volume Logs, metadata buffers written into, 246
voting file(s)
        discovery, 20
        overview of, 13
        recovery, 20–21
        startup processing of, 26
        storing in ASM, 18–20
        third, creation of, 23–24

W

WAIT option
        in rebalance operations, 204
        in SQL scripting, 205–206
Welcome screen, DBCA, 118
write errors
        mirror resilvering and, 228–229
        RDBMS/ASM instances encountering,
            227–228
write operations
        ACFS, recovery and, 247
        during relocation, 233–234

X

XDWK background process, for automated disk
        management, 315–316

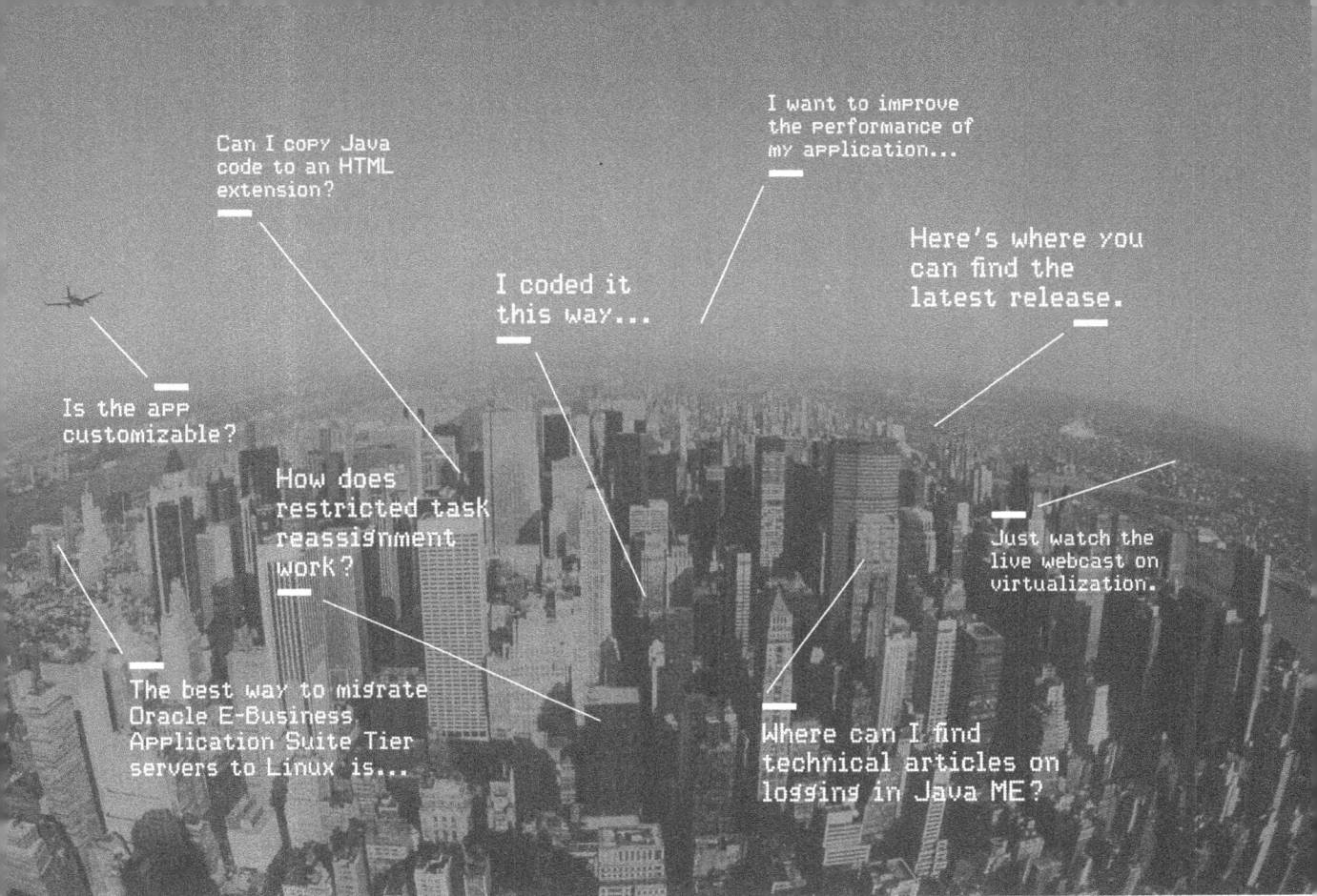

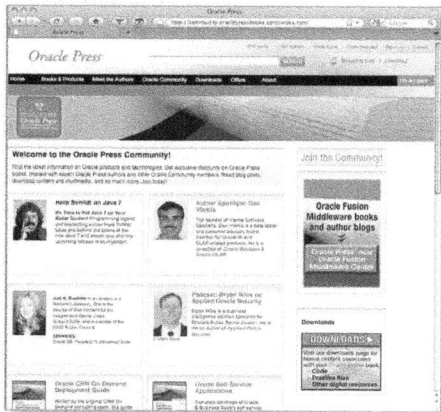

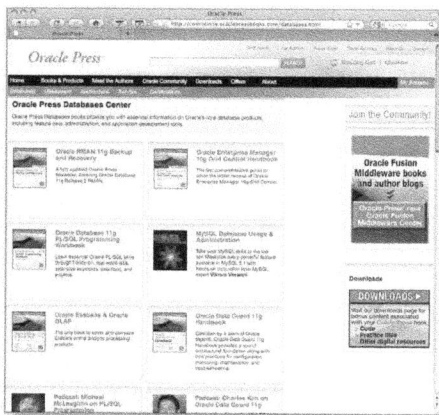

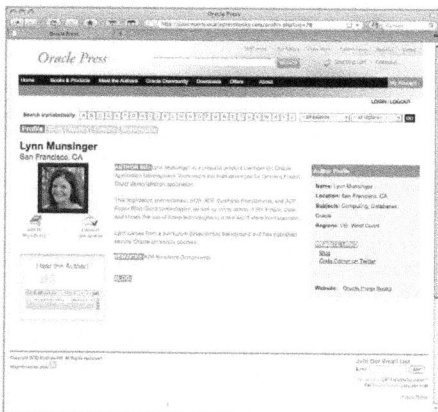

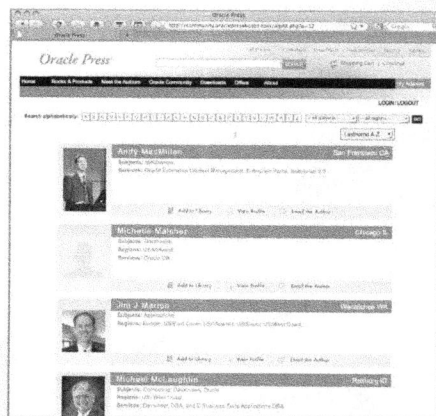